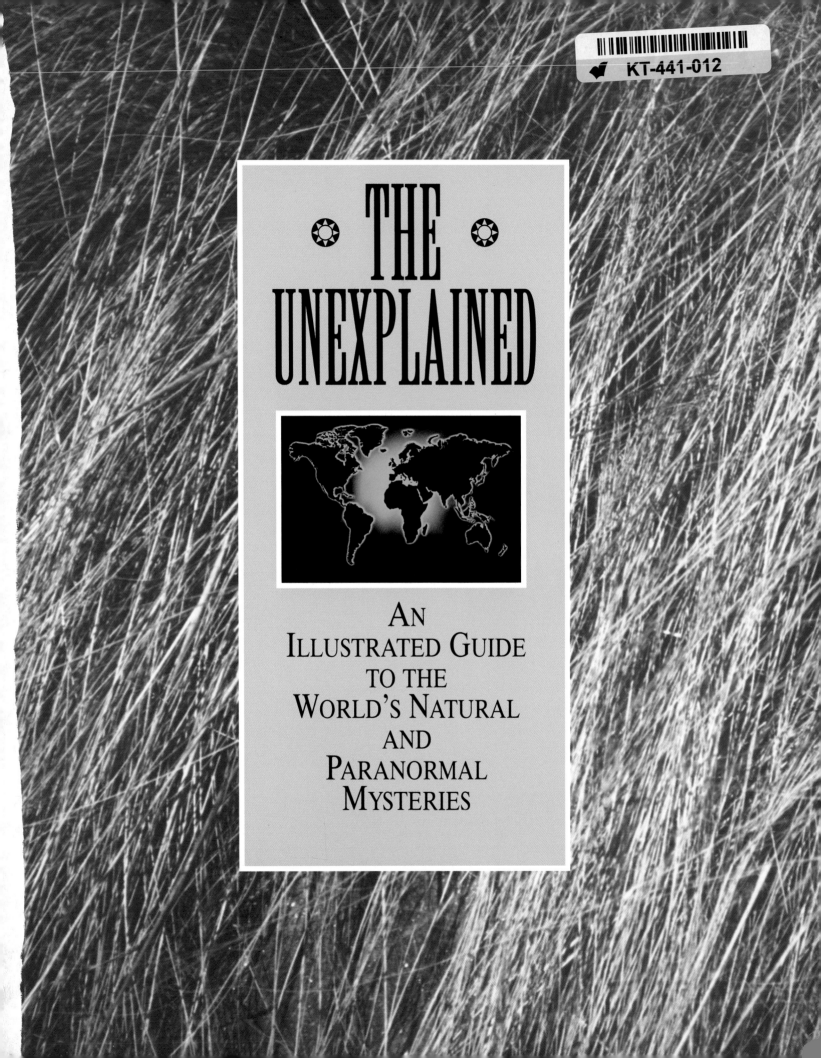

THE UNEXPLAINED

AN ILLUSTRATED GUIDE TO THE WORLD'S NATURAL AND PARANORMAL MYSTERIES

Dedication

To my good friend Mark Chorvinsky, with my warmest thanks for making this book possible for me

THIS IS A CARLTON BOOK.

Text © Dr Karl P. N. Shuker 1996
Design © Carlton Books Limited

This edition published by Carlton Books Limited 1996

A CIP catalogue for this book is available from the British Library.

ISBN 1 85868 186 3

Design and Editorial: Andy Jones and Barry Sutcliffe
Project Editors: Sarah Larter/Tessa Rose
Project Art Direction: Russell Porter
Picture Research: Maja Mihajlovic

Printed in Dubai

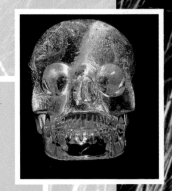

THE UNEXPLAINED

An Illustrated Guide to the World's Natural and Paranormal Mysteries

Dr Karl P. N. Shuker

CARLTON

Contents

Introduction
A PROCESSION OF THE DAMNED

The most beautiful thing we can experience is the mysterious. It is the source of all true art and science.

Albert Einstein, 'What I Believe', *Forum*, October 1930.

Einstein's words remain as valid today as they were 66 years ago. For every

'A' Road along the information superhighway of international mainstream science, there is a myriad of shadowy backwaters leading to the unexpected and inexplicable. As its name suggests, *The Unexplained: An Illustrated Guide to the World's Natural and Paranormal Mysteries* is a global exploration of the strange and

spectacular, but unlike other books in this genre, the structural format of its contents is wholly geographical, i.e. grouping them not by subject but by geographical locality.

This novel approach facilitates the inclusion of not only many highly publicized mysteries from around the world that demand documentation in any book of this nature, but also an unrivalled spectrum of other extraordinary anomalies and enigmas. Subjects in the latter category are no less fascinating than their more famous kindred but, because of their restricted geographical range, they have previously received little coverage or attention. The result is a uniquely diverse panorama of the uncanny and unexpected, in which lake monsters, sacred relics, aliens, ghosts, werewolves, levitating saints, the Little People, ancient cities, ball lightning, abominable snowmen, zombies, and other mystifying phenomena of celebrity status are reviewed alongside an array of hitherto neglected yet equally controversial conundrums.

Where else could you find a winged cat from Manchester and a green cat from Denmark, milk-drinking statues from India, Namibia's flying snake, blue-skinned humans from Chile, Mexican vampire plants, Peruvian glowing mummies, an Egyptian crocodile boy, death-ray stones from the Torres Strait,

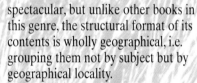

an electric worm from the Gobi desert, phantom South American islands, Ben MacDhui's Big Grey Man, the White River monster, the Dover demon, the Hopkinsville goblins, Hamelin's *real* pied piper, the Mad Gasser of Mattoon, Samoan death clicks, whistling ghosts of Kiribati, earthquake hairs from China, a magnetic mountain from Vietnam, Zululand's asphyxiating tree, a spectral motorbike passenger from Cape Province, the bleeding bread of Bolsena – and other wonders too numerous to mention here?

Mindful of the geographical theme of this book (not to mention the need to prevent it from attaining prodigious proportions!), all the mysteries selected for inclusion are ones that are directly linked to a specific locality, or which are represented by famous examples with precise provenances. Phenomena that fall outside these criteria are excluded; this applies to certain parapsychological subjects such as telepathy, precognition and out-of-body experiences, which generally focus upon individual people whose talents or ordeals have no

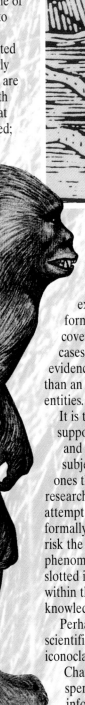

manifestly geographical connection. Also excluded are UFOs and aliens as considered from the more familiar viewpoint, i.e. as extraterrestrial craft and life-forms. In contrast, I *have* included coverage of various theories and cases that feature explanations and evidence proposing an earthly rather than an extraterrestrial origin for such entities.

It is tragic but true that even in this supposed age of peerless scientific and technological sophistication, the subjects contained in this book are ones that most mainstream researchers prefer simply to ignore or attempt to dismiss out of hand without formally investigating them, rather than risk the stigma of association with phenomena that cannot be smoothly slotted into pre-existing pigeon-holes within the corpus of accepted modern knowledge.

Perhaps the best description of these scientific outcasts came from the arch-iconoclast himself, American author Charles Fort (1874–1932), who spent a lifetime gathering eclectic information on what he termed: "A

procession of the damned. By the damned, I mean the excluded. We shall have a procession of data that Science has excluded."

Happily, however, just as a few lone individuals braved scientific ridicule to investigate and ultimately bestow formal respectability upon such erstwhile pariahs as meteorites, insect-eating plants, radioactivity, space travel and the duck-billed platypus among others, so too are there a select number of open-minded researchers today who are boldly studying the mysteries of modern times. Equally, as a scientist myself, I am not content merely to document unexplained data without seeking explanations. Whenever possible, therefore, I have included details of any scientific studies conducted in relation to the subjects in this book, and extensive bibliographical sources for readers wishing to pursue these subjects further.

Come with me upon a cosmopolitan safari in search of magic, marvels and mysteries from the four corners of the globe. For as the fictitious but factually minded Sherlock Holmes once said: "Life is infinitely stranger than anything which the mind of man could invent."

Chapter 1

Great Britain and Ireland

SECRETS FROM THE SCEPTRED ISLE AND THE EMERALD ISLE

IT HAS BEEN SAID THAT THE BRITISH ISLES HAVE MORE GHOSTS THAN ANYWHERE ELSE IN THE WORLD. THIS MAY BE SO, BUT BRITAIN AND IRELAND'S MYSTERIES ARE FAR FROM CONFINED TO CLOSE ENCOUNTERS OF THE SPECTRAL KIND. PLESIOSAURIAN LAKE MONSTERS AND PANTHER-LIKE BIG CATS JOSTLE FOR MEDIA HEADLINES, ALONGSIDE PLAGUES OF PINK FROGS, MOVING STATUES, THE HOLY GRAIL, AWE-INSPIRING MEGALITHS TAPPING INTO SUBTERRANEAN ENERGY SOURCES, MERMAID FUNERALS, GREEN CHILDREN, AND ALL MANNER OF OTHER MYSTERIES AND ENIGMAS.

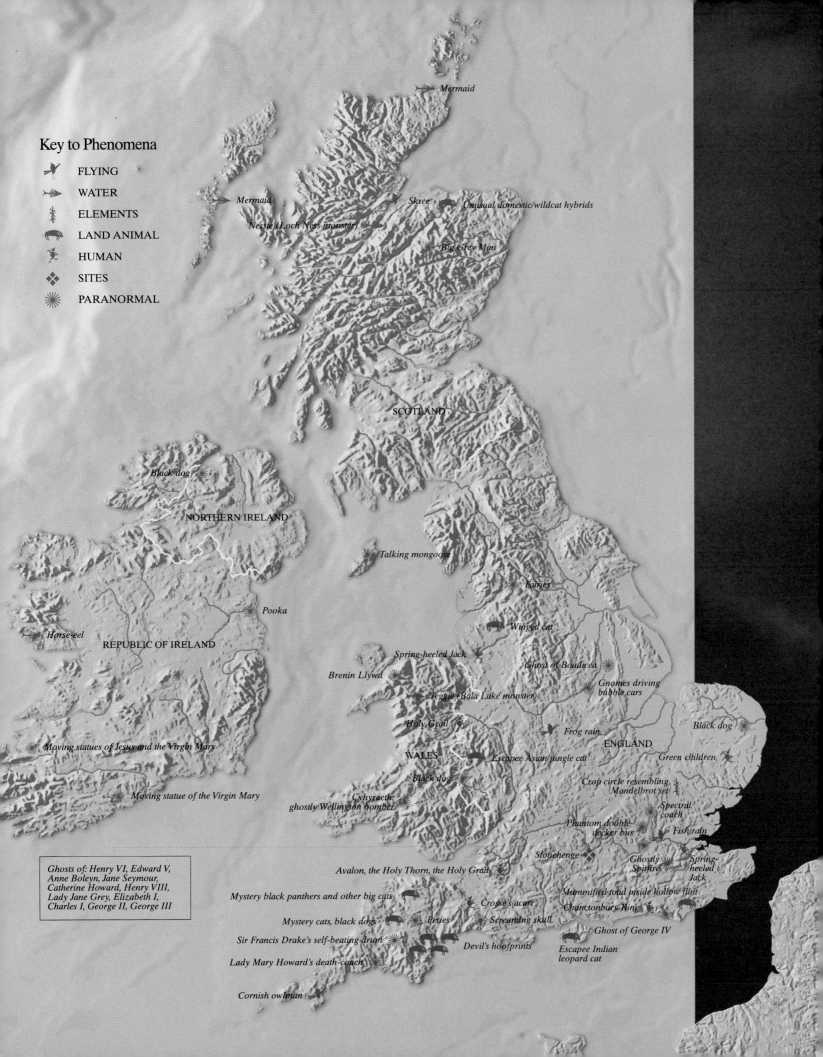

Key to Phenomena

- 🐦 FLYING
- 🐟 WATER
- 🌲 ELEMENTS
- 🐖 LAND ANIMAL
- 🏃 HUMAN
- ❖ SITES
- ✳ PARANORMAL

Mermaid

Mermaid

Skree

Unusual domestic/wildcat hybrids

Nessie (Loch Ness monster)

Big Grey Man

SCOTLAND

Black dog

NORTHERN IRELAND

Talking mongoose

Fairies

Pooka

Winged cat

Horse-eel

REPUBLIC OF IRELAND

Spring-heeled Jack

Ghost of Boadicea

Brenin Llywd

Gnomes driving bubble cars

Teggie (Bala Lake monster)

Holy Grail

Frog rain

Black dog

Moving statues of Jesus and the Virgin Mary

WALES

Escapee Asian jungle cat

ENGLAND

Green children

Moving statue of the Virgin Mary

Black dog

Crop circle resembling Mandelbrot set

Cyhyraeth; ghostly Wellington bomber

Spectral coach

Phantom double-decker bus

Fish rain

Stonehenge

Ghostly Spitfire

Spring-heeled Jack

Ghosts of: Henry VI, Edward V, Anne Boleyn, Jane Seymour, Catherine Howard, Henry VIII, Lady Jane Grey, Elizabeth I, Charles I, George II, George III

Avalon, the Holy Thorn, the Holy Grail

Mummified toad inside hollow flint

Mystery black panthers and other big cats

Crosse's acari

Chanctonbury Ring

Mystery cats, black dogs

Pixies

Screaming skull

Ghost of George IV

Sir Francis Drake's self-beating drum

Devil's hoofprints

Escapee Indian leopard cat

Lady Mary Howard's death-coach

Cornish owlman

British Phantom Fauna

THE EXMOOR BEAST AND OTHER BRITISH MYSTERY CATS

During spring 1983, numerous lambs were allegedly slaughtered by an unknown predator at a farm owned by Eric Ley at South Molton on Exmoor. At the same time, local people were reporting sightings of a black panther-like cat in the area, which was afterwards pursued unsuccessfully by the Royal Marines and was inevitably assumed to have been the beast responsible for the sheep kills. However, naturalists who observed the kills felt that they were actually more dog-like than cat-like in appearance, and stray dogs roaming the moors are only too well known for preying upon sheep and other livestock.

Adding further to the Exmoor mystery was the eventual realization that even if the mystery panther was not the killer, it was not unique either. Other black pantheresque cats were being reported from Exmoor and also from Dartmoor, further south, as well as tawny puma-like animals, and lynx-like beasts with short tails and tufted ears. In January 1986, casts were taken of footprints found at Muddiford, just west of Exmoor, that are clearly those of a big cat – probably a lynx, judging from their 75-mm (3-inch) diameter and circular shape.

As I revealed in my book *Mystery Cats of the World*, large cats belonging to a wide range of different non-native species have been reported from all parts of Britain for many decades.

Former mystery cat – now known to be an unusual domestic/wildcat hybrid – from Kellas, Scotland.

They are evidently escapees from captivity, mostly from private collections, or from private homes where they are kept as exotic pets, or they have been deliberately released by owners no longer willing or able to maintain them.

For many months in 1988, the local people of Ludlow, in Shropshire, had reported seeing a large lynx-like cat prowling the fields and surrounding countryside, but they were not widely believed, their reports dismissed as misidentifications of dogs, domestic cats or foxes. On 3 February 1989, however, Norman Evans discovered the dead body of an extraordinary animal near to his farm at Richard's Castle, Ludlow. It had apparently been killed by a car, and proved to be an Asian jungle cat *Felis chaus*, a sizeable lynx-like species with pointed ears, tawny fur and striped legs, which is not native to Britain or continental Europe. It had clearly escaped from captivity, and could well have been living wild in the Ludlow area for a considerable length of time. Its body has been preserved as a magnificent taxiderm exhibit and constitutes undeniable evidence that non-native, exotic species of wild cat are indeed living in the British countryside.

Other verified examples include: a puma in Scotland (caught alive, October 1980), a leopard cub in Manchester (caught alive, August 1975), a black panther cub in Kent (caught alive, January 1975), a clouded leopard also in Kent (shot dead, March 1976), a lioness in Lancashire (found dead in a lake, May 1980), five Asian leopard cats (Isle of Wight, Cheshire, Dartmoor and two in Scotland), plus at least one other jungle cat (killed by a car in Hayling Island, Hampshire, July 1988).

On Exmoor, however, the beast (or beasts) remains elusive – sightings of

CATS WITH WINGS

In 1975 the *Manchester Evening News* published a photograph of an astonishing cat that had lived in a builder's yard at Trafford Park several years previously. What made this cat so special was the pair of long fluffy wings projecting from its back, clearly visible in the photograph. According to men working in the yard at that time, their highly unusual pet could even raise these unexpected appendages above its body.

Manchester's winged cat is far from unique. Many similar animals have been recorded in Britain, and a few elsewhere too, but until very recently there was no explanation for their "wings". During the early 1990s, however, I learnt of an obscure genetically based skin disorder that provided the long-awaited answer.

Known as feline cutaneous asthenia (FCA), it causes the skin of its feline sufferers to be abnormally elastic, particularly upon the shoulders, back and haunches, readily stretching into long wing-like projections. Not only are these covered in fur, but if they incorporate sufficient muscle fibres, they can be raised up and down. Moreover, these projections will peel off very easily, but without causing bleeding – thus explaining several reports of winged cats that suddenly "moulted" their wings.

Manchester's winged cat.

panthers, pumas and lynxes continue, but so far the animals have eluded all attempts to capture or kill them.

Panther-like big cats on the loose have also been reported from many parts of continental Europe, North America and Australia. In January 1990, for example, a black panther prowling around Rome was seen by several surprised eyewitnesses, and was even filmed by a TV crew, but escaped attempts by the police to capture it.

As for Britain's big cats, this is a saga that seems destined, rather like Rome's panther, to run ... and run ... and run!

✦ FALLING FROGS

One of the oddest enigmas of nature is the widely reported phenomenon of frog rain – that is, unaccountable falls of frogs down to earth from the sky, sometimes in appreciable numbers and usually (but not always) during a shower of rain. Sceptics attempt to explain away this weird occurrence by suggesting that the frogs were merely lurking unseen in ground vegetation and were flushed out of cover by the rain, thereby creating the illusion that they had actually fallen down from the sky with the rain. However, there are many cases on file, including the following one, in which it is clear that the frogs really did fall from above.

In or around 1902, when she was then about eight years old, my grandmother Gertrude Timmins (*née* Griffin) was walking with her mother, Mary Griffin, across a field in what is now the town of West Bromwich, in the West Midlands. As they were walking it began to rain, so they opened their umbrellas, but a few moments later Gertrude felt a great number of quite heavy thumps on top of hers. When she peered out from beneath it, she saw to her amazement that the objects responsible for the thumps were small frogs, dropping down from above, hitting the top of her umbrella, bouncing off it and falling to the ground around her feet. She became quite frightened, but her mother assured her that there was nothing to fear, informing her in a wholly matter-of-fact manner that it was merely a frog rain and that the frogs would stop falling soon – which they did.

The fact that the frogs had been plummeting down on to the tops of the umbrellas proved that they had not simply crawled out of undergrowth at the rain's onset. Nor were there any trees or buildings nearby from which they could have dropped, so the only source of the falling frogs was indeed the sky. This dramatic incident left such a vivid impression in my grandmother's

Mrs Gertrude Timmins, who witnessed a fall of tiny frogs when she was eight.

Rains of bright pink or red frogs were reported in Gloucestershire in 1988.

... AND TOADS IN HOLES

One of the most unusual specimens in the Booth Museum in Brighton is the mummified corpse of a toad. It was discovered inside a hollow flint nodule cracked open by workmen in a quarry at Lewes, East Sussex, in 1899. It must be said that it was donated to the museum by Charles Dawson, prime suspect in the notorious Piltdown man hoax, hence its authenticity is doubtful. However, there are many eminently reliable records, especially from Britain, of hollow rocks that have been found with living toads entombed inside.

One day in 1835, for instance, while standing at the easterly end of a railway cutting near Coventry, John Bruton noticed a block of sandstone fall from a loaded wagon running down to the embankment. As it fell, the block broke across the middle, revealing a hole in the centre, from out of which a living toad dropped to the ground. Bruton ran over and picked up the toad, whose head had been injured by its tumble, and he exhibited it at his local office until it died from its injury ten days later.

mind that right up to her death in 1994, at the age of 99, she could still readily recall all of it.

Following a wet Sunday in June 1979, in Bedford, Vida McWilliam spied countless tiny green frogs hopping across her lawn, and was even more surprised to find her bushes festooned with frogspawn – indicating again that these unexpected visitors had arrived from above rather than below. Just for a change, the frogs that fell over Moseley, Birmingham, during a severe storm on 30 June 1892 were white. And rains of bright pink or red frogs, first reported in Gloucestershire during 1988, have been recorded from several localities in England. These are probably all genetically based colour mutants.

Nor are animal falls limited to frogs. On 28 May 1984, Ron Langton of East Ham, London, discovered a number of small fishes – flounders and smelts – on his roof, which had apparently fallen there during a heavy rainstorm the previous night. Fish falls were also reported from nearby Canning Town during this same period. Elsewhere in the world, even stranger examples are on record, including falls of lizards, snakes, salamanders, snails, grasshoppers, earthworms and jellyfish.

Among those scientists willing to accept that animal falls do occur, the official explanation is that the creatures have been sucked up by a cyclone, whirlwind, waterspout, or similar meteorological disturbance, transported for a time through the air and then dropped to the ground again. Although this is quite reasonable, it does not explain why or how such disturbances are so curiously selective: seldom is more than one type of animal sucked up at any one time. Similarly, it is very rare that any of the undergrowth in the animals' immediate surroundings is lifted up with them.

Many centuries have passed since the bewildering phenomenon of animal falls was first documented, but science has still to succeed in obtaining a satisfactory solution to it.

Mummified toad inside a hollow flint nodule at the Booth Museum, Brighton.

Incarcerated toads are not a peculiarity of a single type of rock. In 1910, a Leicestershire inhabitant discovered a half-grown living example while breaking open a piece of coal. A solid layer of clay 2 metres (6 feet) underground at Broseley, Shropshire, was found to contain a small toad inside when split open by workmen in 1906. Limestone-incarcerated specimens, however, are among the most common. The renowned Victorian geologist William Buckland conducted a grisly experiment by deliberately sealing two dozen toads into separate compartments of rock, some limestone and some sandstone, after which he buried them in his garden for a year. When he dug them up, he found that the entombed toads were dead, but most of those entombed within limestone were still alive.

These findings led to the current accepted theory, which suggests that young toads enter porous rocks, such as limestone, or rocks with an external opening leading to the interior, and become trapped there if they grow larger before attempting to re-emerge. It is worth noting that the Lewes flint contained a small channel through to the outside. Once entombed, the toads' odour entices tiny insects inside, which they then feed upon, and the rock's opening or pores enable air to reach them, so that they can breathe. Moreover, when toads enter a state of hibernation their energy requirements drop notably, which would enable them to survive in an incarcerated state for at least a couple of years if necessary.

This theory recently gained support from a most unusual case that brings the subject of imprisoned amphibians into the modern age. In October 1995 some pupils at Rhyl High School in North Wales were clearing rubbish from an overgrown area near a small pool, when they discovered an old ring-pull can with a 5-cm- (2-inch) long frog alive and well inside. The frog was much larger than the can's ring-pull hole, so it must have entered when it was younger and as the can's sell-by date was May 1994, the frog may well have been trapped inside for more than a year. Clearly, therefore, it had survived by living upon insects and other tiny life forms that found their way inside, and it had remained moist as a result of rain and dew entering through the can's hole.

✸

NESSIE, TEGGIE AND OTHER BRITISH LAKE MONSTERS

With a history of sightings dating back to an encounter with St Columba around AD 580, Scotland's elusive Nessie, the long-necked hump-backed monster of Loch Ness, is probably the world's most famous mystery beast.

One popular identity for the Loch Ness monster is a plesiosaur, seen here doing battle with an ichthyosaur.

A photograph taken by underwater camera in Loch Ness: is this Nessie?

Inevitably, it has been the subject of numerous hoaxes, to the extent that sceptics have cast doubt upon many eyewitness accounts and virtually all photographic evidence obtained of the monster above the surface of the water.

To my mind, however, there are two categories of evidence that offer convincing proof of the reality of a large, unidentified type of creature in Loch Ness. The first category comprises the handful of reports claiming sightings of the monster on land. Not only are these significant in that they provide a view of the creature in its entirety, but also they closely corroborate each other. Perhaps the most important terrestrial encounter with Nessie occurred at 1.30 a.m. on the moonlit morning of 5 January 1934, and featured a veterinary student, in other words. an eyewitness with a knowledge of wildlife, who would have been unlikely to mistake a commonplace creature for something else.

Arthur Grant was travelling from Inverness to Glen Urquhart on his motorbike when he noticed something dark moving in the bushes along the right-hand side of the road. Just as he rode up to it, a long neck bearing a small snake-like head with large oval eyes turned towards him, and then a huge body bounded across the road up ahead and plunged down the steep bank to the loch, entering it with a great splash. In those few amazing moments, Grant distinctly observed two front flippers, with what seemed to be two others further back and a lengthy tail, probably 2 metres (5–6 feet), with a rounded tip. The animal appeared to be 5–6 metres (15–20 feet) long and over 1 metre (3 feet) high. Large flipper-like tracks were later discovered in shingle near to where Grant had seen the mysterious animal go down the bank to the loch.

Grant's description is a good verbal portrait of a plesiosaur – a prehistoric aquatic reptile with a long neck, small head, slender tail, robust body and four flippers. Although plesiosaurs officially died out over 60 million years ago with the dinosaurs, an undiscovered modern-day version is a popular identity not only for Nessie but also for a number of other long-necked freshwater monsters and sea serpents reported from around the world.

The second category of noteworthy Nessie evidence consists of underwater sonar/photographic recordings. These have been obtained by several scientific teams over the years, including researchers from Dr Robert Rines's Academy of Applied Science, based at Concord, New Hampshire. Indeed, this team obtained what I consider to be the most compelling evidence currently on record for the existence in Loch Ness of a very large species of living creature still undiscovered by science.

In the early hours of 8 August 1972, Dr Rines's team was monitoring an area of the loch with sonar equipment and an underwater camera in Urquhart Bay when the sonar detected a shoal of fish moving very rapidly, as if fleeing from something else. Moments later, the sonar recorded a very large solid object, 6–9 metres (20–30 feet) long, pursuing the shoal in a deliberate, purposeful manner. As the object passed by, it triggered the underwater camera, which took a series of photos. When these were developed, two showed a remarkable flipper-like structure, 1.25–2 metres (4–6 feet) long and rhomboidal in shape, attached to a much larger body. Zoological analyses have

Holidaymaker Jennifer Bruce took this photo of Loch Ness in 1982. Unintentionally, she may also have snapped a portrait of Nessie in the waters of Urquhart Bay.

Title page of **A Straunge Wunder in Bongay**, *depicting the mysterious black dog seen in Bungay, Suffolk, in 1577.*

confirmed that the flipper's shape is hydrodynamically efficient, and closely resembles the flippers of plesiosaurs. What is so impressive about this evidence is that it was obtained by two totally objective sources – machines – which simply record what they detect with no interest in whether or not there is a Loch Ness monster and also wholly corroborate each other. The sonar detected a moving body, and the camera photographed it.

Long-necked water monsters have also been reported from several other Scottish lochs, including Morar, Arkaig, Quoich, Oich, Lochy and Lomond.

Mysterious aquatic beasts have been sighted in some of Ireland's lakes too, notably Lough Nahooin and Lough Fadda in County Galway, but these tend to be very different in form. Termed horse-eels, they are usually said to have a horse-like head but a very elongate, eel-shaped body. Intriguingly, this description corresponds well with reconstructions of zeuglodonts – supposedly extinct serpentine whales whose flexible backbone could have readily formed the vertically undulating shape commonly reported for this category of water monster.

Horse-eels have sometimes been

sighted in loughs too small to sustain them for long periods of time, but if they migrate from one lough to another, not residing permanently anywhere, this would not be a problem. It is believed likely that zeuglodonts were able to move about on land albeit only for relatively short distances, unlike other types of whale.

Much less familiar is the Welsh version of Nessie, known as Teggie. Believed to inhabit Llyn Tegid, or Bala Lake, Teggie has been reported since at least the 1920s and has been variously likened to a crocodile or a small plesiosaur. In September 1995, however, a three-day search of the lake by a Japanese film crew using a mini-submarine failed to spot its elusive enigma.

Many sightings of marine counterparts to the horse-eels and long-necked lake monsters discussed here have been reported from the seas surrounding the British Isles. Although not likely to be of the same species, these sea serpents are presumably closely related to them.

❂
BLACK DOGS AND OTHER ZOOFORM PHENOMENA

The Middle Kingdom, a collection of Irish folklore and beliefs compiled by Dermot A. MacManus, contains a modern-day account of a frightening encounter between one of his friends and a sinister entity of a type reported over many hundreds of years. It was Easter 1928, and MacManus's friend, a student on holiday from Trinity College in Dublin, was fishing in a river near his home in County Londonderry when he saw a very large black dog approaching him, paddling its way through the river's shallow stretches. Somehow the student sensed that it was malevolent and he immediately clambered up into the branches of a tree close by. Soon, the creature had reached the spot where he had been sitting, and as it walked beneath the tree it gazed up at the frightened occupant, baring its teeth in a snarling grin. Even worse, however, were its eyes, for they were blazing red in colour, "... which seemed like live coals inside the monstrous head". The student remained in the tree until this terrifying apparition was lost to view around a bend in the river.

This is just one of countless reports describing phantom-like creatures of canine form termed black dogs, devil dogs or hell hounds. There are many local versions – Black Shuck in East Anglia, Skriker ("howler", in Lancashire), Padfoot (Staffordshire), Muckle Black Tyke (Scotland), Mauthe Doog (Isle of Man), Gwyllgi ("dog of darkness", in Wales), Barguest (Yorkshire). Tales of Hergest's black dog from the Herefordshire–Powys border and a pack-hunting Dartmoor form inspired Sir Arthur Conan Doyle's *The Hound of the Baskervilles*.

Nevertheless, these uncanny entities generally share certain well-defined characteristics. They are usually as large as labradors or alsatians, almost invariably black and often with shaggy coats. They exude a distinctly sulphurous odour and their crimson eyes glow like fire. They look solid, yet can vanish at will, sometimes in a fiery explosion, and anybody who touches one of these beasts usually dies shortly afterwards. Even to see one is believed in some areas to be a sure sign of impending doom.

Their relationship with humans is decidedly ambivalent. Some, like the above example, are unquestionably menacing. Perhaps the most terrifying black dog case occurred in August 1577, during a morning service at Bungay church in Suffolk. Without warning, a ferocious black dog materialized in the aisle and attacked the shocked congregation, killing two people and somehow managing to burn another person very severely. Shortly afterwards it repeated its onslaught in nearby Blythburgh church, and when departing through the church door it left behind some prominent scorched claw marks, which are still visible there today. In stark contrast, several accounts record black dogs purposefully accompanying women walking alone down dark, desolate lanes, only to vanish once the women reached home or well-lit areas.

Interestingly, black dogs appear only

A witch rides a black dog in this lithograph from **La Vie Exécrable de Guillemette Babin, Sorcière** *(1926).*

in certain very restricted localities – a specific country lane, or churchyard, or river bank – never seeming to stray outside their established territory. Such territories are often associated with ancient monuments or buildings, or aligned along supposed ley lines, marking out postulated channels of earth energy.

How can we explain black dogs? Hallucinations or simple misidentifications of normal dogs are generally inadequate solutions. Mental projection by the alleged observer is often proposed, but without explaining how or why such projection occurs. Alternatively, perhaps these entities share an origin with nature spirits and other beings deemed by some investigators to be elementals. Many consider black dogs to be cyclical (imprint) apparitions – a form of moving energy trace, possibly the preserved images of real dogs from the past that are somehow triggered by certain meteorological effects, whereupon they run before the eyes of bemused observers like a three-dimensional cinefilm. Yet this fails to explain several reports in which the dog behaved like an interactive apparition, specifically looking at its human observer. Links have even been suggested between black dogs and ball lightning, which might explain the Bungay beast and its scorching effects.

Whatever the answer, answers, black dogs are only the most familiar category in a diverse range of zooform phenomena – a term coined by Jonathan Downes, an Exeter-based investigator of mystery animals, to describe entities that outwardly resemble animals but appear to be supernatural rather than corporeal. Some seem so outlandishly bizarre that they could not possibly be flesh-and-blood, but they were only too real to their horrified observers.

On the eve of the battle of Culloden in the Scottish Highlands, fought between the Duke of Cumberland's troops and the rebellious Jacobites in 1746, a shrieking human-headed monster with burning red eyes and black leathery wings hovered over the terrified soldiers. Called the skree, it could be readily dismissed as fantasy, were it not for the disquieting fact that one of the eyewitnesses was none other than Lord George Murray, a well-respected general renowned for his level-headed outlook.

Another example is a monstrous horse-like beast with the face of an evil, leering man that blocked the path of John Farrell and Margaret Johnson for almost two minutes as they drove along a lonely road near Drogheda in County Louth, Eire, one spring evening in 1966. Only when it suddenly disappeared were its two terrified eyewitnesses able to continue their journey. Irish tradition tells of a fearful supernatural creature called the pooka, which often assumes the guise of a malevolent horse. But pookas are purely mythological – aren't they? Perhaps there are areas in Britain where myths become reality, if only for a short time.

MERFOLK

According to an old Cornish legend, a mermaid fell in love with the melodious singing voice of Matthew Trewhella, a chorister at Zennor church, and lured him into the depths of the sea, where they were married and raised several children. Although many tales of merfolk are indeed nothing more than legends and folklore, there are some extraordinary reports on file that cannot be discounted quite so easily.

Take, for instance, the following letter, published in *The Times* newspaper on 8 September 1809, and written by Scottish schoolmaster William Munro. One summer day around 1797, he was walking towards Sandside Head on the Caithness coast in the northern Highlands when:

... my attention was arrested by the appearance of a figure resembling an unclothed human female, sitting upon a

A mermaid with a manatee. Some scientists still believe that sightings of mermaids have in fact been of manatees.

rock extending into the sea, and apparently in the action of combing its hair, which flowed around its shoulders, and was of a light brown colour. The forehead was round, the face plump, the cheeks ruddy, the eyes blue, the mouth and lips of a natural form, resembling those of a man; the teeth I could not discover, as the mouth was shut; the breasts and abdomen, the arms and fingers of the size of a full grown body of the human species; the fingers, from the action in which the hands were employed, did not appear to be webbed, but as to this I am not positive. It remained on the rock 3 or 4 minutes after I observed it, and was exercised during that period in combing its hair, which was long and thick, and of which it appeared proud, and then dropped into the sea from whence it did not reappear to me. I had a distinct view of its features, being at no great distance on an eminence above the rock on which it was sitting, and the sun brightly shining.

Traditional identities offered for mermaids, such as seals or sea-cows, seem inadequate when faced with this educated eyewitness's in-depth account of an unequivocally human-like entity. The more cynically minded might suggest that Munro had merely chanced upon a lady about to indulge in a spot of nude swimming – and who knows, perhaps they may be correct! This explanation, however, cannot solve the tragic case of the Benbecula mermaid.

As documented in Volume 2 of Alexander Carmichael's treatise *Carmina Gadelica* (1900), in or around the year 1830 some people were gathering seaweed at Sgeir na duchadh in Grimnis, on the Outer Hebridean island of Benbecula, when a strange woman-like entity began frolicking nearby in the sea. After fruitless attempts to catch the creature, a boy threw a stone that struck it heavily in its back. The creature sank beneath the waves, but a few days later its dead body was found washed ashore about 3 kilometres (2 miles) away, at Cuile in Nunton.

According to the detailed description given in *Carmina Gadelica*, the creature's upper portion was about the size of a well-fed, 3–4-year-old child, but with an abnormally developed breast.

Woodcarving of a mermaid (c. 1800).

Its lower body was like a salmon in shape, but lacked scales. Its skin was white, soft and tender, and its long hair was dark and glossy. Not surprisingly, such a remarkable sight drew great crowds, who gazed at it closely and even touched it, and everyone went away convinced that this was truly a mermaid. Indeed, it was so human in form that Duncan Shaw, factor for Clanranald, baron-bailie and sheriff of the district, ordered a coffin and shroud to be made, and its body was formally buried a short distance above the shore from where it had been found – a unique funeral attended by many people. If this had been nothing more than a dead seal or a beached whale, it is highly unlikely that eyewitnesses as knowledgeable about maritime matters as the seafaring inhabitants of Benbecula would have mistaken it for a mermaid, or accorded it a ceremonious funeral.

In 1981, Canadian researchers Dr Waldemar Lehn and I. Schroeder argued that sightings of mermen reported in medieval Norse manuscripts were probably optical illusions – observations of common sea mammals greatly distorted by strong, non-uniform atmospheric refraction. This may be true, but optical illusions cannot be buried in a coffin and a shroud.

In 1960, the British scientist Professor Sir Alister Hardy FRS boldly speculated that humans may have evolved not from bipedal plains-dwelling primates, the orthodox view of our ancestral development, but from aquatic ape-like forms instead. Hardy's radical hypothesis was subsequently expanded by Elaine Morgan in *The Aquatic Ape* and other publications, but has gained little acceptance from the scientific community. Notwithstanding this, such a concept may offer a highly original solution to another longstanding mystery.

Even if *Homo sapiens* is not descended from aquatic ancestors, what if the human family tree contained a water-dwelling offshoot, whose species remained in the sea but evolved and survived in parallel with their terrestrial counterparts? What would such creatures be like today? Perhaps we already know, and perhaps we even have a name for them – merfolk.

'Twixt Heaven and Earth, Present and Past

THE HOLY THORN AND THE HOLY GRAIL

William Blake's immortal poem and hymn, "Jerusalem", refers to the possibility that as a boy Jesus visited Great Britain, with his tin-trading uncle, St Joseph of Arimathea. There are also stories of how, after the death of Jesus, St Joseph travelled to Britain again, founding a small church at Glastonbury in Somerset. Destroyed by fire in 1184, this was replaced by the abbey, which was razed by King Henry VIII in 1539 but whose ruins stand today.

Glastonbury, of course, has an additional claim to mythological fame, for some historians believe it to be the Isle of Avalon, to which King Arthur was taken to be healed when mortally wounded in his last battle. In fact, Glastonbury has been the focus of some intricate interweaving of Arthurian and Christian romances, as will be seen.

According to legend, while St Joseph was at Glastonbury his staff rooted in the ground and burst forth into a great thorn tree. Here too, in the church's well, St Joseph reputedly concealed the Holy Grail – the chalice that Jesus drank from during the Last Supper, and which was used to catch drops of his blood falling from his crucifixion wounds.

So much for legend, but does any of it have a basis in fact? There was indeed a large thorn tree in the grounds at Glastonbury, but puritanical Oliver Cromwell ordered it to be cut down, condemning it as an idolatrous

Detail of window in Kilkhampton parish church, Devon: Joseph of Arimathea carrying the Holy Thorn and the Holy Grail.

image. In 1985, however, one of its descendants was planted on this same spot; others can be found elsewhere in the abbey grounds. Interestingly, their subspecies, *Crataegus oxyacantha praecox*, is not native to Britain, but is found in the Holy Land – support, perhaps, for the legend of St Joseph's journey to Britain?

The history of the Holy Grail is far more complex, confusing and contradictory. Many historians nowadays consider that its Christian associations, so familiar today, are actually a relatively recent invention, and that the real source of the Holy Grail concept can be traced much further back in time than Christianity – as far back as the distant realms of Celtic mythology. Here it is equated with a magic cauldron owned by the god Bran that could restore to life anyone whose slain body was cast into it.

In *The Shroud and the Grail*, Noel Currer-Briggs proposed that there were two separate Grails that have since become confused with each other. One is the chalice that we generally think of today as the Holy Grail. However, the other, which he believes to be the true Grail, was the dish-shaped reliquary casket that had contained the linen sheet wrapped around the body of Jesus after he was removed from the cross, i.e. the Shroud of Turin.

No less conflicting are the many Arthurian tales of the quest for the Grail, believed to possess great healing powers. In the most famous of these, Sir Thomas Malory's *Le Morte Darthur* (1485), the quest was achieved jointly by Sir Galahad (Gawain in some other tellings), Sir Perceval and Sir Bors, who reached the Grail Castle, surrounded by a barren wasteland, to find that the holy chalice was guarded by a wounded,

La Mort d'Arthur by James Archer.

Viroconium, in what is today the county of Shropshire. Here it came under the protection of a local king, whom Phillips believes to have been none other than King Arthur, and remained undisturbed for several centuries, until the Norman invasion, when Arthur's lands – and the Grail – were given to Payn Peveril, a French nobleman.

From then on, the Grail was passed down through successive generations of the Peveril family. In 1850, his last direct descendant, Frances Vernon, married a local historian called Thomas Wright, but their only child, a son, died while still a youngster. What would become of the Grail now? Wright and his wife decided to conceal their precious heirloom. Nevertheless, Wright was concerned that the Grail might be lost forever and so he left behind some cryptic clues to its location – an artificial cave in Hawkstone Park near Shrewsbury – appended to a poem relating to the Grail written by one of his wife's ancestors in the seventeenth century.

After Thomas Wright's death, his wife remarried, and in 1920 one of her grandchildren, Walter Langham, learnt about his family's connection with the Grail. Deciphering Wright's clues, Langham trekked through a maze of tunnels and caves beneath the White Cliff, a ruined chapel at Hawkstone Park. And there, hidden beneath a stone eagle, he discovered a 5-cm- (2-inch) tall goblet hewn from green onyx and very worn. Could this really be the Holy Grail?

Experts are presently nonplussed, and because the goblet is composed of onyx its age cannot be ascertained by carbon dating. Regardless of its identity, however, why had its existence not been made public before now? After Langham found it, the goblet remained in his family, but when it passed into the hands of its current owner, Langham's great-grand-daughter Victoria Palmer, living in Rugby in Warwickshire, she was wholly unaware of its controversial claim to fame. Indeed, until Phillips contacted her in 1995 to tell her that it might actually be the Holy Grail, since when she has consigned it to the safety of a bank vault – it had been residing inside a box of junk in her attic! How very unromantic an end to the history of what may be one of the world's most inspirational religious artefacts!

The 5-cm (2-inch) cup of green onyx believed by Dr Graham Phillips to be the legendary Holy Grail used to collect the blood of Jesus.

immobile keeper, the Fisher King. Only when a certain question relating to the Grail is asked correctly can the Fisher King be healed, the land restored and the Grail obtained. Sir Galahad successfully posed the question, and the trio of knights then transported the Grail by ship to a holy Eastern city called Sarras, where Galahad was crowned king before Perceval returned to the Grail Castle and Bors to Camelot. The Grail's subsequent fate, however, became obscured by countless claims of conspiracies, intervention by the Knights Templar, Cathars and so on.

A very different history has been mooted by the author Dr Graham Phillips in his latest work *The Search For the Grail*. He believes that the Holy Grail was removed from the tomb of Jesus in AD 327 by archaeological scholars sent by the Roman empress Helena, and taken back with them to Rome. In 410, when Rome was under attack from barbarian hordes, the Grail was smuggled out, sent to Britain, which was still under Roman occupation, and placed for safety in the city of

THE LITTLE PEOPLE

One day in July 1917, 15-year-old Elsie Wright took her father's box camera to a woodland glen in Cottingley, Yorkshire, and took her very first photograph: it became one of the most famous, and controversial, images ever exposed to public scrutiny. For the photograph depicted her 10-year-old cousin Frances Griffiths with a group of diminutive winged fairies, dancing in front of her. Two months later, the two girls obtained a second photo, this time portraying Elsie with a gnome. These extraordinary pictures greatly intrigued theosophist Edward Gardner, and they fascinated Sir Arthur Conan Doyle, who was preparing a book called *The Coming of the Fairies* (published in 1922) and was naturally eager to pursue any evidence that might confirm the reality of such entities. As a result, the two girls were given fresh cameras and photographic plates and asked to take some more fairy photos, which in August 1920 they did – three in all. In the last of these the fairies were semi-transparent, as if fading from view, and Elsie claimed that she could not photograph them any more.

For 57 years, this quintet of pictures perplexed the scientific world. Although Elsie and Frances repeatedly swore that they were genuine, most people felt sure that they were fakes and it was well known that Elsie had always been an accomplished painter, but not even photographic experts were able to show how the hoax had been perpetrated. In August 1977, however, writer Fred Gettings solved the mystery. Looking through a children's book called *Princess Mary's Gift Book*, published in 1915 and widely available at that time, he spotted some fairy illustrations that were virtually identical to the fairies in Elsie's first picture.

An account of his discovery appeared in *The Unexplained* (No. 116) in 1982, but the next issue contained an even more sensational coup – an article by fairy researcher Joe Cooper claiming that Elsie and Frances had admitted to

Fairies in flight, with "... the Moon, like to a silver bow/New-bent in Heaven", and Titania, Queen of the Fairies, lying asleep. Arthur Rackham's illustration (1908) for William Shakespeare's **A Midsummer Night's Dream**.

him that they had indeed hoaxed the pictures, using cut-out fairies painted by Elsie. The long-running saga finally came to an end on 17 March 1983, when Frances confessed to *The Times*, which published the news the next day, with a confirmation by Elsie appearing in its issue of 4 April.

Full details of how Elsie and Frances had accomplished the deed were revealed in a comprehensive series of *British Journal of Photography* articles by Geoffrey Crawley, running from 24 December 1982 to 8 April 1983. Perhaps the most remarkable revelation in the Cottingley exposé, however, was that a major clue to the pictures' true nature

had been clearly visible all along. Some of the cut-outs had been held in place by hatpins, and the head of one pin had been noticed by Conan Doyle but identified by him as a fairy navel!

Notwithstanding the demise of these photos as evidence for the reality of fairies, modern-day sightings of the Little People in Britain still occur. In 1928, Mrs G. Herbert recollected seeing a pixie while taking an afternoon walk on the southern edge of Dartmoor as a child in 1897. It resembled a little wizened man about 45 cm (18 inches) tall with a brown wrinkled face and wearing a pointed hat, doublet and knicker-like leggings. As she looked at

The Cottingley fairies: one of Elsie Wright's controversial photographs.

it, the pixie vanished. A similar being was briefly spotted in April 1936 by a car driver when rounding a bend along a quiet Hertfordshire lane.

An unnamed correspondent in the periodical *John o'London's* (June 1933) claimed that on eight occasions during August 1931, she and her eldest daughter had spied some 45-cm- (18-inch) tall female fairies wearing delicate transparent gowns in their Warwickshire garden. Around August 1887 or 1888, teenager Grace Penrose saw three small doll-like figures in identical white gowns, dancing by a well behind her home at Sennen Cove, Cornwall. More recently, during summer 1964, some children claimed that they had watched a number of little green men in white hats hurling stones and clods of earth at each other on a bowling green in Liverpool.

Most bizarre of all, however, must surely be the statement made by a group of 10-year-old children that while walking home from Wollaton Park, Nottingham, one evening in late September 1979, they saw a troupe of about 60 gnomes drive out of the lakeside bushes in 30 tiny red and white bubble cars! The gnomes were described as being only half as tall as the children themselves, with greenish crinkled faces, red tunics, green leggings, and white beards with red tips. Despite rigorous questioning the following morning by their school's headmaster, the children insisted that they were telling the truth. Marjorie Johnson, a former secretary of the Fairy Investigation Society based in Notttingham, disclosed that she had received several other reports of Little People from Wollaton Park, often near to its lake.

Identities proposed for the Little People are numerous. Traditionally they have been deemed to be lost souls or the souls of pre-Christian people, doomed to wander the earth until they ultimately disappear. Others consider them to be fallen angels, or elemental nature spirits inhabiting a different dimension of reality from our physical world, or even visible thought-forms – mentally projected *à la* Ted Serios, America's foremost "thoughtographer".

Some researchers, noting that the overall decline in modern-day fairy reports is matched by the contemporary surge in UFO sightings, suggest that fairies may have abandoned dancing in secluded groves in favour of soaring through the skies in flying saucers. Certainly, encounters with fairies and supposed extraterrestrials do share many similarities.

In 1893, folklorist David MacRitchie expressed the opinion that the Little People were the last remnants of a pygmy race of ancient Britons, and Neolithic pygmies have been nominated as the answer to continental Europe's fairies too. Recalling Dr Carl Sagan's theory that humankind's longstanding belief in dragons stems from archaic racial memories, persisting through millions of years from prehistoric times when the earliest mammals co-existed with dinosaurs, I cannot help but wonder if the Little People are racial memories of our more direct ancestors, the dwarf-like australopithecines, which died out around one million years ago. As all races of *Homo sapiens* are descended from these, this would explain the worldwide belief in Little People.

Even so, the fundamental question is not what the Little People are, but whether they exist. Or to put it another way, in the words of J. M. Barrie: "Do you believe in fairies?"

CROSSE'S ACARI

The author Mary Shelley once attended a lecture in London given by an eccentric electrical researcher from Somerset called Andrew Crosse. Traditionally, the inspiration for her classic horror story, *Frankenstein*, is believed to have been a nightmare, but in his intriguing book *The Man Who Was Frankenstein*, writer Peter Haining proposed that her model for Dr Frankenstein was Andrew Crosse – and for a very good reason. There is some controversial evidence to suggest that during one of his many mysterious experiments with electricity, performed secretly in his secluded country house at Broomfield, this extraordinary man discovered a means of creating life!

As recorded in his own report of the experiment in question, he had been attempting to create silica crystals by permitting a fluid medium, containing hydrochloric acid and a solution of potassium silicate, to pass through a lump of iron oxide, when:

On the fourteenth day from the commencement of this experiment I observed through a lens a few small whitish excrescences or nipples, projecting from about the middle of the electrified stone. On the eighteenth day these projections enlarged, and struck out seven or eight filaments, each of them longer than the hemisphere on which they grew.

On the twenty-sixth day these appearances assumed the form of a perfect insect, standing erect on a few bristles which formed its tail. Till this period I had no notion that these appearances were other than an incipient mineral formation. On the twenty-eighth day these little creatures moved their legs. I must now say that I was not a little astonished. After a few days they detached themselves from the stone, and moved about at pleasure.

In the course of a few weeks about a hundred of them made their appearance on the stone. I examined them with a microscope, and observed that the smaller ones appeared to have only six legs, the larger ones eight. These insects are pronounced to be of the genus acarus, *but*

there appears to be a difference of opinion as to whether they are a known species; some assert that they are not.

I have never ventured an opinion on the cause of their birth, and for a very good reason – I was unable to form one. The simplest solution of the problem which occurred to me was that they arose from ova deposited by insects

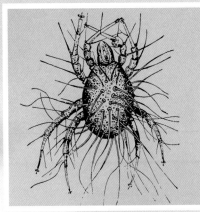

A drawing of one of Crosse's acari.

floating in the atmosphere and hatched by electric action. Still I could not imagine that an ovum could shoot out filaments, or that these filaments could become bristles, and moreover I could not detect, on the closest examination, the remains of a shell ...

I next imagined, as others have done, that they might originate from the water, and consequently made a close examination of numbers of vessels filled with the same fluid: in none of these could I perceive a trace of an insect, nor could I see any in any other part of the room.

If these creatures were indeed acari (i.e. mites), then they were arachnids, not insects, but far more important than their taxonomy is their apparent origin – spontaneously generated from non-living matter, in a solution typically much too caustic to sustain any form of life.

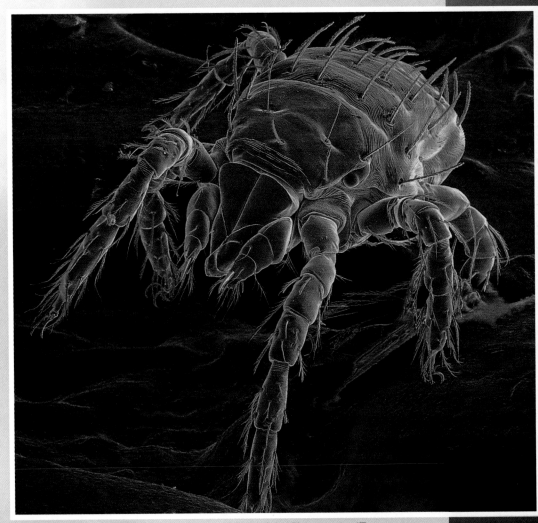

A coloured scanning electron micrograph (SEM) of the Chigger mite (TROMBICULA ALFREDDUGESI), also known as the American harvest mite. Magnification: x 225.

Far from receiving the scientific acclaim that he might have expected from such a sensational result, however, Crosse was subjected to such vitriolic tirades from his peers that he chose to retire from public life, shunned by – and shunning – the world. Yet when fellow electrical researcher W. H. Weeks repeated Crosse's experiments, carefully ensuring that all possible external sources of acari had been excluded from his apparatus, he too succeeded in producing living acari. Even eminent physicist Sir Michael Faraday revealed that he had obtained similar results with some of his own experiments. In 1909, Charles E. Benham urged scientists to repeat Crosse's work to solve this mystery once and for all, but his plea was not heeded. More than 80 years later, the riddle of Crosse's acari remains unexplained.

Perhaps Crosse was just a careless worker who had failed to isolate his apparatus's contents from external contamination. But what if he really did discover the miraculous secret of creating life from the inanimate? A fraud or a Frankenstein – who can say?

IRELAND'S MOVING STATUES

On 14 February 1985, some of the children in a group of 30 who were praying at St Mary's church in Asdee, County Kerry, claimed to have seen the right hand of a statue of Jesus beckoning them and the eyes of a Madonna statue moving. A month later, some children alleged that a statue in their church at Ballydesmond in County Cork had been moving.

Thus began an extraordinary year in which religious icons all over Ireland reputedly exhibited varying degrees of unexpected mobility. The site of the greatest fervour, however, was the shrine at Ballinspittle, County Cork, whose 152 kg (3 hundredweight) statue of the Virgin Mary was claimed by 17-year-old Clare O'Mahoney and her mother to have rocked backwards and forwards as they walked by its grotto on the evening of 22 July. This initiated a flurry of

The statue of the Virgin Mary at Ballinspittle that was reputedly seen to move.

interest, which led to great numbers of people visiting the shrine during the next four months and numerous allegations that the statue was indeed rocking on its heels, sometimes moving its head and shoulders too. Two days after the O'Mahoneys' sighting, it was watched with some alarm by Sergeant John Murray of the Garda Siochana, who stated that it was vibrating from side to side to such an extent that he had wondered if it was going to fall over.

Happily it did not, but events at Ballinspittle nonetheless reached a dramatically violent climax when, during the early evening of 31 October, two men attacked the Madonna with a hammer and an axe, badly damaging its head,

hands and the illuminated halo around its head. After jeering the horrified crowd for being "stupid fools, worshipping a plaster statue", the two men and a colleague who had been photographing their vandalism jumped in their car and drove off. Although soon caught, they were acquitted at their trial on a legal technicality.

In *The Moving Statue of Ballinspittle*, Lionel Beer listed 47 locations in Ireland that experienced reports of moving statues or other phenomena connected with the Virgin Mary during 1985, and a collection of journalistic accounts concerning these remarkable incidents featured in *Seeing Is Believing: Moving Statues in Ireland*, edited by Colm Toibin.

If they did not comprise authentic miracles, the sightings were presumably due to various optical effects. Investigators of the Asdee reports have shown that an illusion of movement can be effected with the two tall statues in St Mary's church merely by staring for a short time at the small round window between the statues and then gazing at either one of them.

Similarly, the glare of lights illuminating various statues in dark conditions might well have stimulated unconscious eye movements in the observers, thereby eliciting illusory movement by the statues. This is a likely explanation for the many claimed sightings that occurred outdoors at night, or inside churches with subdued lighting.

Another illusion is the autokinetic effect, often experienced by mountaineers, in which stationary objects seen at a distance and lacking a detailed background can appear to move. Perhaps this, coupled with the power of suggestion, always a potent force, was responsible for some reports too. After all, the Ballinspittle Madonna stands over 6 metres (20 feet) away from the viewing area, in a dark alcove on a hillside, from where it would surely be difficult for even the keenest-eyed observers to state categorically that they had detected genuine movement.

Last, but certainly not least, while stopping short of citing mass hallucination, it is evident that if there is a sufficient desire to see something, people will see it, whether it is real or not – a psychological situation arising time and time again with mysterious phenomena.

✦

CROP CIRCLES

Few mysteries have gained such a high public profile so rapidly as the occurrence of crop circles. Prior to 1980, these baffling but beautiful geometrical anomalies that mysteriously appear, usually at night, in fields of corn or other crops were known only to a few farmers. Today they are one of the most famous and visually recognizable enigmas of all

time. Their study even has its own name – cereology.

The variety of crop circles is almost endless, but the simplest form consists of a single circle within which all the corn stems are flattened to the ground but not broken, merely bent over at their base. Often the circle has an outer ring whose stems are also bent, but almost invariably in the opposite direction to those within the remainder of the circle. Sometimes the circle is surrounded by an equidistant series of much smaller circles (satellites), which may or may not be linked to the principal circle by channels. Other circles may contain narrow rings of unbent stems, sandwiched between the main body of the circle and an outermost ring of bent stems.

At first, crop circles seemed to be limited to England's southern counties, but once the phenomenon began to receive media attention, many more examples were reported. Soon, much of Britain was represented by sightings, with reports also coming in from overseas. Explanations offered for their occurrence ranged from rutting hedgehogs or badgers, landing marks left behind by visiting UFOs, and bickering flocks of birds, to fungal infections, over-fertilization and covert military involvement featuring secret weaponry trials.

Not only has the number of sightings increased, so too has the complexity of the circles reported. In their bestseller, *Circular Evidence*, engineers-turned-cereologists Pat Delgado and Colin Andrews suggest that the circles are cryptic pictograms created by some higher cosmic intelligence, and were recognized by the Hopi Indians of Arizona as hieroglyphics disclosing that the world was in grave peril.

A rather more prosaic explanation, but increasingly conceded nowadays by investigators, is that the more intricate the circles become, the less likely it is that they are untouched by human hands, not to mention feet, lawn rollers, and ropes anchored to a central stake. How else can we explain, for instance, the startling occurrence near Royston, Cambridgeshire, in August 1991 of a crop circle exhibiting the perfect configuration of a highly complex computer-generated model from chaos mathematics known as the Mandelbrot

The Mowing Devil, a pamphlet from 1678.

set? There is no question that the hoax factor plays a very prominent part in the occurrence of crop circles, as confirmed by various media exposés and statements from self-confessed fraudsters.

Nevertheless, many of the simpler circles are undoubtedly authentic. After all, some have occurred in remote, inaccessible areas, or in localities rarely visited by anyone, and why waste time producing fake examples here?. The most popular, and to my mind the most plausible, solution to these is the plasma vortex theory, proposed by Dr Terence Meaden, formerly associate professor of physics at Dalhousie University in Canada, more recently editor of the *Journal of Meteorology* and a symposium volume entitled *Circles From the Sky*.

According to Dr Meaden, if a hill obstructs a gust of wind, a vortex is formed, which meets stationary air on the hill's lee side to create a spiralling column that sucks in more air and atmospheric electricity. When this makes contact with the crop field, it spirals, flattening the corn into the familiar configuration of a crop circle. The column's electrical charge also produces the high-pitched noise that has been reported by people just before

Dr Meaden with Gary and Vivienne Tomlinson and the crop circles they saw being formed.

encountering a newly formed circle. Meaden's theory succinctly elucidates not only the physical construction of crop circles but also those rare yet fascinating occasions when eyewitnesses have been fortunate enough to witness the creation of a circle.

One such event occurred in August 1991, when Gary and Vivienne Tomlinson were taking an evening walk in Hambledon, Surrey, at the edge of a cornfield. Suddenly, the corn on their right-hand side began to move. A mist hovered above them and they could hear a strange high-pitched sound. Then a very powerful whirling wind began pushing them from above and all sides, until they could hardly stand upright – except for Gary's hair, responding to the localized build-up of static electricity. Abruptly, the vortex split in two, then raced away, shimmering mistily, and leaving behind two shocked eyewitnesses standing in the middle of a classic crop circle, whose corn stems were flattened all around them.

Further support for Meaden's theory has come from a team of Japanese physicists led by Professor Yoshihiko Ohtsuki, who announced in June 1991 that they had successfully generated tiny balls of plasma (ionized air) in the laboratory, formed by electromagnetic interference in the air. When these balls made contact with plates covered in aluminium powder, they created circles and rings corresponding in appearance to crop circles.

Continuing research has also unearthed some very intriguing but hitherto-unrecognized pre-1980 accounts of crop circles. Of particular interest is an illustrated pamphlet from August 1678, in which it is suggested that a "mowing devil" was responsible for an extraordinary configuration in a Hertfordshire oat field that greatly resembles a crop circle. Its present-day significance is indicated by the fact that an 1810 reproduction of this pamphlet was sold to a farmer at a Wiltshire auction in March 1994 for £280.

According to Dr Meaden, however, crop circles may date back considerably further than this. In his book *The Goddess of the Stones*, he boldly speculated that the famous cup and ring decorations favoured by Neolithic artists, ancient mazes, and other vulva-symbolizing geometric designs associated with primeval fertility goddesses may all have been inspired by early man's sightings of crop circles and their energetic creation.

It has often been said that nothing is new in the realms of fashion. The same may also be true, it would seem, in the world of cereology.

Crop formation in the form of the Mandelbrot set near Royston, Cambridgeshire. The formation appeared in August 1991.

GREEN CHILDREN OF WOOLPIT

The remarkable history of the green children of Woolpit was first documented by two medieval English chroniclers – Ralph, Abbot of Coggeshall, and William of Newburgh. One day during the reign of King Stephen (AD 1135–54), two children were found weeping and wandering, lost and forlorn, in the great pits used to trap wolves at the village of Woolpit, in Suffolk. They caused great amazement among the villagers, but this was due not to their behaviour and their unintelligible dialect but to their appearance – for their clothes, their eyes and, most strikingly, their skin were all green! They were taken to the house of local landowner Sir Richard de Calne, which became their home; but despite all attempts to feed them, for quite a time after their discovery these strange children refused to eat anything other than green beans. Sadly, the younger of the two, a boy, died less than a year later, but the other child, a girl, grew strong and spent the rest of her life in the area.

Over the years, the green tinge to her skin gradually vanished, and when she

The village sign depicts the Green Children.

The Woolpit church banner.

reached maturity she married a man from King's Lynn in Norfolk. She also learnt English, and was eventually able to inform the villagers that she and the boy had come from a country called St Martin's Land, where there was no sun, only a permanent hazy twilight. They had been following their flocks when they had entered an underground passageway and stumbled out, on the other side, into the bright sunlight of Woolpit.

Many explanations have been offered for this curious story. Because of the children's green skin (the colour of Faerie) and preference for green beans (food of the dead, according to Celtic lore), some researchers have discounted their history as merely a charming folktale. Others have linked it with England's traditional Green Man or Jack-in-the-Green – a leafy supernatural entity personifying fertility and the rebirth of spring. It has even been suggested that the children had originated from a mysterious subterranean world present beneath the surface of the earth and lacking sunlight, or from some parallel dimension through which they had accidentally stepped into our own.

In recent times, a much more literal, sober interpretation has also been put

forward for consideration. During the 1980s, investigator Paul Harris visited Woolpit and learnt that local people generally believe that the story derives from a legend concerning a medieval Norfolk earl who was guardian to two young children. The earl tried unsuccessfully to poison the children with arsenic and then abandoned them in Wayland Wood, in the area of Thetford Forest on the Norfolk–Suffolk border. Here they would surely have died, thus enabling him to take control of the estate that they were due to inherit when they reached adulthood. According to the Woolpit people, these probably became the green children who were later found, still alive but disoriented and ill. Worth noting here is that arsenic poisoning can cause chlorosis, in which the skin turns green. So too can anaemia, a result of malnutrition, from which the abandoned youngsters were likely to have been suffering. A diet-related origin for their green skin would also explain why the girl's complexion reverted to a normal colour once she began to thrive on proper food.

Harris believes that the story's other key portions have straightforward explanations too. For instance, a few miles north-west of Woolpit is a village called Fornham St Martin, which could explain the identity of "St Martin's Land". Further north is Thetford Forest, whose dark interior would certainly seem twilit and sunless to two young children abandoned in its depths. The forest also contains many Neolithic flint mines and associated passages. Perhaps the youngsters wandered into one of them, which led to Woolpit. Furthermore, in the twelfth century most people did not travel very far, so the dialect of children from a distant village may indeed have sounded strange to Woolpit's inhabitants.

There is one final but intriguing twist to the tale of the Woolpit green children. An almost identical story is on record from nineteenth-century Spain, dating from August 1887 and set in the Catalonian village of Banjos. Indeed, apart from the difference in the locality and time, the only notable discrepancy between the two stories is that in the Spanish version the girl dies too, after about five years. Even their liking for

The Green Man boss in the cloister ceiling of Norwich Cathedral.

beans is mentioned, and to add coincidence to coincidence, the nobleman who cares for them after their discovery is named as Señor Ricardo da Calno – not exactly dissimilar from Sir Richard de Calne!

This story has been unquestioningly recycled in several books; in *The Monster Trap and Other True Mysteries*, Peter Haining repeated a claim made by John Macklin that the documents and statements of the people who saw and looked after the two green children still exist. In 1986, however, Frank Preston revealed that he had written to the British Council Institute in Barcelona regarding this story, but although the institute conducted extensive searches on his behalf, which included contacting Spanish librarians, museums and town hall archives, as well as searching newspapers from August 1887 for relevant accounts, no trace of the story could be found. This is not surprising, because the village of Banjos does not exist. It is imaginary, just like its green children, whose story is clearly a hoax

devised by someone inspired by the Woolpit version to create a more modern counterpart.

SECRETS OF STONEHENGE

The British Isles are plentifully supplied with standing stones, stone circles and other ancient megaliths: Avebury Henge in Wiltshire, the Rollright Stones in Oxfordshire, Long Meg and Her Daughters in Cumbria, Callanish on Lewis in the Western Isles, the Longstone, one of several standing stones on Dartmoor, and the Ring of Brodgar in Orkney are just a few. None, however, is more famous, or more mysterious, than Stonehenge, standing aloof on Salisbury Plain.

Stonehenge consists of two circles, the outer one composed of sarsen stone (sandstone) pillars formerly supporting

lintels (only six remain), the inner one of bluestones. Inside the latter circle are two series of standing stones, each in the shape of a horseshoe. Once again, the outer series is of sarsen stones, the inner of bluestones. None of the circles or horseshoes is complete. Some of the stones have fallen, others are missing altogether. Inside the innermost horseshoe is a single stone, broken in half, called the Altar Stone, and surrounding the outermost circle is a ring of 56 holes called the Aubrey Holes. Intersecting these some 80 yards from the Altar Stone is the Heel Stone.

The sarsen stones are of local origin, but the bluestones are generally believed to have been transported somehow from the Prescelly Mountains in the far south-west of Wales. According to more radical ideas, intermingled with legend, they were brought to Wiltshire from Ireland, via the magical powers of the magician Merlin, and to Ireland from Africa, by giants!

It is popularly but erroneously believed that Stonehenge was constructed by the druids. In fact, Stonehenge was first constructed around 4000 years ago, during the Neolithic "New Stone" Age. It has been modified several times since then, most recently around 1400 BC, during the Early Bronze Age, producing the version that exists in incomplete form today.

This much is fairly clear, but far less certain is the precise function of this awe-inspiring edifice. Just what was Stonehenge – solar temple, lunar observatory, source of healing energy, extraterrestrial monument? Numerous theories, from the arcane to the absurd, have been proposed. A great deal has been written about the supposed alignments of certain of its stones with celestial events, leading to the conclusion that Stonehenge was created as a complex astronomical observatory; and it is true, for instance, that the line between the Heel Stone and the Altar Stone extends to the precise point of midsummer sunrise. More recently, however, as pointed out by Janet and Colin Bord in *Ancient Mysteries of Britain*, researches have exposed flaws in some of these alignments, thus necessitating a re-examination of the role of Stonehenge in this capacity.

Stonehenge – 4000 years old, its purpose is still a mystery.

A very different theory about Stonehenge owes its origin to folklore, which claims that, just like those of many other megaliths, its stones have healing properties. This belief was first documented as far back as the twelfth century AD, in Geoffrey of Monmouth's *History of the Kings of Britain*. Moreover, during the "Dragon Project" research programme initiated in 1978 by earth energy investigator Paul Devereux, it was demonstrated that at least one of the Rollright standing stones in Oxfordshire exhibited rapid fluctuations of magnetic energy and a high magnetic field. What is so interesting about this is that for centuries local people with broken or fractured limbs have visited the Rollright Stones in the belief that the stones will mend them – and modern hospital therapy has revealed that electromagnetism does accelerate the healing process of bone fractures. Is this just a coincidence?

Perhaps such forces were known to the builders of Stonehenge and other megalithic structures, who erected them in sites that could tap into the earth's natural energy sources for this purpose. Again, the "Dragon Project" has shown that many megaliths are situated on or near to geological faults, associated tectonic intrusions or areas releasing radiation.

Considerations of earth energy lead inevitably to the subject of ley lines – straight lines linking prehistoric or pre-Christian monuments, sacred sites and ancient magical localities, and which may visually delineate a vast network of underground channels of earth energy. Although such ideas were first seriously applied to the British Isles as recently as 1921, by amateur investigator Alfred Watkins, in China the reality of lung mei or "dragon paths" (inspiring the name for Devereux's project) has been accepted for countless centuries. Not only that, it

provides an intriguing parallel with the concept of energy meridians fundamental to the practice of acupuncture, another ancient Chinese tradition.

In the West, the subject of earth energy still incites controversy, but many no longer doubt its existence, or its power. One forceful demonstration of the latter was experienced by a very startled youth called William Lincoln on the evening of 25 August 1974. He and three friends had just entered a ring of beech trees encompassing an ancient earthwork circle called Chanctonbury Ring, an intersection of five leys on a hilltop at Washington, West Sussex, when he was suddenly raised more than a metre into the air by an invisible force. Here he remained for at least 30 seconds, suspended horizontally and screaming with fear, before falling down to the ground – a stark reminder, perhaps, of the potency of the past even in the present day?

A Gathering of Ghosts

BRITAIN'S GHOSTLY ROYAL FAMILY

Many of Britain's most famous cyclical (imprint) ghosts are of former monarchs or consorts who seem unwilling, or unable, to relinquish the present for the past. A cyclical apparition is a recurring phenomenon, triggered by certain environmental conditions. At least four are said to haunt various parts of Windsor Castle – Henry VIII in the deanery, Elizabeth I in the library, Charles I in the Canon's House, and George III in the room where he was restricted during his periods of madness. Sightings of George III have also been reported from Kensington Palace, where the spectre of his predecessor, George II, who died here, is sometimes seen gazing at the weather vane. Hampton Court is home to the spirits of three of Henry VIII's six wives – Anne Boleyn, Jane Seymour, who carries a lighted taper as she walks from the Queen's Apartments, and Catherine Howard, giving voice to terror-stricken shrieks.

Anne Boleyn's ghost is either fond of travelling or has a number of replicates because she has been reported elsewhere too. A brightly illuminated, gliding version has been spied on Tower Hill, she was imprisoned in the Tower of London before her execution. Each year on the anniversary of her execution (19 May), she appears at Blickling Hall in Norfolk where she lived for a time as a child, but her arrival foretells her ultimate doom, for she is headless, her head in her lap, inside a coach drawn by four headless horses.

The Tower of London was a prison to other noble personages down through

Anne Boleyn, second wife of Henry VIII

the centuries, and this is reflected in the assortment of apparitions reported there, including Henry VI, the two Princes in the Tower (Edward V and his brother) and Lady Jane Grey. A very different grey lady, believed to be the ghost of Mary I, who overthrew Lady Jane, frequents the tapestry room of Sawston Hall in Cambridgeshire; and Mary's mother, Catherine of Aragon, lives on in Kimbolton Castle, Huntingdon, where she died in 1536.

A more recent member of Britain's ghostly royal family is George IV, who acted as Prince Regent during George III's periods of insanity. He is sometimes seen walking along one or other of two underground passages linking the Brighton Pavilion and the Dome concert hall, which was a stable when he was alive. At the other end of the royal time scale is William II, killed while hunting in the New Forest in 1100, but still seen today on the Cadnam to Romsey road, the route taken by the cart carrying his dead body all those years ago.

Perhaps the most astonishing, and distant, member of Britain's royalty to linger in a contemporary limbo of the lost, however, is none other than Boadicea (Boudicca), Queen of the Iceni, who committed suicide during the first century AD rather than be captured by the Romans. The many centuries that have passed since then have created a Britain immeasurably different from the one she knew, but she has still not abandoned it, for a spectacular apparition of this valiant warrior queen riding her chariot has occasionally been sighted even in modern times, emerging from mist near Ermine Street, a Roman road in Lincolnshire.

✦

TERRIFYING TRANSPORT

Not all ghosts are human or animal; some of the strangest are of the very animatedly inanimate variety! One of the most gruesome examples must surely be the death coach of Lady Mary Howard that reputedly haunts the old King's Way moorland road between Tavistock and Okehampton in Devon. Imprisoned inside is the wan spectre of Lady Howard, daughter of a seventeenth-century estate owner called Sir John Fitz of Fitzford, and the coach itself is constructed from the skulls and bones of her four husbands, all of whom were supposedly murdered by her. Even the coach dog running in front of it is a skeleton.

On the evening of 28 June 1944 at around 9.45 p.m., David Hanchet was cycling home and had just reached the junction of Bell Lane in Enfield Old Town, on London's northern outskirts, when he saw a tall black box-shaped coach driven by a coachman and drawn by a team of black horses suddenly drive straight through a hedge bordering some allotments to his left. Totally silent but outlined by an electrical blue light, the coach ran parallel with the hedge for a while, with its wheels about a foot above the ground, then disappeared through the gates of an old garage. The coachman was wearing a tall black hat, a long whip was at his side, and several people were inside. A young boy riding a bike nearby also saw this extraordinary apparition and fled in terror. This is just one of many sightings of an eerie spectral coach running along Bell Lane, and according to legend it is the coach of King James II's notorious "hanging judge", George Jeffreys, who rides inside.

A much more modern mode of phantom transport was reported by many people during 1936 – nothing less, in fact, than a ghostly No. 7 double-decker bus! Bright red in colour, it raced down St Mark's Road, Kensington, on several occasions in the middle of the night, brightly lit inside and with headlights blazing, but no passengers or

crew could be seen. A number of car drivers coming along this road swerved in panic to avoid it, but the novelty of a supernatural double-decker swiftly vanished when one driver, unnerved by this frightening apparition, crashed into a wall and was killed. Soon afterwards the wall was demolished and the road widened to make the area safer – and the phantom bus was never seen again.

Also on file are recent reports of a ghostly Spitfire seen and heard near Biggin Hill airfield on London's southern fringes, and a spectral Wellington bomber in Dyfed flying over the Towy valley between Llandeilo and Llandovery, where Wellington bombers trained during the Second World War.

Most eerie of all, however, must surely be phantom road accidents, in which the transport is real but the victim a ghost. Driving along the A12 towards Great Yarmouth on the rainy evening of 2 November 1981, Andrew Cutajar was near to Hopton when he saw a grey mist in the middle of the road. As he drew nearer, it resolved itself into the form of a tall long-haired man dressed in a long coat or cloak and wearing old-fashioned lace-up boots. The figure made no attempt to move out of the way, so Cutajar braked to avoid him, but as he did so his car skidded on the wet road and plunged straight into the man – and out the other side! The man was no more substantial than a cloud and just vanished. Cutajar's car crashed into the grass verge, but happily he was uninjured. As for his "victim", it turns out that this is just one of several similar incidents reported from this stretch of road, seemingly haunted by the ghost of a man from an earlier century with no knowledge of modern traffic!

✦

SPRING-HEELED JACK

For a number of years during the nineteenth century, London was terrorized by two veritable fiends in human form known only as Jack, and whose identities remain as much a mystery today as they were then. One was a horrific serial killer – Jack the

Ripper. The other was an even more grotesque figure, who may not even have been human – Spring-heeled Jack.

The saga of Spring-heeled Jack appears to have begun in September 1837, when three women and one man, all in separate incidents and all in or near London, were attacked by a weird cloaked figure with pointed ears, talon-like claws, protruding eyes that glowed like blazing orbs and the ability to spit huge flames from his mouth. Equally bizarre was his capability of leaping immense distances through the air, often clearing walls and sometimes even houses in a single enormous leap and thus foiling all attempts made to capture him.

On the evening of 18 February 1838, teenage sisters Margaret and Lucy Scales were walking home through the Limehouse district after visiting their older brother when a tall phantom-like figure holding a small lamp leapt out of the shadows encompassing the entrance to Green Dragon Alley. Without uttering a word, he opened his mouth and spurted great flames of blue fire into Lucy's face, before bounding out of sight moments later as Lucy fell to the floor, gripped by a quivering spasm of fear that lasted for several hours afterwards.

Two nights later in East London, someone rang the bell at the gate of the house where 18-year-old Jane Alsop lived with her parents. When Jane opened the door, she could see a tall thin figure standing in the shadows, wearing an expansive black cloak and some form of helmet. Thinking that he was a policeman, she stepped forward and the man cried out to her to bring him a light quickly, because his colleagues had captured the infamous Spring-heeled Jack. After fetching a candle, she ran outside with it, but when she gave it to the supposed policeman, she received a terrifying shock. As reported by *The Times* two days later:

He threw off his outer garment, and applying the lighted candle to his breast, presented a most hideous and frightful appearance, and vomited forth a quantity of blue and white flame from his mouth, and his eyes resembled red balls of fire ... He wore a large helmet, and his dress [tunic], which appeared to fit him very tight, seemed to her to resemble white oil skin.

Spring-heeled Jack features on the front cover of a popular 'penny dreadful' (circa late nineteenth century).

foul marshes and suffused with the stink of disease and death. Here, amid abject poverty and squalor, a meagre existence was eked out by the flotsam and jetsam of humanity, among whom was a 13-year-old prostitute called Maria Davis. On that fateful day, while observed by several people close by, Maria was walking along a bridge spanning a particularly vile stretch of marsh called Folly Ditch when Spring-heeled Jack abruptly appeared. Seizing her by the shoulders, he breathed a flurry of flames into her face, then in an almost nonchalant manner he picked up the screaming girl and threw her over the side of the bridge, directly into the marsh below, where her body swiftly sank into its suffocating depths. Before any of the horrified onlookers could do anything, this evil entity had bounded away, as quickly as he had come, leaving the police to dredge the mud and ooze of Folly Ditch in search of Maria's corpse.

Spring-heeled Jack has never been satisfactorily identified. The only contender with any degree of merit was Henry, the Marquis of Waterford, infamous for his sadistic sense of humour. His general build and protuberant eyes corresponded with Jack's, and he is known to have been in the relevant area at the time of several of the attacks. Moreover, once while making one of his famous escapes, Jack's cloak opened and an elaborate crest containing a large gold "W" was revealed. However, whereas Waterford died in 1859, Jack's activities continued

But worse was to come. Almost blinded by the flames belched into her face by this monstrous apparition, Jane staggered back, and her attacker lunged at her with fingers that seemed to her to be made of metal – as sharp as the talons of some great beast or bird of prey, shredding her dress and tearing the flesh on her arms, neck and shoulders.

Screaming with pain and terror, Jane pulled out of his grasp and ran towards the door, but he was quicker and caught her again, raking her skin and pulling out clumps of her hair. Fortunately, her frantic cries alerted her two sisters in the house, who ran outside and freed her.

All three of the women then fled inside and slammed the door, but Jack refused to go away, until in answer to the sisters' frantic cries from an upstairs window some genuine policemen nearby came running. When he saw them, Jack escaped across a field in a series of huge bounds, dropping his cloak in his haste.

So far, his attacks, although terrifying, were not fatal, but all that changed one day in 1845 when Spring-heeled Jack transformed himself from a deranged madman into a callous murderer. At that time, Jacob's Island in Bermondsey was a sleazy slum area containing a number of filthy, decaying houses surrounded by

Jacob's Island, Bermondsey.

for many years afterwards, and as far afield as East Anglia and Everton in Liverpool, scene of his last known appearance, in September 1904.

Equally mystifying are his astounding feats. The common assumption that his immense leaps were achieved using shoes fitted with powerful springs was conclusively (and painfully) disproved when German soldiers wearing such shoes during the Second World War tried to emulate Jack. None succeeded, and almost all of them broke their ankles! Comparing his flame-spitting talent with that of fire-eaters is futile too, because fire-eaters cannot generate fire inside their mouths in the way that Jack did. And how can we explain his razor-sharp metallic talons and his macabre glowing eyes?

Inevitably, some investigators have speculated that Spring-heeled Jack was not human and that he had entered our world from some other dimension or planet. Curiously, a figure very similar in appearance and leaping abilities was observed bounding up into a tree by three people in Houston, Texas, on 18 June 1953. Once in the tree, he simply disappeared and immediately afterwards an unidentified rocket-shaped object was seen and heard rising up through the sky over the rooftops.

Was this a recent visitation from Spring-heeled Jack or another of his kind? If so, let us hope that the twentieth century was less to his liking than the nineteenth, and that he never again returns!

✵ THE BIG GREY MAN OF BEN MACDHUI

With a height of 1309 metres (4296 feet), Ben MacDhui is the loftiest peak in the Cairngorms and the second highest peak anywhere in Scotland. It also has another claim to fame – that of a haunted mountain, because many mountaineers are certain that it harbours a malign humanoid entity, referred to locally as Am Fear Liath Mor, the Big Grey Man.

Ben MacDhui's sinister occupant first came to widespread notice when eminent climber Professor Norman Collie recalled to a stunned audience at the Annual General Meeting of the Cairngorm Club in Aberdeen (December 1925) that in 1891 he had been descending from this mountain's summit through heavy mist when suddenly: "I began to think I heard something else than merely the noise of my own footsteps. For every few steps I took I heard a crunch, and then another crunch as if someone was walking after me but taking steps three or four times the length of my own."

At first Collie tried to make light of such fancies, but the sound persisted, though its agent remained hidden in the mist. As he continued walking "... and the eerie crunch, crunch, sounded behind me, I was seized with terror and took to my heels, staggering blindly among the boulders for four or five miles". Vowing never to return there alone, he remained convinced that there was "something very queer about the top of Ben MacDhui".

This chilling account, coupled with the unquestionable reliability of Collie himself, attracted great media attention. Moreover, other mountaineers began to confess that they too had experienced similar sensations of uncontrollable yet inexplicable fear and panic while on Ben MacDhui (some had scarcely avoided plummeting over the edge of its cliffs in their terror and overwhelming compulsion to leave as quickly as possible) and had come away with the

vivid impression that a malevolent, paranormal presence existed here, which sought to frighten away anyone venturing upon this lonely, desolate peak. There have even been sightings of a huge, man-like figure, strains of ghostly music and laughter have been heard wafting across its shadowy slopes, and many accounts of heavy footsteps like those heard by Collie have been documented.

Reports are not wholly confined to Ben MacDhui either. One day during the early 1920s, while coming down alone from Braeraich in Glen Eanaich, which is close to Ben MacDhui, experienced mountaineer Tom Crowley heard footsteps behind him. When he looked around, he was horrified to see a huge grey mist-shrouded figure with pointed ears, long legs and finger-like talons on its feet. He did not stay for a closer look.

Wales's answer to the Big Grey Man is the Grey King, also known as the Brenin Llwyd or Monarch of the Mist. Said to frequent Snowdon, Cader Idris, Plynlimon, and other lofty peaks, this awesome entity was greatly feared in times past as a child-stealer, and even the mountain guides were nervous of venturing into its domain.

Explanations offered for the Big Grey Man are very diverse. They range from a yeti-like man-beast, a mystical holy man, a geological holograph, and an optical illusion comparable to the famous Brocken spectre, to a marooned extraterrestrial, a visitor-induced energy trace image, an electromagnetic

Ben MacDui looks tranquil enough, but does it harbour a sinister presence?

phantom, and a hallucination engendered by oxygen deficiency.

There is also another noteworthy possibility. In view of the vast variety of unexplained phenomena reported from Ben MacDhui over the years, could this mountain be a "window" area – an interface between different dimensions or alternate worlds? If so, there is a good chance that such a significant portal would have a guardian, to deter would-be intruders or trespassers. Is it just coincidence that this is the precise effect so successfully accomplished by Ben MacDhui's mysterious Big Grey Man?

SCREAMING SKULLS, WAILING BANSHEES ... AND A TALKING MONGOOSE

Many ghostly phenomena are predominantly visual, but Britain can boast some emphatically audible examples too. One of the most macabre is the screaming skull of Bettiscombe Manor, Dorset. Several different versions of its history have been documented, but according to the most familiar one it is the skull of a West Indian black slave, whose master, John Frederick Pinney of Bettiscombe Manor, promised to send his body to his homeland for burial when he died. Sadly, however, Pinney broke his promise, burying him in Bettiscombe churchyard instead. Every night from then on, the churchyard and manor echoed with the sounds of terrible screams and groans, until the corpse of Pinney's slave was disinterred and brought into the manor. The sounds stopped, but at some time in the future the corpse mysteriously vanished, except for its yellowing skull. Since then, according to local lore, the skull has been taken out of the manor on several occasions – and each time the area has been plagued by devastations, including livestock deaths,

THE CORNISH OWLMAN

During 1976, several children and teenage girls independently spied a strange feathered "owlman" near the church at Mawnan, a small village on the south coast of Cornwall. Judging from the sketch made by eyewitness June Melling, 12, who saw it hovering over the church tower on 17 April, it resembled a man with feathered wings, pointed ears and a black beak. By contrast, it appears much more owl-like in a drawing prepared by Sally Chapman, one of two teenage girls who reportedly observed this entity on 3 July, as it stood amid some pine trees in the woods near the church and then took flight. According to Sally and fellow eyewitness Barbara Perry, it was like a big owl the size of a man, with glowing red eyes, pointed ears and pincer-like feet. Sally's description and sketch recall the European eagle owl *Bubo bubo*, an extremely large species not native to Britain but a frequent escapee from collections, with bright orange eyes, prominent ear tufts and huge talons on its feet. Further sightings occurred near Mawnan church in 1978, after which it seemed to vanish from existence.

During the late 1980s, however, a teenager whom I shall identify only as Gavin (now an undergraduate zoology student) was walking with his girlfriend one summer evening through woodlands in the vicinity of Mawnan when they saw the owlman standing on a thick branch in a large conifer tree, with its wings raised. Grey and brown in colour, with glowing eyes, it seemed around 1.25 metres (4 feet) tall, and they discerned two huge toes on the front of each foot. When the creature saw its eyewitnesses, "...its head jerked down and forwards, its wings lifted and it just jumped backwards. As it did its legs folded up." Its behaviour once again calls to mind a very large owl, although Gavin is not sure what it was. Some researchers deem the owlman to be a zooform entity, or simply a hoax. The simple truth is that we just don't know.

Birdman monster. Seen on 3rd July, quite late at night but not quite dark. Red eyes. Black mouth. It was very big with great big wings and black claws. Feathers grey.
B. Perry 4th July 1976.

I saw this monster bird last night. It stood like a man then it flew up though the trees. It is as big as a man. Its eyes are red and shine brightly. Sally Chapman 4/7/76.

F. Marion Crawford's classic ghost story **The Screaming Skull** illustrated by L. Ward in a 1936 edition.

· I·SAW·THE·BANSHEE·FLYING· · WILD·IN·THE·WIND·OF·MARCH ·

A banshee, illustrated by Florence Harrison (circa 1910).

exceptionally violent weather that destroyed crops, and unearthly screams, all of which have ceased once the skull has been returned.

A chilling tale, but whether there is any truth to it is quite another matter. When the skull was examined by Professor Gilbert Causey of the Royal College of Surgeons, he stated that it was in fact the skull of a prehistoric woman. If so, it may have come from one of the ancient barrows on the Dorset Downs.

Other screaming skulls have been documented at Burton Agnes Hall in Yorkshire, Wardley Hall in Manchester, Calgarth House beside Lake Windermere, Warbleton Priory Farm in Sussex and Higher Farm at Chilton Cantelo in Somerset.

According to Irish lore, the banshee is a supernatural entity in the form of a weeping woman who haunts certain ancient Irish families (even outside Ireland), and whose terrible wailing cry warns of an impending death within the family or its circle of friends. Perhaps the most dramatic recent case occurred on 22 November 1963, when Boston businessman James O'Barry, descended from an Irish family who emigrated to the USA in 1848, allegedly heard the banshee's fearful shriek just after noon. Later that day, O'Barry learnt that one of his friends had been assassinated: his friend was President John F. Kennedy.

A Welsh equivalent to the banshee is a disembodied moaning cry known as the cyhyraeth or death sound, which haunts a number of old Welsh families. It has recently been reported in the region of the River Towy. Another audible augury of doom is a drum that once belonged to Sir Francis Drake. Now housed at Buckland Abbey, once Drake's home, it is said to beat of its own accord at times of national crisis. Events at which the drum has supposedly sounded include the surrender of the German fleet in Scapa Flow in the Orkney Islands in 1918, and the retreat from Dunkirk in June 1940.

Perhaps the most bizarre vocal apparition documented in Britain was a talking mongoose called Gef, which purportedly haunted the Irving family's isolated farmhouse, Doarlish Cashen, on the Isle of Man's western coast, during the 1930s. Although many people visited their home and heard Gef, only the Irvings claimed to have seen him clearly. Some investigators believe that Gef was a mischievous poltergeist, whereas others have concluded that the Irvings' teenage daughter, Voirrey, was an accomplished ventriloquist.

DEVIL'S HOOFPRINTS

The Times is not known for carrying unreliable or sensationalized information, which is why the general public and scientific world alike took particular notice of a report that appeared in its 16 February 1855 issue, from which the extract below is drawn:

Considerable sensation has been evoked in the towns of Topsham, Lympstone, Exmouth, Teignmouth, and Dawlish ... It appears that, on Thursday night last [8 February] there was a very heavy fall of snow in the neighbourhood of Exeter and the south of Devon. On the following morning the inhabitants of the above towns were surprised at discovering the footmarks of some strange and mysterious animal, endowed with the power of ubiquity, as the footprints were to be seen in all kinds of unaccountable places – on the tops of houses and narrow walls, in gardens and courtyards, enclosed by high walls and palings, as well as in open fields. There was hardly a garden in Lympstone where these footprints were not observable. The track appeared more like that of a biped than of a quadruped, and the steps were generally eight inches in advance of each other. The impression of the foot closely resembled that of a donkey's shoe, and measured from an inch and a half to (in some instances) two and a half inches across [38–63 mm]. Here and there it appeared as if cloven, but in the generality of the steps the shoe was continuous, and, from the snow in the centre remaining entire, merely showing the outer crest of the foot, it must have been convex.

It was not long before the more superstitious-minded voiced the opinion that these bewildering prints were of diabolical origin, and so they became known as the devil's footprints or hoofprints. This was but one of many explanations proffered, including unusual meteorological effects, or the tracks of otters, rats, herons, wood mice, an escaped kangaroo, swans, cats, dogs, badgers, hares, donkeys, or even a still-undiscovered species of albatross-like bird making a fleeting visit from its secret polar domain.

The most recent, and certainly the most novel, solution proposed was that of Manfri Frederick Wood in his book *In the Life of a Romany Gypsy*, claiming that according to Romany recollections the tracks were the product of a well-orchestrated exercise featuring seven Romany tribes using more than 400 sets of measure stilts with size 27 boots at their base! The purpose was to scare superstitious Didekais and Pikies from the area.

No known meteorological effect can create these "hoofprints", and all but one of the animal contenders are too large. Moreover, according to certain other reports of that February night's strange event, some tracks passed through drain-pipes and tiny holes in hedges, and even stopped abruptly in the middle of open fields.

The only creature whose tracks are small enough, and can also explain these anomalies, is the wood mouse *Apodemus sylvaticus*. This species is extremely adept at climbing up and over all manner of surfaces and structures. It can also run through drain-pipes and squeeze through minuscule gaps. And a wood mouse scampering across a white, snow-covered field would soon be spotted and snatched off the ground by any owl close by, thus bringing its tracks to a sudden end.

Reviewing this case in 1964, zoologist Alfred Leutscher revealed how the wood mouse's four paws collectively produce a horseshoe-shaped print when hopping through snow, just like those found in Devon, and he recalled seeing in Epping Forest many such tracks made in the snow by wood mice during the severe winter of 1962–63. It was an exceptionally severe winter when the tracks occurred in Devon, so with less food available than normal the area's wood mice may have been unusually bold in searching for nourishment – a plausible scenario that also explains why such tracks have not been seen very often since.

*The wood mouse (*APODEMUS SYLVATICUS*) is extremely agile.*

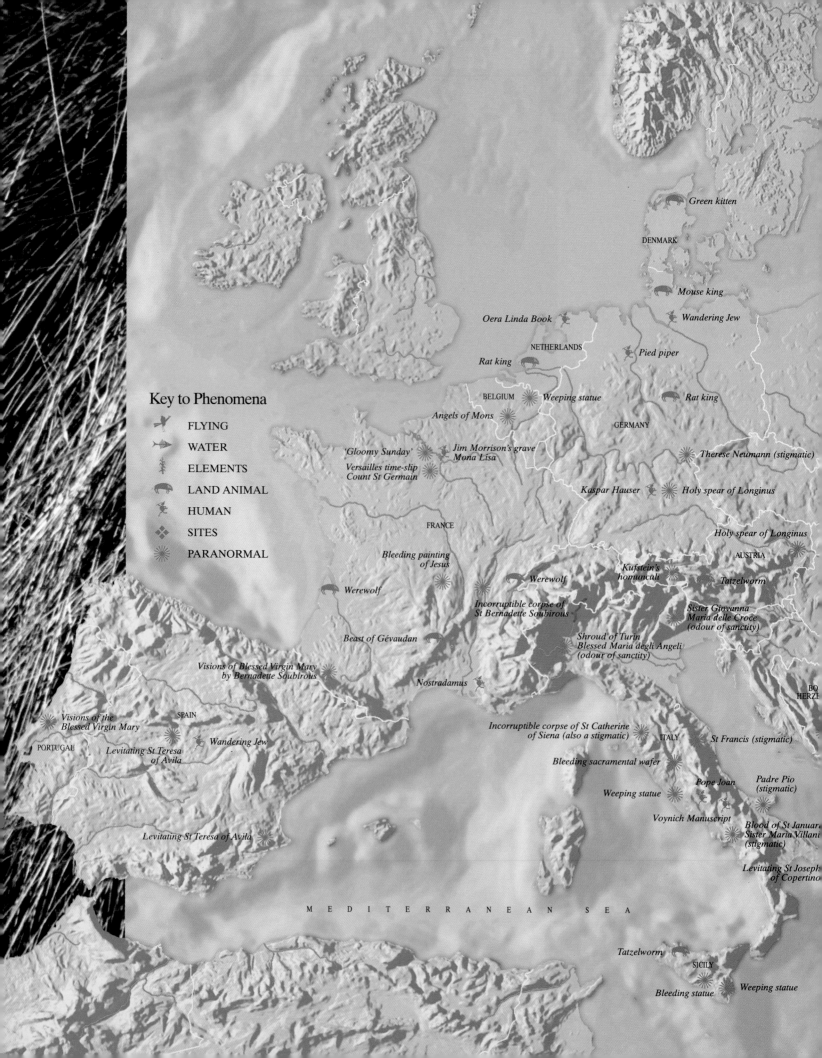

Key to Phenomena

- FLYING
- WATER
- ELEMENTS
- LAND ANIMAL
- HUMAN
- SITES
- PARANORMAL

Green kitten

DENMARK

Mouse king

Wandering Jew

Oera Linda Book

Pied piper

NETHERLANDS

Rat king

BELGIUM   *Weeping statue*

Angels of Mons

Rat king

GERMANY

'Gloomy Sunday'   *Jim Morrison's grave*
Mona Lisa

Therese Neumann (stigmatic)

Versailles time-slip
Count St Germain

Kaspar Hauser   *Holy spear of Longinus*

FRANCE

Holy spear of Longinus

Bleeding painting
of Jesus

AUSTRIA

Kufstein's
honunculi   *Tatzelworm*

Werewolf

Werewolf

*Sister Giovanna
Maria delle Croce
(odour of sanctity)*

Incorruptible corpse of
St Bernadette Soubirous

Shroud of Turin
Blessed Maria degli Angeli
(odour of sanctity)

Beast of Gévaudan

Visions of Blessed Virgin Mary
by Bernadette Soubirous

Nostradamus

BO
HERZE

Visions of the
Blessed Virgin Mary

SPAIN

*Incorruptible corpse of St Catherine
of Siena (also a stigmatic)*   ITALY   St Francis (stigmatic)

PORTUGAL

Wandering Jew

Levitating St Teresa
of Avila

Bleeding sacramental wafer

Pope Joan   Padre Pio
(stigmatic)

Weeping statue

Voynich Manuscript   Blood of St Januar
Sister Maria Villani
(stigmatic)

Levitating St Teresa of Avila

Levitating St Joseph
of Copertino

M E D I T E R R A N E A N   S E A

Tatzelworm

SICILY

Bleeding statue   Weeping statue

Incorruptible
corpse of
St Andrew Bobola

POLAND

ROMANIA

Vampires
Prince Vlad Tepes

eding statue;
ssed Virgin Mary
ons

❂ Chapter 2 ❂
Continental Europe

HISTORIC REALMS OF MARVELS AND MIRACLES

EUROPE – A CONTINENT OF PROUD HISTORY AND GREAT
MYSTERY, WHERE RELIGIOUS MIRACLES AND SACRED
CHRISTIAN RELICS STAND ALONGSIDE DARKER WONDERS
AND PAGAN RIDDLES; A WORLD OF DYNASTIES AND
DECEPTION WHOSE LANDS ARE WELL-EXPLORED, YET
RETAIN MANY CRYPTIC SECRETS. LET US LOOK MORE
CLOSELY AT SOME OF THESE ENIGMAS AND SEE WHAT
THEY WILL REVEAL.

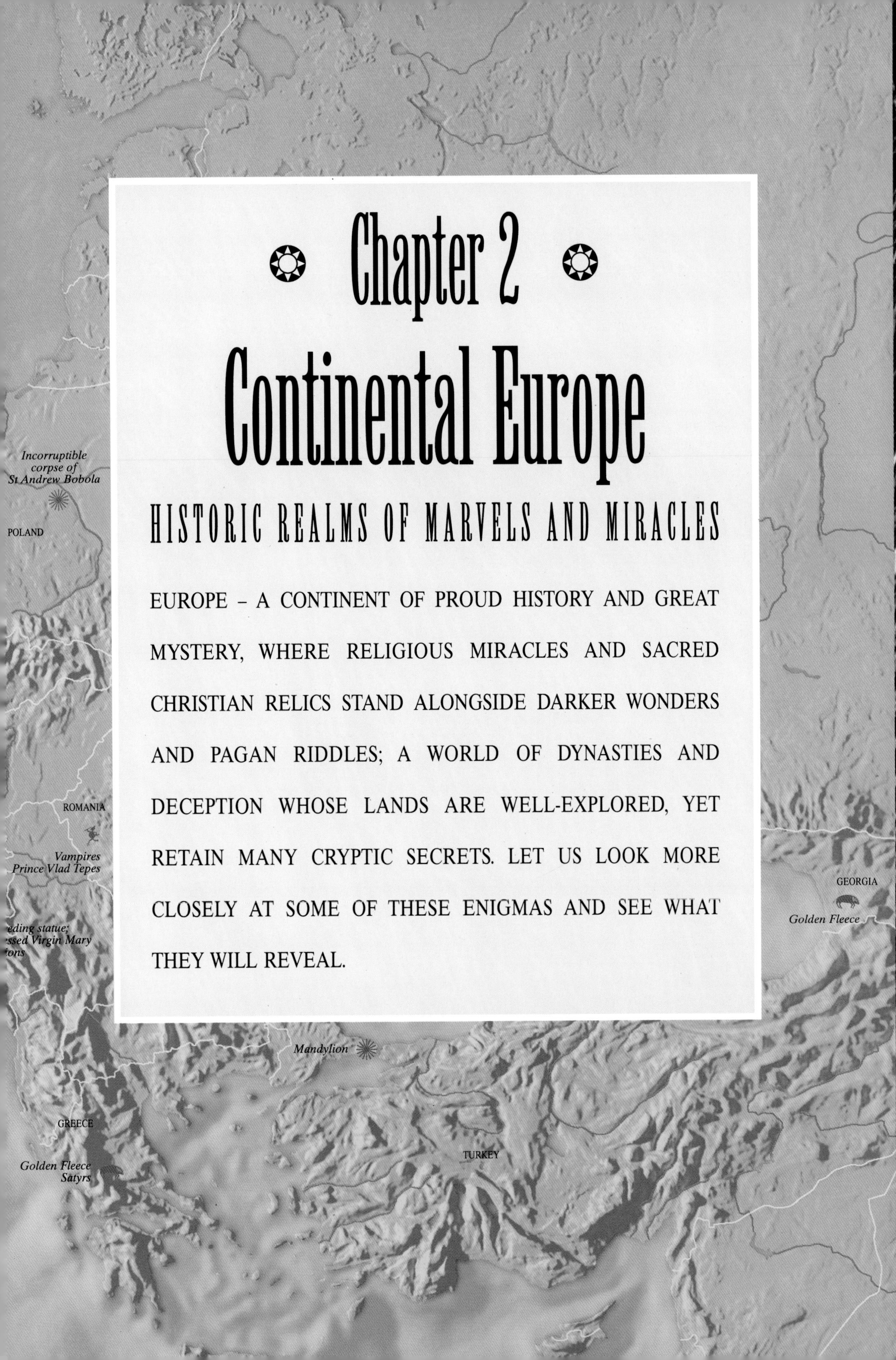

GEORGIA

Golden Fleece

Mandylion ❈

GREECE

Golden Fleece
Satyrs

TURKEY

Rat Kings, Tatzelworms and Other Baffling Beasts

✦

RAT KINGS

On 13 July 1748, German miller Johann Heinrich Jager found that his mill at Gross Ballheiser (also spelt "Grossballhausen") contained more than just flour when a bizarre aggregation of 18 living rats fell out from between two stones underneath the cogwheels. Remarkably, the rats were all inextricably linked to one another by their tails, which were intertwined in a knot of gordian proportions. This type of conjoined collection of rats is called a rat king or roi de rats, possibly a corruption of rouet de rats – "rat wheel", and quite a number of examples have been documented in Europe during the past few centuries.

Perhaps the most dramatic case on record featured the discovery by some farm workers in December 1822 of two rat kings together, within a hollow beam in the attic of a barn in the eastern German village of Döllstedt. One of the kings contained 28 rats, the other had 14. Yet even these do not compare to the monstrous example found desiccated and hairless in a miller's chimney at Buchheim, Germany, in May 1828. Its rats, probably not adults, comprised an amazing 32 individuals in total. This emperor among kings was duly preserved for posterity and is now

a prized possession of the Altenberg Mauritianum.

In *Rats*, Martin Hart devoted a chapter to rat kings and listed 56 different examples, 38 of which he considered to be authentic (some fake rat kings have been deliberately manufactured over the years to sell at high prices to unwary curio collectors).

A rat ring or roi de rats – the result of a bizarre intertwining of the creatures' tails.

All but one feature the black rat *Rattus rattus*; the exception is a king of 10 young field rats *R. brevicaudatus*, found in Bogor, Java, on 23 March 1918. A king of young wood mice *Apodemus sylvaticus* was discovered in April 1929 at Holstein, and there are a few squirrel

kings on record too. The most recent rat king seems to be a seven-specimen example found by Dutch farmer P. van Nijnatten in his barn at Rucphen, North Brabant, in February 1963.

How can rat kings be explained? Some French investigators have proposed that the linking of specimens may occur before the birth of a litter, so that the litter's rats are born as a king. If so, this would be similar to the little-known phenomenon of cat kings – litters of kittens born with grossly intertwined umbilical cords. As some of the largest rat kings have contained adults, however, a prenatal origin cannot explain all, if any, such kings. After all, as the members of a king are unlikely to be able to obtain much food, they surely could not survive from birth to maturity in an inseparably linked condition.

Alternatively, if a group of rats find themselves in a confined damp space, they may huddle close to one another, pressing and wrapping their tails together, so that the tails adhere in a knotted mass. In a bid to uncover the kings' secret, the Rucphen specimen was X-rayed, which revealed that the tails were indeed knotted, resulting in some tail fractures and signs of a callus formation. These indicated that the knot had occurred quite some time in the past, but just how the knot had formed remains a mystery.

THE ALPINE TATZELWORM

One day during the summer of 1921, a poacher and a herdsman were hunting on Hochfilzenalm mountain in southern Austria when they saw a bizarre animal watching them. Resting on a rock, it resembled a grey worm, 60–90 cm (2–3 feet) long and as thick as a man's arm. The poacher decided to shoot the creature and pointed his rifle at it, but just as he did so it leapt at the men, performing a considerable aerial arc and revealing that it possessed two short front legs. Needless to say, the men fled at once, leaving their uncanny adversary far behind.

This is just one of countless reports on file describing a seemingly undiscovered species of reptile or amphibian native to the Swiss, Bavarian and Austrian Alps of Central Europe,

and referred to by the local inhabitants of this alpine terrain as the tatzelworm (clawed worm) or stollenworm (hole-dwelling worm). Judging from a report from farmers describing a strange cat-headed serpentine beast with only two front limbs that was seen attacking a herd of pigs near Palermo, Sicily, in 1954, creatures resembling the tatzelworm might also exist in parts of southern Europe.

Science may have narrowly missed the chance of uncovering the tatzelworm's identity in 1924, for this was when two travellers in the Mur Valley discovered what seemed to be the partial skeleton of a 120-cm-(4-foot) long lizard. It was looked at by a veterinary student, who suggested that it comprised the remains of a roe deer carcase, though this was disputed by its finders because of discrepancies between its features and those of deer. Unfortunately the skeleton was afterwards discarded without anyone else examining it. Interestingly, just two years later a creature said to resemble a giant lizard was encountered by a 12-year-old shepherd boy at precisely the same spot where the controversial skeleton had been found. The boy was so terrified by the experience that he refused to tend sheep there for the rest of that summer.

The description given by the poacher and herdsman in 1921 fits that of most tatzelworms on record, with one notable exception. Different eyewitnesses have given different limb counts. Some claim that this species has only a single, front pair of legs; others say that it has two pairs of legs; a few say that it has no legs at all. In general appearance it is likened to a worm-like lizard or salamander. None of these identities is impossible. There is a group of widely distributed lizards called skinks, some of which have two pairs of small limbs, others just a single tiny front pair. Similarly, while most salamanders have two small pairs, the North American sirens have only a front pair.

Some zoologists have favoured a relationship between the tatzelworm and the American Gila monster *Heloderma suspectum*, a species of poisonous lizard, or with the glass snake *Ophisaurus apodus*, a large legless lizard from southern Europe.

In 1954, Sicilian farmers reported seeing a cat-like creature with a serpent's body.

THE MARK OF THE WEREWOLF

Before scientific advances began to sweep aside the Dark Ages' all-embracing shadows of superstition, ignorance and religious fanaticism, much of Europe's population lived in very real fear of werewolves – humans who could transform themselves into wolves. In those days people had great faith in the reputed power of the plant wolfsbane (monkshood) to ward off these evil shapeshifters. Another practice was to shoot suspected individuals with blessed silver bullets.

Traditional measures for determining whether a person was a werewolf involved looking out for signs that were as vague as they were numerous. Suspicion could fall upon anyone with any of the following traits: protruding teeth, hairy hands or feet, ears that were pointed and small or positioned low and towards the back of the head, unusually long third fingers, thick eyebrows joining on the bridge of the nose, and long curved fingernails tinged with red. People eating the brains or roasted flesh of a wolf, or the meat from a sheep killed by a wolf, were certain to become werewolves; this was also the dire fate awaiting those who drank from puddles forming in wolf footprints or at water-holes frequented by wolves.

All in all, it is surprising that anyone escaped suspicion and it certainly explains the extraordinary abundance of werewolf trials during the Middle Ages. France, for instance, staged an incredible 30,000 trials just between the years 1520 and 1630, as confirmed in public records still existing from that period.

One of the most famous of these trials featured a recluse called Gilles Garnier. During the summer of 1573, the partially devoured corpses of several slaughtered children were found in the area of Dôle, and a number of local peasants claimed to have spied a strange wolf-like beast with Garnier's face. In November of that year a group of villagers, following the sound of a young girl's terrified screams, discovered her, still alive but badly wounded, in the clutches of a huge wolf fitting this description. Although the wolf escaped, Garnier was arrested a few days later, together with his wife. At the trial, Garnier freely confessed to two of the killings attributed to this creature, and even stated that he had taken home a portion from the body of one of his victims, which was duly eaten by his wife. Not surprisingly, both defendants were found guilty and were burned alive in January 1574.

Bearing in mind that the direct physical transformation of a human into a wolf –or any other creature – is a fundamental biological impossibility, it seems far more likely that Garnier was simply insane. Indeed, he may not even have committed the crimes: recluses lacking friends or influence have always been popular as scapegoats for the evil deeds of others.

Some werewolf trials adopted a more enlightened attitude, as with Jacques Rollet from Caude in western France, who had murdered and eaten several people before he was captured in 1598 while dismembering yet another victim. After hearing his claim that he could transform himself into a wolf and seeing that he was clearly mentally subnormal, the judge committed him to a lunatic asylum. A similar case featured Jean Grenier, a mentally retarded teenage shepherd from the Bordeaux region, who bragged that while in the guise of a wolf he had killed and devoured more than 50 children. Following his trial in 1604, Grenier was given into the care of a local Franciscan monastery where he spent the rest of his life.

Rollet, Grenier, possibly Garnier too, and many other so-called werewolves were undoubtedly suffering from a bizarre but long-recognized mental condition called lycanthropy in which sufferers fervently believe that they can actually turn into a wolf at will. They also behave like wolves, howling at the moon and attacking people using their teeth and nails. Even today, cases of this grotesque, pitiful delusion are occasionally reported from Europe.

Nevertheless, some people in medieval times may have believed that they were turning into wolves not because of lycanthropy but because they had taken various hallucinogenic substances. Some, derived from such plants as henbane and deadly nightshade, are well known for inducing illusions and were widely used for witchcraft purposes. In addition, a grain-contaminating fungus called ergot secretes a compound similar to LSD that causes hallucinatory sensations of shape-shifting. This is very relevant to the prevalence of medieval werewolf claims, because during that period uncontaminated grain was reserved for the aristocracy; peasants wishing to make bread had to use grain contaminated with ergot. Little wonder, then, that some were convinced that they could change themselves into wolves.

Rabid wolves foaming at the mouth, or somebody unfortunate enough to have been bitten by one and thus displaying the same symptoms, are also likely to have been mistaken for werewolves. It is certainly the case that two further supposed traits of werewolves are their frothing mouths and their ability to turn anyone they bite into a werewolf.

In 1990, Hugh Trotti offered what may well be yet another, quite fascinating insight into the werewolf myth. An ancient Egyptian god of death was the jackal-headed deity Anubis, worshipped by a cult whose priests wore a wolf-like mask representing him. This cult eventually transferred to Rome and by the first century AD statues of a jackal-headed human figure called Hermanubis were numerous there. Germanic troops recruited into the Roman armies would have observed priests of Hermanubis wearing their wolf-like masks and seen the jackal-headed statues and would undoubtedly have remembered and spoken of them after the Roman Empire's fall. In turn, as suggested by Trotti, distorted accounts of these could eventually have inspired legends of humans who were able to assume the form of wolves.

⬡

GROW YOUR OWN HOMUNCULI

Even today, the alchemists of medieval times remain famous for their supposed, though unconfirmed, ability to transmute base metals into gold, using the fabled philosopher's stone. Less well-remembered, yet even more controversial, is their alleged artificial creation of tiny living humanoids, known as homunculi. Recently, however, Paul Thompson published an engrossing review of this largely forgotten arcane subject in *Fate* (September 1994), which contains some remarkable revelations.

Alchemists claimed that the culture medium required for the growth of homunculi contained several biological fluids such as sputum or egg-white, and sometimes inorganic fluids like dew; but the two substances most commonly cited as essential were human blood and semen, both of which are widely believed in primitive or non-scientific societies to harbour the vital essence of life. Also required was horse manure, whose heat-releasing properties were utilized to incubate the medium.

Bearing in mind that all of the above ingredients are readily obtainable, why was the production of homunculi a skill restricted to alchemists? The answer is

Theophrastus Paracelsus.

that the recipes always seemed to contain one vital ingredient that was exceptionally complex and difficult to prepare. For example, in the homunculus recipe contained within the treatise *De Natura Rerum*, written by the sixteenth-century Swiss scholar Theophrastus Paracelsus, "the arcanum of human blood" was included: essential but esoteric, its constituents were known only to the alchemical fraternity.

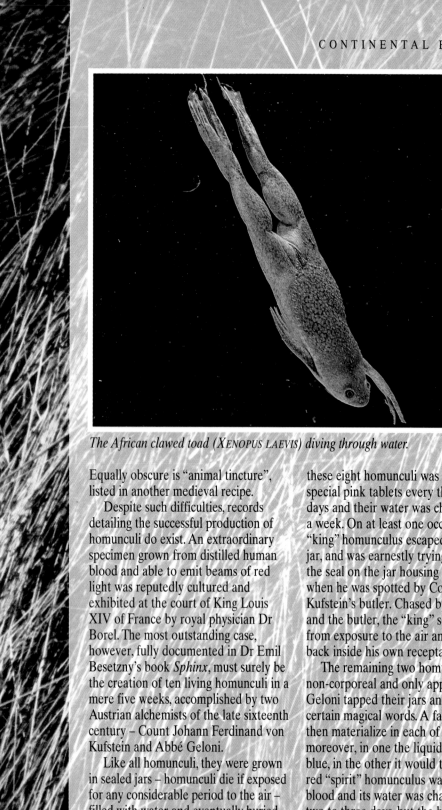

*The African clawed toad (*XENOPUS LAEVIS*) diving through water.*

Equally obscure is "animal tincture", listed in another medieval recipe.

Despite such difficulties, records detailing the successful production of homunculi do exist. An extraordinary specimen grown from distilled human blood and able to emit beams of red light was reputedly cultured and exhibited at the court of King Louis XIV of France by royal physician Dr Borel. The most outstanding case, however, fully documented in Dr Emil Besetzny's book *Sphinx*, must surely be the creation of ten living homunculi in a mere five weeks, accomplished by two Austrian alchemists of the late sixteenth century – Count Johann Ferdinand von Kufstein and Abbé Geloni.

Like all homunculi, they were grown in sealed jars – homunculi die if exposed for any considerable period to the air – filled with water and eventually buried under heaps of manure. They were treated, as usual, with some special, but unspecified, solution, which doubled the size of eight of the homunculi, producing a series of 30-cm- (1-foot) tall specimens.

No two homunculi looked the same and to each was fixed an identity. Eight were physical manikins, known respectively as the king, queen, knight, monk, nun, seraph, miner and architect, and clothes pertinent to their identities were manufactured for them. Each of these eight homunculi was fed with special pink tablets every three to four days and their water was changed once a week. On at least one occasion, the "king" homunculus escaped from his jar, and was earnestly trying to remove the seal on the jar housing the "queen" when he was spotted by Count Kufstein's butler. Chased by Kufstein and the butler, the "king" soon fainted from exposure to the air and was put back inside his own receptacle.

The remaining two homunculi were non-corporeal and only appeared when Geloni tapped their jars and chanted certain magical words. A face would then materialize in each of them; moreover, in one the liquid would turn blue, in the other it would turn red. The red "spirit" homunculus was fed on blood and its water was changed every two to three days, but the blue "spirit" homunculus was never fed and its water was never changed.

All ten homunculi would answer questions concerning future events, invariably predicting correctly the outcomes, and they were observed by many people. These included some very notable personages, like Count Franz Josef von Thun and Count Max Lamberg. Surely, however, such bizarre man-made entities could not really have existed – or could they?

I cannot help but wonder whether these particular homunculi were nothing more than large amphibians brought back by travellers from the tropics. One likely candidate is the African clawed toad *Xenopus laevis*, a common species, vaguely human in shape, which lives permanently in water – perhaps explaining why the "king" fainted soon after escaping from its jar.

No one knows what happened to nine of the homunculi after Geloni and Kufstein ultimately went their separate ways. However, an event occurred that may have left behind some tangible evidence of the tenth. Once, the jar containing the "monk" homunculus was accidentally dropped, smashing as it hit the floor and killing its humanoid inhabitant. His body was afterwards buried in the grounds of Kufstein's Tyrolean residence – but where is this today? If only we knew its locality, the soil around it could be sifted, as suggested by Paul Thompson, and who knows what remains might be found?

One thing is certain: if a 30-cm-long skeleton is ever found under these circumstances, Thompson would be very interested to learn more about it – and so would I.

THE GOLDEN FLEECE – DID IT REALLY EXIST?

One of the most familiar stories in Greek mythology features the quest by the hero Jason and his party of fellow adventurers aboard the *Argo* to obtain the Golden Fleece at Colchis (now part of Georgia). This was the fleece of Chrysomallus, a magical winged ram sent by Hermes to carry away some children from Ino, their evil stepmother. Ino had planned to sacrifice them in the hope of appeasing the gods during a great famine in Boeotia, ancient Greece.

Traditionally, this tale has been dismissed either as total fiction or as a distorted telling of an early search for gold in which an ordinary fleece was used as a sieve to trap gold particles washed down the river Phasis. In 1987, however, Dr G. J. Smith, a researcher in physical chemistry at Melbourne University in Australia, offered up for consideration a radically different theory, which proposed a much more direct, if highly unusual, basis in reality for the allegedly mythical Golden Fleece.

In modern times, farmers often feed their sheep upon leaves during periods of famine. Consequently, Smith suggested that in ancient Greece farmers experiencing such a situation may well have provided their sheep with the leaves of the extensively cultivated olive tree *Olea europaea*. The leaves of this species contain an acid from which chemical compounds known as pentacyclic triterpenoids are derived; sheep that ingest certain of these compounds are known to secrete through their skin's sweatglands a reddish substance called lanaurin, which stains their fleece a distinctive golden colouration.

This has led Smith to speculate that the story of the Golden Fleece may have originated from sightings of sheep that had been fed extensively upon olive tree leaves during the period of severe famine prevalent when this myth apparently arose, and which, therefore, may well have possessed golden, lanaurin-stained wool. It is hardly the most romantic explanation for such a stirring legend, but undeniably thought-provoking.

✴

THE BEAST OF GÉVAUDAN

Between June 1764 and June 1767, a considerable number of horrific murders, mostly of women and children, took place in a district of Lozère, in south-eastern France, called Gévaudan. On those few occasions when the assassin was spied, it proved to be a huge wolf-like beast, which dispatched its victims by savagely tearing out their throats before devouring their bodies or simply ripping them apart. To quell the rising tide of panic, in February 1765 King Louis XV sent to Gévaudan a famous hunter called Denneval, accompanied by six highly trained

bloodhounds, but they did not meet with success.

Seven months later, however, it seemed as if the Beast of Gévaudan's bloody reign of terror had finally come to an end, when the king's personal gun-carrier, Antoine de Beauterne, tracked what was assumed to be the creature to a quarry at the bottom of the Bèal Ravine, near the village of Pommier. Here it was shot dead and its immense body, more than 1.5 metres (5 feet) long and weighing 65 kg (143 lb), was transported in triumph to the court of the king. It proved to be a massive black wolf, but it was not the Beast, for the killings continued.

Then on 19 June 1767, another huge wolf was shot, this time at Mount Chauvet by Jean Chastel, after which the killings finally ended. Many people, however, believe that there was more to the history of the Gévaudan Beast than a bloodthirsty, possibly even rabid, wolf. In *La Bête du Gévaudan*, Gérald Ménatory suggested that many of the killings may in fact have been the work of one or more human serial killers, capitalizing upon reports of man-killing wolves to conceal their own murderous attacks.

There is one other theory, even more chilling. Could the Beast of Gévaudan have been a werewolf – performing its gruesome acts as a wolf, and afterwards transforming back into a man to elude discovery? Inevitably, scientists have little time for such an identity. Are we to assume, therefore, that it was just a coincidence that the killings came to an end when Chastel shot the Mount Chauvet wolf ... with a blessed silver bullet?

A woodcut impression of the Beast of Gévaudan, which terrorized Lozère in south-eastern France during the 1760s.

Jason and Medea with the Golden Fleece, in a German engraving.

DENMARK'S GREEN KITTEN

In autumn 1995, Pia Bischoff was surprised to discover a two-month-old kitten outside a hayloft in Dybvad, north-western Denmark. When she took a closer

look at it, however, she was even more surprised – because this curious kitten's fur and claws were bright green! All attempts to wash off its strange hue have been in vain. Vets who have examined the animal and researchers at the university hospital in Copenhagen who have studied samples of its fur claim that it may have been green ever since it was born, noting that the copper patina extends from the tip to the follicle of every hair.

Although this odd colouration could be due to a mutant gene, it seems more likely that the kitten (or even its mother while pregnant) has somehow come into contact with copper-contaminated water. Several years ago, in a town in southern Sweden, water derived from some corroded copper pipes was unmasked as the culprit responsible for the hair of several blonde women turning green!

A satyr portrayed on a fragment of an amphora dating from the sixth century BC.

SEX AND THE SATYRS

In Greek mythology, satyrs were semi-humans with the hairy legs, hooves, tail and short horns of goats; but did they have a basis in reality? This unexpected prospect was raised in a stimulating paper published in the scientific journal *Human Evolution* in 1994 by Dr Helmut Loofs-Wissowa from the Australian National University's Faculty of Asian Studies.

In ancient classical art, satyrs were frequently portrayed with a prominently erect penis, even when engaging in non-sexual activity. Indeed, it was this characteristic that earned them their reputation for sexual licentiousness. However, Dr Loofs-Wissowa believes that this is all fallacious and that in fact the satyrs were displaying a physiological condition known as the penis rectus, in which the penis assumes a horizontal position even when flaccid. Among modern humans this condition is only recorded from the bushmen of South Africa, but it is often portrayed in prehistoric cave art, including some Upper Palaeolithic examples from Europe, in which the figures exhibiting the penis rectus condition are hairy humanoids.

There are two very intriguing aspects to this. One is that anthropologists have argued that these hirsute figures are representations of Neanderthal man *Homo neanderthalensis*, which is believed to have died out at least 30,000 years ago. The other is that sightings of hairy troll-like humanoids are often reported in many parts of Asia, and these are believed by some scientists to be relict, modern-day Neanderthals, eluding formal scientific discovery. Of particular note here is that eyewitness descriptions of these mystifying entities have often mentioned the odd fact that they seem to have permanently erect penises, apparent even when spied indulging in non-sexual activity such as eating or walking. This suggests that they are in reality displaying the penis rectus condition.

Combining all this information, Loofs-Wissowa suggests that the penis rectus condition is clearly a marker in human palaeontology, i.e. indicating the identity of Neanderthals. And, as a direct consequence, he boldly proposes that satyrs might actually have been latter-day Neanderthals. He notes that many features attributed to satyrs in artistic representations differentiate them from modern humans but ally them to Neanderthals. These include their hairy body, upturned nose, prominent eye ridges, round head, strong neck and, most noticeable of all, their exhibition of the penis rectus condition, hitherto wrongly identified as an indication that satyrs possessed a hyperactive sex drive.

This is a very novel idea, but it still leaves unexplained the small matter of the satyrs' hooves and tail, not to mention their horns....

VAMPIRES

The vampire myth is a complex concept that has evolved from many different sources. Archaic superstitions, grisly discoveries of premature burials featuring unfortunate sufferers of catalepsy (a form of unconsciousness whose victims appear dead), psychopathic killers with an insane craving for blood, lurid tales of real blood-drinking vampire bats with which the followers of Cortés regaled their aghast public upon their return to Europe from the Americas – these are just a few of its interwoven strands.

The vampire's "evolution" from the early mythological concept of a vitalized corpse to a visibly human entity was greatly assisted by Bram Stoker's novel *Dracula*. His inspiration for the fictional count was a real person from the fifteenth century – Prince Vlad V of Wallachia, now part of Romania, and adjoining the vampires' supposed stronghold, Transylvania. Nicknamed Dracula after his family's emblem, a dragon, "dracul" in the Wallachian tongue, which also means "devil", Prince Vlad was greatly feared for his sadistic bloodlust. His favourite method of dealing with real or imagined foes was to impale their living bodies on stakes, for which he earned another nickname, "Tepes" – the Impaler. He is even believed to have dined upon their flesh and may have drunk their blood too.

There might be more to Vlad Tepes and his vampire connection, however, than murderous insanity. In some allergic reactions to a given substance, sufferers also develop an addiction to that same substance, and if deprived of it they can react in a highly bizarre, deranged manner. In 1985, Idaho physician Dr Thomas McDevitt suggested that the Wallachian tyrant may have suffered from an allergic reaction of this nature in relation to blood, explaining his obsession with blood-letting and the hideous methods that he devised to achieve it. Moreover, portraits of the prince depict him with dark circles beneath his eyes, puffy cheeks and a sallow pallid complexion – classic characteristics of some types of allergy victim.

Publicly aired in 1982 by Professor David Dolphin from the University of British Columbia in Vancouver, another medically inspired explanation for vampires is that they are suffering from a congenital blood disorder known as iron-deficiency porphyria, subsequently dubbed "the Dracula disease". The metabolism of sufferers is very inefficient in combining iron with complex compounds called porphyrins to yield haem, an intrinsic component of the blood pigment haemoglobin. As a result, their skin becomes increasingly impregnated with iron-free porphyrins, which are stimulated by daylight to incite a chain of reactions causing skin lesions and other disfigurements. To avoid this, sufferers tend to emerge only at night. Further increasing their vampire-like traits, another outcome of this disease is a tightening of the gums, which causes the teeth to protrude.

Bearing in mind that any haem which *is* present in the system of this disease's sufferers is exceedingly valuable, substances that destroy haem and thus remove precious iron from their bodies can be lethal to such

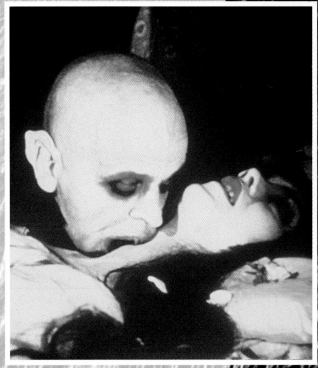

Fount of inspiration: twentieth-century horror films still feed on the vampire myth.

people. It is an interesting coincidence that a common food containing a substance, which activates the haem-destroying enzyme, cytochrome P450 also happens to be a famous vampire-dispelling agent – garlic!

The true vampire (DESMODUS ROTUNDUS), a native of tropical America, is indeed a blood-drinking bat.

Historical Mysteries

Voynich Manuscript

Amid the vast store of knowledge contained within the Beinecke Rare Book and Manuscript Library at Yale University is a unique medieval manuscript lavishly illustrated with colour paintings of strange plants and astronomical symbols, not to mention a varied selection of nude women. The only problem is that the ornate script of this book's 200-page text is written in a wholly unknown language that has withstood all attempts in modern times to decipher it.

This baffling tome is known as the Voynich Manuscript, named after New York book dealer Wilfred M. Voynich who purchased it in 1912 from the library of a Jesuit college in Frascati, Italy. Accompanying the manuscript was a letter dated 1666, written to the famous Jesuit scholar Athanasius Kircher by his former tutor Marcus Marci. In his letter, Marci claimed that the manuscript's author had been identified as Roger Bacon, an outstanding English scientist/alchemist from the thirteenth century, by one of the manuscript's previous owners, Holy Roman Emperor Rudolph II (died 1612).

After purchasing the manuscript, Voynich made copies available to many of the world's leading code-breakers, including teams employed in wartime cypher interpretation, as well as ancient language researchers – but all to no avail. Not only is the language resolutely incomprehensible, most of the illustrated species of flowers do not even exist!

When Voynich's widow died in 1960,

Strange plants feature in the Voynich manuscript.

the manuscript was sold to book dealer Hans Kraus, whose attempts to market it ended in such disappointment that in 1969 he donated the exasperating tome to Yale University. Among the identities offered to explain it are that it represents an attempt to devise an artificial language, an extravagant hoax, an example of spirit-mediated automatic writing or an exceedingly peculiar herbal catalogue.

The only person to achieve the slightest degree of success in exposing its secrets is Yale University's own Professor Robert S. Brumbaugh, who considers it to be an alchemical work; such works are well known for their elaborate symbolism and cryptic text. A few scribbled calculations in the manuscript's margins led him to formulating a code whereby he was able to decipher some of the names of those few illustrated plants in it that do exist, and also certain stars. Aside from that, the text's contents continue to remain a complete mystery.

I wonder if Yale University has considered the idea of self-publishing the Voynich Manuscript, selling it in their bookshops and any others willing to stock it, and announcing in a blaze of media publicity that a handsome prize will be given to anyone who succeeds in deciphering the manuscript and making their methods available for independent scrutiny? Bearing in mind Roger Bacon's fame for accurately predicting many major scientific inventions and principles centuries before they were conceived, however, perhaps some researchers have voiced the opinion that his extraordinary manuscript might well contain secrets that are best left undiscovered, even in this modern age.

The Voynich manuscript, written in a wholly unknown language.

⬖
ATLAND – THE "OTHER" ATLANTIS

The mysterious Oera Linda Book chronicles the supposed history of a northern continent called Atland, wholly distinct from Atlantis but equally lost today. A semicircular land mass sited off the Netherlands' Frisian coast, idyllic Atland had a subtropical climate and contented people, until a great catastrophe in 2193 BC destroyed the island and many, but not all, of its inhabitants. Those who survived travelled elsewhere, establishing some of the world's most significant civilizations, including those of the ancient Egyptians, Greeks and Indians.

As if all of this were not sufficiently radical, other fascinating insights into the Atlandian era include the origin of its own civilization as an offshoot from that of Atlantis, destroyed several millennia earlier, Frisian heroes as the original models for the Norse deities, a visit to Atland by the Greek hero Ulysses (Odysseus), the development of our numerical symbols not from the Arabic but from ancient Frisian, and Atland's use of Britain as a penal colony!

If its contents are indeed true, the Oera Linda Book would require historians to rewrite considerable portions of humanity's history, so what is known about this revolutionary document's own history and origin? It first attracted modern-day attention in 1848 when a Frisian antiquarian called Cornelius Over de Linden (i.e. Oera Linda) showed the manuscript to Dr E. Verwijs, Librarian of the Provincial Library of Leeuwarden in Friesland. The manuscript, written on cotton paper using iron-free black ink, had supposedly been copied in 1256 from a previous version and had been in the Oera Linda family ever since.

Verwijs was keen to see the book published, but when he approached the Frisian Society to sponsor such an undertaking, it refused, condemning the work as a hoax. In 1876, however, an eminently respectable London publisher, Trubner & Co., did publish it, with the original Frisian script printed alongside an English version by William R. Sandbach (derived in turn from a Dutch translation, by Dr J. O. Ottema, of the Frisian). Not unexpectedly, however, historians were virtually unanimous in their opinion that the manuscript was a complete fraud, differing only in their ideas as to who was the perpetrator, with Cornelius Oera Linda, Verwijs, or both, among the leading contenders.

And there its history might well have ended – unknown, briefly revealed, then forgotten once more – had it not been for Robert J. Scrutton, who restored it to public attention via his own books, *The Other Atlantis* and *The Secrets of Lost Atland*. Nevertheless, the erstwhile existence of Atland and the pioneering activities of its survivors have still largely failed to gain any official acceptance, though a rare vote of support for them appears in *Unsolved Mysteries: Past and Present* by Colin and Damon Wilson.

Yet who can be surprised? Any work that overturns every traditional concept of human advancement, offering what is in effect an entirely alternative history of the world but with scant independent support for its claims, is unlikely to be enthusiastically received by the academic community. Even the

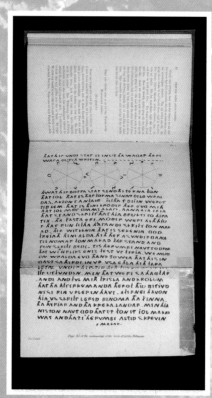

Part of the Oera Linda manuscript reproduced in the 1876 publication.

adherents of Immanuel Velikovsky's own highly individual, but exhaustively researched views of human history as expounded in *Worlds in Collision* and other works, are deeply suspicious of this book's authenticity – and they of all people might have been expected to show some sympathy for a work that challenges orthodox beliefs, had it shown any real promise of scholarly plausibility. So RIP Atland and the Oera Linda Book ... again.

✸

THE WANDERING JEW

During the Middle Ages, one of the most tenacious legends circulating through Europe was that of the Wandering Jew, Cartaphilus, originally employed as a porter by Pontius Pilate. According to the legend, after Pilate had delivered him to the Jews for crucifixion, Jesus was being dragged out of the judgement hall when he paused for a moment to rest. Seeing this, Cartaphilus cruelly struck him on the back with his hand and jeered, "Go quicker, Jesus, go quicker; why do you loiter?" In reply, Jesus looked back at the porter and said, "I am going, and you will wait till I return." (In some versions of the legend, Jesus was struck by Cartaphilus as he staggered past bearing his cross.) Since that day, Cartaphilus has roamed the world unceasingly, unable to die until the Last Judgement.

This stark tale was first documented in the book of the chronicles of the abbey at St Albans, England, which was copied and continued by Matthew Paris. He recorded that in AD 1228, the abbey was visited by a certain archbishop from Armenia, who told the monks that Cartaphilus had eaten at his table and that they had often spoken together. Apparently, he was now known as Joseph, following his baptism by Ananias (who also baptized the apostle Paul). A similar account of the Armenian archbishop's testimony was penned in 1242 by Philip Mouskes, who later became Bishop of Tournay.

During the sixteenth century, reports of the Wandering Jew were numerous and widespread. In 1505, he reputedly assisted a weaver called Kokot to find a

The Wandering Jew, from an illustration in **Le Juif Errant** *(1845).*

treasure that had been hidden in the royal palace in Bohemia 60 years earlier, during the Jew's previous visit there. Not long afterwards, he supposedly spoke with the Arab hero Fadhilah after the capture of the city of Elvan by the Arab. On that occasion, the Jew gave his name as Bassi Hadhret Issa.

During the winter of 1547, he was spied in a Hamburg church by a student called Paul von Eitzen, later to become Bishop of Schleswig. A tall man with long hair, despite the freezing weather the Jew was barefoot and dressed only in threadbare clothing, a description frequently given by eyewitnesses. Listening solemnly to the sermon, he

sighed and beat his breast whenever the name of Jesus was mentioned. Afterwards Eitzen sought him out, learning that he now called himself Ahasuerus, and listening in awe as the Jew regaled him with extensive details of his life and those of the countless famous people encountered by him during his unending travels. Again, the Jew's seemingly vast knowledge of history, as well as his ability to speak in many languages, was alluded to in numerous other eyewitness narratives too. Moreover, he never laughed, refused all offers of money or gifts, and harshly rebuked anyone speaking of God or Jesus in a blasphemous manner.

VERSAILLES TIME-SLIP

During the afternoon of 10 August 1901, two middle-aged English spinsters, college principal Charlotte "Annie" Moberly and headmistress Eleanor Jourdain, were walking through the gardens of the Palace of Versailles, seeking a building called the Petit Trianon. Looking around, they suddenly found that all the other people nearby seemed to be wearing strange clothes, resembling those worn in pre-Revolution France during the eighteenth century. On the steps of a summerhouse was a man, also dressed in this anachronistic style, whose face was visibly pockmarked by smallpox, which was common in the 1700s. And when they reached the Petit Trianon, Moberly (but not Jourdain) saw a woman in an elaborate eighteenth-century gown, who was sketching: the woman greatly resembled King Louis XVI's consort, Marie Antoinette!

The gardens at Versailles in the mid eighteenth century.

In their subsequent book, *An Adventure*, the two women expressed no doubt that they had either spied ghosts from the 1780s or had travelled back in time to that period. Other people came forward to announce that they too had experienced similar sights in the Versailles gardens. Moreover, schoolteacher Clare M. Burrow had allegedly walked through a gate here that was later shown to have been sealed up for over a century.

In *The Ghosts of the Trianon*, Michael H. Coleman concluded that the two women had probably come unsuspectingly upon a rehearsal for a theatrical pageant with actors in period costume, but how can that explain Miss Burrow's sealed gate? Similarly, the women claimed to have seen a plough, but were told by the gardeners that there was no plough in the gardens; such a plough did exist here, however, during the reign of Louis XVI. Is that just a coincidence, or do these gardens truly offer a window – even a doorway – into the past?

Eleanor Jourdain.　　　　*Charlotte Moberly.*

The Jew was supposedly seen by many people in Hamburg at that time, inspiring the German publication of a popular pamphlet outlining his history (a reflection of this period's anti-Semitism?) and also, much later, a series of dramatic wood-cuts by Gustave Doré.

In 1575, the secretary Christopher Krause and Master Jacob von Holstein, legates to the court of Spain, claimed to have met the Jew while travelling through Madrid. By the close of the century, he had also been reported from Vienna, from Cracow and Moscow in 1601, Lubeck in 1603, and Paris in 1604. By 1633 he was back in Hamburg, Brussels in 1640, Leipzig in 1642, Munich in 1721, and at the beginning of the 1800s he was travelling through Scandinavia. The most recent report comes from Salt Lake City, Utah, in 1868.

What are we to make of such a strange affair? Perhaps the most perceptive comment was made by John Allan in *Mysteries*: "... there is no shred of evidence for its truth. Apart from anything else, since Christ was prepared to forgive his killers as he hung on the cross, it seems monstrously out of character for him to condemn one man eternally for a single blow."

✷

THE PIED PIPER OF HAMELIN – FOLKLORE OR FACT?

The year was 1284, and the town of Hamelin in Lower Saxony, Germany, was besieged by a plague of rats. The despairing townsfolk offered a sizeable reward to anyone who could rid them of these rodents. One day a stranger arrived, dressed in garish two-tone attire, and by skilful playing of his musical pipe he lured the rats into the river Weser, where they all drowned. However, the ungrateful people refused to pay him his reward, so the piper began to play again, but this time it was not the rats but the town's own children who were called forth. Still playing, the sinister piper led 130 of them away, eastward out of Hamelin and on towards a hill called Koppen, which opened as they approached and closed up again when they had entered. Neither the piper nor the children were ever seen again.

There are many historians, especially in Germany, who believe that this famous fairy tale has a firm basis in fact. In Hamelin itself is a street called Bungelosen Strasse. This is the street through which the children supposedly ran when called by the piper's bewitching music; ever since, it has been forbidden by law to play any form of music here. It also bears an inscription recalling the piper's dreadful deed and fixing its date as 26 June 1284.

In 1982, Maurice Shadbolt revealed how, while investigating the pied piper myth at Hamelin, he visited the home of retired schoolteacher Hans Dobbertin, who has spent much of his life attempting to trace Hamelin's lost children and is now certain of their true fate. Dobbertin's theory hinges upon the key fact that in medieval times, German colonization of eastern territories was greatly encouraged, not only because they were eminently suitable for settlement, but also because their Slav and Hungarian overlords needed all the help they could obtain to prevent their lands from being overrun by the savage Tartars.

According to Dobbertin, the vanishing pied piper was most probably Count Nicholas von Spiegelberg, a German colonizer with longstanding connections in the Hamelin area. As for Hamelin's lost "children", Dobbertin and Shadbolt consider it much more likely that these were actually a group of disaffected teenagers, out of work and eager to make a new start elsewhere, who were encouraged by Spiegelberg to seek their fortune in the east of the country.

Dobbertin believes that Spiegelberg and the "children" journeyed north-east, eventually boarding a ship that sank, drowning everyone aboard, near a Pomeranian coastal village called Kopahn, now contained within Poland. He considers that over the course of several centuries, the name "Kopahn" became confused with that of "Koppen", the hill beyond Hamelin.

Spiegelberg was last seen on 8 July

The Pied Piper of Hamelin in an illustration by Arthur Rackham (1939).

1284, at the Baltic port of Stettin, several days' journey from Hamelin. Of particular note is that Stettin, like Kopahn, was a port along the route habitually taken by German colonizers travelling to the Baltic region. Even the piper's pied attire recalls the ornate outfits worn by German noblemen like Spiegelberg.

But what of the earlier portion of the legend, in which the piper rids Hamelin of its rats? Shadbolt believes this to be an entirely separate event. He claims that it was merely an example of rat removal involving the playing of a high-pitched tin whistle of the type frequently used for this purpose by

English rat-catchers; this was later erroneously tagged on to the tragic deaths of the town's teenagers when their ship sank near Kopahn. As a result, a wholly new story was created whose strange qualities have persisted long after the more prosaic reality had been forgotten.

Interestingly, a similar theory has been outlined by various other historians, but nominating Bishop Bruno of Olmütz (now Olomouc) as the piper figure, anxious to obtain colonizers for his diocese in Bohemia. They point out the many similarities in family names between the town records of Olomouc and Hamelin.

✦ WHATEVER HAPPENED TO THE LIZARD KING?

On 3 July 1971, Jim Morrison – lead singer with The Doors, and one of the world's most enigmatic rock stars – died of a heart attack in his bath. Or did he? Every year, fans old and new visit the Parisian cemetery of Père Lachaise, to see the grave in which he was buried. Or was he? For over 20 years, rumours have been circulating about the sensational possibility that the death of this mystical 1960s icon was a stage-managed sham – that in reality Jim shed his leather-clad

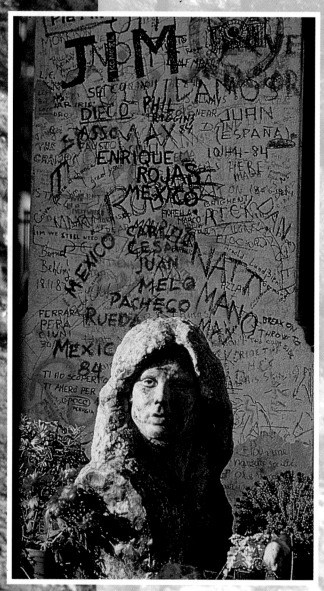

Memorial to Jim Morrison at Père Lachaise cemetery, Paris.

Lizard King persona and took on a new identity elsewhere.

Claims regarding this new identity are as varied as they are numerous, as reviewed in "Rumors, Myths and Urban Legends Surrounding the Death of Jim Morrison", an absorbing article by Thomas Lyttle in *Secret and Suppressed* (1993). Some of these stories tell of a mysterious businessman supposedly involved in banking transactions at San Francisco's Bank of America. Others allude to a frequenter of certain controversial bars and night-clubs in Los Angeles. Who is the secretive star of various radio programmes in Louisiana? Could Jim be a James-Bond-style intelligence agent with CIA links? According to yet another line of speculation, he is presently working as a minicab driver in Camberley!

Nevertheless, the concept of a faked death is not as outlandish as it might initially seem. Certainly, Jim was weary of his rock-star image, which he felt was responsible for his failure to achieve his aspired status as a serious poet. He had also publicly expressed a desire on many occasions to change his identity, to disappear and reappear as someone different.

But there is more to consider than just the necessary motive and inclination. Why was the media not informed of his death for six days – two days *after* the funeral itself? Isn't it rather strange that his parents were prevented from seeing his body, and that even his manager, the person who made the official announcement of his death, did not see it? Instead, he saw only Jim's widow Pamela, a sealed coffin (which a fellow Doors member claimed to be too small to hold Jim's tall body) and a death certificate made out by a local French doctor who has steadfastly refused to give interviews on the subject.

In addition, there was no autopsy of his body, the funeral was attended by just a few very close friends amid intense secrecy, and attempts since then by fans to obtain permission for the body to be dug up and formally examined have always been blocked. As for Pamela, the one person who would certainly know the truth, she died three years after Jim, without releasing any information.

Even those who accept that Jim's death was genuine are in disagreement

about its precise nature. Some discount a heart attack in preference for such diverse alternatives as: a drug overdose; assassination by covert intelligence agencies in the USA or France; death via spider venom used in magic initiation rituals, Jim was fascinated by many forms of occult practices, particularly voodoo; and supernatural murder via long-distance witchcraft perpetrated by a jilted lover in New York!

Thomas Lyttle offered a thought-provoking opinion from Ray Manzarek, keyboard player with The Doors: "If there was one guy that would have been capable of staging his own death – getting a phony death certificate and paying off some French doctor ... And putting a hundred and fifty pound sack of sand into a coffin and splitting to some point on this planet – Africa, who knows where – it is Jim Morrison who would have been able to pull it off."

Jim was famous for his macabre sense of humour: did he have the last laugh after all?

✦ STRANGE MUSIC

Certain famous European songs have some very strange tales to tell, far stranger than any of their lyrics, but few are more unnerving than the history of the song "Gloomy Sunday".

It was written in Paris one rainy Sunday in December 1932 by the Hungarian composer Reszo Seress, on the day after his girlfriend had ended their engagement. Intensely depressed, Seress was contemplating just how very gloomy this particular Sunday was when a hauntingly sad tune that was totally unknown to him began to play in his mind. Shocked out of his despair by this unexpected event, Seress jotted down the tune and entitled it "Gloomy Sunday". The words that he penned for it told the tragic story of a man whose lover had recently died and who was now considering suicide in order to be united with her again.

The first publishers to whom Seress took "Gloomy Sunday" turned it down, claiming it to be too melancholy. Indeed, one of them felt that it might be better if people never heard it. This opinion proved to be very prophetic, for once the song was published its unrelentingly sad strain soon gained a notorious reputation for inciting people to commit suicide.

The first known instance occurred in spring 1933, when a youth sitting in a Budapest cafe asked the band to play "Gloomy Sunday". After they had finished playing it, he promptly went home and shot himself. In a chilling account of this song's dark history by Tane Jackson in *The Unknown* (May 1987), several other alleged cases are given, though no names of the people concerned are mentioned, testifying to the fatal attraction of "Gloomy Sunday". Its victims even included singers who had incorporated its deadly refrain in their repertoires.

In one of the most disturbing cases, a London flat was broken into by neighbours after hearing the mournful melody of "Gloomy Sunday" playing incessantly inside. There they found the flat's owner, a young woman, lying dead on the floor from an overdose, with a gramophone endlessly playing the fatal song.

By the late 1930s, "Gloomy Sunday" had incited such a degree of public alarm that the Hungarian government discouraged public performances of it. Needless to say, this came as a great relief to many musicians, who had seriously begun to fear for their own continued well-being whenever they had to play Seress's uncanny composition. Many radio stations, including the BBC, considered banning it (a number of local stations in the USA did refuse to play it), and several families of suicide victims whose deaths were linked to this sinister song (over 200 in total) attempted unsuccessfully to ban it entirely.

The English version of "Gloomy Sunday" was written by Sam Lewis, and in 1941 a record of it was released by Billie Holliday. By then, however, the song's notoriety had lessened: with the coming of the Second World War there were many far more dramatic events to engage popular attention. Even so, its malign influence had not entirely ceased.

Gordon Beck, of Salisbury in Wiltshire, who served with 76 Squadron at RAF Yeravda in Poona, India, during 1946, recently recalled how one of his

The composer Tartini receives diabolic inspiration in this contemporary engraving.

fellow pilots would become very upset if ever he heard him playing his record of "Gloomy Sunday" (a version by the Artie Shaw Orchestra, with a female vocalist), the pilot claiming that it made him feel suicidal. Beck thought little of this, until he began flying too and discovered to his alarm that he could not get the song's haunting melody out of his head; it penetrated his mind even above the noise of the aeroplane's engines. Never again did Beck play "Gloomy Sunday".

How can the disturbing effect of this eerie song be explained? Perhaps, as suggested by Tane Jackson, Seress had expressed his own profound emotions of grief so successfully in the song that it somehow amplifies those of people listening to it who are similarly depressed, inducing them to take their own lives as a means of escaping their sadness. This disturbing prospect is not as unlikely as it might seem. In *The Secret Power of Music*, David Tame reveals that music can exert some astounding effects upon humans, influencing stress, heart rate, digestion and other metabolic processes, as well as our emotional and mental well-being.

Perhaps the most poignant cases

linked with "Gloomy Sunday" are those of the two people who were responsible for its creation. Its composer, Reszo Seress, committed suicide in 1968 by leaping off a building, after confessing that he had never been able to write another hit song. As for the girl who had jilted him all those years ago, she had already been found dead, alongside a sheet of paper on which she had written the words "Gloomy Sunday".

Another supposedly unlucky song is "I Dreamt That I Dwelt in Marble Halls", from Rudolf Friml's operetta *The Bohemian Girl*. Believed to bring bad luck to anyone who hears it, this song stirs up much the same feeling of dread among singers (some of whom perform it only with great reluctance) as the Shakespearean play *Macbeth* does among actors, who prefer to call it simply "the Scottish Play". Yet no one seems to know how or why this song gained its ill-starred reputation.

Some songs, rather like "Gloomy Sunday", seem to be written by the subconscious rather than the conscious mind. One night while asleep, the Italian composer Guiseppe Tartini dreamed that the devil was playing an exquisite tune to him on a violin. Waking up,

THE OUROBOUROS OF ORGANIC CHEMISTRY

One of the most famous aromatic compounds in organic chemistry is benzene, whose molecules each consist of six carbon atoms and six hydrogen atoms: but what is benzene's molecular structure? Today, the answer to this question is well known, but during much of the nineteenth century it was a profound mystery.

One night, after yet another fruitless attempt to discover the structure, German chemist Friedrich August Kekulé fell asleep and dreamed a bizarre dream in which the various atoms of benzene were cavorting all around him, combining and recombining in a dizzy phantasmagoria of shapes. Suddenly, right before his amazed eyes, they united to form an ouroboros – a snake-like dragon that clasps its own tail in its mouth, forming a ring. Instantly, Kekulé awoke and knew that at last he had found the answer: the six carbon atoms of benzene were linked to one another not in a line, or in a series of branched connections, but in a closed ring! And he was right.

Tartini attempted to write down the tune from his dream, and although he claimed that the result was greatly inferior, it became his most famous work – "The Devil's Trill". Similarly, in *Yesterday and Today*, Ray Coleman revealed that one late morning in 1963, the tune for what was destined to be one of the world's most frequently recorded songs came to its composer in a dream. The composer was Paul McCartney, and the song was "Yesterday".

✦

COUNT ST GERMAIN

Count St Germain is surely the quintessential "man of mystery". Although he was well-acquainted with many of the most eminent figures of eighteenth-century Europe, no one knew anything about him. His real name, his origin, background, the source of his inestimable wealth, even his age – all were shrouded in controversy, which he made no attempt to dispel.

He first came to attention in 1710, when seen in Venice by a youthful Countess von Georgy, who estimated him to be 45–50 years old. She saw him again in the late 1750s, only to discover that he did not look a day older than when she had first met him in Venice.

From 1737 until 1784, he travelled widely through Europe and beyond, visiting and offering (with varied degrees of success) all manner of advice and assistance to King Louis XV of France and other leading figures of the day. In 1743 his arrival at Versailles was a sensation, with countless stories and rumours circulating about this exotic-looking stranger, garbed in the most expensive clothes and literally dripping with spectacular diamonds – festooning his fingers, filling his pockets, and used by him in preference to money.

As the years passed by, the mysteries surrounding this charismatic count grew ever stranger. He refused to eat in public. He claimed to have lived for untold centuries and to have personally encountered the Holy Family. He was a welcomed member of many of the most esoteric occult societies. When asked about his immense wealth he spoke of how he had attained the alchemists' fabled philosopher's stone for converting base metals into gold, hinted of secret processes for creating enormous diamonds, of studies conducted in the Egyptian pyramids and meetings with the learned mystics of the Himalayas. He was said to possess healing powers,

Count St Germain – master alchemist or artful charlatan?

to undergo out-of-the-body journeys, and he visibly trembled with fear before fleeing from the room when, on one occasion, he was referred to as a devil. He even claimed to possess the alchemical elixir of eternal life – and it was not just his stories and his never-ageing appearance that gave people reason to believe this.

On 27 February 1784, Count St Germain died. He was buried at Eckernförde in Germany on 2 March, but not even death, it seemed, could suppress this irrepressible enigma for long. In 1785, he (or someone exactly like him) made a well-attested appearance at an occult conference in Wilhelmsbad. In future years he was seen many times – with fellow occultists, or advising Marie Antoinette, or visiting Sweden's King Gustavus III and many others too.

Even the twentieth century may not have escaped his personal attention. In January 1972, a Parisian man called Richard Chanfray, ostensibly in his mid-40s and claiming to be the count, appeared on television, and with the aid of a camping stove performed what seemed to be a successful transmutation of lead into gold. In November 1992, veteran traveller Douchan Gersi claimed to have met a mysterious person in Haiti called St Germain, who dematerialized in Gersi's hotel room, 100 miles away from Port-au-Prince, then reappeared 32 minutes later holding a book that Gersi had left behind in another hotel – at Port-au-Prince.

The saga of Count St Germain is a strange story indeed, inviting comparisons with figures from the past and the future, from fiction and from fact – Baron Munchausen and the Wandering Jew, Faust and Fulcanelli, with even a dash of Dorian Gray thrown in for good measure. Was Count St Germain simply a smooth-talking charlatan, or a master alchemist who had achieved occult successes far beyond the dreams of science? Do the recent incidents merely indicate that the romance of the count's cryptic history has inspired a modern-day generation of pretenders to his throne, or is it conceivable that the twentieth century has indeed witnessed the latest activities of the genuine article? Of course, they say that old legends die hard, but then again, so too do old habits ...

THE PROPHECIES OF NOSTRADAMUS

In print for over 500 years, and second, therefore, only to the Bible for continuous publication, are the prophecies of a sixteenth-century French seer from Saint-Rémy called Michel de Notredame, better known to the world as Nostradamus. Supporters are convinced that he has accurately predicted many significant events in Europe, and elsewhere too, including Hitler's invasion of Poland, the Great Fire of London and the recent civil war in Yugoslavia. Sceptics consider that any such "accuracies" merely reflect the great influence of hindsight upon the prophecies' translators and the interpretations of these translations.

The fundamental problem lies in the fact that in order to avoid possible accusations of witchcraft, Nostradamus deliberately concealed his predictions' true meaning in a welter of obscurity. They comprise 965 quatrains penned in a cryptic mixture of Latin, Greek, French and his native Provençal, their wording is purposely ambiguous and contains numerous invented words that do not exist elsewhere, and the time-sequence of the quatrains is not ordered.

Inevitably, the translations and interpretations differ greatly: a given quatrain can yield several wholly separate predictions. Even one of the more lucid examples, referring to a devastation of London's people by thunderbolts, has been variously interpreted as foretelling the burning of martyrs by Queen Mary I, the Great Fire of London or the Blitz in 1940.

Among the delights predicted by Nostradamus for the end of the twentieth century are another world war (which Europe will lose), and European decimation by a terrible plague. Accurate prophecies or artefacts of imaginative interpretation? It won't be long before we find out.

PORTRAIT DE MICHEL NOSTRADAMUS, Astronome célèbre.

Michel Nostradamus naquit à Saint-Remy, petite ville de Provence, le 14 décembre 1503, à l'heure de midi; il émit fils de Jacques Nostradamus, notaire royal de cette ville, et de damoiselle Renée de Saint-Remy; il était petit-fils, sent paternel que maternel, de médecins et mathématiciens célèbres; il fut reçu docteur en l'université de Montpellier, dont il exerça la charge de professeur. Ce grand homme a vécu sous les règnes de Louis XII, François Ier, Henri II et Charles IX, dont il fut médecin; il retourna à Silon, autre ville de Provence, et y mourut en bon chrétien, après avoir été tourmenté par la goutte qui, dégénérée en hydropisie, le suffoqua au bout de huit jours, ayant prédit l'heure et le jour de sa mort, qui arriva entre trois et quatre heures du matin, le 2 juillet 1566.

THE SMILE ON THE FACE OF THE MONA LISA

For many people, Leonardo da Vinci's world-famous painting, "The Mona Lisa", is simply a portrait of the wife of Francesco del Giocondo, a wealthy Florentine merchant. Certain investigators, conversely, claim that her enigmatic smile hides some startling surprises.

Why, for instance, is this particular painting so alluring? Dr Leopold Bellak, a psychology professor at New York University, has analysed her face using the Zone System, whereby the left and right sides are studied independently, as are the top and bottom halves. Bellak concludes that her full cheeks suggest sensual indulgence and her weak chin implies a lack of self-control – flirtatious enough, perhaps, to attract the eye of any red-blooded male?

Perhaps not. As revealed by Tim Walker in an excellent review of Mona Lisa mysteries (*Daily Mail*, 21 October 1993), American computer artist Lillian Schwartz and Maudsley Hospital registrar Dr Digby Quested believe that her face yields a very different message – for they claim that it is actually a mirror image of Leonardo da Vinci's own face!

Although it is known that Leonardo penned many notes in mirror-image writing, the concept of a transvestite Mona Lisa is still something of a shock; but worse is to come. The picture was stolen from the Louvre in 1911, and when later recovered it was X-rayed to check its authenticity. That was confirmed, but the X-rays also revealed that the Mona Lisa had apparently possessed a beard at one time, which had later been painted over.

If the Mona Lisa is a disguised portrait of Leonardo, however, then he may well have been even more remarkable a man than hitherto supposed. According to Dr Kenneth Keale, a consultant at Ashford Hospital, Middlesex, her cheery smile, youthful complexion, generous body proportions and the way in which her robe falls into her lap all show that the person depicted in this painting is heavily pregnant!

Pregnancies aside, she (or he?) may not have been in the best of health when posing for the portrait. In the view of Californian medical specialist Dr Kedar Ardour, her captivating smile is in fact the result of a type of facial paralysis called Bell's palsy, which explains its lop-sided shape. This is aided and abetted, according to Maryland dentist Dr Joseph Borkowski, by the equally tragic fact that she had somehow lost her front teeth, which is why her lips droop at the corners. But before we lose sight altogether of the mystique associated with the Mona Lisa, we should perhaps be thankful that the portrait was ever painted at all. In the opinion of Japanese heart specialist Dr Haruo Nakamura, noting the yellow pigmentation in the corner of her left eye, the person posing for this picture possessed high cholesterol levels and could have suffered a heart attack at any moment. So much for the healthy foods of earlier ages!

Mona Lisa, painted by Leonardo da Vinci c. 1503. Is this in fact a disguised portrait of the artist?

KASPAR HAUSER

As far as the rest of the world is concerned, Kaspar Hauser literally stepped into existence on 26 May 1828 when, as an incoherent 16- or 17-year-old, he staggered into Nuremberg's Unschlitt Square, wearing expensive but tattered clothing and ill-fitting boots, and clutching an envelope addressed to "the Captain of the 4th Squadron, 6th Cavalry Regiment".

Taken there by a cobbler who had spotted him, he handed his envelope to the captain, who found that it contained two letters. These stated that throughout his life he had been locked away from the outside world and contact with other humans, and that he should now be trained as a cavalry soldier like his father. Reacting in a bizarre manner to inanimate objects such as a clock and a candle flame, which he seemed to believe were alive, and dismissed by the captain as a simpleton, he was taken to the police station, but when given a pen and paper he wrote "Kaspar Hauser". This was assumed by everyone to be his name.

Attempts were made to teach Kaspar to talk, read and write, and he responded with astonishing speed, becoming fluent in all three within just a few weeks. He confirmed that he had spent his entire life imprisoned in a darkened place, sleeping or sitting on straw and tended to by persons unseen, yet he seemed remarkably healthy under the circumstances. In August 1829, Kaspar's autobiography was published, but it contained no new details about his past and was not a success. Shortly afterwards, however, he hit the headlines when on 7 October he suffered a mysterious wound to his brow, which he said had been inflicted by a man with "a black face" (a mask?). Yet no one else had seen such a person.

During the next few years Kaspar toured Europe in the company of Lord Stanhope, an English aristocrat, but his life was soon to come to a highly controversial end. On 14 December 1833, at Ansbach near Nuremberg, Kaspar stumbled into the house of a local teacher called Dr Meyer, bleeding from a severe stab wound in his chest and claiming to have been attacked in the park. He showed Meyer a wallet supposedly given to him by his attacker immediately before the incident, which contained a meaningless message in mirror writing. Yet when the police went to the site of the incident, only Kaspar's footprints could be found.

Monument erected to the memory of Kasper Hauser, a youth without a past.

On 17 December, Kaspar died, avowing to the end that the wounds were not self-inflicted.

Over 150 years of speculation have failed to shed any light upon his identity, his strange claims and behaviour, or the significance of the two attacks. Was Kaspar a fraud who enjoyed the glamour that his stories had brought for him in Nuremberg, or was he an equivalent of sorts to the many "feral children" who have survived in the wild without any human parental care? If the latter is true, how can his amazingly swift understanding of reading and writing be explained, and what was the reason for his years of isolation? Were his "attacks" self-inflicted, to maintain public interest in him, or could they have been sinister attempts to silence him by those who feared what he may reveal as he became more articulate?

Kaspar Hauser was buried beneath a headstone that spoke only of a youth without a past, who was robbed of a future. Such is the sum total of our knowledge concerning one of the most enigmatic figures from modern times.

*Kaspar Hauser as portrayed in the **Magasin Pittoresque** in 1837.*

Religious Enigmas

STATUES AND PAINTINGS THAT WEEP OR BLEED

Is it possible that artefacts in the shape of humans can also display certain aspects of human behaviour? An extraordinary but not infrequent occurrence is the bizarre phenomenon of religious statues that allegedly weep or bleed, reported particularly, though not exclusively, from Catholic countries in Europe and sometimes featuring paintings too.

One of the most famous examples is the small, mass-produced plaster Madonna that began weeping profusely on 29 August 1953 at the home of its owners, Angelo and Antonietta Iannuso, at Syracuse in Sicily. Even after its eyes were dried, it would straight away begin to weep again. This remarkable statue soon attracted crowds of sightseers, and several infirm people who touched its tears, including Antonietta herself, claimed to have been miraculously cured of their ailments. Bemused scientists took samples of the statue's tears for analysis and duly announced that these samples were found to be indistinguishable from genuine human tears. Following this, the Catholic Church

formally recognized the statue's weeping as a miracle, and today the Iannusos' little plaster Madonna is housed in its own specially created shrine, which attracts many worshipping visitors every single year.

In 1980, another Sicilian plaster statue of the Virgin Mary received considerable attention when blood

Weeping statue of the Madonna at Maasmechelen, Belgium.

began to trickle from its cheek. This Madonna was set in a rock wall near Niscima, and although it attracted great crowds it was initially viewed with scepticism by Bishop Alfredo Garsia. He banned its veneration and insisted that it

be sealed inside a glass case. This was done, but the statue continued to bleed. Eventually the bishop decided to view it for himself, and emerged from its shrine greatly excited by what he had seen.

A bleeding Madonna was reported from Maropati, Italy, in January 1971, though on this occasion it was not a statue but a painting, at the home of a lawyer. After the painting had been bleeding daily for several days, the local police decided to investigate and took it away for examination, locking it overnight in a box. When they unlocked the box the next morning, the painting was still bleeding, and analyses revealed that it was human blood.

From 1911 to 1915, a painting of Jesus in a church at Mirebeau-en-Poitou, France, exuded blood from his brow, palms and heart. Samples of this blood, analysed at the Lister Institute in London, were found to be human and of a rare blood group.

In 1994, an Italian priest called Father Pablo Martin purchased a plaster Madonna at the Marian shrine at Medjugorje in Bosnia-Herzegovina. He gave it to a friend, Fabio Gregori, who placed it in a home-made shrine in his garden at Civitavecchia, a port 50 miles north of Rome. In February 1995, Gregori claimed that the statue had begun to weep tears of blood – an announcement that drew huge crowds

Crowds await the return to Civitavecchia of the weeping Madonna after its release by fraud investigators.

to his garden to watch and to worship. Reports of at least eight other bleeding or weeping icons in Italy also emerged during this period.

In April 1995, magistrate Antonio Albano ordered Gregori's Madonna to be seized and a fraud investigation was launched. The Gemelli Hospital in Rome conducted DNA tests on samples of the blood wept by the statue. These revealed that the blood was human – and male. None of Gregori's family would agree to give blood samples for comparative analyses, however, so in June, following a sustained public campaign, the statue was returned to Civitavecchia, where it was given a new home in the local church of St Agostino.

Recent photographs of a weeping Madonna statue at Maasmechelen in Belgium and another one in Brooklyn, New York, are particularly interesting. Not only do they plainly depict tears trickling down the statues' cheeks and brimming upon their chin, but they also suggest that the two may have originated from the same mould because the statues themselves appear identical in form, only their attached head-dresses are different. If the two statues do share the same origin, could this somehow explain their shared capacity for weeping?

There is a notable precedent here. In July 1995, chemistry researcher Dr Luigi Garlaschelli from Pavia University published an extremely eye-opening paper in *Chemistry in Britain*, for it painstakingly revealed how to create an effective weeping or bleeding statue:

What is needed is a hollow statue made of porous material, such as plaster or ceramic. The icon must be glazed or painted with some sort of impermeable coating. If the statue is then filled up with a liquid [surreptitiously, through a tiny hole in the head, for example], the porous material will absorb it, but the glazing will stop it from flowing out. If the glazing, however, is imperceptibly scratched away on or around the eyes, tear-like drops will leak out, as if materialising from thin air. If the cavity behind the eyes is small enough, once all the liquid has dripped out there are virtually no traces left in the icon. When I put it to the test, this trick proved to be very satisfactory, baffling all onlookers.

But that is not all. After being refused permission to examine the celebrated Syracuse Madonna, Garlaschelli obtained an exact copy of it from the manufacturer and he discovered that it not only was made of glazed plaster but also had a cavity behind its face. These findings, coupled with his published blueprint for creating weeping and bleeding statues, would seem to explain the mechanism by which the Syracuse Madonna could weep water or some other readily obtained fluid; but how, as queried by Mario Magnano, rector of the Syracuse Madonna's shrine, can it explain the fully verified fact that this statue weeps real human tears?

Back in 1987, however, physicist Dr Shawn Carlson from the Lawrence Berkeley Laboratory in California claimed that he had devised a means of making statues and paintings shed human tears; in a public demonstration he produced a weeping Mona Lisa. He will not disclose his technique, however, until he has patented it, as he plans to market novelty weeping icons.

After centuries of wonder, has another example of the miraculous finally been demoted to the realms of the mundane by the advancement of science?

VIRGIN VISIONS

Visions of the Blessed Virgin Mary (BVM) are far from uncommon. Two of the most famous modern cases occurred in Europe. The first began on 11 February 1858, at Massabielle, near the southern French village of Lourdes, when a 14-year-old shepherdess called Bernadette Soubirous saw a shining figure resembling a girl dressed in white, in front of a grotto. Bernadette saw the vision 18 times and the figure eventually referred to herself as the Immaculate Conception, which identified her, according to the local priest, as the Blessed Virgin Mary. During her ninth vision, Bernadette was instructed by the white figure to dig in the earth at the grotto, and when she did so she discovered an underground spring, whose waters have been claimed ever since to possess healing powers.

Bernadette died in 1879 and was later canonized. Today, Lourdes is a place of pilgrimage for sick people from all around the world, and many miraculous cures have been claimed.

On 13 May 1917, while herding sheep in a pasture near Fatima, in Portugal, three children experienced

Jacinta and Francisco Marto and Lucia dos Santos.

the sky. Afterwards, its astonished audience realized that their rain-drenched clothes were totally dry. Yet no one outside Fatima appeared to have witnessed the sun's departure from its normal course.

"Dances of the sun" were also reported during an unprecedented five-year period of visions, spanning 1981–85, when children at Medjugorje in Bosnia-Herzegovina claimed to have seen the Virgin Mary each day, yielding over 2000 visions in total.

Kevin McClure, in *The Evidence for Visions of the Virgin Mary*, and Father René Laurentin, in *The Apparitions of the Blessed Virgin Mary Today*, feel that many eyewitnesses truly believe that they have seen what they claim to have seen, but there is rarely any objective support for their testimony. In the opinion of Father Laurentin: "Without the receptivity of a subject there would be no apparitions, but ... subjectivity can lead to illusory apparitions."

Bernadette Soubirous sees a shining figure in front of a grotto near Lourdes.

the first of six visions featuring the brilliant figure of a lady above a tree. She told Jacinta and Francisco Marto and Lucia dos Santos that she was from heaven and would appear to them there on the thirteenth day of every month until October. Word spread regarding the children's visions and each month on the 13th they were accompanied by more and more adults. Yet although the children claimed to see the lady clearly, the adults could discern only a small cloud above the tree. By August, the young trio's words had begun to be doubted and they were arrested, but on 19 August they

received another vision of the lady, who told them that they would see her one more time, on 13 October.

Despite a heavy bout of rain, around 70,000 people gathered that day, but only the three children perceived the lady, who identified herself as Our Lady of the Rosary. Then, without warning, an incredible sight supposedly occurred, but was seen by only some of the crowd. The sun began to rotate, two or three times, emitting revolving beams of coloured light, after which it seemed to plummet towards the earth, nearer and nearer to its petrified observers, before veering back up into

INCORRUPTIBILITY

Not only the lives, but also the deaths, of certain European saints were miraculous, inasmuch as their corpses defied the normal laws of decay, remaining resolutely incorrupt without the assistance of embalming fluids or any other artificial aids to preservation.

A relatively modern example is that of St Bernadette of Lourdes, who died in 1879. Her corpse was exhumed in 1909 and again in 1919, but when it was examined by the sisters of the Chapel of St Joseph, in Nevers, they found no sign of decomposition, even though it was so damp that one of her crucifixes had rusted and another was coated with verdigris. Now on exhibition, it remains just as fresh today. Indeed, observers could be forgiven for thinking that she was merely asleep. Other Christian figures whose bodies were exhumed during this century and were found not to have decayed include Blessed Paula Frassinetti, Blessed Maria Assunta Pallotta and St Jean Vianney, the Curé of Ars. Further back in history, the body of St Cuthbert, of Lindisfarne in north-east England, who died in AD 687, was found to be still uncorrupted in the sixteenth century.

In 1922, Red Army troops in Poland broke open the tomb of St Andrew Bobola in the church at Pinsk and hauled out his body. Despite the fact that he had died in 1657, his body was still well-preserved, it had been on public display as recently as 1917. Taken to Moscow, it was later returned, and is now housed in his own church in Warsaw.

Some incorruptible corpses are those of stigmatics – people who have mysteriously developed bleeding wounds corresponding to Jesus's crucifixion wounds (see pp. 73–75). One of the most unusual cases is that of St Catherine of Siena, as revealed by Joan Carroll Cruz in *The Incorruptibles*, which lists more than 100 cases of corporeal incorruptibility.

After developing stigmata in 1375, St Catherine prayed for them to disappear and leave her only with their pain. This duly occurred, but following her death in 1380 the stigmata could be seen beneath the surface of her skin. Moreover, even though her coffin had been regularly soaked with rain, when exhumed in 1430 her body had not decayed. With papal permission, the corpse was then dismembered to yield sacred relics, a holy process called translation. The most recent translations occurred in 1855, at which time her remains, by then almost 500 years old, were still remarkably well-preserved.

Certain soils and humidity conditions can delay or distort the processes of decomposition, as can saponification, the conversion of body tissues into a soap-like structure beneath a toughened outer skin, but rarely explain those cases in which corpses have remained incorrupt even though they have been buried, or directly laid, alongside others that have decayed normally. Some incorrupt corpses, furthermore, are those of persons who died from ailments such as gangrene or from unhealed wounds that might have been expected to accelerate, not retard, putrefaction. As yet, there is no satisfactory explanation for corporeal incorruptibility.

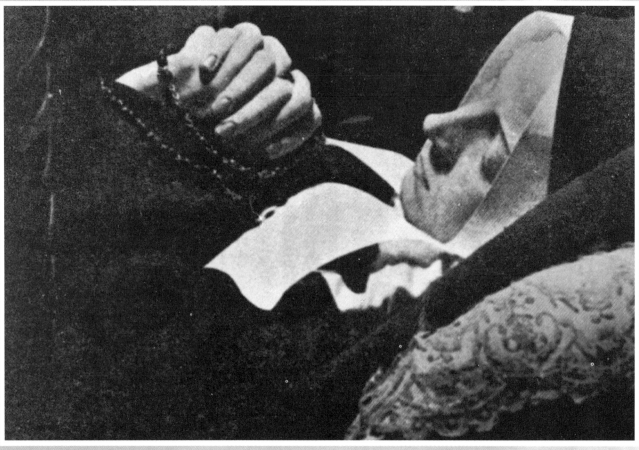

The incorrupt body of St Bernadette of Lourdes.

ANGELS OF MONS

On 29 September 1914, a wholly fictional story entitled "The Bowmen", written by Arthur Machen, appeared in London's *Evening Standard*. The theme of his story was a First World War miracle concerning the outnumbered British Expeditionary Force who had recently retreated from Mons, a Belgian town close to the French border. The troops were rescued from the oncoming German army by a heavenly host of Agincourt bowmen led by St George, who confronted the Germans and sent them fleeing in terror. Soon afterwards, however, the newspapers were filled with reports from British soldiers avowing that this had indeed happened, despite Machen's subsequent attempts to convince them otherwise.

Sceptics sided with Machen, dismissing such reports as fantasy inspired by his story, and Machen made good use of the furore when publicizing his subsequent novel *The Bowmen*, which duly became a bestseller. Since then, most researchers have discounted the "Angels of Mons" affair, denying that it was ever a genuine mystery, but in the early 1990s Kevin McClure published a booklet entitled *Visions of Bowmen and Angels*, which revealed that it was all far more complex than had hitherto been recognized.

After comprehensively surveying the considerable amount of material dealing with the subject, McClure discovered that there were two quite separate categories of accounts claiming divine intervention. One category featured reports of bowmen, the other reports of angels (plus a few "strange clouds"). McClure believes that whereas the bowmen accounts certainly derived from the publication of Machen's original story, reports in the angel category preceded it. Furthermore, the bowmen were said to have been actively invoked by the British troops and to have battled against the Germans with weapons and sonorous war-cries, killing many of them. In stark contrast, the angels allegedly appeared unbidden and unarmed, and merely stood as a passive

The "Angels of Mons" as depicted by Alfred Pearce.

silent barrier, their presence alone being sufficient to ward off the British troops' foes.

This is not all. McClure uncovered reports from French soldiers too, claiming that Joan of Arc and St Michael had materialized to assist their escape from German troops. Strangest of all, a number of British and French soldiers also spoke of a mysterious figure dubbed the "Comrade in White", who had miraculously healed several men and had even shielded some from close-range bullets. They believed that he was Jesus.

McClure concludes that the "Angels of Mons" affair is a genuine mystery after all, rescued from a premature burial, and he could well have a point.

POPE JOAN

Today, the possibility that there had once been a female pope, or papess, is known to many people only from reading Lawrence Durrell's light-hearted novel, *Pope Joan*. For centuries, however, the erstwhile existence of such a person was believed to be an indisputable fact.

The story went that in about AD 818 a girl called Joan was born to English missionaries at Ingelheim, near the German city of Mainz. As she grew older, it became clear that Joan was extremely intelligent and eventually she disguised herself as a man, called herself John Anglicus and gained entry into a local

monastery where she studied assiduously. Later, she travelled to Rome, still dressed as a man, and became so celebrated for her intellect that when in 855 Pope Leo IV died, she was enthusiastically elected as Pope John VIII.

Her papal reign proved a great success, except for one catastrophic mistake. She fell in love with her valet – a mistake made in private, but whose outcome would soon become only too public. One day, two years after becoming pope, she was leading a procession through Rome, from St Peter's basilica to the Lateran palace, surrounded by throngs of excited people. The route between the Colosseum and St Clement's church led down a narrow alley and it was here that suddenly, to the spectators' dismay, the pope collapsed on the ground, evidently in great pain. To their even greater horror, however, when attendants rushed to the pope's aid, "he" was revealed to be a "she": the pope was a woman! More than that, she was in the act of giving birth! Aghast at the sight of such cumulative heresy, the frenzied crowd dragged Joan and her new-born child away and stoned them to death.

For centuries afterwards, the alley where this dreadful exposé had occurred was avoided by papal processions and the ceremonial enthronement of new popes gained a bizarre and novel custom. Before the pope was throned, he had to sit upon a special marble chair with a hole in its seat, the *sella stercoraria*, and be examined by physicians to ensure that he

Pope Joan gives birth during a procession, in this illustration from a medieval chronicle.

LEVITATING SAINTS

Levitation is the controversial ability of certain persons to defy the law of gravity and rise up in the air, sometimes momentarily, but often for prolonged periods, hovering several feet or more above the ground without any visible means of support. In Europe, the Church traditionally looked upon this strange talent as a diabolical practice, hence it was both perplexed and embarrassed by the many attested incidents concerning levitating saints and other notable Christians. These have included: the levitation of St Edmund, then Archbishop of Canterbury, in or around 1242 at Canterbury; St Teresa of Avila during 1680 in Madrid; an Arabian Carmelite nun called Sister Mary at around 1700 in Bethlehem; St Adolphus Liguori in the church of St John in Foggia during 1777; Father Suarez in 1911 at Santa Cruz, southern Argentina; and over 200 other Catholic saints.

Undoubtedly the most extraordinary of these was St Joseph of Copertino, born in Apulia, Italy, in 1603, who became a Franciscan monk at 22 after years of inflicting gruesome tortures upon himself to achieve a state of religious ecstasy. Eventually his periods of ecstasy resulted in uncontrollable, accident-prone spasms of levitation, which he termed "my giddinesses", but which often caused mayhem and embarrassment to the Church authorities.

For instance, after shrieking with joy one particularly pleasant morning, he promptly soared up into an olive tree from which he had to be extricated by a company of monks carrying a tall ladder. On another occasion, he burnt himself on the candle flames when a prayer-induced state of ecstasy transported him through the air during Mass and deposited him upon the altar. And he greatly startled Pope Urban VIII by floating several feet above the ground in front of him.

Not surprisingly, Joseph was eventually requested by the monks to conduct his prayers and meditation in future within the privacy and safety of

was truly a man. When they had confirmed that he was, a deacon would shout to the crowd, "*Habet!*" ("He has!"), and all the crowd would rejoice, exclaiming "*Deo gratias!*" ("Thanks be to God!").

As for John VIII, or Pope Joan, all trace of his/her brief pontificate were erased from Church records by moving forward the enthronement date of the replacement, Benedict III, to 855. And when another pope called John was enthroned several years later, he took Joan's title of John VIII. Even a bust entitled "John VIII, a woman from England", housed in Siena cathedral, was renamed "Pope Zachary" by Pope Clement VIII (1592–1605).

Her scandalous history does occur in the medieval chronicles of Anastasius the Librarian, Marianus Scotus and Sigebert de Gemblours,

among others. Many Protestant writers also publicized it during the sixteenth century, in a bid to malign the papacy. Ironically, it was the extensive treatise of Calvinist historian David Blondel in 1647 which finally confirmed that the entire history of Pope Joan was without foundation. Indeed, even its presence within the above-noted medieval works appears to have been a perfidious insertion by later writers.

In *The Female Pope*, Rosemary and Darroll Pardoe speculate that the Pope Joan myth was inspired by a real but equally unusual person – Nicetas, a eunuch Patriarch in Constantinople (AD 766–80). His story may have been wilfully modified by papal opposition in the mendicant orders, to draw attention to the intense corruption in the papacy at that time and in the process spawned a persistent if fallacious female pretender.

St Joseph of Copertino airborne in front of Pope Urban VIII.

levitation, it was "as if a great force beneath my feet lifted me up". St Teresa was a sixteenth-century Carmelite nun renowned for her great humility. She believed her fully authenticated bouts of levitation or "raptures" to be a visible sign of God's favour but prayed that he might reveal to her his grace in a manner which would not become known to others, so that she might not be set apart from, or considered in any way worthier than, her sister nuns.

Perhaps levitation is actually a collective term for several different phenomena, but whose visible outcome is the same – the acquisition of a weightless condition. Until science is willing, or able, to investigate this extraordinary matter in detail, however, the answer is likely to remain, quite literally, up in the air!

St Teresa of Avila.

his own cell. Until his death in 1663, he allegedly levitated more than 100 times and was canonized because his remarkable ability was deemed to be the work of God.

Scientists, sceptical of such feats of weightlessness, generally discount all levitations as clever illusions, drug-induced hallucinations, a popular explanation for the claims by witches in medieval times that they could fly through the air on broomsticks, or mass hypnotism induced among the audience by the person performing the supposed levitation. Very different explanations, however, are provided by those claiming to possess this baffling ability.

Daniel Dunglas Hume, a famous medium and levitator in Victorian England, affirmed that his acts of levitation were mediated by invisible, intangible spirits, who gently lifted him upwards and supported him in the air, so that he was never afraid of plummeting to the ground. More recently, American writer Helene Hadsell attributed her single, unplanned experience of levitation to an overwhelming surge of euphoria that she experienced one morning after waking up and setting out to attend the morning service at the nearby chapel.

St Teresa of Avila stated that when she attempted to resist an onset of

The Spear of Destiny and Other Sacred Relics

Europe's history is liberally sprinkled with miracles, mysteries and mythology relating to a diverse array of sacred relics. The following is just a small selection.

The holy spear, also known as the lance of Longinus and the spear of destiny, is said to be the spear that a Roman centurion called Gaius Cassius Longinus thrust into Jesus's side when he was on the cross, causing blood to spurt from the wound. At least four different spears have been claimed to be the true holy spear. One was taken to Paris by St Louis following his return from the Palestine crusades during the thirteenth century. A second was sent to Pope Innocent VIII by the Ottoman sultan Bajazet II in 1492 and placed in one of the piers supporting the dome of St Peter's basilica. A third, held at Cracow, Poland, was merely a copy of the fourth, and most famous, spear, whose own history is very complex.

Some researchers claim that it was found at Antioch in AD 1098, during the First Crusade. According to Arthurian romance, it was brought to Britain with the Holy Grail by Joseph of Arimathea after the death of Jesus (see pp. 21–22), and was seen to drip blood in the Grail Procession observed by Sir Perceval at the Grail Castle. Others believe that it was once personally carried by Charlemagne during many successful battles in the ninth century. In any event, it was later owned successively by a series of Saxon monarchs before passing literally into the hands of Frederick Barbarossa, conqueror of Italy during the twelfth century. From him, the spear ultimately found its way into the ownership of the Habsburg dynasty and was displayed in Vienna's Hofburg Museum until as recently as 1938. That was the year in which Austria was annexed by Germany, under Adolf Hitler. As revealed by Trevor Ravenscroft in *The Spear of Destiny*, Hitler was so obsessed by the legends of great power attributed to the spear and to all who owned it that he ordered it to be taken from the Hofburg museum and later hid it in a special vault at Nuremberg.

The holy spear reputedly possesses healing powers, and has always been associated with the power to grant success in battles to all who carried it. Charlemagne allegedly died shortly after accidentally dropping it; so too did Barbarossa. And on 30 April 1945, the very same day that the spear was retrieved from its underground vault by

St Januarius portrayed here with the phials of his blood held at Naples cathedral.

the victorious American troops in Nuremberg, in his own concealed Berlin bunker Adolf Hitler committed suicide.

St Januarius is believed to have been the thirteenth bishop of Benevento, who was executed during a period of Roman persecution in c. AD 305. Naples cathedral owns what is said to be a sample of the saint's clotted blood, contained in two sealed phials enclosed within a glass case. The larger of these two phials is the source of a famous miracle – namely, the mysterious liquefaction of the blood inside the phial when the glass case is rotated during mass by the officiating priest, in full view of the crowd and television cameras. This occurs several times a year and has been witnessed by millions of people since 1389.

According to one eyewitness, physician Dr Giorgio Giorgi, who witnessed the transformation in 1970 while standing only a metre (3 feet) away, it "happened suddenly and unexpectedly. The liquid itself had become much brighter, more shining; so many gaseous bubbles appeared inside the liquid ... that it seemed to be in a state of ebullition."

Sometimes the miracle fails to occur and this is deemed to be an omen of impending disaster – except in December, which rarely hosts a successful liquefaction. This has led some scientists to speculate that external temperature controls the

The Odour of Sanctity

Certain European saints and other holy persons are known to have exuded an exquisite, unearthly scent, referred to as the odour of sanctity, which has never been explained.

No one ever needed to ask where the Blessed Maria degli Angeli could be found within the convent, for the sweet fragrance perpetually manifested by this eighteenth-century Italian nun was so powerful that she could be traced by the strength of her scent alone. Maria believed it to be a sign of heavenly grace, but was embarrassed that it had been bestowed solely upon her, not upon her sisters too. She even tried to hide its perfume by placing foul-smelling objects in her cell, but this was unsuccessful because her odour of sanctity was far more potent.

Similarly, from the moment that Sister Giovanna Maria della Croce placed a wedding ring on her finger (symbolizing her marriage to Christ) when taking her final vows at Rovereto, Italy, in or around 1625, a mysterious scent of indescribable beauty exuded from that finger, and continued to do so for many years. Even items that she touched would be impregnated by her odour of sanctity for several days afterwards. As time passed, this glorious scent was emitted not just from her ring finger but from her entire body and even from her clothes, which would retain the fragrance long after she had last worn them.

blood's transformation, but studies of temperature fluctuations in relation to the blood have shown no correlation.

In 1991, Pavia University announced that one of its chemical researchers had simulated the miracle under laboratory conditions. The researcher was Dr Luigi Garlaschelli, who has more recently revealed a mechanism to explain weeping statues (p. 64). His artificial blood is a dark brown jam-like gel containing chalk and hydrated iron chloride, sprinkled with salt water. When slowly shaken, it soon liquefies, but solidifies again when left to stand. As the blood samples in Naples cathedral have never been formally analysed, there is no scientific verification that they are genuine blood, and Garlaschelli claims that a gel like his own could easily have been prepared even in medieval times. Moreover, in 1921 Dr Frederick Williams reputedly watched a chemist in the Naples hospital dispensary concocting a sample of this "blood" specifically for the cathedral: it contained beef bile and sodium sulphate.

Another medieval miracle recently investigated by science is the bleeding bread of Bolsena, in which bright red blood appeared on the sacramental wafer during a thirteenth-century mass at Bolsena in Italy – an event that inspired Pope Urban IV to inaugurate the annual Feast of Corpus Christi. In 1994, however, Dr Johanna Cullen from George Mason University in Virginia succeeded in recreating the miracle in a petri dish, by incubating some sacramental bread with a bacterium called *Serratia marcescens*, which thrives on starch and is known to produce a vivid red pigment. In three days, several blood-red spots had indeed appeared on the wafer, corresponding well with the description of the Bolsena bread. It seems likely, therefore, that the latter had merely been contaminated with this bacterium.

On 15 July 1995, Father Christopher Jenkins, a priest at St Francis Xavier's church in Hereford, unexpectedly suffered a massive stroke and slipped into a deep coma. Doctors were convinced that he was close to death. However, an oak casket on the church altar contained a sacred relic believed to possess great healing powers – the

The severed hand of St John Kemble – cause of a miracle in July 1995?

severed hand of St John Kemble, a priest executed in 1679 and canonized in 1970. Wasting no time, Father Anthony Tumelty, an assistant to Father Jenkins, placed the hand upon the sick man's brow. Soon afterwards, Father Jenkins awoke from his coma and was later able to eat, talk and walk again.

Not all miracles are of medieval occurrence. And the miracle of St John Kemble's hand is one for which no scientific explanation can be offered, other than the power of faith.

✦

THE SHROUD OF TURIN

The Shroud of Turin is a pale sheet of linen measuring 4.34 metres (14 feet 3 inches) long by 1.09 metres (3 feet 7 inches) wide, which bears the faint, life-sized image of a crucified man, portrayed from both the front and the back. For several centuries, many people have believed this cloth to be the sindon or burial shroud in which the body of Jesus was wrapped after his death, and that the human impression preserved upon it is none other than the image of Jesus himself.

The Turin Shroud's earliest confirmed occurrence in history is when

it was displayed by its then owner, a knight called Geoffrey de Charny I, at Lirey, France, in 1353. It later passed to his grand-daughter Marguerite, who gave it in 1453 to Duke Louis of Savoy. The Shroud narrowly escaped destruction in 1532, when the chapel in which it had been housed by the Savoys caught fire, but apart from a few scorch marks it survived intact. In 1578 it was presented to Turin cathedral and is stored here inside an ornate seventeenth-century altar.

Although the front and rear image of a man can indeed be discerned when looking at the Shroud, this is not particularly distinct, which may be why science showed little interest in it, until 1898. That was when Secondo Pia became the first person to take photographs of it – photographs that were to astonish the world. No longer was the Shroud's image faint and unexciting: when viewed as a negative, it was transformed into a detailed and profoundly moving depiction of a man who had suffered the extreme horror of death by crucifixion. Clearer than ever before were the marks of the nails through his bleeding wrists and the wounds in his feet, as well as multiple weals across his back consistent with lashes from whips used by Roman soldiers at the time of Jesus. There too were the bloody impressions of thorns encircling his brow and a bleeding gash

A detailed, life-size image of a crucified man appears on the Turin Shroud. Is this the face of Jesus ...

in his side made by a pointed weapon.

The man was tall, thin, bearded and seemed to be 30–40 years old. For countless people, there could no longer be any doubt. This was truly the image of Jesus and the Shroud, therefore, was indeed his sindon – but how had it reached Europe from the Holy Land?

In *The Turin Shroud*, Oxford researcher Ian Wilson proposed that the Shroud was one and the same as an equally mysterious relic called the mandylion. This was a smaller piece of cloth, bearing a miraculous image of Jesus's face. It is believed to have been taken from Jerusalem, via Edessa, to Constantinople, but was reputedly destroyed during the city's sacking in 1204 by crusaders. According to Wilson, however, the mandylion was actually the Shroud, folded into three sections, with the topmost section showing only the face. He suggested that instead of being destroyed, it found its way into the ownership of de Charny, who displayed it in its entire, unfolded state, thus "transforming" it into the Shroud.

... or of Leonardo da Vinci?

An intriguing theory, but one discounted by Noel Currer-Briggs in *The Shroud and the Grail*, who claimed that the mandylion was a totally separate relic, identifying it as the soudarion – a small cloth laid over Jesus's face after the crucifixion. In 1988, scientific tests took place that vindicated this distinction between the mandylion and the Shroud.

With the Catholic Church's permission, small samples were taken from the Shroud and given to three laboratories in Oxford, Tucson and Zurich, to determine their age by carbon-14 dating. In a paper in *Nature* (16 February 1989), the teams announced that their findings closely corresponded and placed the date of the Shroud's manufacture at AD 1260–1390.

The Shroud was not the sindon of Jesus after all. Instead, it was only of medieval origin, explaining why there was no good evidence for its existence before the thirteenth century. What the tests did not explain, however, was when, or how, the Shroud's image was created.

Scientific analyses conducted during the 1970s had already shown that the image is three-dimensionally correct, indicating that it was the result of the Shroud being wrapped around a human body. Intriguingly, the image does not penetrate through the linen (which a painted image would have done), but is present only within its uppermost fibres. Even more remarkable, however, is that the image is most clearly visible when viewed as a negative. It was this that inspired Lynn Picknett and Clive Prince to pursue the amazing possibility that the Shroud's image was the result of a very early experiment in photography – performed by none other than Leonardo da Vinci.

In *Turin Shroud: In Whose Image?*, they proposed that Leonardo's interest in optics and his secret membership of a sect called the Priory of Sion led him to create the Turin Shroud as a "relic" with which to mock the Christian belief in Jesus's resurrection, and that he did this using some century-old linen and a corpse upon which he had meticulously duplicated Jesus's crucifixion wounds. He created the Shroud's image using materials and techniques available in his day, which can achieve good photographic results (as Picknett and Prince verified by using them to create their own passable Shroud image). But Leonardo's ultimate sacrilege was to superimpose upon the impression of the crucified corpse's body the image of his own face! Certainly, there is a very strong similarity between the face on the Shroud and Leonardo's, and this would also explain the oft-noted "detached" appearance of the Shroud face.

Not everyone, however, is convinced by this theory. Some believe that the image is indeed that of Jesus and was created by an explosion of divine energy from his body at the moment of resurrection. Shortly after the carbon-14 results were released, Dr Thomas Phillips from Harvard University's High Energy Physics Laboratory expressed doubts about their accuracy by claiming that the body wrapped in the Shroud had radiated energy, yielding the image, and had also generated a burst of neutrons, which would have affected the dating procedures.

After more than 600 years, the last word on the Shroud of Turin has yet to be spoken.

✦

STIGMATA

The year was 1224, the day was 14 September – Holy Cross Day – and St Francis of Assisi was kneeling devoutly in prayer near his humble retreat on Monte Alvernia, profoundly contemplating the terrible suffering of Jesus on the cross. Gazing upwards, he saw a fiery-winged seraph descending from heaven, in the form of a crucified man with the gracious face of Jesus. Seeing him nailed to the cross imbued St Francis with infinite sorrow and compassion, and they began a long period of secret converse. Afterwards the wondrous image faded away, and St Francis instantly began to develop bleeding wounds in his hands, feet and side that corresponded to the crucifixion wounds of Jesus.

Such wounds, which seem to develop of their own accord and do not become septic, are known as stigmata. St Francis is widely believed to have been the first person to develop them, but since that day many others have been documented too, frequently from Europe, mostly women and usually (though not invariably) of the Catholic faith.

Stigmatics often retain their stigmata throughout their lives, but some notable exceptions have also been documented. Therese Neumann was born at Konnersreuth, Bavaria, in 1898, and during her youth suffered various severe ailments that were miraculously cured on the anniversaries of significant days in the life of St Thérèse of Lisieux. She also developed the five typical stigmata (hands, feet and side), together with brow wounds mirroring those inflicted upon Jesus by the crown of thorns. Each Friday she would lose almost a half a litre (a pint) of blood from them and over 3.5 kg (8 lb) in body weight, in a remarkable duplication of Jesus's passion, but even more remarkably, the wounds had always completely healed again by Sunday.

Certain variations in the forms of the stigmata are also on record. The most dramatic and diverse were those of a Breton peasant called Marie-Julie Jahenny. As listed by Ian Wilson in *The Bleeding Mind*, she developed the five typical stigmata on 21 March 1873 and within the next 12 months she gained the crown of thorns wounds, an imprint on her left shoulder, dorsal hand and foot wounds, cord-like wrist marks, an emblematic pattern over her heart, scourge-like stripes on her arms, legs and ankles, and a stigmatic ring.

In the sixteenth century, St Catherine Dei Ricci developed a scar on her right shoulder recalling the type of wound that the carrying of a crucifixion cross would have yielded. In 1979, after experiencing a vision of Jesus

and receiving stigmata in her hands and side, Vera d'Agostino from Pescara province in Italy developed bleeding weals all over her body,

St Francis receives stigmata from the seraph in this painting by Giotto.

resembling the wounds that would result from a scourging, as inflicted upon Jesus at his crucifixion.

In an alleged case of internal stigmatization, Sister Maria Villani, a Dominican nun from seventeenth-century Naples, claimed that during a

state of ecstasy, her heart and side were pierced by a fiery spear of love carried by an angel. She died many years later, shortly after which an autopsy was

conducted upon her body. When her chest cavity was opened, a stream of hot smoke surged up from her heart. Several minutes passed before the surgeon dared place his hand inside the cavity to extract the heart, which contained an old wound that looked as

Padre Pio celebrating Mass in 1955. Pilgrims flocked to the monastery of San Giovanni Rotondo, hoping for his blessing.

if it had been made by a sharp pointed object, like a spear.

The most famous recent stigmatic was Padre Pio (1887–1968), a Capuchin monk from the monastery of San Giovanni Rotondo, near Foggia, Italy. After experiencing stinging pains in his hands while praying on 20 September 1915, during the week of the anniversary of St Francis's stigmatization, this celebrated holy man gained the five typical stigmata on 20 September 1918, which remained throughout his life, often bleeding profusely and causing him great pain. Padre Pio was also credited with many miraculous cures and even with the baffling ability to appear simultaneously in two different localities (bilocation).

Stigmatics have usually experienced great physical and emotional suffering during their early years, and some continue to exhibit hysteria or extreme religious fervour throughout their lives. Investigators seeking an explanation for

stigmata believe that it is this disturbed, frenetic state of mind that induces the development of these wounds through psychosomatic processes, especially if the person possesses notable psychic powers. According to D. Scott Rogo in *Miracles*: "The sufferer literally directs psychokinesis onto his own body. This forces lesions to open in the flesh."

Scientists no longer doubt that the power of suggestion, especially when functioning subconsciously, can achieve remarkable results. As Ian Wilson revealed, under hypnosis some subjects have been induced to weep tears of blood, others have spontaneously developed rope-like weal marks on their skin, have prevented open wounds from bleeding or have become immune to pain. One pertinent case features a temporary stigmatic from California called Cloretta Robertson, who, unlike most stigmatics, is Protestant and black. In 1972, aged 10, and just a week after reading a

religious book dealing with the crucifixion of Jesus, she developed a bleeding stigma in her left palm, and four others intermittently appeared and vanished during the next 19 days. Had the book's subject triggered a psychosomatic response creating the stigmata? If not, the timing of their development is a remarkable coincidence.

One final point should be added. Many portrayals of crucifixions erroneously depict the crucified persons nailed to the cross through their hands. In reality, they would have been nailed through their wrists because their hands would not have been strong enough to support the weight of their body. Yet almost invariably, stigmata arise not in the wrists but in the hands, thereby corresponding with the popular, but incorrect, image of crucifixion and indicating once again that the development of stigmata is induced by mental suggestion.

BLACK SEA

Noah's Ark

TURKEY

Sirrush
(controversial
Babylonian
"dragon" on
Ishtar Gate)

MEDITERRANEAN SEA   Witches' winds

JORDAN

Booming
sands

ISRAEL

Star of Bethlehem   IRAQ

Great Pyramid;
Sphinx

Ark of the
Covenant's location (1)

Mummified
crocodile boy

Lot's wife/Pillar of
salt transformation

EGYPT

Shrieking statue

RED SEA

Mountain tiger

SUDAN

MALI

Stranded corpse of
unidentified sea-serpent

CHAD

Ark of the Covenant's
location (2)

GAMBIA

Were-hyaenas

Extraterrestrial origin for
Dogons' astronomical knowledge

Four-tusked elephants

Death bird (mystery
blood-drinking bat)

Were-hyaenas

Leopard men

ETHIOPIA

SIERRA
LEONE

GHANA

NIGERIA

Prester John's Land

'Were-pterosaur'

Pygmy elephant

CAMEROON

SOMALI
REPUBLIC

Olitiau

Were-pythons

CONGO
REPUBLIC

Dinosaur-like mokele-mbembe
and emela-ntouka; pygmy elephants

Nandi bear

Aquatic elephant; four-tusked
elephants; giant snake

KENYA

ZAIRE

Were-leopards

SOUTH

ATLANTIC

OCEAN

Crowing crested cobra

Modern-day manna

Pterodactyl-like
kongamato

MALAWI

ANGOLA

ZAMBIA

Crowing crested cobra

Lost continent
of Lemuria

ZIMBABWE

MADAGASCAR

Key to Phenomena

NAMIBIA

BOTSWANA

Roaring sands

FLYING

WATER

Winged serpent

ELEMENTS

Asphyxiating poison tree

LAND ANIMAL

SOUTH AFRICA

HUMAN

Sea monster with long trunk
washed ashore at Margate

SITES

PARANORMAL

Phantom motorbike hitch-hiker

Flying Dutchman

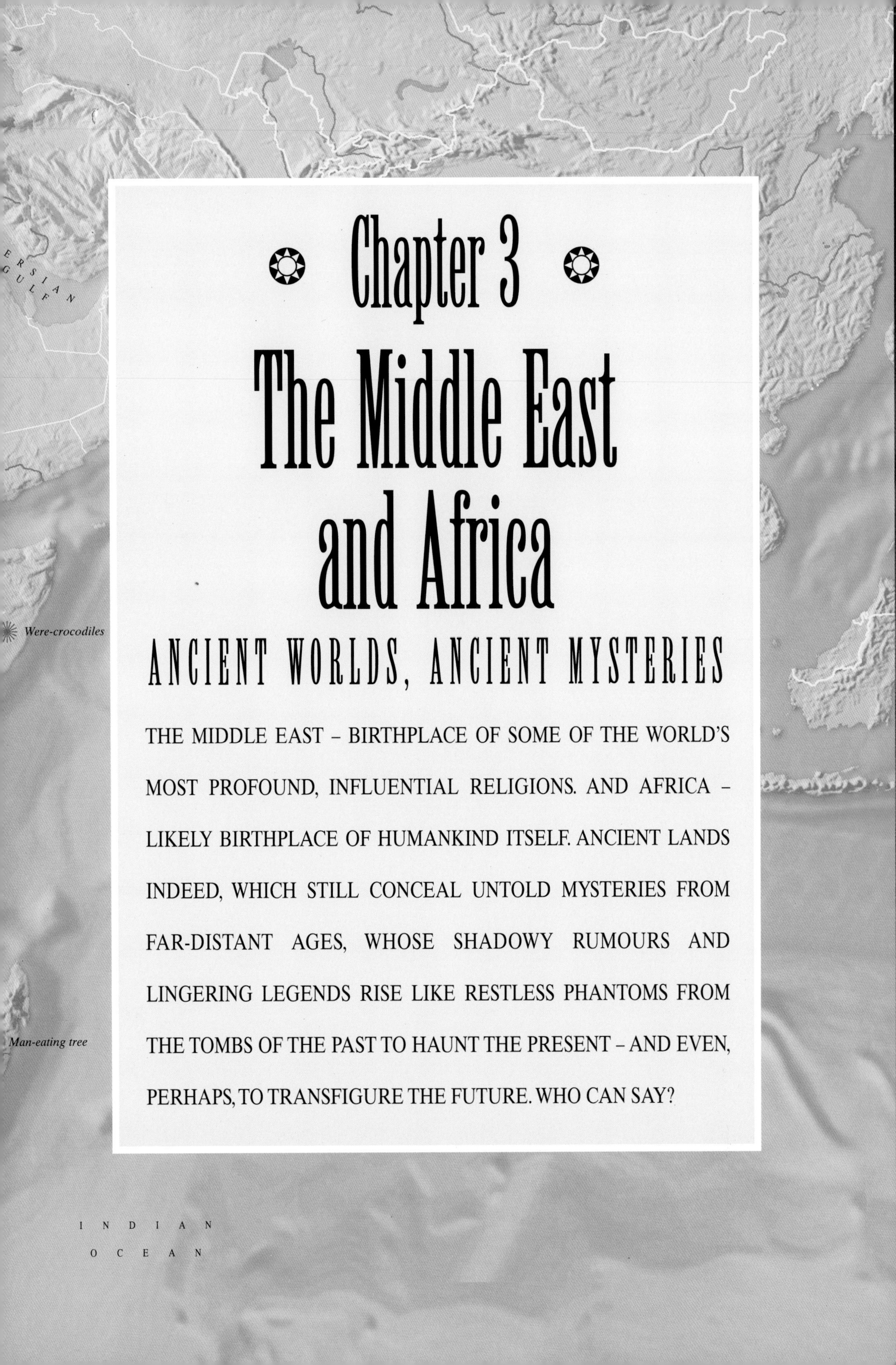

Were-crocodiles

Man-eating tree

Chapter 3
The Middle East and Africa

ANCIENT WORLDS, ANCIENT MYSTERIES

THE MIDDLE EAST – BIRTHPLACE OF SOME OF THE WORLD'S MOST PROFOUND, INFLUENTIAL RELIGIONS. AND AFRICA – LIKELY BIRTHPLACE OF HUMANKIND ITSELF. ANCIENT LANDS INDEED, WHICH STILL CONCEAL UNTOLD MYSTERIES FROM FAR-DISTANT AGES, WHOSE SHADOWY RUMOURS AND LINGERING LEGENDS RISE LIKE RESTLESS PHANTOMS FROM THE TOMBS OF THE PAST TO HAUNT THE PRESENT – AND EVEN, PERHAPS, TO TRANSFIGURE THE FUTURE. WHO CAN SAY?

INDIAN
OCEAN

Riddles from the Past

IN SEARCH OF THE LOST ARK – FROM INDIANA JONES TO VENDYL JONES

In the movies, actor Harrison Ford plays rugged archaeologist Indiana Jones who rediscovers one of the Bible's greatest lost treasures – an event that Vendyl Jones hopes to transform from fiction into fact. Claiming to be the real-life inspiration for the Indiana Jones character, since the early 1990s this elderly Baptist minister from the USA has been actively searching for his film counterpart's legendary prize – the Ark of the Covenant.

According to the Bible, this sacred relic was the magnificent wooden chest (overlain outside and inside with pure gold) that contained the two tablets of stone upon which God had inscribed the Ten Commandments. Constructed from acacia by Moses at Mount Sinai around 1250 BC following precise divine instructions, the Ark was 114 cm (3 ft 9 in.) long by 69 cm (2 ft 3 in.) in width and height, with a heavy lid of gold bearing a pair of shining cherubim. Golden rings were attached to the Ark's sides, through which were passed long poles, enabling it to be carried upon the shoulders of a privileged team of bearers, and in this manner it was transported by the nomadic Israelites during their desert wanderings.

It evidently contained more than tablets of stone, however, for whenever the Israelites went into battle, the Ark

To the Philistines, the ark of the covenant became a deadly prize.

allegedly emitted divine energy that devastated their enemies. Not for nothing was it described in the Bible as the sign and the seal of God's presence on earth. During one confrontation, the Philistines captured it, but their success was short-lived, as they were rapidly smitten by a horrendous plague, inflicting them with cancerous tumours. Soon afterwards, they willingly relinquished their deadly prize, sending it on its way strapped in a cart drawn by two cows, which took it to the borders of Beth-shemesh, a Levitical town of North Judah. Here the Israelites reclaimed it, taking it to Kiriath-Jearim.

Twenty years later, King David transported it to Jerusalem. There in 955 BC King Solomon placed it inside a sacred room called the Holy of Holies, within the first Temple, specially erected on Mount Moriah as a resting place for this miraculous artefact.

According to one tradition, it was later stolen by Menelik, son of Solomon and the Queen of Sheba, and transported to what became Axum in northern Ethiopia. According to another, however, shortly before the Temple was destroyed by the Babylonians in 587 BC the Ark was removed by the prophet Jeremiah, who hid it in an undisclosed cave amid the surrounding countryside. A third possibility is simply that it was destroyed.

Yet whichever (if any) of these theories is true, the outcome was the same: sometime prior to the first Temple's destruction, the Ark had utterly vanished, as far as the records were concerned. Suddenly, it was the

Vendyl Jones sitting on a section of wall he uncovered near Jericho. Jones believes this to be part of an ancient Israelite city which once housed the ark of the covenant.

also claimed to be on the scroll's inventory. By May 1992, he and his team seemed to be drawing even closer to their objective, having unearthed what they believed to be temple incense in one of the caves, but their hopes were shattered when within a fortnight of this latest discovery, the Israeli Antiquities Authority halted their excavations and refused to extend their research permit. No specific reason was given for this abrupt action – so for the present, Jones's attempts to find the lost Ark have been thwarted and he now spurns his 'Indiana' nickname.

Intriguingly, during much the same period that Jones was seeking the Ark in the West Bank, another investigator was claiming that he had already found it – in Ethiopia. In *The Sign and the Seal* and *Fingerprints of the Gods*, British journalist Graham Hancock recounted his arduous quest for the Ark of the Covenant, a quest that led him to Axum, in accordance with the Menelik theory of the Ark's post-Solomon destiny. However, Hancock's researches convinced him that Menelik did not steal it. Instead, he believes that it was retained inside the first Temple until around 650 BC, when its own priests – concerned that it might be destroyed by Judea's King Manasseh, an idol-worshipping pagan – took it to a newly completed Jewish temple at Elephantine, in Egypt. There it was guarded until 410 BC, when the temple was razed. Fortunately, the Ark was rescued and its fleeing bearers transported it to Lake Tana in Ethiopia, from where in AD 350 King Ezana took it northward to Axum. Here, a special abode was established for it – the church of St Mary of Zion. Except for periods of medieval turmoil when it switched localities several times while this church was alternately being destroyed and rebuilt, it has remained here ever since.

So why is it supposed to be lost? How can there be any mystery surrounding the Ark if it can readily be viewed in its present resting place? In fact, as Hancock was to learn the hard way, this is not as easy as it might seem. Tracing the Ark to the church of St Mary, he discovered that although a replica (covered by elaborate drapery) is borne aloft during a public outdoor

lost Ark, its fate an abstruse mystery for scholars everywhere – and then along came Vendyl Jones.

In March 1992, as director of the Institute for Judaic Christian Research in Texas, Jones led an archaeological investigation within the then Israeli-occupied West Bank's famous Qumran Caves, in which the Dead Sea Scrolls were discovered during 1947. In 1952, a controversial scroll, called the Copper Scroll, was unearthed. This allegedly lists many sacred items formerly contained

within the second Temple in Jerusalem (built by Herod the Great and destroyed in AD 70 by the Romans under Titus), together with the localities to which they were removed prior to the Temple's destruction. One of the relics reputedly listed is the Ark of the Covenant.

How it came to be in the second Temple has not been disclosed, but Jones was certainly intent upon revealing the Ark itself, gaining encouragement from his success during 1988 in uncovering a small anointing jug procession celebrating the feast of Timkat, the genuine Ark is permanently concealed within the qeddusa qeddusan (equivalent to a Jewish temple's Holy of Holies), which is strictly out of bounds to all but a single person – the guardian of the Ark.

The Ark's importance, coupled with the power of the Ethiopian Orthodox Church and the country's government, ensures that no one violates this dictum – explaining how a softly spoken, bearded monk, the Ark's current guardian, can effectively keep the entire world at bay, preventing everyone (including Ethiopia's own ruler) from gazing upon the sign and seal of God's presence on earth. And when the monk dies, the successor whom he has chosen on his death-bed will continue this time-honoured tradition.

Even attempting to catch an unauthorized glimpse of one of the Ark's many replicas, housed in several other Ethiopian temples, is fraught with difficulty. When Hancock tried to sneak a look at the replica within the Holy of Holies at Gondar, he swiftly found himself confronted by a vengeful party of furious clerics waving their fists at him and declaring him to be "... a very bad man"! Not surprisingly, he made no attempt to view the real thing. Instead, he had to be satisfied with the advice of its guardian in 1991, a monk called Gebra Mikhail: "I believe that the Ark is well described in the Holy Bible. You can read there."

Just as great a mystery as the Ark's present locality is its identity. After all, it flattened mountains, it levelled the walls of Jericho and it instantly killed an unfortunate helper of King David called Uzzah who placed his hand on it when it seemed about to fall off an ox-drawn cart taking it to Jerusalem. The Ark was also held responsible for the terrible sickness, disfiguring boils and widespread deaths suffered by the Philistines after seizing it from the Israelites – all symptoms of radiation sickness, in the opinion of certain researchers today.

Several identities for the Ark have been offered, including a form of electrical battery, a miniature nuclear reactor, even an advanced food manufacturer that created manna (see p. 103) during the Israelites' long desert

PRESTER JOHN'S LAND

Prester John. The story of a priest-king captured the Byzantine imagination.

During AD 1165, many of the most eminent royal courts of Europe were aflame with curiosity ignited by the circulation of a letter addressed to the Byzantine Emperor Manuel, for the letter had purportedly been written by one of the world's most mysterious rulers – an enigmatic and inestimably opulent priest-king known only as Prester John.

According to rumour and legend, Prester John was the Christian monarch of an unlocated Eastern land brimming with wealth and wonders of every kind. Here could be found unicorns and dragons, the fountain of youth gushed forth its revitalizing waters for all of this realm's citizens to partake, and fireproof clothing was woven from cocoons spun by salamanders in the manner of asbestos silkworms. Incredible fact or imaginative fiction?

Opinion eventually swayed towards the latter option when persistent searches failed to uncover any concrete evidence for the reality of the priestly ruler and his kingdom. Accordingly, his letter was denounced as a hoax and Prester John's Land has long since vanished from maps and atlases. Nevertheless, some researchers believe that the stories may have been inspired by Ethiopia, a Christian country since the fourth century AD, and they suggest that "John" was a corruption of "Zan", the royal title of Ethiopia.

journey in search of the promised land.

Intriguingly, a sacred artefact much less familiar than the Ark but more than a little reminiscent of it reached Asturias in Spain from Jerusalem, via Egypt, during the ninth century. Known as the Arca Santa, it is housed in Oviedo Cathedral, safely ensconced within a special chamber erected for it by Alfonso the Chaste. Just like the Ark, this mysterious chest is said to possess frightening powers: according to historian Ean Begg, when a group of priests opened it in about AD 1030 they were promptly struck dumb.

Whatever and wherever it is, the Ark of the Covenant has fascinated mankind for untold centuries. Perhaps one day, somehow, its secrets will be unveiled – but bearing in mind that nothing created even by today's standards of technology can duplicate its formidable array of talents, will we be able to control the powers that our studies of the Ark may unleash?

Perhaps Gebra Mikhail's advice is well founded.

NOAH'S ARK

Many scientists have traditionally dismissed the account of Noah's Ark and the great flood in the biblical Book of Genesis as an allegory, rather than a description of a factual occurrence. Nonetheless, there have been repeated assertions not only that Noah's vast sea vessel was real, but also that in recent times it has actually been discovered.

During the summer of 1916, Lieutenant Vladimir Roskovitsky, a Russian pilot, claimed to have sighted the hull of a huge ship lying half-submerged in the upper slopes of Mount Ararat in eastern Turkey – popularly believed by biblical scholars to be the mountain upon which Noah's Ark came to rest after the flood. Researchers sent by the tsar located and studied the strange craft, but their detailed report was supposedly lost

*Noah's ark, here the inspiration for **Sending Forth the Dove** by nineteenth-century artist Gustave Doré.*

for Noah's Ark in Genesis, but it does not appear to contain any wood or other physical remains. Fasold has argued that this is because the Ark has become fossilized; geologists counter that it is just an oddly shaped uplift of earth (syncline), an Ark simulacrum rather than the Ark itself. Indeed, it has even been suggested that this striking structure may have *inspired* the story of Noah's Ark – a thought-provoking reversal of traditional concepts. In the meantime, however, Fasold and a team of Turkish scientists continue to study Al Judi's Ark-shaped anomaly, in the hope of confirming that one of the Bible's greatest wonders is more than just a myth.

✡

A SHRIEKING STATUE AND A PILLAR OF SALT

The following lines appeared in a poem called "The Sphinx" by Oscar Wilde:

*Still from his chair of porphyry gaunt Memnon strains his lidless eyes
Across the empty land, and cries each yellow morning unto thee.*

Their words tell of an extraordinary vocal statue that for over 200 years had often emitted a strident shriek, like the breaking of a harp string. It is the eastern member of a pair dubbed the Colossi of Memnon but depicting the seated Pharaoh Amenhotep III. Each more than 15 metres (50 feet) high, these immense sculptures were hewn from sandstone and erected in c.1500 BC, yet still stand today amid the ruins of Thebes (Luxor), close to the Nile's western bank.

In 27 BC, a severe earthquake partially destroyed the eastern statue, whose upper half crashed to the ground. Until then, the statue had been totally silent, but seven years later the historian Strabo visited Thebes and reported hearing it emit at sunrise a muted but perfectly audible bell-like sound. Between then and AD 196, this sound was heard by many other visitors too

during the Russian Revolution.

In the early 1950s, several clear photographs of a ship-like shape in a gulley were allegedly obtained from a helicopter less than 30 metres (100 feet) above Ararat by American oil engineer George Jefferson Greene. In 1962, however, he was murdered in mysterious circumstances while working in Guyana, and his Ark photographs were never seen again.

In 1955, French industrialist Fernand Navarra excavated a sample of ancient timber from a hull-like structure visible beneath a glacier on Ararat. Navarra believes this to be part of Noah's Ark, yet according to American radiocarbon-dating analyses the timber was only about 1400 years old, i.e. not of biblical age. During the 1980s, former astronaut James Irwin led several expeditions to Ararat in search of the Ark, but met with little success.

The most publicized "arkeological" investigations, however, feature an extraordinary ship-shaped object of impressive size discovered not on Ararat itself, but just 32 kilometres (20 miles) away, in the Akyayla range and immediately below the mountain of Al Judi – which happens to be the peak named as the Ark's last resting place by the Qur'an. First reported in the late 1950s during an aerial survey by the Turkish Air Force, this curious object was the focus of several expeditions in the 1980s and 1990s. Their participants included American shipwreck specialist David Fasold and archaeological researcher Vendyl Jones (later to seek a very different biblical Ark – the Ark of the Covenant, see pp. 79–81).

Resembling a ship-shaped hill bounded by a raised ridge, this eye-catching enigma's dimensions correspond fairly well with those given

The Colossi of Memnon, two sandstone statues showing the seated Pharoah Amenhotep III in the ruined city of Thebes. The statue on the right is the shrieking statue.

(and usually at sunrise), including Juvenal and Emperor Hadrian. Some even recorded their experiences on site, inscribing them upon the side of the statue. In c. AD 200, however, Emperor Septimius Severus supervised the statue's belated repair, replacing its fallen upper half with a new, freshly carved version – after which it never "spoke" again.

It is plausible, therefore, that the sound was an unusual side-effect of the damage experienced by the statue during the earthquake and was nullified by the new repair work. Several explanations have been formulated. These include: noises made by the escape of expanding, sunrise-warmed air from inside exposed cracks in the statue; unequal expansion of various sections of the statue's lower half warmed by the sun, causing them to rub audibly against one another; conversion of former ultrasonic emissions into audible emissions by the earthquake's damaging effects; and even fake sounds created surreptitiously by Egyptian priests to gain prestige or money (or both). Frustratingly, we shall never know the truth.

Another long-standing mystery is whether Lot's wife really did turn into a pillar of salt when she looked back at the burning city of Sodom, as claimed in the biblical Book of Genesis. Today the famous Dead Sea, believed by some theologians to be the site of this vanquished city, has many columnar deposits of salt, which could have inspired the story.

Pillars of salt in the Dead Sea. Did these inspire the story of Lot's wife?

Pyramids, especially the Great Pyramid of Cheops, have long inspired fascination.

However, a much more literal explanation was offered in 1988 by chemical researcher Dr I. Klotz from Northwestern University in Illinois. He claimed that Lot's wife was killed by a biblical "greenhouse effect" sparked off by the inferno destroying Sodom.

According to Klotz, as soon as she turned around she would have been hit by a powerful blast of radiation and hot air containing a high level of carbon dioxide, from the fiery conflagration engulfing Sodom. This would have triggered a lethal series of chemical reactions inside her body, combining calcium with the carbon dioxide, culminating in an immense, and almost instantaneous, pervasive crystallization of calcite – thus converting the hapless Mrs Lot into a rigid block of calcite, a substance loosely termed "salt" by ancient Hebrews.

✦

PYRAMIDOLOGY AND PYRAMID POWER

Since its supposed creation in c.2600 BC, the Great Pyramid of Cheops (Khufu) at Giza in Egypt has probably engendered more conjecture than any other artificial edifice on earth. Two of its most controversial subjects are pyramidology and pyramid power.

"Pyramidology" is a term that has been coined to describe efforts by various investigators to prove that the Great Pyramid's dimensions are encoded with a vast amount of advanced scientific data and prophecies. The person most responsible for bringing this belief to public attention was Charles Piazzi Smyth, Astronomer Royal for Scotland, whose on-site studies of the pyramid led in the 1860s to his preparation of *Our Inheritance in the Great Pyramid*, the first of a series of highly detailed tomes. In these, Smyth unveiled all manner of startling metrical data apparently incorporated within the dimensions of the Great Pyramid: for example, its perimeter indicates the length of the earth's solar year, its height to base area ratio equals pi, its height multiplied by 10⁹ yields the distance between the sun and the earth, and so forth.

These claims seemed highly impressive, until other researchers checked them and discovered that they were far from precise. Indeed, in order to obtain some of them Smyth had resorted to the invention of a totally new unit of measurement – the pyramid inch (= 0.999 imperial inch or 25.146 mm). Furthermore, any values incorporating the height of the pyramid were, by definition, only approximations because the pyramid's top is missing! The secret prophecies embodied by its dimensions were not exactly inspiring either. For instance, depending upon the specific set of measurements used, several different predictions for the year of Jesus's Second Coming have been made, including 1881, 1911 and 1936, and the date of God's Final Judgement was supposed to occur on 20 August 1953.

Equally contentious but far more intriguing are the claims surrounding pyramid power. These stemmed from a visit to the Great Pyramid in the 1930s by a French holidaymaker, Antoine Bovis, who was very surprised to find that the corpses of small animals which had died inside it had not decomposed, despite the prevailing humidity, but were still well preserved. Back home, he experimented with cardboard pyramids and found that vegetables placed inside them stayed fresh longer than vegetables placed inside non-pyramidal containers.

In due course, Bovis's findings came to the notice of Karel Drbal, a radio technician in what was then Czechoslovakia, who pursued a different line of investigation. Instead of using vegetables, he placed razor blades inside a model pyramid, and was amazed to discover that blunt ones became sharp again. Drbal was so impressed that in 1949 he applied to the patent office in Prague to register his own pyramid as an invention for resharpening razor blades.

Understandably, the office's scientists were very sceptical about such a radical claim and refused to grant him a patent until further tests had been completed to their satisfaction. These took ten years, but were evidently successful, because in 1959 Drbal duly received his

patent, registered as No. 91304, and a factory in his homeland has been churning out cardboard (now styrofoam) pyramids for the resharpening of razor blades ever since. One of the patent's conditions is particularly interesting: the blade's longitudinal axis must lie in the direction of the earth's magnetic field for the sharpening effect to occur.

Nevertheless, other researchers are greatly divided in their opinions on "pyramid power". Some have allegedly failed to obtain any significant results and deny that such a phenomenon exists. Conversely, Dr Lyall Watson, author of *Supernature*, asserts that by placing a double-edged razor blade directly under the apex of a cardboard pyramid oriented so that its base lines face magnetic north–south and east–west, and with the blade's cutting edges facing east and west, he has been able to use the same blade daily for up to four months. However, he notes that the blade must not simply be placed on the ground inside the pyramid, but instead upon a stand or platform a third of the pyramid's own height, and that the pyramid should be kept well away from electrical devices during the experiment.

A similar report appeared in the *Daily Mail* (28 December 1995), when J. A. Dempsey of Chester, England, affirmed that a cardboard pyramid would fully regenerate a razor blade in three days, which enabled him to use the same cheap disposable razor for 18 months. The relative proportions of his pyramid (and Watson's) matched those of the Great Pyramid, and he placed the blade in a north–south alignment inside it, parallel to one of its faces, and standing on a matchbox so that the blade rested at a third of the pyramid's height from its base.

The mechanism by which such effects might be achieved is still a mystery, though Watson has speculated that perhaps the pyramid's shape generates an internal magnetic field which encourages the regrowth of crystals along the edge of the blunt razor blade. Experiments using a Gauss meter have indicated that magnetic induction is indeed occurring, and electromagnetic dehydration may result from the force field created by such induction, all of

which could explain the above-cited patent condition, and the necessity for keeping model pyramids away from electrical fields, since these would interfere with their magnetic activity.

✡

THE STAR OF BETHLEHEM – A CHRISTMAS MYSTERY

For many centuries, astronomers have speculated about the identity of the enigmatic star of Bethlehem, which appeared in the east, led the three wise men to the stable where Jesus had been born and remained stationary overhead as a holy beacon, according to the Gospel of St Matthew. A fascinating range of suggested solutions is currently on offer.

The most popular idea was voiced by German astronomer Johannes Kepler. He believed the star to be a conjunction (alignment) of the planets Jupiter and Saturn in the constellation of Pisces. This rare event would have had astrological as well as astronomical significance.

Many theologians believe that the three wise men – the Magi – were astrologers, whose studies had foretold a great happening heralded by an unusual celestial event in the east. In astrology, Jupiter is the planet of royalty, and Saturn and Pisces are both connected with the Israelites. Hence a conjunction of these planets in that constellation would have indicated a forthcoming occurrence of great significance and regal association for the Jewish people.

Moreover, in *The Star of Bethlehem Mystery*, Sheffield University astronomer Dr David Hughes revealed from a study of ancient Babylonian and Chinese star records that during 7 BC the Jupiter–Saturn alignment took place three times – a triple conjunction. In other words, a highly unusual, noteworthy celestial event took place, and in the year believed by a number of notable researchers to be the true year of Jesus's birth. The first of these

The journey of the Magi led by a star in the east is an enduring theme of Christian art. This mosaic is in San Apollonia, Ravenna.

conjunctions was on 27 May (which would have been the incentive for the Magi's journey westwards from Persia), the second on 15 September (seen by them when they arrived at Damascus), and the third on 1 December (pointing out their required destination in Bethlehem).

In December 1995 American astronomer Dr Michael Molnar put forward an alternative theory, linking astronomical events at the time of Jesus's birth to astrological symbolism on Roman coins. He proposed that the star was a double occultation (eclipse) of Jupiter by the moon.

Another postulated identity is a supernova or exploding star. Liverpool University astronomer Dr Richard Stephenson learnt from ancient Chinese texts that one supernova occurred in the correct portion of the sky during the spring of 5 BC, another favoured date for Jesus's birth. A supernova also occurred on 23 February 4 BC, which led

the American mathematician A. J. Morehouse to propose that the star was actually a three-stage event, comprising the Jupiter–Saturn conjunctions and the two separate supernovae.

St Matthew stated that the star moved through the sky and "... came to rest over the place where the child was", but adherents of the theories discussed above believe that this movement was just an optical illusion. However, a more literal explanation was aired in 1991, when Professor Colin Humphreys of Cambridge University's Materials Science Department claimed that the star was a comet, one that had been reported during the spring of 5 BC. In contrast, he was unimpressed by solutions evoking the triple conjunction of Jupiter and Saturn, stating that the two planets would always have appeared separate from one another.

In the past, various attempts had been made by other scientists to identify the star with Halley's comet,

but these failed. For although it was indeed brightest at the latitude of Bethlehem, this particular comet arrived in 11 BC, which was at least four years too early.

A final line of speculation regarding the star focuses upon one of seven paintings allegedly painted by St Luke. It portrays the Madonna and Child, and is exhibited in the Church of Our Lady of Expectation on St Thomas's Mount, near Madras, India. In this painting, the star of Bethlehem is depicted as an elliptical object with wing-like structures at its rear end and a core encircled by rays, and is the basis for the most unusual identity for the star suggested so far – an alien spacecraft. This novel concept, publicized by the author Robin Collyns in 1974, is also the theme of Irish pop star Chris de Burgh's haunting Christmas song "A Spaceman Came Travelling", but it is hardly music to the ears of orthodox science.

RIDDLES OF THE SPHINX

From the time of the ancient Egyptians of the New Kingdom (c.1400 BC) right up to the founding of modern Egyptology just over a century ago by Sir Flinders Petrie and others, the consensus of opinion regarding the age of the Great Sphinx of Giza had always been that it predated the Fourth Dynasty of Egypt (which began in c.2550 BC). Twentieth-century researchers, on the other hand, are adamantly convinced that it was built in c.2500 BC, during the reign of the Fourth Dynasty pharaoh Khafre (Chephren), and that its face is that of Khafre himself.

Consequently, considerable reverberations echoed through the Egyptological community when in 1991 Boston University geologist Dr Robert Schoch published some thought-provoking evidence indicating that the earlier opinions had been correct after all and that the Great Sphinx probably dated back to 7000–5000 BC. More specifically, he claimed that the core body of the sphinx dated back to this period, concluding that this mighty colossus was built in several stages, beginning with the core and reaching completion considerably later with the sculpting of the rear portion. Most Egyptologists assume that the sphinx had been built as a guardian for the pyramids, yet if Schoch is correct, it had existed for several millennia before these great structures had even been erected.

Schoch was led to his dramatic conclusions by the type of weathering exhibited by the sphinx, for whereas other sculptures in the area display the expected sand and wind abrasion, the sphinx's weathering pattern seems consistent with erosion caused by water – and the last period of flooding and extensive rainfall here was the Nabtian Pluvial, occurring between 12,000 and 3000 BC. His pre-dynasty dating for the sphinx was corroborated by seismic analyses too, and he is presently hoping to obtain permission from the Egyptian

DOGON ASTRONOMY

The Dogon are a tribe of poor, cave-dwelling, farming people in southern Mali in West Africa – hardly the likeliest source of advanced astronomical data. Yet according to a study of these people during 1946–50 by French anthropologists Marcel Griaule and Germaine Dieterlen, published in 1950, the Dogon priests know of a tiny secret star that they call *po*. They state that it is composed of an exceedingly heavy substance and orbits the brilliant dog-star Sirius in a 50-year cycle, pursuing an elliptical path.

There is indeed such a star – Sirius B, first recorded scientifically in 1862, and so dense that a cubic metre of its matter weighs about 20,000 tonnes. Moreover, its orbit is just as the Dogon describe, which makes all the more remarkable the fact that Sirius B is totally invisible to the human eye and was photographed for the first time as recently as 1970.

So how do the Dogon know so much about it? Their explanation is even more remarkable, for they claim to have received their astronomical information (which also includes knowledge of Saturn's rings and the four major moons of Jupiter) from a race of amphibious space beings called the Nommos that visited the earth long ago from the Sirius star system!

In *The Sirius Mystery*, researcher Robert K. G. Temple supports an extraterrestrial origin for the Dogon data, but others are very sceptical. American cosmologist Dr Carl Sagan considers it far more likely that they gained their knowledge from travelling Europeans around 1930 – a time when details of Sirius, its tiny companion star and other astronomical data later divulged by the Dogon to the French

Dogon dancers.

anthropologists had become familiar in the Western world. It's a very plausible solution, but one that may yet be disproved in a highly sensational manner. The Dogon also speak of a *second* star orbiting Sirius, at right angles to Sirius B. They call it *emme ya* ("sun of women"), but it is presently unknown to science: so what will scientists say if one day they discover that this star really does exist?

The Great Sphinx of Giza: does this fascinating monument considerably pre-date the Pyramids?

government to take samples from the sphinx for radioisotope dating, using chlorine–36.

Schoch also disbelieves the theory that the sphinx shares Khafre's face, citing evidence presented by New York forensic expert Frank Domingo that readily distinguishes the two, and which shows the face of the sphinx to be distinctively "African" (i.e. negroid).

Although his researches are the most scientific, Schoch is not the only recent worker to suggest that the Sphinx is pre-dynastic. In *Serpent in the Sky*, self-taught Egyptologist John Anthony West proposed a minimum date of 10,000 BC for its creation, but his theory that its creators were survivors from Atlantis served only to alienate his ideas from the

Egyptological community. Journalist Graham Hancock has claimed in *Fingerprints of the Gods* that the sphinx may indeed have been built in pre-dynastic times, by a great civilization that formerly existed, he believes, in a once-habitable portion of Antarctica and later travelled by sea to resettle in other areas of the world, including the Nile Valley.

Regardless of whether or not this sounds feasible, we must acknowledge that if the sphinx is truly pre-dynastic, then it was evidently built by an advanced race of people other than the ancient Egyptians: but who were they? Just like its mythological Greek counterpart, the Great Sphinx of Giza is highly skilled at posing profoundly difficult riddles.

LEMURIA – LOST HOMELAND OF THE LEMURS ... AND HUMANITY?

Numbering more than 20 different species, the lemurs are a group of primitive primates found only on Madagascar and a few smaller offshore islands. Their closest relatives are the bushbabies and pottos of tropical Africa, plus the lorises of the Indian subcontinent and South-east Asia, and they are classified with them as the prosimians. But how can the strangely discontinuous zoogeographical distribution of the prosimians be explained?

During the 1860s, zoologists freshly embracing the tenets of Darwinian evolution favoured the possibility that Africa, Madagascar, India and South-east Asia had been connected by a continent bridging the Indian Ocean and housing the first prosimians. This continent, they suggested, later sank beneath the waves, thus isolating the prosimians in their widely separated present-day localities.

English zoologist Philip L. Sclater called this hypothetical "lost" continent Lemuria, and further scientific interest in it was generated during the 1870s when German scientist Ernst Haeckel suggested that Lemuria may even have been the origin of humanity. We now know that the prosimians' disparate distribution was a product of continental drift – that Africa and India had once been in direct contact with one another before splitting apart many millions of years ago, thereby rendering the concept of a sunken linking continent superfluous. Unfortunately, however, long before this had been revealed, several notable occultists had already seized upon Haeckel's views regarding Lemuria as the cradle of humankind to cultivate their own unique and exceedingly alternative scenarios of humanity's development.

Most famous of these scenarios was that of Madame Helena P. Blavatsky, founder of the Theosophical Society. She claimed to have been in psychic contact with ethereal beings who had revealed to her the true history of humanity, which had indeed begun on Lemuria.

According to Blavatsky, the Lemurians were the third of seven Root Races (each passing through seven subrace stages) to inhabit the earth; modern-day humanity is the fifth one. The Lemurians began as grotesque entities resembling brute apes with three eyes and an egg-laying hermaphroditic mode of reproduction. Evolving into more advanced subraces, some eventually migrated to Atlantis and became the fourth Root Race. Lemuria itself was destroyed by horrendous volcanic explosions and

The strange distribution pattern of lemurs prompted theories of a lost continent.

Atlantis, later, by black magic.

Blavatsky died in 1891, but other fantastic details were revealed by her followers, and as recently as 22 May 1932 the *Los Angeles Times Star* carried an account written by reporter Edward Lanser, who claimed to have spied a settlement of Lemurians living in

seclusion on the slopes of Mount Shasta in California. It is ironic that even though in reality Lemuria was never anything more substantial than an incorrect notion aired by some nineteenth-century zoologists, today its name is better known than those of many genuine ancient lands.

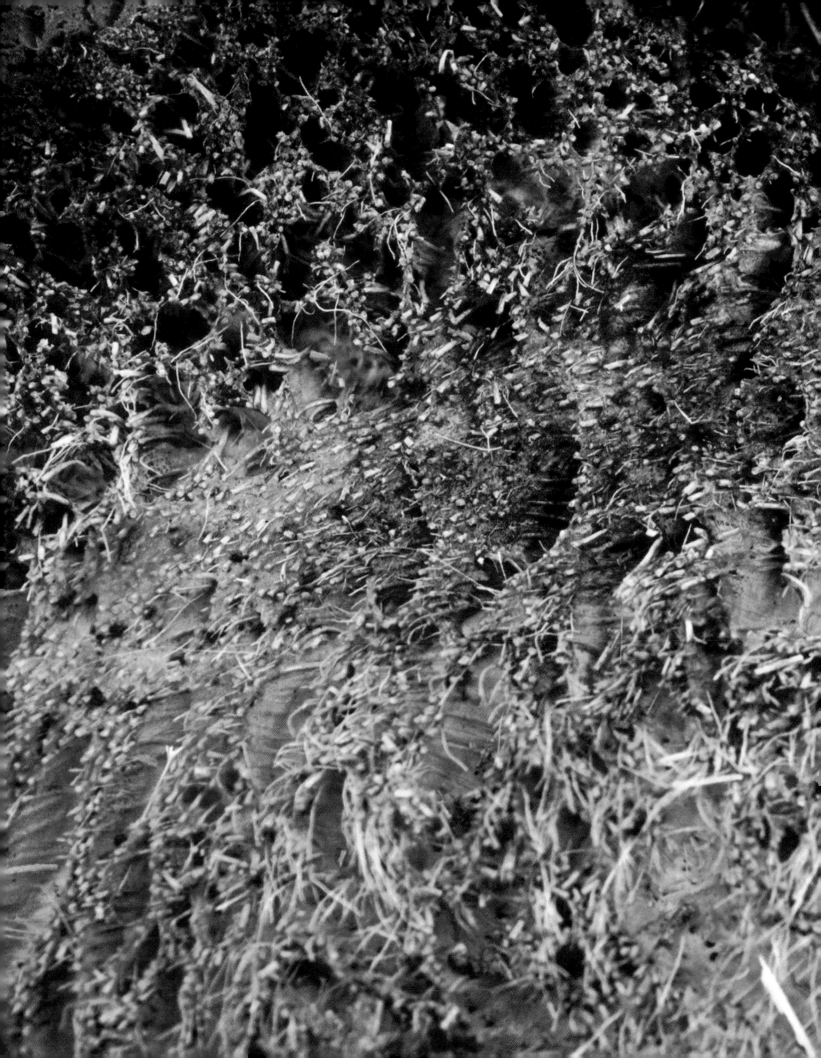

Cryptic Creatures of Every Kind

LIVING DINOSAURS AND OTHER PREHISTORIC SURVIVORS

As discussed in my book *In Search of Prehistoric Survivors*, it seems increasingly likely that there may be undiscovered modern-day descendants of some of prehistory's most famous animals existing in various of the more remote areas of tropical Africa.

The most dramatic prospect must surely be the existence of a living species of dinosaur, and the enigmatic animal currently attracting most attention with regard to this possibility has already inspired several recent scientific expeditions to the immense Likouala swamplands in the People's Republic of the Congo (formerly the French Congo), where it reputedly dwells. It is known to the pygmies and to Western settlers there as the mokele-mbembe.

Eyewitnesses describe it as a very large aquatic beast, approximately 9 metres (30 feet) in total length and reddish-brown in colour, with a burly elephant-sized body, relatively short,

thick legs, a lengthy tail, a slender elongate neck terminating in a small head, and very characteristic three-toed footprints. This description is irresistibly reminiscent of a sauropod dinosaur, like the famous *Apatosaurus* (previously called *Brontosaurus*) and *Diplodocus*. Indeed, when scientists have shown

Dr Karl Shuker wearing the "Operation Congo" T-shirt.

illustrated animal books to native observers of the mokele-mbembe, who have no palaeontological knowledge, they have unhesitatingly selected (and without any prompting) pictures of sauropods as the closest portrayals of this mystery beast.

A surviving sauropod is the identity most favoured by the mokele-mbembe's principal investigator, renowned biologist Professor Roy P. Mackal, recently retired from Chicago University, who led two expeditions to the Likouala during the 1980s in quest of this exciting creature. Two important British expeditions – "Operation Congo" (in 1986) and "Operation Congo 2" (in 1992) – have also searched for it, led by explorer Bill Gibbons.

Sadly, no conclusive scientific proof of the animal's existence has so far been obtained, but this is not really surprising, considering that its habitat is so inhospitable that even the locals avoid it as much as possible. Clearly, the mokele-mbembe is a species that only the most doggedly persistent (and environmentally resistant!) of seekers is ever likely to discover and identify. Perhaps the best hope lies in uncovering recent skeletons of this great beast.

Adding veracity to the eyewitnesses' testimony, similar creatures (known by such names as badigui, amali and n'yamala) have been recorded elsewhere in tropical Africa too, including the Central African Republic and Gabon. Of especial interest is the fascinating theory that the dragon-like sirrush portrayed on the famous Ishtar Gate of ancient Babylon is a distorted depiction of a mokele-mbembe (being based upon travellers' stories rather

The remote Likouala swamplands of the People's Republic of the Congo are said to contain an animal called the mokele-mbembe. Could this be a living species of dinosaur?

than direct observations by the gate's creators), for some of the gate's distinctive glazed bricks may well have come from Central Africa where reports of long-necked water monsters abound.

Another Likouala mystery beast with dinosaurian overtones is the emela-ntouka ("killer of elephants"), which is said to be an elephant-sized amphibious beast with a powerful ivory horn on its nose. Although the possibility that it is some form of semi-aquatic rhinoceros has been proposed in the past, its overall appearance and life-style do not correspond very satisfactorily with this identity. Consequently, taking into account its distinctive horn (very different from those of rhinos, which are

composed only of compressed hair), heavy tail (not a rhino feature) and reputed habit of disembowelling elephants that invade its marshy habitat, Mackal has cautiously suggested that the emela-ntouka may actually be a surviving ceratopsian – that is to say, a horned dinosaur related to the famous *Triceratops*.

One of Africa's most feared mystery beasts is the ferocious Nandi bear of Kenya. Several zoologists have speculated that certain reports may have featured a supposedly extinct beast known as a chalicothere. Technically, this slope-backed relative of the horses was a hoofed mammal (ungulate), but instead of possessing hooves it had huge claws, used for digging up roots. Although officially extinct since the Pleistocene (ending 10,000 years ago), a living species of chalicothere would compare closely with some Nandi bear descriptions, and an enraged individual may even be capable of some of the Nandi bear's murderous attacks.

As a herbivore, however, a chalicothere would not devour its victims. In contrast, some of those slain by the Nandi bear have been eaten, but

there is another possible prehistoric survivor that could explain these cases very satisfactorily. As large as a lion, the short-faced hyaena *Hyaena brevirostris* lived in Africa during the Pleistocene and was a much more active hunter than today's scavenging species. Significantly, many Nandi bear eyewitnesses liken it to a giant hyaena but with a shorter, bear-like face (hence this mystery beast's name). If the short-faced hyaena has indeed survived amid the depths of East Africa's forests, we surely need look no further for the identity of the rapacious Nandi bear!

The tigre de montagne or mountain tiger of northern Chad, West Africa, may also be a prehistoric survivor. According to the Zagaoua people of Ennedi, this unidentified animal is as large as a lion, with red fur and white stripes, no tail, and a huge upper pair of fangs that project conspicuously from its mouth. When an old Zagaoua hunter was shown pictures of various animals,

The feared and ferocious Nandi bear.

living and extinct, he positively identified the mountain tiger as *Machairodus* – the African sabre-toothed tiger, officially believed to have died out over a million years ago! Chad is still little-explored zoologically and its mountain ranges are not readily accessible. Could a relict population of sabre-tooths have survived here, undisturbed by time and avoided by humans? Perhaps an intrepid scientific team will one day provide the answer.

✦

LIZARD BIRDS AND DEATH BIRDS

Some of Africa's strangest secrets are borne upon dark wings of fear and mystery.

Eyewitness descriptions of the emela-ntouka suggest a surviving ceratopsian.

Reports of the kongamato accurately describe a type of prehistoric pterosaur.

The Kaondé people living around western Zambia's Jiundu swamp are convinced that its secluded interior conceals a terrifying "lizard bird" called the kongamato. They liken it to a long-tailed lizard or crocodile with bat-like wings and a beak filled with teeth, which happens to be an excellent description of a rhamphorhynchid – one of prehistory's famous flying reptiles, the pterosaurs! And when shown various illustrated animal books, they have consistently selected pictures of pterosaurs as being accurate depictions of the kongamato.

Nor is this an idiosyncrasy of the Kaondé. Identical beasts have also been reported from Angola, Mount Kenya, Zaire, Tanzania and Zimbabwe. Even eminent South African zoologist Professor J. L. B. Smith believed it possible that they do exist, and his opinion is of great relevance: in 1938, he co-discovered a living coelacanth, an archaic fish hitherto believed to have died out with the pterosaurs and dinosaurs at least 64 million years ago. The concept of twentieth-century pterosaurs is undeniably very radical, but if any have indeed survived, it is precisely the type of impenetrable, unexplored terrain afforded by localities such as the Jiundu swamp where we could expect them to have remained undetected by science.

The kongamato should not be confused with the olitiau – a winged horror from Cameroon's Assumbo Mountains. Zoologists Gerald Russell and Ivan Sanderson spied an olitiau one evening in 1932, during the Percy Sladen Expedition. Without warning, it suddenly appeared out of the darkness and skimmed across the river in which Sanderson was standing, forcing him to duck down out of reach of its open jaws, brimming with teeth. A startled Sanderson affirmed that it was an enormous bat, all-black in colour, with a flattened monkey-like face and an estimated 3.5-metre wing-span (about 12 feet). (This is more than twice that of the currently recognized record holder, a species of New Guinea fruit bat.)

In 1936, archaeologist Byron de Prorok was travelling through southern Ethiopia when he learned of Devil's Cave, a reputedly accursed cavern near Lekempti, which was home to a flock of gruesome winged creatures called death birds. After bribing his informant, a young local guide, to take him to this greatly feared place, de Prorok entered its dark, forbidding domain in search of these mysterious creatures, but all that he encountered was a flurry of bats. When he re-emerged, however, he was informed that these were the death birds and that they earned their evil name from their vampirish taste for human blood.

As proof of this claim, he was taken to a nearby camp occupied by goatherds, who were forced to inhabit this lonely region to tend the goats. While there, he saw that many of the goatherds had wounds on their limbs that resembled small puncture marks. They claimed that these had been made by the death birds, which fly silently to their camp at night and drink their blood while they are asleep. One goatherd in the camp appeared to be close to death, little more than a skin-covered skeleton, in blood-stained clothes and blankets.

Zoologically, what makes this account so remarkable is that only three species of bat are known to live upon blood: these are the vampire bats, which are found exclusively in the New World. There is no known species of blood-

Ivan Sanderson, a zoologist, recorded a description of a huge bat-like creature in Cameroon's Assumbo Mountains.

consuming bat in the Old World, so if de Prorok's report and the goatherds' claims are accurate, there could well be a very dramatic new species of bat still awaiting discovery in Ethiopia's aptly named Devil's Cave.

Two of the most bizarre accounts of winged wonders from Africa were recently brought to light by John L. Vellutini. The first of these appeared in Mary H. Kingsley's *West African Studies*, and reads as follows:

The most peculiar form of witch power I have heard of as being found inside a patient was on the Ogowe from two native friends, both of them very intelligent, reliable men, one of them a Bible reader. They said that about two years previously a relation of theirs had been badly witched. A doctor had been called in, who administered an emetic, and there appeared upon the scene a strange little animal that grew with visible rapidity. An hour after its coming to light it crawled and got out of the basin, and finally it flew away. It had bat's wings and a body and tail like a lizard. This catawampus, my informant held, if it had not been disturbed by that emetic, would have grown up inside the man and have eaten its way through the vitals.

This grotesque little vignette is very reminiscent of the "water wolf" folklore prevalent in Yorkshire, England, telling of a strange lizard-like beast that can reputedly grow inside a person's stomach if they inadvertently drink river water containing the creature's eggs. It also recalls the infamous "urban legends" of people ingesting octopus eggs, and so forth.

Vellutini's other report was from Sir Allan Cardinall's *In Ashanti and Beyond*.

When I was at Goaso [in Ghana] a certain chief, whom I got to know well, told me one evening, in answer to a query as to his health, that he was very worried. He had had bad news; two of his friends in distant villages were seriously ill; it was his fault, and he did not know what to do. Asked to explain, he averred that of late, when he went to sleep at night-time, he had assumed the shape of an enormous bat – a winged crocodile he described – and had visited

these and other friends, and had been eating them; hence their illness; what was my advice? Now he firmly believed this, and offered many sacrifices. The dream kept recurring and, as its substance was common knowledge, public opinion at his suicide a few months later, after I had been transferred, was that he had been a wizard; that he knew it, and he had taken his life in a rather heroic way.

A "winged crocodile" more readily brings to mind a pterosaur than a bat. Yet even the prospect of a living pterosaur of straightforward corporeal nature, such as the kongamato, is exceedingly radical – let alone a dream-infiltrating were-pterosaur!

ELEPHANTINE ENIGMAS

Exceptionally small yet fully adult elephants have been reported for over a century from several African countries, including Zaire, the Central African Republic, Cameroon, Gabon and Liberia. A few living specimens have

even been exhibited in zoos, such as New York's Bronx Zoo, once home to a famous male pygmy elephant called Congo. Standing a mere 1.12 metres (3 feet 8 inches) at the shoulder when captured as a six-year-old in Congo (then the French Congo) during 1905, Congo was still only about 2 metres (less than 7 feet) tall when he died 10 years later. The local people have their own specific names for these pint-sized pachyderms, recognizing them as a wholly discrete variety from the much larger normal elephants. Science, conversely, has tended to dismiss them either as rare freaks of nature – stunted, dwarf individuals of no taxonomic significance – or as incompletely grown juvenile specimens displaying precocious tusk development.

In 1989, however, German zoologists Drs Wolfgang Böhme and Martin Eisentraut announced that the pygmy elephant should be classed as a valid species in its own right (*Loxodonta pumilio*), citing many anatomical and behavioural findings in support of their claim. These included confirmation that tusked specimens were indeed adults and not juveniles, the discovery of a dead female containing a full-term foetus (again refuting the juvenile

London Zoo briefly exhibited a pygmy elephant.

The marshlands of Zaire are reportedly home to a water elephant.

identity), and filmed sightings of pygmy elephant herds (discounting the "freak" dwarf identity).

Even more controversial is the water elephant of Zaire. Standing about 2 metres (6–8 feet) tall at the shoulder, this strange animal is said to have fairly short legs, a smooth shiny skin like that of a hippo, an elongate neck twice the length of the normal African elephant's and a noticeably oval-shaped head with only a short 60-cm- (2-foot) long trunk and no tusks. Reported from the marshlands between Lakes Mai-Ndombe (formerly Leopold II) and Tumba, it reputedly remains hidden in deep water during the day, but comes out on to land at night to graze upon rank grass. Remarkably, the water elephant seems very similar in form to some of the earliest, long-extinct members of the elephant family tree, such as *Phiomia* and *Moeritherium*: could they have given rise to a little-modified but reclusive present-day equivalent?

Many African myths tell of fabled elephant kings with four tusks instead of the usual two, but freak four-tusked elephants do exist. The best-known example is a specimen shot at Lukula in Zaire on 6 August 1947, whose head was sent to the Musée du Congo Belge in Belgium. Each of its four huge tusks weighed about 23 kg (50 lb). Another four-tusker was seen, but not shot, on 18 May 1917 by Abdul El-Farag Ali in the

Sudan, and naturalist Armand Denis saw the skull and tusks of a specimen that had been found dead in the Ituri Forest in Zaire. Strangest of all, however, was the Central African three-tusked elephant noted by David Livingstone and killed on 1 May 1870, for the extra tusk grew from the base of the animal's trunk.

✦

GAMBO AND TRUNKO

Based upon sightings of some very crocodilian sea serpents, there is a remote but tantalizing possibility that a lineage of highly specialized sea crocodiles or thalattosuchians has persisted into the present day from the Mid-Cretaceous Period (approximately 110 million years ago). Unlike other crocodilians, their streamlined bodies lacked scales, their limbs had become paddle-like in form, and a large fish-like fin was present on their tail's upper surface.

One of the most compelling reports in relation to this line of speculation featured the dead but virtually undamaged and non-decomposed carcase of a strange sea creature found washed ashore on a Gambian beach on 12 June 1983 by wildlife enthusiast

Owen Burnham. According to his description, the animal (later nicknamed "Gambo") was about 4.5 metres (14–15 feet) long and relatively slender in shape, dark on top but much paler below, with very long jaws containing 80 pointed teeth, and a pair of nostrils at the upper jaw's tip. It also had a short neck, two pairs of paddle-shaped limbs and a long pointed tail.

Although not corresponding with the description of any species known by science to be alive today, Burnham's account corresponds well with a thalattosuchian, and particularly so if we assume that Gambo had originally possessed a tail fin but that this had been torn off at (or after) its death. If only Gambo's carcase had been preserved for formal examination.

Tragically, however, while Burnham was still examining it, some local people came along and decapitated the carcase, with the intention of selling its head as a tourist souvenir, before burying the rest of its remains in the sand. How ironic it

"Gambo", the strange sea creature found and described by wildlife enthusiast Owen Burnham.

"Trunko", a bizarre marine animal seen battling with whales off a beach in South Africa in 1922.

would be if the scientifically priceless skull of a modern-day species of sea crocodile is currently gathering dust on someone's mantelpiece!

On the morning of 1 November 1922, visitors to the beach at Margate, South Africa, were treated to an amazing spectacle out at sea: two whales could be clearly observed engaging in battle with a thoroughly bizarre sea monster with snowy-white fur and a huge elephantine trunk. As the titanic battle progressed, the monster seemed to weaken, and three hours later it was dead. During the evening, its lifeless body was washed ashore and proved to be truly colossal, measuring just over 14 metres (47 feet) in length, and including a 3-metre (10-foot) tail. Apart from its luxuriant 20-cm- (8-inch) long fur, however, the most remarkable feature of this beast was that it did not possess a distinct head; instead, it bore only the trunk-like appendage, 1.5 metres (5 feet) long, that had been visible during its fatal encounter with the whales.

Needless to say, there is no animal known to science, either from the present or the past, that bears any resemblance to Margate's "marine elephant" (dubbed "Trunko"). This makes it all the more frustrating that throughout the 10 days during which its carcase lay beached on the shore, no scientist took the trouble to come along and examine it. Finally, as if in disgust, the waves carried it back out to sea again and it was seen no more.

"Furry" sea-monster carcases usually prove to be the decomposed remains of sharks, in which the "fur" is actually their exposed connective tissue fibres, but this cannot explain the Margate corpse because Trunko was seen with its fur while still alive, fighting the whales. In short, what could have been a major zoological discovery was simply ignored and was allowed to be lost forever.

✵
SECRET SERPENTS

Africa may harbour some spectacular snakes still evading scientific recognition. A very dramatic incident supporting this possibility occurred in 1959 and featured Belgian aviator

The crowing crested cobra, reminiscent of the mythological cockatrice.

Colonel Remy van Lierde. While flying a helicopter at an altitude of approximately 150 metres (500 feet) above a patch of vegetation and some termite hills in the Katanga (now Shaba) region of Zaire, he saw a huge python-like serpent emerge from a hole in the ground and rear upwards, directly towards his helicopter. What makes this so outstanding a report, however, is not so much the creature's belligerent behaviour as its stupendous size. Following careful analysis of background topography in some photos that van Lierde obtained of this snake in action, its total length was estimated to be at least 12–15 metres (40–50 feet) and possibly as much as 60 metres (200 feet)!

Even more astonishing are rumours of a bizarre serpent gifted with the remarkable ability to crow like a cockerel, and which further parallels this farmyard inhabitant by being adorned with facial wattles and a prominent horny coxcomb on top of its head. More than a little reminiscent of the mythological cockatrice and referred to as the crowing crested cobra (though it does not possess a hood), this amazing creature has been frequently and soberly reported across much of tropical Africa. It is known by many different local names, including inkhomi ("killer"), and can grow up to 6 metres (20 feet) long. In 1944, Dr J. O. Shircore of Karonga, Malawi, claimed that he owned the preserved remains of the coxcomb and part of the neck from one of these snakes; and in May 1959, John

Knott accidentally ran over one while driving home from Binga in Southern Rhodesia (now Zimbabwe). According to Knott, the snake's crest was symmetrical and could be raised via five internal prop-like structures.

Most incredible of all, however, must surely be the flying snake of Namibia. Its existence is common knowledge to the Namaqua people in the southern portion of this country, but it has been seen by several other people too. In 1942, teenager Michael Esterhuise was in the mountains at Keetmanshoop when he threw a stone at what he thought was a large monitor lizard inside a rocky crack, but which proved to be a very large snake with a pair of wing-like structures projecting from the sides of its mouth. On a separate occasion, one of these serpents launched itself from a rocky ledge and soared down towards Esterhuise, hitting the ground with great force. Esterhuise fled, but the creature's tracks remained and were examined by acclaimed naturalist Marjorie Courtenay-Latimer, who confirmed that they were consistent with the marks that a snake would have made. This incredible beast is also said to bear a bright light in the middle of its brow, but that may simply be a patch of highly reflective scales. Moreover, in Asia there is a familiar species of "flying" snake that can glide from tree to tree by spreading its ribs and flattening its body into a ribbon-like parachute. So perhaps the light-emitting flying snake of Namibia is not quite so unlikely after all.

✵
WERE-LEOPARDS AND CROCODILE BOYS

The belief that evil spirits and certain humans can transform themselves into animals is rife throughout much of Africa. Reports of were-hyaenas or hyaena men, who mercilessly devour unfortunate humans and their livestock, are very common in the West African countries of Mali and Nigeria. Indeed, in the Bornu language of north-eastern Nigeria there is even a specific word for this type of shape-shifting – bultungin, which translates as "I change myself into a hyaena". In southern Africa, hyaena men are said to be very handsome, but possess two separate mouths – one for talking and one with huge teeth for cracking human bones (this mouth must always be concealed from intended victims, for obvious reasons!).

Were-leopard traditions occur in Zaire and also in Sierra Leone, West Africa – home to some of the secret and greatly feared leopard-men societies. Their members claim the ability to transform themselves into leopards, dress in leopard skins and maul their hapless victims to death in the gruesome manner of their feline namesakes, using horrific metal talons.

While exploring the Congo Republic in the 1980s, Bill Gibbons (referred to on p. 91) heard some amazing tales of witch-doctors who could supposedly transform themselves into huge pythons. Elsewhere, the Somali Republic is known for its stories of were-crocodiles, and David Livingstone encountered many reports of were-lions, especially from the Makololo of the Upper Zambezi region, who referred to them as the pondoro.

In March 1992, Turkish archaeologists announced the discovery of an extraordinary ancient Egyptian mummy in the vaults of the

Were-leopards and leopard-men societies are greatly feared in Zaire and Sierra Leone.

famous Topkapi Palace in Istanbul. It was concealed inside a wooden sarcophagus, and when carefully unwrapped it was found to comprise the upper parts of a young boy fused to the lower half of a crocodile!

The explanation for this bizarre specimen is still unknown. Some researchers have speculated that the boy may have been killed and partly eaten by the crocodile, and that in order for him to possess a complete body with which to pass into the next world, his parents arranged for his reptilian murderer to be killed and for the section of its body corresponding to the devoured portion of their son's to be attached to the boy's remains. However, this theory seems to be no less bizarre than the mummy itself!

A more plausible possibility is that the mummy was deliberately created as a sacred artefact or offering by worshippers of Sebek, ancient Egypt's crocodile-headed god of rivers and lakes. It may even have been produced as a clever fraud for exhibition purposes. Similar monstrosities used to be popular in American carnivals. One, known as Jake the Alligator Man and comprising the upper half of a monkey skeleton skilfully attached to the lower half of a small alligator, is still owned by Marsh's Free Museum in Long Beach, California.

Jake the Alligator Man: Long Beach postcards also feature more conventional types of sunbathing.

From the Shadows of the Dark Continent

THE FLYING DUTCHMAN

The supernatural history of the *Flying Dutchman* allegedly began in the 1600s, when this ship was sailing from Amsterdam to Batavia (now Jakarta) in Java, captained by a fearless and extremely experienced Dutch mariner called Hendrik Van der Decken. All went well until they encountered a terrible storm while attempting to sail around South Africa's Cape of Good Hope. Every effort made aboard the ship to combat the elements and continue their journey was in vain, but Van der Decken dismissed his crew's frantic pleas to turn the ship around. Instead, shouting blasphemous oaths skyward, he swore vehemently to defy even the Almighty and succeed in navigating onwards through the storm to Table Bay.

Suddenly, a heavenly figure appeared on deck – the Almighty himself or the Angel of the Lord? – but Van der Decken refused to touch his hat in deference and brazenly shot at the figure with his pistol. In response, his divine visitor sternly proclaimed that he and his ship would never again find rest. Henceforth they would be cursed to sail the seas until the end of eternity and would bring disaster to those who

encountered them. And so it was, for once the crew had died, they were replaced by animate skeletons, serving forever more on a ghost ship commanded by the undying figure of Captain Van der Decken.

This could be swiftly dismissed as a rather histrionic legend that inspired Wagner's equally dramatic opera *Der fliegende Holländer* (1843), were it not

*The phantom **Flying Dutchman**, cursed to sail the seas for eternity.*

for the fact that many sober sightings of the cursed craft are on record and most are from the Cape of Good Hope. In March 1939, Helene Tydell and about 60 other sunbathers at False Bay near the Cape itself spied the *Flying Dutchman* sailing slowly across the sea (even though there was no wind) before abruptly vanishing in full view of its audience. In September 1942, it was watched for some 15 minutes by four

members of a family sitting on their terrace at Mouille Point, Cape Town, as it sailed towards Table Bay, leaving a strange incandescent glow in its wake.

Further afield, both the ship and its captain were reputedly witnessed in February 1857 by crewmen aboard the *Joseph Somers* off the south Atlantic island of Tristan da Cunha. According to its legend, the *Flying Dutchman* brings doom to those who meet it, and shortly afterwards the *Joseph Somers* somehow caught fire, killing many people aboard.

The most famous *Flying Dutchman* sighting was accompanied by unforeseen tragedy too. It occurred on 11 July 1881 in Australian waters between Melbourne and Sydney, and one of the 13 observers was 16-year-old Prince George, Britain's future King George V. Although serving as a midshipman on HMS *Baccante*, he actually saw the phantom ship while aboard HMS *Inconstant* (to which he had recently been transferred when the *Baccante* developed rudder problems), and he entered it by name in the *Inconstant*'s log. According to his account, the *Flying Dutchman* glowed with a strange red light, and its masts, spars and sails were clearly visible. The prince was not the first *Inconstant* crewman to spy it: the seaman claiming that grim honour fell from the rigging the next day and was killed instantly.

Sceptics claim that such sightings are

THE MIDDLE EAST AND AFRICA

nothing more than mirages of real ships sailing elsewhere, but eyewitnesses consistently describe a vessel that is incongruously old-fashioned in appearance. Very different from modern ships, it closely recalls a seventeenth-century Dutch East Indiaman – the precise identity of the *Flying Dutchman*.

✦

THE HIKER AND THE BIKERS

One of the most eerie of ghostly phenomena is the phantom hitch-hiker. A typical scenario features a car or lorry driver stopping to pick up an ostensibly real hitch-hiker, who inexplicably dematerializes at some stage during the subsequent journey and is later identified from the bewildered driver's description as someone local who died several years earlier.

A novel twist to this chilling tale occurred in Cape Province, South Africa, during the late 1970s, because more than one driver was involved in that particular case, and instead of travelling in cars or lorries, at least two of them were riding motorbikes!

It began one evening in April 1978 when army biker Corporal Dawie van Jaarsveld was driving along the road near De Rust. He saw a young woman standing beside the road so, pulling up, he asked her if she would like a lift to the nearby town of Uniondale, which was on his planned route to his girlfriend's house. She mumbled a reply

Corporal Dawie van Jaarsveld, one of at least two motorcyclists to encounter a ghostly pillion rider on the same stretch of road near Uniondale, South Africa.

that he couldn't hear clearly through his crash helmet, and then got on behind him, so he gave her a spare helmet to wear, plus a spare radio earpiece so that she, like him, could hear the music playing on his radio.

Ten miles further on, his motorbike's back wheel skidded, so Dawie paused to check whether he had a puncture – and was amazed to find that his passenger had disappeared. Yet she had clearly not fallen off, because the helmet that she had been wearing was strapped on to the passenger seat, and to his even greater surprise, when he took off his own helmet he found that the spare radio earpiece he had given her was fitted to his other ear!

Greatly unnerved, Dawie stopped at a cafe and telephoned his girlfriend, informing her of his spine-chilling experience. His story was later checked by researcher Cynthia Hind, who confirmed that everyone who had seen him at the cafe remembered that he had indeed seemed very frightened, and his girlfriend verified this too. But that was not the end of the story.

On 4 April 1980, while riding his motorbike by the spot where Dawie had picked up his vanishing passenger, Andre Coetzee felt someone put their arms around his waist from behind and he had the distinct impression that there was someone riding pillion on his bike. In panic, Andre accelerated rapidly and promptly felt something strike him three times on his helmet. Not until he had reached over 160 k.p.h. (100 m.p.h.) did the unseen presence depart.

Continuing investigations, meanwhile, had uncovered stories of several car drivers during the past few years who had all picked up a young woman in this same locality and at much the same time of year. The woman had always mysteriously vanished, and greatly resembled Dawie's passenger, not only in looks but also in her clothing.

Eventually, a pilot came forward to disclose that his fiancée, Maria Roux, had been killed in a car accident on 12 April 1968 – at the precise location where the phantom female hitch-hiker was annually being reported. And Maria Roux's description, including the clothes that she had been wearing when killed, matched those of the hitch-hiker.

MONSTROUS TREES

When the amazing Venus flytrap was first brought to scientific attention during the 1760s, sceptical botanists initially refused to believe that this extraordinary plant could actually capture and consume insects, until they saw it happen. A century later, in 1878, Polish biologist Dr Omelius Fredlowski received a letter from German explorer Carle Liche who claimed to have seen a much bigger and deadlier carnivorous plant while visiting Madagascar: he asserted that he had watched in horror as local inhabitants sacrificed a living woman to this monstrous tree!

Liche likened the tree to a pineapple, but standing 2.5 metres (8 feet) high and thick in proportion, with eight leaves hanging from its apex, each about 3.5 metres (11–12 feet) long and tapering to a sharp point. A clear treacly liquid with highly intoxicating properties trickled into a pair of concave plates arranged one inside the other. These comprised the apex of the tree, and from beneath the rim of the bottom plate a series of hairy green 2.5-metre- (8-foot)long tendrils stretched out in every direction. Above these, six extremely thin tentacle-like feelers, each over 1.5 metres (5–6 feet) long and white in

colour, reared up to the sky, twisting and twirling incessantly like sinister serpents.

Suddenly, after the people had offered up prayers to the tree, they encircled one of the women amongst them and forced her to climb its trunk. Once she had reached the apex, surrounded by its dancing feelers, she bent down and drank the viscous fluid exuding there and became wild with hysterical frenzy. But when she tried to jump down, the tree instantly came to life, and with the merciless fury of starved serpents its feelers quivered over her head, then fastened themselves all around her, wrapping her within their ever-tightening folds.

Soon her screams were replaced with a gurgling moan, and slowly the tree's eight great leaves rose upwards until they too had forced themselves against her body, pressing closer and closer until a revolting fluid trickled down from between them, composed of the scarlet blood and oozing viscera of the tree's victim mingled with its own creamy viscous intoxicant. The leaves retained their upright position for 10 days, after which, as discovered by Liche when he walked by one morning, they became prone once more, with the hairy green tendrils outstretched and the deadly feelers floating above. As a silent reminder of the horrors that had recently been perpetrated here, however, a white human skull lay at the base of the tree.

Predictably, many scientists are very

sceptical about Liche's lurid account. Yet when Salmon Osborn, a former governor of Michigan, visited Madagascar in the 1920s to seek this botanical horror, he learnt that the tree was apparently well known to the locals and missionaries there, and that for many centuries Madagascar had been known as "the land of the man-eating tree". Even so, he never encountered it – but that is probably just as well!

Speaking of Madagascan missionaries, on 2 November 1882 one such person, the Reverend G. W. Parker, published some fascinating news in *Nature* concerning another very mysterious but equally dangerous tree. Called the umdhlebi and said to exist in Zululand, South Africa, it was described by Parker as "a villainous-looking tree" with large glossy tapering leaves, dark green and brittle, as well as fruits resembling long black pods with a red tip, and a peculiar bark that hangs down in large flakes, revealing a fresh growth of bark underneath.

According to Parker, however, the umdhlebi's most striking attribute was "... the power of poisoning any living creature which approaches it; the symptoms of poisoning by it being severe headache, blood-shot eyes, and delirium, ending in death." Goats or sheep are sacrificed to it by the Zulu people, who bravely attempt to collect any of its fruits that fall to the ground, for these supposedly yield the only known antidote to the tree's malign effects.

Fruit collection can only be achieved without loss of life if the umdhlebi is approached from its windward side, fuelling speculation that it releases a deadly gas, possibly absorbed from its substratum. Yet Parker claimed that although it prefers barren rocky ground, this species will grow on all kinds of soil, not exclusively upon those that exude carbonic acid gas. For obvious reasons, the area surrounding an umdhlebi is never inhabited by humans.

Parker also alluded to a seemingly related Zululand shrub that is said to share the umdhlebi's asphyxiating ability, but has smaller leaves and bark that does not peel. To date, however, neither of these murderous species has been formally described by science.

Audrey II, the plant with an appetite for blood in Frank Oz's film **Little Shop of Horrors.**

SANDS THAT BOOM AND ROAR

Two of Africa's most renowned mineralogical mysteries are the booming sands of Jebel Nagous mountain on the Sinai Peninsula and the roaring sands of the Kalahari Desert in southern Botswana.

"Jebel Nagous" translates as "mountain of the bell" and is well-named. Several large banks of sand rest upon its steep slopes, and one – Seetzen's Bell Slope – emits sonorous booming noises whenever its sand slides down. This sand is composed principally of quartz and calcareous sandstone in very fine, well-rounded grains and its sounds were described in 1889 by the investigator H. Carrington Bolton as "... a musical tone resembling the lowest bass note of an organ with a tremolo stop". The larger the bulk of sliding sand, the louder the sound, but the sand must be dry. The precise booming mechanism involved is still unknown, but the rapidly sliding bank of sand appears to vibrate rather like the diaphragm in a loudspeaker.

The Kalahari's roaring sands lie at the south end of an elongated expanse of whitish sand dunes near the desert's south-eastern corner, and produce two different sounds. One is their famous roar, occurring when the sands are pushed forward in a heaped-up manner; the other is a hum when they move slowly down a slope. Even samples of this sand taken to Pretoria in bags would roar if the bags were tilted sharply when half empty, but in bags left open the roar disappeared after a few weeks. This may have been due to absorption of Pretoria's atmospheric water vapour by these samples, because wet sand will not roar.

✡

MANNA – FOOD FROM THE GODS?

According to the biblical Book of Exodus, during the Israelites' 40-year journey through the wilderness from Egypt to the Holy Land they were sustained by a miraculous "bread" that God provided and which fell in great quantities from heaven. White in colour and called manna, it looked like coriander seed and tasted like wafers made with honey: but what was it? Even today, there is no universally accepted answer to this question.

One possibility voiced by several researchers is that manna was an edible species of lichen called *Lecanora esculenta*, which grows upon rocks but is readily dislodged by wind currents and can be transported considerable distances through the air. Samples from a reputed modern-day fall of manna were collected by an Angolan scientist and sent to some European colleagues who confirmed that they were composed of lichens.

The most widely supported explanation at present, however, is that manna is the gummy, sweet-tasting secretion excreted by two species of coccid hemipteran bug. Related to the famous cochineal insect, they feed upon a desert shrub known as the tamarisk tree *Tamarix mannifera*, burrowing into its bark. This theory was proposed long ago by Greek monks living in the Sinai region traversed by the Israelites, and has been very popular among scholars ever since. The insects' exudation soon dries, becoming a sticky white solid that often falls to the ground from the tamarisk as sparkling crystalline granules, and it is well known that nomadic Bedouins eat it during their travels. Nevertheless, it seems difficult to believe that sufficient quantities could occur to sustain a very large group of people each day for 40 years, and it is not adequately nutritious to comprise their principal source of food.

Worthy of note is yet another source

The Israelites gather manna from heaven in this painting from 1520.

The manna ash FRAXINUS ORNUS.

of manna – the manna ash tree *Fraxinus ornus*. The manna exuded by this tree is the source of a crystalline carbohydrate known variously as manna sugar or mannite, which is extracted from it by the use of alcohol, and also occurs in many other plants, including brown seaweeds and onions.

The most extraordinary explanation for manna was put forward by George Sassoon and Rodney Dale in *The Manna Machine*, in which they proposed that it was an algal culture manufactured daily by a high-technology food processor – which was none other than the mysterious ark of the covenant (see pp. 79–81). Bearing in mind, however, that this book evolved from an April Fool's article written by these selfsame authors for *New Scientist* in 1976, it is difficult to know how seriously they expect their idea to be taken by others.

✪

SHARAV AND SIROCCO – THE WITCHES' WINDS

The ancient Babylonians believed that certain diseases were carried to humankind upon the hot dry breath of demons, and even today we still speak,

albeit colloquially, of the "ill wind that brings no one any good". Moreover, the arrival of certain winds has long been associated with inexplicable local outbreaks of various medical ailments, crime and even suicide.

These winds are referred to as witches' winds or even devil winds. One of the best-known examples is the sirocco, whose warm breath blows each spring from the Sahara and the Arabian Peninsula eastwards across the Mediterranean towards Italy and Spain.

The sirocco has many different regional names, such as the sharav (Israel), khamsin (Egypt), chili (Tunisia) and leveche (Morocco). Since 1960, its Israeli incarnation, the sharav, has received great attention from Dr Felix Sulman at the Hebrew University in Jerusalem. His researches have unfurled some of its age-old secrets and have been succinctly reviewed in Fred Soyka's *The Ion Effect*, and in *Heaven's Breath* by Dr Lyall Watson.

In the Middle East, the sharav's deleterious influence upon mental and physical health is so well known that some judges adopt a more lenient stance in relation to violent crimes if they were committed during a visitation by this ill wind. Similarly, doctors know of many illnesses that invariably increase in frequency whenever the sharav is passing through their region.

By 1971, Dr Sulman had shown that there are three distinct categories of "sharav sufferer", each exhibiting a different biochemical response to its baleful breath. One major category consists of people whose urine contains abnormally high levels of a hormone called serotonin – a powerful mood-controlling substance. Serotonin normally acts as a natural tranquillizer, but if too much of it is produced, it has precisely the opposite effect, causing irritability, migraine, sleeplessness – all classic symptoms of people exposed to the sharav.

Sufferers in the second major category are perpetually weary and display a markedly decreased ability to produce the hormone adrenaline, normally secreted when the body needs to deal with a stressful situation. The inference here, therefore, is that prolonged exposure to the sharav has

Statue of the Babylonian demon Pazuzu, whose hot breath carried illness to humans.

overworked these persons' adrenal glands, reducing their efficiency.

In the third category are sharav sufferers whose hormone-secreting thyroid gland is not functioning normally, owing once again to excessive stimulation by the sharav.

But how does it bring about these physiological effects? The answer appears to be that hot dry winds like the sharav, and particularly those carrying great quantities of dust or sand (as does the sharav), accumulate an excess of positive ions, i.e. positively charged air molecules. When present in unusually high concentrations, positive ions induce a variety of medical ailments – ailments corresponding with those reported by sharav sufferers.

The accumulation of positive ions no doubt explains similar ill effects associated with other witches' winds, such as the berg (South Africa), kubang (Java), föhn (Switzerland), chinook (Rocky Mountains), mistral (France), brickfielder (New South Wales) and Santa Ana (Sierra Nevada). Furthermore, the effects of some of these, notably the föhn, may be due not only to positive ions but also to sferics – electromagnetic waves of atmospheric origin.

Chuchunaa (man-beast)

Tunguska explosion

RUSSIA

BLACK SEA

CASPIAN SEA

Almasty/kaptar
(man-beast)

Letayuschiy chelovek
("flying human")

Giant yeti (dzu-teh)

Almas (man-beast)

MONGOLIA

Death worm
(allergorhai-horhai)

Bar-manu (man-beast)

CHINA

Three types of yeti

TIBET   Tumo (temperature elevation);
                      lung-gom

Yeren
(man-beast)

Milk-drinking statues

Milk-drinking
statues

Shambhala; Agharti

Quake hairs

Blue tigers

PAKISTAN

Rustless
iron pillar

Pygmy and true yetis
(teh-lma and meh-teh)

NEPAL

Milk-drinking
statues

Buru (giant lungfish)

Bear-reared
child   Devil cat

HONG KONG

Giant yeti (dzu-teh)

BANGLADESH

Milk-drinking statues

INDIA

Wolf-reared
children

Milk-drinking
statues

Giant yeti (dzu-teh)

Fakir magic, including
levitation, rope trick

MYANMAR

King cobra worshipping
dance; giant yeti (dzu-teh)

VIETNAM

Tiger-reared
child

Hope Diamond

Quake
hairs

THAILAND

Flying "bat-woman"

Klaasen's uncanny green jade Buddha;
milk-drinking statues

Devil bird; horned jackal

SRI
LANKA

Key to Phenomena

⚘ FLYING

🐟 WATER

⚘ ELEMENTS

🐗 LAND ANIMAL

⚘ HUMAN

◈ SITES

✳ PARANORMAL

I N D I A N   O C E A N

Milk-drinking
statues

Cobra taming

SINGAPORE

BORNEO

Batutut
(man-beast)

SUMATRA

Orang pendek (man-beast)

Prophesied eruption
of volcano

KRAKATOA

Ahool (giant bat)

JAVA

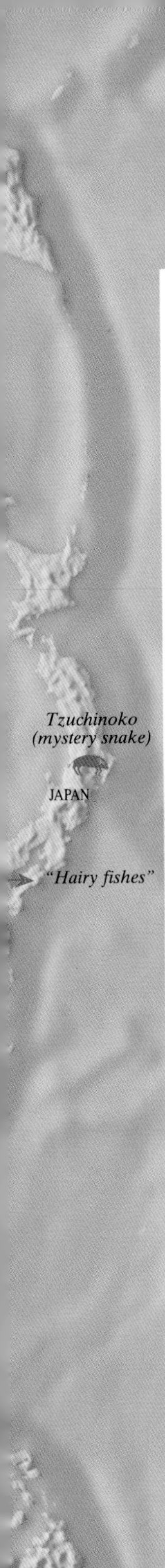

Chapter 4
Asia

THE OCCULT AND THE ORIENT

IT IS FITTING – INDEED, IT IS INEVITABLE – THAT THE WONDERS OF ASIA SHOULD BE AS INSCRUTABLE AND AS EXOTIC AS OTHER FACETS OF THIS LANGUID, MESMERIZING CONTINENT. HERE, ACOLYTES OF THE MYSTERIOUS AND MYSTICAL FROM EVERY CORNER OF THE GLOBE PAY RESPECTFUL HOMAGE TO THE VENERABLE AND VENERATED SECRETS THAT ARE TO BE DISCOVERED AMID THESE ILLUSIVE LANDS OF DREAMS AND DELIGHT.

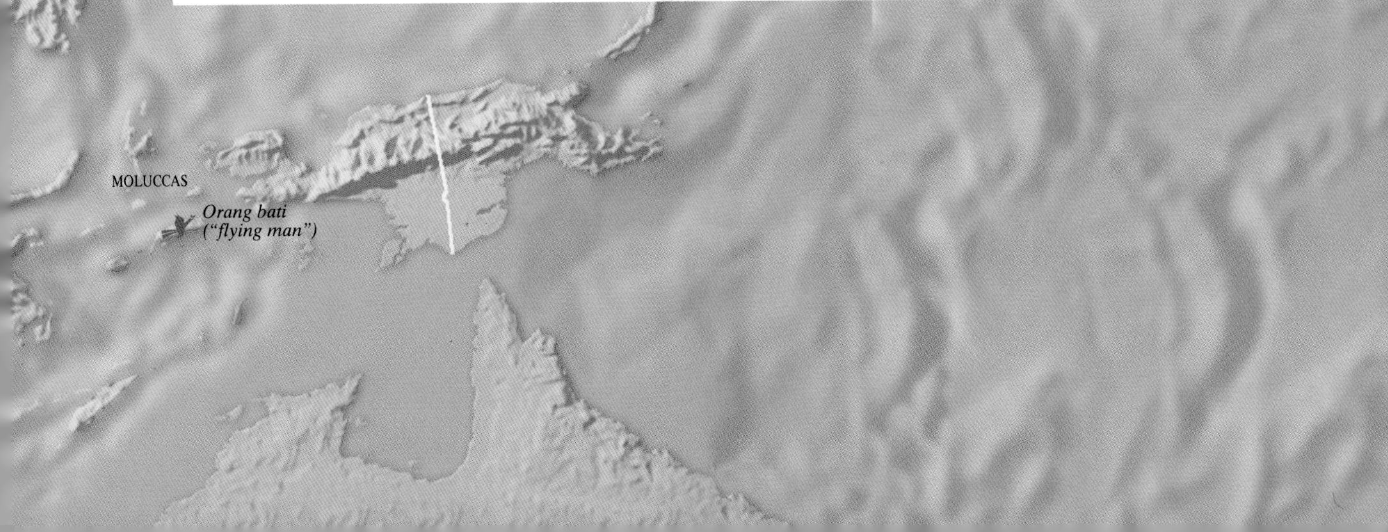

Tzuchinoko (mystery snake)

JAPAN

"Hairy fishes"

MOLUCCAS

Orang bati ("flying man")

Strange Talents, Secret Knowledge

TIBETAN WISDOM

Tibet has inspired many fictional accounts telling of lost lands like Shangri-La and endowing its lamas with uncanny powers – but is the reality of Tibet even stranger than fiction?

There is a long-standing Buddhist belief that somewhere amid Tibet's lofty domain is a true Shangri-La – a tranquil holy world called Shambhala, consisting of a lush, fertile valley encircled by tall snow-capped mountains. A repository of esoteric knowledge pre-dating all modern civilizations, Shambhala is where the Buddha was instructed in the ancient wisdom, and is populated by a race of enlightened super-humans, yet is hidden from the view of most mortals. Even aeroplanes can fly over it without detecting its presence, but several cryptic tunnels are said to connect this wondrous land with the Dalai Lama's palace, the Potala.

Certain Eastern traditions and researchers, however, suggest that Shambhala is located beyond Tibet. According to Taoist mythology, for instance, this secluded land is called Tebu and is situated somewhere between Tibet and Szechwan. After studying Middle Eastern and Greek texts, the historian Geoffrey Ashe placed Shambhala much further north, in the remote Altai Mountains bordering southern Russia and north-western Mongolia.

Madame Helena Blavatsky, founder of the Theosophical Society (see p.89) favoured southern Mongolia's Gobi Desert, whereas Hungarian philologist Cosma de Körös looked to the west, proposing Syr Daria in Kazakhstan as a likely locality. According to some

Detail from a Tibetan "Wheel of Life".

believers, however, Shambhala has no physical existence on earth, but belongs to a separate dimension or higher level of consciousness, to be found not by the body but only by the mind and spirit.

Allied to the traditions of Shambhala is the notion that all the continents are linked by a maze of underground passages radiating from a vast subterranean world called Agharti, allegedly situated somewhere beneath Tibet or elsewhere in Asia. In *The Lost World of Agharti*, Alec Maclellan recalled stories claiming that Agharti is home to an ancient "super race", which remains concealed from our own world on the surface of the planet, yet seeks to control it by means of a mysterious but immensely potent force called "vril power".

Much of this stems from a strange book by English occultist Edward Bulwer-Lytton called *The Coming Race*, published in 1871, around which a great deal of controversy has raged as to whether it was a wholly fictitious novel or a story based upon fact. Someone who was most certainly persuaded by its account of an arcane subterranean race endowed with mystical power, however, was Adolf Hitler. As revealed by Maclellan, Hitler was eager to gain possession of the Aghartians' secret vril power, which, he believed, would guarantee the success of his grandiose schemes for world conquest and the establishment of a Thousand Year Reich. The Vril Society was the name of a leading occult society in Nazi Germany, and Hitler dispatched several scientific expeditions in search of subterranean lands, but none was ever found.

Also said to involve mysterious powers are some extraordinary physical feats performed by Tibetan Buddhist

One of many mystical facets of Tibetan Buddhism is the belief that a person's soul may be reincarnated several times before its ultimate liberation. This is depicted here in a traditional tanka or "Wheel of Life", shown in the grasp of demon Mara, the Tempter.

The Dalai Lama. Cryptic tunnels are said to connect his palace, the Potala, with the wondrous land of Shambhala.

monks and still unexplained by Western science. One of their most amazing talents is tumo – the ability to raise their body temperature so dramatically that they can survive an entire winter inside a bleak mountain cave surrounded by snow, yet dressed in just a single robe or even naked.

Tumo is acquired only by formal yogic training, and the final test to determine whether the student has successfully gained this esoteric skill is nothing if not decisive. Not only must the student sit naked all night upon a frozen mountain lake, he must also dry, using only his own body warmth, a robe that has been dipped through a hole in the ice into the lake's chilling waters and then wrapped around him. Each time the robe becomes dry, it is plunged back into the water and then wrapped around the student again – a procedure which is repeated throughout the night until daybreak.

In 1981, Dr Herbert Benson from Harvard Medical School attached temperature sensors to some Tibetan Buddhist monks adept at tumo, and confirmed that some were able to raise the temperature of their fingers and toes by as much as 8°C (15°F), with lesser increases recorded from other portions of their body. He concluded

that tumo must involve dilating the blood vessels in the skin, a reaction precisely converse to the skin's normal response to cold.

No less astonishing is lung-gom – a mode of training that enables lamas to run at incredible speeds across the snow, apparently by reducing the weight of their body, and involving intense, continuous concentration. Western observers have recorded amazing speeds of up to 19 kilometres (12 miles) in 20 minutes accomplished by lung-gom runners. In *With Mystics and Magicians in Tibet*, explorer Alexandra David-Neel, who spent 14 years studying in Tibet, recalls seeing one of these runners and wanting to photograph and talk to him, but being prevented from doing so by her Tibetan companion. For he warned her that any such interruption would break the lama's concentration and, in so doing, kill him instantly.

A final Tibetan mystery surrounds a singular book called *Sungods in Exile*, which claims that a Tibetan tribe called the Dzopa are in fact the physically degenerate descendants of a race of aliens from the Sirius star system who crash-landed in Tibet during AD 1017 and subsequently interbred with the local people! Found among the Dzopa

was a strange metal disc now known as the Lolladoff plate, which can gain or lose weight at will and is covered in abstruse inscriptions. This book was supposedly written by a mysterious Oxford scholar called Dr Karyl Robin-Evans, who visited Tibet in 1947 but died in 1974, and was edited by David Agamon. Some researchers have assumed it to be authentic, others are much more sceptical. At the very least, its notions are certainly far removed from Shangri-La!

✵

DANCING WITH THE COBRA KING

Often featuring a near-mystical, uncanny rapport between disciple and deity, one of the oldest examples of animal veneration is ophiolatreia – snake worship – which takes many forms, but none more dramatic, or dangerous, than the deadly dancing performed by the snake priestesses of Myanmar's famous serpent cults. The focus of their veneration is the king cobra *Ophiophagus hannah*, which, attaining a total length of up to 5 metres

Deadly dancing: at the climax of her dance with a cobra, a Myanmar snake priestess bends forward to kiss it.

(16 feet), is the world's largest species of venomous snake. It is also one of the most aggressive, and when about to strike can raise its head and the front portion of its body at least a metre (3 feet) off the ground. Faced with such a formidable creature, most people would lose no time in placing as great a distance between themselves and this serpent as possible! But a Myanmar snake priestess has a very different ambition in mind – to dance with her reptilian god.

And so, once a wild king cobra has been located, the priestess begins her extraordinary performance just a metre or two in front of it, skilfully employing her long dress in a matador-like manner to deflect the potentially fatal lunges with its deadly fangs that the snake attempts whenever she moves within striking range. Soon her dress is wet and stained with golden drops of venom, but the greatest danger has still to be faced. At the climax of her dance, the priestess suddenly bends forwards and kisses the cobra – sometimes on its head, sometimes directly on its lips! She

repeats this incredible feat twice and then backs slowly away, rejoining the other worshippers and leaving the cobra to glide swiftly away. The dance is over, the deity gone.

How is such an astounding performance achieved? Training from an early age with non-poisonous species or with "cold" (de-fanged) cobras may be involved in order to gain the requisite knowledge of snake behaviour and movement so that its actions can be predicted with split-second timing. Similarly, the priestess's dance may be specifically orchestrated to dazzle or even mesmerize the cobra, reducing the speed and accuracy of its strikes. Whatever the explanation, the ritual of dancing with cobras is the product of very ancient tradition.

One of these dramatic ceremonies was attended by the naturalist Armand Denis in 1939, during a filming trip to the Far East; but while undertaking another assignment in Asia, he witnessed a second, even more extraordinary encounter between king cobra and human.

Just before the outbreak of the Second World War, Denis was filming in Singapore; in order to complete the wildlife film that he had been working on he advertised locally for a number of king cobras, a common species in that area. Eventually, he received about a dozen, all adult and extremely belligerent. He placed them in a securely fastened crate with a fine wire-netting top, whose mesh they profusely drenched with their potent venom as they struck at it repeatedly in their fury at finding themselves held captive in this manner.

Not long afterwards, a young Chinese boy, dressed in a strange white garb with deep sleeves, arrived at the hotel and gravely volunteered his services to Denis as a snake-handler, provided that Denis would give him one of the king cobras at the end of the filming sessions. Although he naturally doubted the boy's capability to handle such dangerous snakes as these in safety, Denis was sufficiently intrigued by his serious demeanour and outlandish offer to allow him to take a look at the cobras, while they writhed irritably but impotently within the confines of their locked crate. The boy soon focused his attention upon one especially large and aggressive specimen, which he considered to be very beautiful and which, he assured Denis, he would have no problem in handling. Needless to say, Denis promptly reminded him that this was a lethal creature that no one would dare to handle in its current, highly emotional state; only after it had quietened down during several days of captivity could it be considered in any way safe to deal with, and only then for filming purposes.

The boy merely smiled, however, and asserted confidently that it would be very easy for *him* to handle it now and in complete safety. He then began to prise up one corner of the crate. Denis, very much alarmed, implored him to leave the snake alone. In response, the boy paused and withdrew from the folds of one of his long sleeves a small vial of strange green liquid, which, when uncorked, released a fragrance vaguely reminiscent of freshly cut grass. He poured some of this into his mouth and then leaned down to the crate, until his

face was well within the cobra's striking range. Hardly daring to look, Denis could only stand and await the inevitable, instantaneous strike that would swiftly bring death to this foolish child. Instead, it was the boy who acted first, and in a very unexpected manner.

Leaning even closer to the crate, he suddenly spat the liquid out of his mouth, spraying it liberally all over the face, head and body of his chosen cobra! The boy waited for about a minute, and then – to Denis's even greater surprise, and absolute horror – he casually reached into the crate and lifted the cobra out, his hands around the middle of its body's great length, holding this huge deadly serpent with no more concern than any other child might display when holding a length of cord or a skipping rope. By some uncanny means, the green liquid had rendered the cobra totally passive. True, it reared its fist-sized head upward to gaze evenly at its young captor, but it made no attempt to strike at him.

After a time, the boy placed the cobra back into the crate, bowed solemnly to the dumbfounded Denis, and walked out of his room, promising

to come back the following morning and handle all the cobras in the crate – but he did not return, and Denis never saw his mysterious visitor again.

The mechanism at work here is even more mystifying than the secret of cobra dancing, for science knows of no substance that can passify cobras in this manner. A century ago, some journals claimed that in parts of Ohio rattlesnakes could be repelled by the leaves of the white ash tree, but this remains unproven by modern scientific techniques.

✵

FAKIR MAGIC

Some of the most famous feats of physical prowess demonstrated by Indian fakirs defy all the accepted maxims of Western physiological science – or do they?

From the earliest times, Western visitors to India and elsewhere in Asia have been baffled by the astonishing sight of near-naked fakirs lying on beds of nails without incurring any injuries.

Unlike the West, the East has never experienced problems in accepting the phenomenon of levitation.

A yogi with his head buried in sand at Agra, India. When this photograph was taken, his breathing had stopped and his heart-rate was two beats a minute.

The secret of this remarkable performance is that it is, of course, just an illusion, but not of the optical variety. The fakir really does lie on the nails and they really do press into him, but he is safeguarded by a canny understanding of certain basic physical principles long known to Western scientists but rarely appreciated by laymen. Therein is the illusion – namely, his Western observers' mistaken belief that the nails must surely pierce his body.

In autumn 1981, Professor Larry D. Kirkpatrick, a physicist at Montana State University, personally duplicated the fakirs' act of lying on a bed of nails in front of an audience of students on the college campus at Bozeman. He even permitted a burly American football player in full gear to sit on his chest while still lying upon the nails. And the purpose of this engrossing demonstration? It was to emphasize the significant relationship between weight

distribution and pressure, i.e. the greater the number of nails supporting his body, the smaller the amount of pressure exerted by his body's weight on each nail. Consequently, as long as the bed has more than a certain minimum number of nails (this number is directly proportional to the weight of the person lying on them), the amount of pressure that the body exerts upon any given nail is not great enough to cause the nail to puncture the skin.

Unlike the West, the East has never experienced problems in accepting the phenomenon of levitation – another feat demonstrated by fakirs. Far from pretending that it does not exist or is merely a hoax and condemning those performing it as pagan (once the typical reaction of European religions), if Asian youngsters are spied achieving acts of levitation they are then methodically trained by older, experienced practitioners in order to develop and control their powers.

One of the most meticulously observed cases of levitation on record from Asia took place during 1936 in southern India, and was depicted in the *Illustrated London News* (6 June 1936) by a series of stunning photographs taken by an eyewitness, P. Y. Plunkett. It featured a fakir called Subbayah Pullavar and occurred at around 12.30 p.m. before about 150 people.

After pouring water in a circle around the tent in which he would be performing the levitation, the fakir stepped inside the tent, where he remained hidden from view for a few minutes. The tent was then removed and the onlookers saw to their amazement that he was suspended horizontally in the air, in a trance, resting his hand upon a cloth-covered stick, about a metre (3 feet) tall, which he seemed to be using not for support but rather for balance. Naturally, the observers passed their hands through the space underneath him to test for any hidden wires or suchlike, but nothing was found.

Many photos were taken, and after about four minutes the tent was replaced around the fakir, to shield him from view again during his descent. However, Plunkett was able to discern him through its thin walls and saw him swaying for a short time, still in mid-air, before sinking downwards very slowly but remaining horizontal, taking about five minutes to reach the ground. This extraordinary performance has never been satisfactorily explained.

Even more controversial is the infamous Indian rope trick. There have been countless stage and screen versions, ably facilitated by sophisticated special-effect techniques, but many visitors to the East claim to have witnessed it in the open air. Yet no formally authenticated "al fresco" exhibition ever appears to have been documented, though in view of the trick's ostensibly gruesome nature, this is perhaps not surprising.

The fakir throws one end of a long hemp rope up into the air, where it remains suspended, like a stiff vertical pole. He then orders his boy assistant to climb the rope, which he does – only to vanish from sight when he reaches the top. His voice, however, remains and insults the fakir, who, furious at his assistant's temerity, climbs the rope and also disappears. Moments later, the severed limbs and torso of the boy fall to the ground, the fakir reappears at the top of the rope and climbs down, carrying the boy's head. After arranging his dismembered form on the ground, the fakir suddenly kicks it – and the boy stands up, alive and totally unharmed! The show is over and the baffled audience departs.

Several explanations have been offered. Mass hallucination is a popular contender, its supporters citing the fakir's continuous monologue during the performance as a subtle means of lulling the audience into a receptive state of mind. Another proposed solution is that the rope trick has never actually been performed and is nothing more than Eastern folklore.

In *The Unexplained*, however, Marc Cramer sought to explain it as a clever illusion, performed at night with lanterns to aid the deception. It entails

Indian rope trick performers "Karachi and Kyder" photographed in 1935.

the cryptic support of the rope by a hidden wire, the temporary disappearance of the two performers at the rope's summit as an optical effect of the night-time darkness beyond the range of the lanterns' glare, and the "dismemberment" of the boy as devious subterfuge utilizing the corpse of a recently killed monkey and a specially painted wooden head. Photos do exist of fakirs with vertical ropes, but these may well incorporate bamboo "joints", which can lock into place to yield a stiff pole, but will unlock at a simple shake to yield a normal-looking rope.

Searching for Snowmen and Digging for Death Worms

IN THE FOOTSTEPS OF THE YETI

The popular image of the yeti or abominable snowman is that of a large shaggy man-beast briefly sighted as it strides across a snow-swept mountain landscape, leaving behind giant footprints in its wake. However, researches by zoologists Ivan T. Sanderson and Dr Bernard Heuvelmans, and also by cryptozoologist Loren Coleman, have revealed that yetis can be categorized into three totally separate morphological types, with quite distinct habitats.

The first type is the pygmy yeti or teh-lma, which stands about a metre (3–4 feet) tall. Clothed in very thick red fur with a slight mane, of omnivorous diet (revealed by its droppings), and leaving behind 13-cm- (5-inch) long humanoid footprints, the teh-lma is indigenous to the lower, tropical valleys of the Himalayas in Nepal and Tibet, and the upper Brahmaputra region. In Sanderson's opinion, the teh-lma may comprise a very primitive race of small hairy human – a sort of proto-pygmy.

The second type of yeti is the "true" yeti or meh-teh. This is the creature most commonly referred to in sightings of so-called abominable snowmen. A very sturdy, man-sized entity of omnivorous diet and standing 1.5–1.8 metres (5–6 feet) tall, it has a conical head, a very wide lipless mouth, protruding jaw, and is covered in short thick fur, generally reddish-brown but sometimes grizzled. Although native to the same geographical localities as the teh-lma, the meh-teh generally inhabits the upper montane forests, but

In 1960, Sir Edmund Hillary tells journalists of his hopes to find a yeti on his next Himalayan expedition.

occasionally ventures across snowfields when seeking food, creating the familiar "snowman" tracks. Its feet are short but very broad and the second toe is longer than the big toe, which readily distinguishes meh-teh footprints from those of humans. The meh-teh could be a specialized species of orang-utan, modified to live on the ground amid high-altitude mountain forests.

The third and most imposing type of yeti is the giant yeti, known variously as the dzu-teh ("hulking thing"), rimi, tok or nyalmo. Although the Nepalese people have heard of it, the giant yeti is not native to their country or to the Himalayas, occurring instead in the highest, most rugged ranges of eastern Tibet, Sikkim, Bangladesh, Myanmar, Manchuria and north Vietnam. Extremely shy despite its great size, this spectacular creature is habitually bipedal, omnivorous and stands 1.8–2.7 metres (6–9 feet) tall. It has a flat head, a beetling brow with an upturned fringe of hair across it, long powerful arms, huge hands and a long shaggy coat, black or dark grey in colour. Unlike those of the meh-teh, its feet are very humanoid in shape, but leave tracks revealing the presence of two pads under the first toe on each foot.

Interestingly, this is also a characteristic of tracks left by America's mystery man-beast, the bigfoot or sasquatch, and descriptions of the giant yeti and the bigfoot are extremely similar – so much so, in fact, that cryptozoologists believe it likely that the two belong to one and the same species. As to the identity of that species, the favourite contender is a huge ape-like creature called *Gigantopithecus*, which formerly lived in central Asia, but officially died out around 300,000 years ago. However, no satisfactory reason for

Yeti footprint discovered in 1951 on a Nepalese glacier at an altitude of 5,800 metres (19,000 feet). This is from a meh-teh or true yeti.

and has never been seen again. Even more sensational is the claim made in 1953 by a Tibetan lama called Chemed Rigdzin Dorje Lopu that he had examined two mummified 2.5-metre- (8-foot) tall specimens of the rimi or giant yeti. One was housed in the monastery at Sakya, the other in the monastery at Riwoche in Kham Province, but this was before China's annexing of Tibet, followed by the razing of many Tibetan monasteries.

Not all findings are so elusive, however. In 1959, a yeti expedition to Nepal organized by a Texan oil millionaire, Tom Slick, returned with some yeti faecal droppings. These were found to contain a hitherto unknown form of parasitic nematode worm; since animal species often possess parasites unique to themselves, this offers support for the belief that at least one type of yeti, just like its parasite, is indeed a species new to science.

THE REAL BATMAN?

The Sundanese people of western Java tell of a gigantic bat called the ahool, named after its thrice-uttered flight call. The bat spends its days concealed in caves behind waterfalls, but skims across jungle rivers at night in search of large fishes that it scoops out of the water with its feet. Its head is monkey-like, but its face is flattened like a man's, its dark eyes are large, its grey furry body is said to be as big as that of a one-year-old child, and its enormous wings span about 3.5 metres (11–12 feet) when fully extended. This is roughly twice the wing-span of the world's largest known species of bat. Nevertheless, evidence for the ahool's reality may not be restricted to native stories. One evening in 1927, naturalist Dr Ernst Bartels distinctly heard one of these outsize bats utter its diagnostic triple cry as it flew over his house.

Rather more humanoid, at least according to local tradition, is the orang bati ("flying man") of Seram. Although this Indonesian island is the second largest in the Moluccas group, its

its extinction has so far been put forward; and at the time of *Gigantopithecus*'s existence, Asia was linked by a land-bridge to Alaska. Many other animal species crossed this bridge, entering and establishing themselves in the New World, so why not *Gigantopithecus* too?

If *Gigantopithecus* did indeed do this, and has persisted there right up to the present day while successfully eluding scientific detection, this could explain reports of the bigfoot. Similarly, elusive surviving populations in its original Asian homeland could explain the giant yeti.

Reports of various yeti relics or remains periodically filter into the West, but when investigated, the reality has been rather less than anticipated. In 1960, a supposed yeti scalp was seen at Khumjung monastery by Sir Edmund Hillary, who was leading a three-month yeti expedition to Nepal. He was permitted to borrow it for examination in Europe, where it was found to be from a mountain-dwelling goat-

antelope, the serow *Capricornis sumatraensis*. It was thereafter denounced as a hoax, but this is somewhat short-sighted. The "yeti scalp" is worn in religious Nepalese ceremonies by a person taking the part of the yeti. Hence the scalp is meant merely to *represent* the yeti; there is no necessity for it to have been actually derived from one. But whereas the Nepalese are aware of this, Westerners often mistakenly assume that "yeti scalps" must be from yetis, which would perhaps explain the Khumjung confusion.

Another Nepalese monastery, this time at Pangboche, formerly possessed a peculiar preserved hand, allegedly from a yeti. Samples of skin and bone from this were analysed by the anthropologist Professor W.C. Osman Hill and by a team at the University of California in Los Angeles. Results indicated that they were from a still-undescribed species of primate. Photos of the hand still exist, but the hand itself was mysteriously stolen from the monastery in May 1991

The orang-bati – a giant bat, or something more?

BLUE TIGERS AND DEVIL CATS

Some of Asia's most cryptic mysteries are of the feline variety. Still eluding formal confirmation of their existence, for example, are the exotic blue tigers of Fujian, in south-east China. These beautiful animals have occasionally been sighted, but no skin or specimen has ever been obtained for scientific study. The closest anyone came to achieving this was in September 1910, when Harry R. Caldwell, a Methodist missionary who was also an expert hunter and a diligent seeker of blue tigers, spied one at close range.

According to his description of it in *Blue Tiger*: "The markings of the animal were marvellously beautiful. The ground colour seemed to be a deep shade of maltese, changing into almost deep blue on the under parts. The stripes were well defined, and so far as I was able to make out similar to those of a tiger of the regular type."

The blue tiger's attention was focused upon something in a ravine just below where it was sitting, and when Caldwell leaned forward he saw that it was watching two children gathering vegetation there. Caldwell realized that if he were to shoot the tiger from where he was, he might put the children at risk, so he moved his position in order to change the direction of his shot. In so

interior, occupied by dense rainforests, remains largely unexplored. In June 1986, the tropical agriculturalist Tyson Hughes visited Seram during his work and while there he gathered some detailed reports of the orang bati from the indigenous people, who were visibly terrified of it. They claimed that these entities are human in form and stand almost 1.5 metres (4–5 feet) tall, but have black wings, red skin, a long thin tail, and emit mournful wails. Large numbers inhabit various long-dead volcanoes on Seram, but at night they fly across the forest to the coast, where they abduct children from Uraur and other villages there. The helpless infants are carried back to the orang batis' mountain strongholds, never to be seen again. Could the orang bati be a giant bat – or something more? If nothing else, it calls to mind a bizarre report logged from Vietnam.

Earl Morrison was one of three U.S. marines on guard duty near Da Nang in South Vietnam during a summer evening in 1969, when they reputedly saw an incredible entity flying slowly towards them. To their astonishment,

they could plainly see that "it" closely resembled a naked woman about 1.5 metres (5 feet) tall, with black furry skin and ebony wings! Attached to these wings were her fingers, hands and arms. Before she vanished from view, she passed close enough to the three men for them to hear her wings flapping. Traditional explanations for this report suggest misidentifications of some large bird or bat, possibly due to stress resulting from living in a war zone – but in view of the orang bati accounts, who can say?

Also requiring consideration are similar, long-standing reports of bat-winged humanoids from the Primorskiy Kray Territory (Russian Far East). Here, they again have their own specific name – the letayuschiy chelovek, translated as "flying human". One was spied several years ago in the immense taiga forest by a hunter called A. I. Kurentsov when it flew over his fire, and reports often refer to their eerie cry, resembling a woman's scream but ending in a lugubrious howl. Real-life batmen? The taiga is big enough to hide many wonders.

Tigers have a compelling beauty. Rare sightings of blue tigers suggest a truly exotic animal.

doing, however, he lost sight of the blue tiger, which silently vanished into the depths of the jungle.

During his searches for these wonderful creatures, Caldwell was sometimes accompanied by his son, John, who recalled seeing strands of blue fur on several occasions along Fujian's mountain trails, and also by the famous American zoologist Roy Chapman Andrews. It is likely that these tigers' spectacular colour is due to the same pair of mutant, or abnormal, genes responsible for the striking colouration of the domestic cat breed known as the Maltese.

More evil than exotic is another feline enigma referred to as a devil cat. Father John Morrison, a Catholic priest, was called out many times during his years at the mission in Patna, India, to deal with these seemingly invisible but very audible mystery beasts. His first experience of a devil cat occurred in spring 1940, when one of his students, Eugene, told him that his house was being plagued by strange noises. In particular, he had often heard the loud cry of a cat, yet no cat seemed to be present anywhere nearby. Father Morrison visited Eugene's house and sprinkled holy water in the rooms. While he was there, the sounds ceased, but as soon as he left, they began again.

One afternoon, Eugene's wife, Cecilia, ran to Father Morrison in a very frightened state, begging him to come to their house and do something about these noises. Suddenly, however, while she was still telling him about them, an eerie cat-like cry echoed from the roof of Morrison's own house. It was an extraordinary sound, which he likened to a combination of a cat's shriek and the shout of a peacock.

Straight away, Morrison went with Cecilia to her home and sprinkled holy water all through her house, over the verandah and even on an empty house nearby. Then he went back to his own home and did the same there. After that, he called upon St Michael for help, by way of the prayer that is spoken after Mass in Catholic churches. The cry of the devil cat was not heard again either in Father Morrison's house or in that of Eugene and Cecilia.

✦ EXOTIC FAUNA FROM THE EAST

Among the many inscrutable secrets of the Orient are a veritable menagerie of mystery beasts still eluding zoological recognition. One of the most infamous is the Sri Lankan devil-bird, which earns its name from its hideous cry, likened by some to the shrieks that would be made by a young boy being slowly strangled! This macabre creature has been dismissed by many scientists as either the Sri Lankan brown wood owl *Strix leptogrammica ochrogenys* or the Sri Lankan eagle owl *Bubo nipalensis blighi*, but neither identification is based upon sightings of these species in the act of emitting the devil-bird's spine-chilling cries.

In addition, the Singhalese, Tamils and many Westerners on the island all denounce these "official explanations", especially any involving the brown wood owl. This is so familiar a species here that there seems little possibility that it could be responsible for the devil-bird's shrieks without this fact having been established long ago. Other suggested identities range from one or more of the island's eagles, to a species of nightjar, or even a water rail.

Another unusual animal from Sri Lanka is the horned jackal; this is a jackal with a small horn projecting from the back of the skull. These horns are probably nothing more than physically induced abnormalities, but they are prized as lucky talismans by the local people.

One of the world's most sensational creatures may be concealed amid the sands of the southern Gobi desert. It is known as the allergorhai-horhai or Mongolian death worm, and was sought unsuccessfully a few years ago by a European team of explorers led by Ivan Mackerle. It is said to resemble a large fat worm, up to 1 metre (4–5 feet) long and dark red in colour, with spike-like projections at both ends. It spends much of its time hidden beneath the desert sands, but whenever one is spotted lying on the surface it is scrupulously avoided by the locals, for good reason.

The Mongolian death-worm, said to squirt virulent poison and possibly able to electrocute its victims.

If anything approaches too closely, the death worm can squirt a stream of virulent poison which is said to be extremely corrosive and kills almost instantly – presumably by burning its way through the flesh and into the bloodstream of its victim. Moreover, the death worm can also kill in a second, much more mysterious manner.

During Mackerle's expedition, their local interpreter informed them that many years earlier, when he was a boy, a team of Western geologists visited this same area. During their stay, one of them was poking idly into some sand nearby with an iron rod when he abruptly dropped down dead. Moments later, the sand that he had been poking began to move and from out of it wriggled a huge fat worm – an allergorhai-horhai.

Astonishing as it may seem, if this story is true (and many similar ones are on file, some involving camels walking through the sand), the only way in which the worm could have killed in that manner was by electrocution. Several different groups of electricity-generating fishes are known, but the

The African lungfish PROTOPTERUS DOLLOI *could be a distant relative of the Himalayan swamp monster, the buru.*

worm would be the first terrestrial species with this ability. Perhaps a truly shocking secret awaits disclosure beneath the Gobi's silent sands.

In 1987, cryptozoological researchers Michel Dethier and Ayako Dethier-Sakamoto brought to Western attention reports of a Japanese mystery beast called the tzuchinoko. Known for centuries to the Japanese, it is an

Possibly a mutant variant of the pit viper, the tzuchinoko is a mysterious Japanese snake.

unusually short and thick-bodied snake with a prominent dorsal ridge. Judging from certain features, such as small but well-defined facial pits, horn-like projections above its eyes, a well-delineated neck and a triangular cross-sectional shape when viewed head-on, the tzuchinoko may be an unusual mutant variant of the pit viper *Agkistrodon halys*, or it could be a wholly separate species.

Strangest of all from Japan, however, is a river-dwelling species of amphibious "hairy fish", up to 1.5 metres (4–5 feet) long and covered with scales, but with human-like hair on its head. Sometimes coming out on to land, these creatures will play and fight with one another, giving voice to loud cries, but are very aggressive towards humans, readily attacking and killing them, yet without devouring their bodies afterwards. Could these "hairy fishes" be a distorted description of fur seals, transplanted in folklore from their marine environment into a freshwater equivalent?

In 1948, Ralph Izzard (at that time a correspondent for London's *Daily Mail*) and explorer Charles Stonor journeyed to Rilo, an eastern Himalayan valley close to the Dafla Hills in Assam, in search of a mysterious swamp-dwelling monster known to the local Apa Tani people as the buru. It was said to be 3.5–4 metres (11½–13½ feet) long, with a roundish, elongate body and tail, making it somewhat serpentine in appearance, and with limbs described by some eyewitnesses as being little more than paired flanges. Unfortunately, its two investigators failed to encounter this puzzling animal, and it now appears to be extinct.

Cryptozoologists have traditionally assumed that the buru was some form of monitor lizard. However, as I pointed out in *Extraordinary Animals Worldwide*, the creature with which it compared closest in overall morphology and lifestyle is a giant lungfish. Indeed, according to local reports it was never seen out of water and buried itself in the mud at the swamp's bottom during the dry season. Monitor lizards never do this, but South American and certain African lungfishes do. Oddly, although lungfishes are known to exist in South America, Africa and also Australia, no living species has ever been discovered

in Asia. Yet there seems no good reason why they should not occur there too. However, quite apart from the buru, reports have recently been collected by Chicago University biologist Professor Roy Mackal in Vietnam regarding a mysterious fish that seems to be a 1.8-metre- (6-foot) long species of lungfish. So perhaps these strange creatures do exist on the Asiatic continent after all.

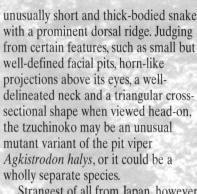

ALMAS, ORANG PENDEK AND YEREN – LIVING TROLLS OF ASIA

According to palaeontology, Neanderthal man *Homo sapiens neanderthalensis* was a stocky, muscular subspecies of human with jutting jaws, heavy brow ridges, and low-vaulted skull, which formerly lived in many parts of Eurasia but had died out entirely around 30,000 years ago. Is it possible, however, that folklore and legends of troll-like beings are based at least in part upon relict populations of Neanderthals still surviving in remote parts of Asia?

Reports of mysterious "wildmen" covered in hair but otherwise closely resembling basic Neanderthal morphology have reached Western science from many different regions, where they are quite familiar to the local people. Mongolia's version, for example, is referred to as the almas, and inhabits the Altai Mountains. In the Caucasus, it is the almasty or kaptar, the nasnas or dev in Iran, and the chuchunaa in Siberia's Verkhoyansk Range. In Pakistan, it is the bar-manu, and reports are on file from several other southern Asian countries too.

During the past three decades, some of these "neo-Neanderthals" have received serious attention from Western scientists. In her authoritative book *Wildmen*, English anthropologist Dr Myra Shackley recorded her field investigations of almas sightings in Outer Mongolia during 1979, and was

sufficiently impressed by the testimony of local eyewitnesses to state: "I am now prepared to accept the reality of the almas." Worth noting is that the area from where the almas reports were emerging also contains fossil Neanderthal remains.

Russian anatomist Dr Marie-Jeanne Kofman has spent over 30 years researching the Caucasian almasty, whose history includes an extraordinary event. During the second half of the 1800s, a female almasty with dark skin covered in reddish hair was caught in the forests of Mount Zaadan. She possessed high cheekbones, protruding jaws and other classic Neanderthal features, and was dubbed Zana, but was unable to speak. Zana lived for the remainder of her life in the village of Tkhina, during which time she became pregnant by at least one of the village men and gave birth to five children. She died in the 1880s.

In 1964, Russian scientist Dr Boris Porshnev visited the region and spoke to two persons claiming to be Zana's grandchildren. They told him that, unlike Zana, their parents (her offspring) were able to speak and resembled other humans in the village except for their dark complexions. Offspring of Neanderthals and modern humans would certainly have been fertile: indeed, some anthropologists believe that the Neanderthals vanished not through actual extinction but by interbreeding with modern humans until their separate identity was lost.

Since the late 1980s, Jordi Magraner from the National Museum of Natural History in Paris has been seeking the bar-manu in Pakistan. At the eighth meeting of the Language Origins Society held at Selwyn College, Cambridge, on 9 September 1992, he and co-researcher Dr Anne Malassé presented an impressive dossier of eyewitness sketches and accounts testifying to its continuing existence in the northern Chitral region of Pakistan.

In 1994, Debbie Martyr, a journalist from London, spent five months in Kerinci Seblat National Park in western Sumatra, seeking an elusive variety of man-beast known as the orang pendek ("short man") or sedapa. Sightings of these 1-metre- (3-foot) tall, tailless, hairy beings, which resemble

HOMO SAPIENS NEANDERTHALENSIS, supposedly extinct for 30,000 years though remarkably alive in the "wildmen" of legend and folklore.

brief sightings of what they are convinced was a genuine orang pendek. Once, she even viewed it through the lens of her camera, but as it was utterly immobile she assumed that it was an inanimate object and momentarily turned away; when she turned back, the "object" had vanished. Only then did she realize that she had seen one of Sumatra's living leprechauns! She revisited Sumatra in 1995 in a further attempt to track down this elusive creature, and plans to continue doing so until she has confirmed the reality of the orang pendek. In the meantime, however, she may have been beaten in the race to obtain a photograph of it by fellow investigator Pak Buya, who has snapped a shot of a small humanoid being covered in brown hair.

Some primatologists have suggested that the orang pendek could be a relict form of *Homo erectus*, the direct ancestor of modern humans; others favour the identity of a highly specialized species of anthropoid ape adapted to walk on two legs.

Yet another mystery man-beast from Asia is the yeren, frequently reported from the Shennongjia Mountains in central China and believed by cryptozoologists to be either a surviving species of *Gigantopithecus* or a lingering mainland population of orang utans. Descriptions portray a shaggy, red-haired ape-man standing 1.5–1.8 metres (5–6 feet) tall, with very large feet. In recent years, yeren hair samples found on trees and bushes have been analysed by proton-induced X-ray emission (PIXE) spectrometry, to discover the relative concentrations of the elements contained in them. The resulting profile proved to be totally different from that of any known species in China, with an exceptionally (but consistently) high iron/zinc ratio.

In 1994, while visiting the Shennongjia region, journalist Bob Chisholm was shown a film of a strange dome-headed being with ape-like ears, claimed by locals to be the hybrid offspring of a male yeren and a human woman. However, a Western-trained doctor in Beijing identified it as an extremely abnormal human, suffering from microcephaly.

broad-shouldered apes but walk on their short hind legs, have been reported for centuries from this Indonesian island (and also from Borneo, where it is called the batutut). Without a specimen to examine,

however, science has consistently denied their existence, dismissing such accounts as misidentifications of large gibbons, bears or orang-utans.

Nevertheless, during their search Martyr and her colleagues made two

Eastern Esoterica

The Diamond of Doom and a Disturbing Figurine

Like a radiant star of icy blue fire, it sparkled in the brow of an Indian temple idol – until it was impiously plucked out by a thieving Hindu priest, whose punishment for this unholy act was a slow and agonizing death. Thus, according to legend, began the dark history of a singularly famous, and infamous, gem. We know it as the Hope Diamond, but many of its luckless owners have come to look upon this sinister stone as the Diamond of Doom.

It was apparently unearthed in the Golconda mines by the Kistna River in south-west India, and made its European debut in 1642, when it was bought by a French merchant called Jean-Baptiste Tavernier. In 1668, he sold it to King Louis XIV for a handsome profit, but this was soon forfeited in rescuing his son from colossal debts. Tavernier travelled to India in the hope of recouping his losses, but was mauled to death by a pack of wild dogs.

Meanwhile, the dreaded diamond passed successively into the hands of several royal owners, and each suffered

a grim fate. King Louis XIV, formerly a monarch of unparalleled magnificence, lost much of his empire and all his popularity. Princess de Lamballe was beaten to death, and both King Louis XVI and Queen Marie Antoinette were executed.

Years later, a Dutch diamond cutter skilfully diminished its eminent proportions, but not its evil influence.

To many of its owners, the Hope Diamond became the Diamond of Doom.

His son stole the cut stone from him, and the distraught diamond cutter committed suicide. In 1830, this jinxed jewel gained its official name, when it was purchased by a very affluent banker called Henry Hope. Even so, one of his descendants, Lord Francis Hope, was almost penniless when he sold it, after his wife had cursed the diamond for the failure of their marriage. As for its

buyer, French broker Jacques Colot, he went insane and committed suicide, and its next two owners were both murdered!

A Turkish sultan who purchased the gem in 1908 for $400,000 stabbed his wife shortly afterwards, and was overthrown. And the entire family of Edward McLean suffered grievous calamities in the years following McLean's purchase of this doom-laden diamond in 1911.

It is said that the only way to rid oneself of an object associated with bad luck is not to sell it but to give it away, which is why it is interesting to note that the only person who did not experience misfortune once the Hope Diamond had entered his possession was American jeweller Harry Winston. After buying the diamond from the estate of the ill-fated McLean family, he did not sell it again. Instead, he donated it to the Smithsonian Institution, where it remains to this day – a priceless mineralogical wonder, whose piercing blue rays conceal a violent history stained crimson with the blood and anguish of previous owners.

A precious object of an altogether different kind had an equally mysterious power. In *Through the Jungle Very Softly*, Ludwig Koch-Isenburg recounted the strange history of a small Buddha figurine elegantly carved from green jade. Thirty years earlier, a Dutch

colleague called Klaasen had been so mesmerized by its artistry that he had stolen it from its secret resting place. The figurine had stood at the feet of an enormous ancient statue of Buddha, carved out of the rock inside a jungle-shrouded ravine grotto used as a temple in Thailand. Klaasen successfully smuggled it back home with him to Holland, but although he was a fervent collector of works of art, the sight of the figurine sitting on his desk brought him no joy, only an inexplicable feeling of unease. In little more than a year, he was so disturbed by the figurine's presence that he returned to Thailand, taking the uncanny statuette with him, to replace it at the feet of the giant Buddha. And there, while doing so, Klaasen met a Buddhist monk, who smiled and told him that he had seen him steal the figurine the previous year, but knew that it would enlighten him and that he

would then restore it to its true abode.

Another Eastern enigma is the solid iron pillar, 6.4 metres (21 feet) tall, that stands in a courtyard at Mehauli, near Delhi, India. What is so odd about this pillar is that except for a superficial layer of rust, it shows no corrosion – even though it is around 1600 years old. It was erected during the fourth century AD, to mark the victory of King Chandra Gupta II over his enemies, but the precise nature of its structure is controversial. According to the historian Francis Hitching, it is a single piece of pure iron. Yet in a *New Scientist* article (3 January 1985), Dilip Salwi claimed that it also contains small amounts of carbon, silica and phosphorus, and that it was created from several separate pieces of hot wrought iron, which were hammered together in a furnace by a now-extinct Indian technique called forge welding.

MAGNETIC MOUNTAINS

One of the many fanciful stories in the *Arabian Nights* collection tells of a magic mountain consisting entirely of lodestone, to which all items made of iron are irresistibly drawn. Yet similar claims have also appeared in certain factual works. The earliest seems to be the 13-volume *Geography*, written by the Egyptian scholar Claudius Ptolemaeus in the second century AD. This work mentioned a sea-encircled mountain in the Far East, close to

"the Islands of the Satyrs", which was wholly composed of lodestone. Its presence was lethal to passing ships because its magnetic properties drew out all their iron nails, causing them to fall apart and sink.

A comparable account occurred in a book by the Chinese writer So Sung from the eleventh century. Referring to the promontories and peninsulae of the coast of what is now southern Vietnam, he spoke of shallow stretches of water containing numerous mounds of lodestone, whose iron-attracting talents pulled apart the iron-sheathed bottoms of foreign ships sailing by.

No such mountains, islands or other lodestone landmarks have been recorded in recent times, however, so at present these tales must be relegated to the realms of folklore again.

*Agib ascending the lodestone mountain illustrated in a nineteenth-century edition of the **Arabian Nights**.*

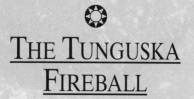

THE TUNGUSKA FIREBALL

In the early morning of 30 June 1908, an enormous fireball roared through the sky above Siberia and exploded with such colossal force north-west of Lake Baikal that in the remote Tunguska region directly below, an expanse of sturdy forest covering about 2000 square kilometres (800 square miles) was razed to the ground and set ablaze like a flimsy pack of cards. Such was the power of the thunderous blast that microbarographic records later revealed that our entire planet had twice been circled by atmospheric shock waves emanating from Tunguska. People 65 kilometres (40 miles) away had been thrown into the air, reindeer herds had perished in fiery winds, and for days afterwards the sky was lit by an eerie red glow, visible as far away as Britain.

Examinations of the shattered landscape have failed to find any trace of an impact crater that would be expected if a meteorite had crashed – the explanation offered by Tunguska's first investigator, the Russian geologist Leonid Kulik. Moreover, in the years that followed, new trees germinating in this area showed an abnormally accelerated growth rate, leading some investigators to the conclusion that they had been mutated by radiation. This led other Russian investigators to consider the radical possibility that a nuclear-powered alien spacecraft had exploded, but there is no conclusive evidence for increased radiation levels here.

A popular idea is that a comet exploded above Tunguska, thus melting the comet's icy head and explaining why no notable fragments of rock or iron have been reported, which would have been the case had the explosion been due to a meteorite or small asteroid. However, no records of an approaching comet were documented. Moreover, in 1993 Christopher Chyba and colleagues at the NASA Goddard Space Flight Center in Greenbelt, Maryland, claimed that the explosion was too low for a comet, proposing instead the vaporized disintegration of a stony asteroid

Lake Cheko in central Siberia, close to the centre of the Tunguska Fireball, is now the site of a laboratory set up to explore the phenomenon.

27 metres (90 feet) in diameter. An alternative "space-age" solution is that a tiny black hole tore through the sky, plunging down into the body of the earth without leaving any meteorite-type impact crater, and emerging out of the opposite side somewhere in the North Atlantic. No Atlantic disturbance at the appropriate time was recorded, however, so unless the black hole destroyed itself while passing through the earth, this theory is not tenable.

An explosion of anti-matter has also been proposed, but so little is known about this that it cannot readily be argued one way or the other. Almost 90 years have passed since that fateful morning at Tunguska, but the mystery of what happened there is still unresolved.

✵

MILK-DRINKING STATUES

One of the most unusual religious phenomena to have occurred for many years began on Thursday 21 September 1995 at a Hindu temple in New Delhi. This was during the season of pitr baksh, when devout worshippers place an offering of milk for their ancestors' souls in front of a white marble statue of the elephant-headed deity Ganesha, the genial Hindu god of practical wisdom.

Today, however, to the amazement of the worshippers, the statue suddenly began to drink the milk, imbibing it through its trunk!

Word of this unprecedented miracle rapidly spread far and wide – and so too did the miracle. Before the end of the day, from Hindu temples all across India, Hong Kong, Nepal, Indonesia,

Krakatoa continues to erupt today, but not with the deadly force of 28 August 1883.

Bangladesh, Thailand, Singapore, and even from temples in Africa, the Middle East, Europe, North America and Australia, reports had emerged of milk-drinking effigies.

A 45-cm- (18-in) high statue of Ganesha busily sucked milk from a spoon at the Khampur Shiv Mandir temple in Chandigarh, Punjab. Milk vanished from the hands of worshippers offering it to the Ganesha image in Ludhiana, also in the Punjab. In Britain, the Vishwa temple in Southall attracted considerable media and public attention when a 30-cm- (12-in) high statue of the bull Nandi, ridden by the Hindu deity Shiva, began sipping milk from a spoon. Even a bronze statue of the cobra deity Shash Naag duly imbibed in the Shri Ram Mandir temple, also in Southall.

Some claims were simply incredible. Numerous cartons and bottles of milk had reputedly been drunk by figurines of Krishna, Ganesha and Brahma at a temple in Hong Kong's Happy Valley. A single small silver statue of Ganesha had somehow managed to consume 20 litres!

Yet the miracle ended as swiftly as it had begun. By the next day, Friday 22 September, most of the idols worldwide

THE KRAKATOA PROPHECY

The colossal volcanic eruption that virtually destroyed the tiny island of Krakatoa, situated between Sumatra and Java, on 28 August 1883 would have remained unknown to the Western world for several days, had it not been for a detailed, accurate account of the catastrophe written by reporter Ed Samson and featured in the *Boston Globe* newspaper on 29 August. Amazingly, however, the account was based entirely upon a recent dream by Samson (a fact not known to the *Globe* when publishing it) and he had called the island Pralape. Yet, as the real island was named Krakatoa, "Pralape" seemed to be an invention of his dream – until it was later discovered that over 150 years earlier, Krakatoa had indeed been called Pralape!

Hindu devotees in Dhaka, Bangladesh, offer milk to the elephant-headed god Ganesha as statues of the deity worldwide begin to drink.

took the view that the explanation was likely to be a mechanism functioning in the reverse manner to that offered as a solution to weeping statues (see pp. 63–64). Indian physicist Dr Das Bangia pointed out that in cases when liquids appear to be absorbed by marble or other forms of permeable stone, what is actually happening is that molecules in the marble's rough surface create a capillary channel, which sucks in droplets quite rapidly. These then spread into a very thin layer that is difficult to see, particularly if the marble is white, as is the case with many Hindu statues.

Needless to say, however, absorption by capillary action could not account for the enormous quantities of milk supposedly drunk by some statues. Exaggeration, or hallucination? Nor, of course, can it explain milk-drinking by metal statues.

✦

FERAL CHILDREN

Accounts of children reared by wild animals are not limited to fictional examples like Mowgli of *The Jungle Book* and the classical legend of Romulus and Remus. Many fully authenticated true-life cases have also been recorded. Probably the most famous of these began one evening in October 1920, near to the village of Midnapore in eastern India.

For quite a time, the villagers had lived in fear of two human-like "phantoms", which, they claimed, periodically emerged from various holes in a clearing close by, terrifying everyone with their grotesque appearance. In a bid to solve this mystery, the Reverend Joseph Singh promised to seek out these phantoms, and on the evening in question he was perched precariously up a tree overlooking the holes, little expecting to see anything, but fulfilling his promise to the villagers. After a while, however, two adult wolves came out of the holes, followed by several cubs and, to the Reverend's amazement, the two dreaded phantoms!

As they drew nearer, Singh became even more amazed: they were not ghosts or demons at all. They were two

were evidently satiated, because they refused to drink any more milk. A few reports emerged during the weekend, after which the phenomenon was over.

Worshippers had no doubt that it was

a miracle. In response, cynics questioned how the drinking by statues of a precious food like milk in parts of Asia racked by poverty could be deemed miraculous. As for the scientists, they

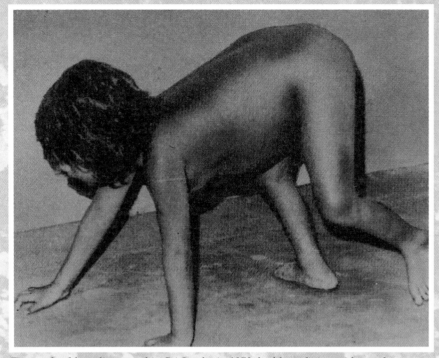

Tissa, a feral boy discovered in Sri Lanka in 1973, had been living with monkeys.

young girls! Incredibly, they had been living with the wolves in their den, adopted as "honorary cubs" by these fierce beasts and cared for alongside their own offspring. One of the infants was only eighteen months old, the other was about seven.

On 17 October, the two girls were captured and taken to an orphanage, where the staff began the arduous task of "converting" back into humans a pair of children who would only sit and howl, or run around on all fours like puppies. The staff named the younger girl Amala, and the older girl Kamala. Sadly, Amala died just a year later, without learning to stand or to talk, but Kamala lived until she was 16. During that time she gradually acquired some basic human traits: she gained a rudimentary vocabulary of at least 30 words, she learnt how to walk and to stand upright, and she acquired a liking for cooked food. Long before this, however, she had touchingly demonstrated that despite her canine upbringing, her human identity had never been totally obliterated; when Amala had died, two tears trickled down Kamala's cheek.

Another report of a feral child also comes from India. Variously referred to as Shamdeo, Ramu and Baloo (after the *Jungle Book* character), this child had been reared by a female bear in a cave within the state of Uttar Pradesh, and was captured in May 1972 by a hunter who had found him playing with some wolf cubs near to the bear's cave. He was eventually looked after by nuns at Prem Divas, Mother Teresa's Home for the Destitute and Dying in Lucknow, where he died in February 1985 after developing cramps. He was about 17 years old, and had been renamed Pascal.

Perhaps the most astounding case on record featuring a child reared by a wild animal is one that came to the attention of an Indian magistrate during the early years of this century. While he was serving at that time in the Central Provinces of India, a ferocious man in his forties was dragged before him in chains, roaring and raging in such a violent, scarcely controllable manner that the greatly shocked magistrate made enquiries about his background and thereby uncovered the astonishing secret of the man's past.

Many years earlier, some villagers in this region had come upon a large tigress, accompanied by two cubs and what, to their amazement, appeared to be a human boy! As they peered closer, they could see that it was indeed a boy, five or six years old, and so they captured him and took him back to their village, where they confined him in one of their huts. His adoptive

mother did not forsake her "cub" so easily, however, because for several nights afterwards the tigress would enter the village and prowl agitatedly around the hut containing him, until in fear for their own safety the villagers finally killed her.

From then on, the boy was reared by the head villager and ultimately acquired human characteristics, but he possessed a ferocious temperament and was able to walk unafraid and unmolested among wild tigers in the jungle. The boy had eventually grown up into a man – the very same man who was now standing in chains before the magistrate.

Like all the other histories recounted here, the tragic case of the tigress and her human cub reveals that the fundamental distinction between man and beast is far from being as clear as we may like to think, for it is blurred by something even more fundamental – love.

QUAKE HAIRS

The following excerpt is from an account in *Scientific American* for 1848, describing a violent earthquake that occurred at Chantibun, eastern Thailand, on 13 May of that year:

During the shock, there spontaneously came out of the ground a species of human hairs in almost every place – in the bazaars, in the roads, in the fields, and the most solid places. These hairs, which are pretty long, stand upright and adhere strongly to the ground. When they are burned, they twist like human hairs and have a burned smell which makes it to be believed that they are really hairs; they all appeared in the twinkling of an eye during the earthquake. The river of Chantibun was all rippling, and bubbles rose to the surface, so that the water was quite white. It is thought that these hairs may have been produced by electricity.

"Quake hairs" have been reported from other Asian earthquakes too. Some Chinese quake hairs have been identified as fibres from a native tree, the hemp palm *Chamaerops fortunei*. In many other cases, however, their origin and identity have remained a mystery.

H U D S O N

B A Y

CANADA

QUEEN
CHARLOTTE
ISLANDS

Caddy ➤

Caddy ➤

VANCOUVER
ISLAND

Ogopogo

*Manipogo
(lake monster)* ➤

*Kenneth Arnold's sighting
of nine UFOs*

*Landing site of
Venusians seen by
Samuel Thompson* ➤

*White
bigfoot*

Bigfoot

Ball lightning

P A C I F I C
O C E A N

Sliny Slim (lake monster)

Minnesota iceman

Monster bird of prey

Bigfoot

*Pedro the midget mummy/
The Nimerigar*

Big-hoot (giant owl)

*Giant red-haired
mummified humans
(Si-Te-Cahs)*

Giant human skeleton

*Frog-faced
humanoid
monster*

Monster bird of prey

Death of James Dean

*Dancing blue lights
in graveyard*

UNITED STATES

Mad Gasser

Moth...

Sky-beasts (living UFOs)

*Meeting place of
George Adamski
and Venusian*

Big-hoot (giant owl)

Goblin-like ETs

*Brown
Mountain
spooklights*

Scaly reptile-man

*White River
monster*

Lizard M...

Florida globster

Ball lightning

Marfa spooklights

G U L F   O F
M E X I C O

Key to Phenomena

- FLYING
- WATER
- ELEMENTS
- LAND ANIMAL
- HUMAN
- SITES
- PARANORMAL

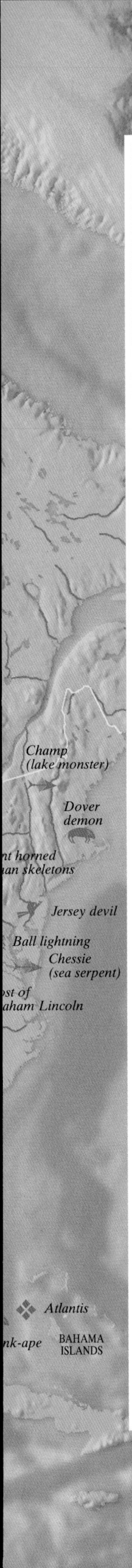

Chapter 5

North America

NEW LANDS, FORGOTTEN SECRETS

BEHIND A FAÇADE OF FAMILIARITY AND MODERNISM, NORTH

AMERICA IN REALITY CONTAINS MANY FEATURES THAT ARE

NEITHER FAMILIAR NOR MODERN, ARISING INSTEAD FROM

OTHER TIMES, AND PERHAPS OTHER DIMENSIONS TOO. LIKE

A GOBLIN UNIVERSE IN WHICH ALL THINGS ARE POSSIBLE,

THERE IS AN ALTERNATE, UNOFFICIAL WEST – A WORLD

WHERE JAMES DEAN AND ABRAHAM LINCOLN RUB

SHOULDERS WITH LIZARD MEN AND MOTHMEN, WHERE THE

SKIES HOST MYSTERIOUS VISITATIONS, THE OCEANS WRITHE

WITH SERPENTINE MONSTERS, AND HAIRY GIANTS STILL LURK

AMID THE SHADOWS OF THE FORESTS.

Champ
(lake monster)

Dover
demon

nt horned
an skeletons

Jersey devil

Ball lightning
Chessie
(sea serpent)

ost of
aham Lincoln

❖ *Atlantis*

nk-ape BAHAMA
ISLANDS

Visitors from Outer, and Inner, Space

LIZARD MEN

One of the most bizarre creatures reported in recent times is undoubtedly a nightmarish entity from South Carolina, which has been aptly nicknamed Lizard Man. According to eyewitnesses, it walks on its hind legs, stands just over 2 metres (7 feet) tall, and has glowing red eyes and green scaly skin. It has only three toes on each foot and three fingers on each hand, but every toe and every finger has a 10-cm- (4-inch) long black claw at its tip.

Lizard Man first made its presence felt at around 2 a.m. on 29 June 1988. This was when 17-year-old Christopher Davis was changing a flat tyre on his car near Scape Ore Swamp, which is just outside the backwater village of Bishopville in South Carolina's Lee County.

Chris was placing the jack into his car boot when he spied something very large running on its hind legs towards him, across a field close by. As it drew near, Chris jumped inside his car and tried to slam the door shut, but the horrifying reptile-man seized it from the other side, gripping the mirror as it attempted to wrench the door open! And when Chris tried to escape by accelerating hard, his scaly attacker jumped on to the car's roof! Luckily, it soon fell off as the vehicle sped away.

When Chris arrived home he was trembling with fear, the roof of his car bore a series of long scratches and the wing mirror was severely twisted.

The massive media publicity generated by this incident led to many other Lizard Man reports emerging

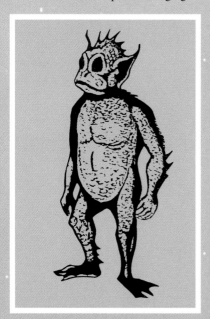

A scaly humanoid biped emerged from the waters of Thetis Lake, British Columbia, in August 1972.

during the summer of 1988, but the same could not be said for Lizard Man itself, who eventually disappeared without ever having been satisfactorily explained.

Interestingly, this bizarre episode is far from being unique. Long before Chris Davis's frightening experience, many other parts of North America had also hosted encounters with reptilian man-monsters, astonishingly similar in appearance to the amphibious "gill-man" starring in Hollywood's classic *Creature from the Black Lagoon* movie.

On 19 August 1972, for example, Robin Flewellyn and Gordon Pike were allegedly chased away from the beach around Thetis Lake in British Columbia, Canada, by a 1.5-metre- (5-foot) tall bipedal monster with six sharp points on its head, which had unexpectedly surfaced in the lake.

Four days later, at around 3.30 p.m. on 23 August, Russell Van Nice and Michael Gold could only watch in amazement when what was presumably the same creature suddenly stepped out of the lake, looked around and then walked back into the water, disappearing from sight. According to their description, it was humanoid in shape, but with scaly silver skin, huge ears, the face of a monster and a pointed projection on its head.

In 1977, a State Conservation naturalist called Alfred Hulstruck claimed that a scale-covered man-beast regularly emerged at dusk from the red algae-choked waters of Southern Tier in New York State. Five years earlier, in March 1972, two policemen saw a frog-faced humanoid creature, about the size of a dog, plunge into Little Miami River near Loveland, Ohio. In this same area, back in 1955, a respectable businessman claimed that he had seen a quartet of 1-metre- (3-foot) tall, frog-faced creatures squatting under a bridge like fairytale trolls.

Another longstanding tradition of scaly humanoids features the fish-men of Inzignanin, near Chicora – an area sandwiched between North and South Carolina. These beings were said to be covered with scales and had webbed hands. Most distinctive of all, however, were their tails, which were as thick as a man's arm, about 45 cm (18 inches) long and relatively inflexible, like those of crocodiles or alligators. According to local lore, they lived only on raw fish and therefore soon died out when the area's fish supplies became exhausted.

Equally strange was the 2-metre- (6-foot) tall, fluorescent-eyed monster that clawed Charles Wetzel's car on the evening of 8 November 1958 as he drove by the Santa Ana River near Riverside, California. Although often placed in the bigfoot (i.e. ape-man) category of mystery beasts, it was much more akin to the reptilian monsters, as noted by the writer Loren Coleman, because it was covered in leaf-like scales and had a protrusible beak-like mouth.

Needless to say, no real-life creatures of the "Black Lagoon" variety have ever been proven by science to exist on earth, either during the present or the past. Yet, if the course of evolution had taken a different turn, our planet may indeed have been home to life forms of this type. In 1982, the scientific journal *Syllogeus* published a very unusual but highly original paper by two well-respected Canadian palaeontologists, Dr Dale A. Russell and Dr R. Séguin from the National Museum of Natural Sciences in Ottawa. Its subject was the fascinating possibility that, if the dinosaurs had never died out, they would have eventually given rise to a dinosaurian counterpart of human beings.

In their paper, Russell and Séguin speculated about the likely appearance of such a creature and suggested that it would have stood upright on its hind legs, with three fingers on each hand. They even constructed a model of this

'dinosaur man' – and what is so amazing about it is that in overall appearance it is remarkably similar to the descriptions of Lizard Man and other reptilian man-beasts reported from modern-day North America!

✵

THE JERSEY DEVIL

One of the most extraordinary monsters on record from the USA became a major news story in January 1909, when it was seen by numerous people in the state of New Jersey and also in the area of Pennsylvania bordering New Jersey. Some of its eyewitnesses tried to convince themselves at first that it must have been some form of hideous giant bird, but they finally admitted that many of its features were far stranger than any observed in a bird, and the creature soon became known as the Jersey devil.

E.W. Minster, a postmaster from Bristol in Pennsylvania, gave a particularly detailed first-hand description of this mysterious monster. He had caught sight of it on the morning of 17 January 1909, after hearing an eerie sound coming from the direction of the Delaware River. According to Minster, the Jersey devil

*In January 1909, the **Philadelphia Evening Bulletin** carried this drawing of the Jersey devil based on the eyewitness descriptions of Mr and Mrs Nelson Evans of Gloucester City, New Jersey.*

was flying diagonally across the river and looked like a large crane at first, but was glowing brightly like an immense firefly. It had a long slender neck that it held outstretched in flight, two pairs of legs (the front pair was shorter than the hind pair) and two long thin wings. Strangest of all, however, was its head, which resembled a ram's because it bore a pair of curled horns. And as it flew, it uttered a bloodcurdling cry, which Minster described as a combined squawk and whistle, beginning very high and piercing but ending very low and hoarse.

At the same time that sightings of this incredible creature were being reported, strange marks resembling hoofprints were being discovered in the area too, and not just on the ground. Some were even spotted on the roofs of houses! Then, not long after these reports had come to an end, it seemed as if the mystery of the Jersey devil had finally been solved. An exhibition in Philadelphia's Arch Street Museum claimed that it had on display a genuine Jersey devil, which had recently been captured alive! Sadly, however, it proved to be nothing more remarkable than a kangaroo that had been decorated with bright green stripes and which had a pair of fake bronze-coloured wings strapped to its shoulders! It was, of course, a hoax – whereas almost a hundred years later, the real Jersey devil has still not been captured or conclusively identified. The mystery continues ...

Separate sightings, similar sights: Bill Bartlett produced a watercolour (above) and John Baxter a drawing (inset) of the strange being which each saw independently on the night of 21 April 1977.

⬟

THE DOVER DEMON

The last thing that 17-year-old Bill Bartlett expected to see when driving with two friends through Dover, Massachusetts, at around 10.30 p.m. on 21 April 1977 was a creature from another dimension. Yet that is what he may have done, at least in the opinion of some investigators – and judging from Bill's description of what he saw, they could have a point!

Driving along, his car's headlights suddenly illuminated a peculiar entity picking its way along a stone wall at the side of the road. As can be seen from the picture that Bill later prepared, which is reproduced here, the creature had a disproportionately large head, shaped like a water melon, with two big, protruding eyes that glowed orange, but it did not seem to have a mouth, nose or ears. Its body was small, its neck and limbs were long and thin, and its fingers and toes were slender and supple. The creature appeared to be hairless, but its peach-coloured skin was rough in texture. It stood about 1 metre (3–4 feet) high, and was observed only by Bill (his two friends were not looking in the right direction to see it).

Unknown to Bill, however, his strange sighting would soon be substantiated by an entirely independent eyewitness. Less than two hours later, 15-year-old John Baxter was walking home little more than a mile from the locality of Bill's encounter when he saw a strange figure coming towards him. After receiving no reply when he called out to it, John paused, and as he did so the figure ran away down a gully. John chased after it and when he was about 9 metres (30 feet) away, he could see it clearly, standing upright on its hind legs and gripping the trunk of a tree. When he spied its

brightly glowing eyes staring at him from an otherwise featureless face, however, John decided to let caution supersede curiosity and he walked briskly back to the road. Once he reached home, he too made a visual record of what he had witnessed, and as can be seen here, his wholly independent illustration corresponds very closely indeed with Bill's.

At around midnight on 22 April, what writer Loren Coleman has subsequently called "the Dover demon" was seen again, this time by 15-year-old Abby Brabham while being driven home by Will Taintor, 18, who only spied it very briefly. Abby's description matched those of Bill and John in every respect except one: when she observed it, its eyes were glowing green, not orange. And thus ended the curious case of the Dover demon – for it has never been reported again and has never been satisfactorily identified.

If the descriptions of it are accurate – and they are certainly very consistent – the Dover demon does not resemble any species known to science, either from North America or elsewhere. It may not, however, be *entirely* unknown. The Cree nation of eastern Canada speak of a mysterious race of pygmy entities called the Mannegishi, who delight in playing tricks upon travellers. According to the Cree, the Mannegishi have round heads, long thin legs, arms with six fingers on each hand, and they live between rocks in the rapids. Excluding the finger count discrepancy, this description is reminiscent of the Dover demon.

✶

PEDRO – WYOMING'S UNEXPLAINED MIDGET MUMMY

One day in October 1932, after spending several weeks seeking gold in a ravine at the base of the San Pedro mountains, about 100 kilometres (65 miles) south-west of Caspar in Wyoming, Cecil Main and Frank Carr spotted some indications of gold in one of the ravine's thick stone walls. The only way to determine whether the wall really did contain gold, however, was to blast it apart with dynamite, and so this is what they did. Once the resulting clouds of dust had begun to disperse, the two men peered through the yawning hole left behind and discovered that the wall had been hiding a small cavern. It was a natural cave, about 4.5 metres (15 feet) long but only 1.2 metres (4 feet) high and wide. Inside was a small ledge, and to the astonishment of the prospectors, they could see a tiny pixie-like creature sitting cross-legged upon it, with its arms folded across its waist. Looking closer at this extraordinary being, however, they discovered that it was no longer alive. In fact, it was a mummy, but unlike any ever seen before.

First and foremost, it was exceptionally small, less than 18 cm (7 inches) high as it sat there and with a total height of only 35 cm (14 inches). Yet it did not seem to be a child. Its face resembled that of a smirking old man, with a low brow, a broad flat nose, large eyes (one of which was half-closed) and a very wide mouth with thin lips. Its skin was a tanned, bronze colour, heavily wrinkled, its body was barrel-shaped, its hands were large and its long fingers

Pedro: X-rays revealed within the mummy a man-like skeleton just 35 cm (14 inches) tall.

bore minute but readily visible fingernails. The top of its head was abnormally flat and covered in a dark, gelatinous substance, eclipsing all but a fringe of hair around its edge.

The bewildered prospectors carefully lifted this enigmatic little effigy off its ledge and took it back with them when they eventually returned to Caspar, where it attracted an immense amount of interest. It became known as Pedro (after its mountain origin) and was eventually purchased by Ivan Goodman, a car dealer in Caspar. When scientists first learnt of its discovery, they were somewhat sceptical, suspecting a hoax. Nevertheless, after being shown the mummy by Goodman, anthropologist Dr Henry Shapiro from the American

Museum of Natural History was intrigued enough to organize an X-ray examination for it. If this mysterious midget was simply a hoax, carefully constructed externally but with no internal substance, X-ray analysis would swiftly expose it as such.

Instead, however, the X-ray plates confirmed that Pedro possessed an irrefutably man-like skeleton, despite its tiny stature. It exhibited a complete set of ribs, fully formed arms and legs with all bones readily discernible, a backbone that had once been perfectly formed but which had subsequently suffered an injury, and also a fractured left collar-bone. Indeed, it seemed as if this little person had met its death through some violent attack, accounting not only for those injuries, but also for its flattened head and the dark gelatinous substance. When examined, it was found that the skull had been smashed by an extremely heavy blow, and the dark substance was exposed brain tissue and congealed blood.

As for Pedro's age, despite the severe damage its skull was sufficiently intact to reveal that its fontanelle (a soft space between the skull's bones) was closed. This is an adult characteristic; in babies and small children, it is still open. Moreover, Pedro also had a full set of teeth, the most distinctive of which were its large, noticeably pointed canines. Its overall morphology, internally and externally, indicated that it was about 65 years old when it died, and in Shapiro's opinion it was not from recent times, but dated far back into history.

In 1950, Goodman died and Pedro became the property of Leonard Wadler, but later vanished from the headlines and today its location is unknown. In 1979, Pedro's X-rays were shown to Wyoming University anthropologist Professor George Gill, who announced that it had probably been a grossly malformed infant or foetus suffering from anencephaly – a severe condition in which most of the cranium and brain have failed to develop. Sometimes, moreover, the portion of brain that *has* formed is exposed, with no protective bony covering. This could account for Pedro's flattened head and its covering of congealed blood and brain tissues, but anencephaly cannot explain Pedro's adult features and dentition.

In 1993, French zoologist Dr François de Sarre suggested to me that Pedro may have been a foetus suffering from microcephaly (abnormal cranium and brain formation), but on to whose skeleton the skin of an adult man had been carefully moulded – in the same way that the Jivaros do when they produce their famous tzantzas or shrunken heads.

Professor Gill thought that Pedro may have belonged to a race of unknown prehistoric native American people. However, many modern native American groups claim that this continent was, and still is, home to a very aggressive race of pygmies or Little People, whose descriptions closely tally

with Pedro. In particular, the Shoshone nation of Wyoming speak of the Nimerigar, who would attack them with tiny bows that shot poisoned arrows. According to some traditions, these pygmies even kill their own kind when they become ill, by beheading them or smashing their skulls – just like Pedro's skull had been smashed. It would be strange indeed if the true identity of Pedro proved to be a euthanased elf.

✪

FLYING SAUCERS AND UFOS – ALIEN SPACECRAFT OR ELUSIVE SKY-BEASTS?

Many sightings of supposed flying saucers and UFOs are simple misidentifications of certain earthly or astronomical objects, including weather balloons, the planet Venus, light-reflecting fog or clouds, distress flares, flocks of geese or even swarms of insects reflecting light, lenticular clouds, aeroplane vapour trails, low-flying aeroplanes and meteors.

As for the remainder, most people assume that any "genuine" flying saucers and UFOs are alien, extraterrestrial spacecraft; but what if at least some of them are extraordinary living creatures, native to our planet yet undiscovered by science? Largely unconsidered elsewhere, this fascinating idea has received appreciable attention from researchers in North America.

Few ecological niches on land or in the water are not occupied by animals modified for existence here – but what about the sky? Although certain insects and birds spend much of their time in flight, there are no animals that live their entire lives airborne in the sky, adapted for an exclusive existence in the atmosphere encircling our planet – or are there?

It is well known that the term "flying saucer" was coined by a reporter documenting Idaho businessman Kenneth Arnold's sighting of nine flying disc-shaped objects near Mount Rainier, Washington, while piloting a Callair aeroplane on 24 June 1947. Less well known is that Arnold considered these objects to be living organisms: "sort of like sky jellyfish".

Nor was he alone in his opinion. A month later, John P. Bessor from St Thomas, Pennsylvania, submitted a similar theory, which he had developed in 1946, to the United States Air Force. Far from dismissing it as unrealistic, the officer who replied to Bessor described

A lenticular cloud above Joshua Tree National Monument, California. Eddying wind, often near mountains, is the usual cause of lenticular or "lens-shaped" clouds.

Taken in Oregon in 1950, this photograph shows the archetypal "flying saucer".

his notion as "one of the most intelligent theories we have received".

The sky-beast concept gained further impetus in 1955 with the publication in the USA of a detailed appraisal of this idea by Countess Zoe Wassilko-Serecki, a prominent liberal-minded thinker. She proposed that planet earth's upper atmosphere is populated by enormous bladder-like beasts with glowing bodies composed of energy enveloping a central core of solid matter. They exhibit the ability to change their shape at will, from a spherical configuration when stationary to a cigar-like form when moving, absorbing energy to fuel their non-corporeal beings. In the years following her statement, during which UFO sightings have become increasingly common, a notable number have indeed featured distinctly cigar-like shapes recalling the appearance of the sky-beasts predicted by the countess.

In addition, her ideas won praise from zoologist Ivan Sanderson, one of America's most celebrated investigators of mystery beasts. And in the early 1960s, scientist and hydrophone inventor John M. Cage from New Jersey drew comparisons between incidents involving dolphins following ships with sightings of UFOs trailing aeroplanes, postulating that these latter entities were in reality intelligent life-forms that

fed upon negative electricity.

The most famous and extensive exploration of the sky-beast theory for UFOs, however, is that of Trevor James Constable, a radio officer in the US merchant marine. In 1978, he published his investigations and findings in a very absorbing book, entitled *Sky Creatures*.

According to Constable, some reported UFOs are indeed gigantic, undiscovered native life-forms highly modified for a wholly aerial existence within the earth's atmosphere. He named these exceedingly specialized organisms "critters" and described them as single-celled (like amoebae), but encased within a mica- or metal-like outer covering, and existing in a wide range of sizes – from as much as nearly a kilometre (half a mile) in length down to a few centimetres at most. The reason that these critters are seen only infrequently, explained Constable, is that they often reflect infra-red light (invisible to the human eye). Because they change colour, under certain conditions critters will reflect visible light and it is then that they "become" UFOs. It seems that they can be photographed using infra-red cinefilm and an appropriate filter, and Constable's book includes many photos of alleged critters, obtained in the Mojave Desert in California.

In 1992, the concept of living UFOs, sometimes termed "bioforms", also received publicity outside the USA, through British author Andrew Collins's book, *The Circlemakers*. Collins reported how, while seeking an explanation for the formation of crop circles (see pp. 27–28), he uncovered the work of a hitherto-obscure scientist called Wilhelm Reich, who claimed to have discovered a mysterious type of energy termed orgone. Collins suggested that orgone may well hold the key to the crop circle mystery, claiming that all the phenomena documented in relation to modern-day crop circles have also been recorded in association with Constable's critters. In turn, if critters are composed of orgone, their occasional contact with the earth's surface could thus explain the circles' creation.

Critters, always assuming that they do exist, may not be the only form of atmospheric sky-beast native to our planet. During the Second World War, an early form of UFO was often encountered by fighter pilots, who reported seeing small balls of brilliant white or reddish light dancing around and pacing their aeroplanes in a manner that seemed uncannily intelligent, even playful – almost as if they were curious about the nature of the planes.

These balls of light became known as foo fighters, and were believed to be a secret weapon of the enemy, until it was discovered that American, British, German and Japanese pilots were all seeing them. Similar objects can sometimes be detected by radar too, whereupon they are referred to as gizmos or angels. Constable believes that foo fighters may be very primitive sky-beasts, less sentient than their giant-sized relatives.

There is no doubt that the concept of UFOs as living sky-beasts is exceedingly radical and would probably be dismissed out of hand by the more conservative members of the scientific community. Consequently, the last word should go to a leading biologist at the Wright-Patterson Air Force Base at Dayton, Ohio, which is the headquarters of the US Air Force's UFO investigations. In view of the controversial nature of this subject, he prefers to remain anonymous, but his opinions speak for themselves:

*"Sort of like sky jellyfish" is how one eyewitness described nine flying disc-shaped objects in 1947 – and perhaps no less fantastic in appearance than this sea jellyfish, which appears in Dr Richard Lydekker's **The Royal Natural History** (1894–6).*

When you toss a pebble into a pool, you see the water animals – the nymphs, crawfish, minnows, water insects – streaking away in fright. But almost before the ripples have died in the pool they are back, investigating curiously. Perhaps events on this earth – atomic explosions, rocket flights into the stratosphere and so on – have been like the pebble tossed into the pool. They have disturbed the stratosphere, perhaps have sent ripples into the fabric of space itself. And the space animals, in curiosity, are coming down to investigate.

As a zoologist, I had always been perplexed by the absence of exclusively sky-dwelling life-forms on our planet, especially given the incredible ingenuity demonstrated by evolution in successfully populating everywhere else with living things. If Constable, Cage and other proponents of the sky-beast scenario are correct, however, perhaps I no longer need to be perplexed – merely frustrated that I have yet to glimpse any examples of evolution's best-kept but most amazing secret of all.

❂

VISITORS FROM VENUS – EXTRA-TERRESTRIALS OR INTER-DIMENSIONALS?

A surprising number of Americans have reputedly been visited by aliens *claiming* to be from other planets in our solar system, particularly Venus; but are these alleged extraterrestrials all that they seem to be, or is their true origin much closer to our own than we realize?

The most famous reported visitation from Venus took place during the early afternoon of 20 November 1952 in the Californian desert near Desert Center, when 61-year-old UFO enthusiast George Adamski supposedly encountered a sandy-haired humanoid

Venusian. With slanting grey-green eyes, tanned hairless face, and wearing a shimmering one-piece garment, this distinctive figure communicated via sign-language and telepathy with Adamski for almost an hour, before making its departure aboard a scout ship hovering nearby. According to Adamski, he succeeded in taking photos of this ship, and some of his colleagues had been observing his contact with the Venusian through binoculars, at a distance of about 1.5 kilometres (1 mile).

In his books *Flying Saucers Have Landed* and *Inside the Space Ships*, Adamski alleged that he met the Venusian on several subsequent occasions and was taken on to its ship, travelling aboard it to the far side of the moon, where he spied cities, forests, mountains, lakes and a furry four-legged animal. In later years, he even claimed to have visited the ringed planet Saturn to attend an interplanetary conference!

Inevitably, Adamski's accounts drew short shrift from the scientific community and such scepticism has been adequately justified by astronomical research since his death in 1965. For example, America's manned lunar landings, beginning in 1969 with Apollo 11, revealed the moon to be a barren lifeless world, far removed from his descriptions of advanced lunar civilizations and natural grandeur. Equally, as Saturn has been shown to be a gas planet composed principally of hydrogen, how it could function as a venue for a cosmic conference attended by Adamski, or any other humanoid form of life, is hard to imagine.

Even his famous photos of the Venusian scout-ship have failed to withstand the test of time. The common scientific consensus nowadays is that these were actually fakes, depicting models made from bottle coolers and chicken feeders.

As for Venus being the home planet of Adamski's olive-eyed, smooth-skinned visitor, it would be truly astounding if any humanoid civilization could exist on such a planet. Its fiery surface temperature of 480°C (896°F), baleful vista of volcanoes, omnipresent thunder and lightning storms, and sulphuric acid rainfall have inspired astronomers to liken this infernal world

One of George Adamski's famous photographs: a Venusian interplanetary carrier with five scout-ships – or a model made from bottle coolers and chicken feeders?

to a traditional image of hell!

In an attempt to circumvent this latter impasse, a number of researchers into the esoteric have suggested that Venusian humanoids may normally inhabit a dimension of higher "atomic vibration" than the physical three-dimensional level in which we live. For them this is a totally real and substantial dimension but one from which they must "step down" when wishing to manifest themselves to planet earth dwellers. Yet even if all this is true, another issue equally difficult to resolve is the diversity of eyewitness descriptions concerning Venusians.

In 1950, Samuel Thompson saw a troop of nude diminutive Venusians with blond waist-length hair and dark skin, playing merrily in a glade near Markham, Washington, while their spaceship hovered close by. Although they were benevolent like other supposed Venusians, in Thompson's opinion they seemed extraordinarily childlike: indeed, his description is more reminiscent of elves or some other traditional race of Little People than of ETs.

Certainly they were in great contrast to the highly sophisticated, fully humanoid Venusians who regularly contacted Howard Menger throughout

his life, following his initial meeting as a 10-year-old boy with a beautiful golden-eyed female Venusian near his New Jersey home in 1932. According to Menger, Venusian technology is 2500 years more advanced than our own, and the Venusians are vegetarians, whose specially processed foodstuffs possess a far greater nutritional content than their counterparts on planet earth.

The Aetherius Society is dedicated to storing up spiritual energy in mountain-contained "batteries" that can be discharged to trouble spots anywhere on planet earth for the easing of suffering. The society was founded in 1954 by George King, a former London taxi driver. King claims to be the earth's representative on a Saturn-based council called the Interplanetary Parliament, and also to be in communication with an unseen Cosmic Master called Aetherius, living on Venus. According to this society, Venusians are 2–2.75 metres (7–9 feet) tall, with long pale hair and cinnamon skin, eyes that lack pupils, and tiny feet. They no longer need to eat, their energy intake is accomplished merely by breathing; Aetherius, apparently, has not eaten for over 3000 years!

So who, if anyone, is correct out of the above selection of those claiming contact with Venusians? Is there any

way of reconciling these and other conflicting testimonies? In their absorbing book *Life Beyond Planet Earth?*, Janet and Colin Bord offer some compelling speculations.

Many ufological sceptics believe that the variety of forms and life-styles of Venusians described by their earthly eyewitnesses indicates that these alien encounters were really hallucinations or visions induced by fear, stress, drugs or even dietary stimuli. However, as noted by the Bords, illusion may be as important as delusion. That is, some encounters with Venusians may be genuine, not imaginary, but the Venusians purposefully adopt whichever guise they consider to be the most influential for a given situation or eyewitness.

Perhaps the most thought-provoking aspect of the Venusian visitations, however, is that these beings might not even be from Venus at all. It is very interesting that most encounters with aliens claiming to have journeyed here from Venus – or from other planets within our solar system – occurred *before* space-probes had been sent out from the planet earth, exposing these worlds to be incapable of sustaining the existence of advanced forms of life. Since then, as the Bords have pointed

George Adamski supposedly met a sandy-haired humanoid Venusian near Desert Center, California, in 1952.

out: "alien entities have continued to make contact with Earth people, but they have stopped claiming to come from our Solar System. As Mankind reaches out into the Universe, so the entities retreat – and change their tactics."

But why? Why do they apparently not wish us to learn their true origins? Perhaps, as the Bords suggest, their true home is far closer to us than we currently realize – a parallel planet earth sharing the same space as our own, yet existing in a separate dimension. Since its inhabitants can visit us on our planet (but not vice-versa), however, theirs must be much more advanced, socially and technologically. Even so, they may be afraid that their planet's existence would be threatened if ever a means of entering it were discovered by our more aggressive culture. And so, by spinning tales to us of populated extraterrestrial worlds, our visitors lure our minds away from the far likelier concept of interdimensional travel.

There is one other notable explanation that also eradicates an extraterrestrial origin for these supposed Venusians. Is it possible, as some UFO researchers have speculated, that they are actually from our own planet's future? Are these entities our own far-distant descendants, a highly evolved, advanced race of humans that may actually be visiting us to prevent us from embarking upon deleterious projects, or to study us as examples of

their own less sophisticated, more barbaric past? Any consideration of time travel necessarily conjures up all manner of mind-bending paradoxes involving the future influencing the past, but there is little doubt that whatever they are, and wherever they have come from, our friendly neighbourhood Venusians are decidedly interested in our activities. It would be equally interesting, not to mention reassuring, to know the reason for their curiosity.

✸

THE GOBLINS OF HOPKINSVILLE

Many of the world's most celebrated cases of alleged encounters with extraterrestrials (ETs) have occurred in North America. Yet even these have attracted great scepticism from some investigators, so that their authenticity is still unresolved. There is, however, at least one very notable exception to this trend – the astonishing case of the Hopkinsville goblins.

On the evening of 21 August 1955, at their farmhouse in the hamlet of Kelly, close to Hopkinsville, Kentucky, the Suttons (seven adults and three children) were entertaining a visitor, a local friend called Billy Ray Taylor. At around 8 p.m., Taylor stepped outside to fetch some water from a well in the

backyard, where he observed a silver object skim across the farmhouse and land about 100 metres (300 feet) further away in a gully hidden by trees. When he told the Suttons about this, they were amused but not convinced. Shortly afterwards, however, their dog, which was outside, began barking in such a frantic, hysterical manner that Taylor and one of the Suttons' sons, Elmer, went out to investigate. They were greatly shocked to see a glowing goblin-like creature floating towards them! They were carrying rifles, so both men shot the entity, but instead of falling to the ground it simply flipped backwards and scurried away.

It was soon back, however, and this time it was accompanied by at least one other of its kind. During the next 3–4 hours, the Suttons were besieged by these macabre "space goblins", which appeared in nearby trees, scrambled over their farmhouse and peered in at them through the windows. One of the creatures even leaned down from the porch roof, and with a taloned hand snatched at the hair of Taylor, who was standing underneath!

According to descriptions given by the Suttons in subsequent interviews, each of the "goblins" stood 75–105 cm (2¹/₂–3¹/₂ feet) tall, was principally bipedal and glowed silver. Its domed head was disproportionately large and bore two short antenna-like structures. It also had a pointed chin, a conical nose with a rounded knob at the tip and a pair of huge, pointed, elephantine ears. Its big, bulbous, laterally sited eyes glowed yellow, and its extremely wide mouth's upper lip was tucked beneath the lower lip. There was no neck.

The goblin's body had a powerful chest, but the rest of the torso was very thin, and its arms and legs were positively spindly. The arms were extremely long too, so that its broad hands almost touched the floor even when the creature was standing upright. Each hand had four webbed, clawed fingers. Its legs were much shorter than its arms but were exceedingly thin and terminated in circular feet that resembled suction cups. There was no tail.

Merely to be confronted by such entities would be alarming enough, but the most unnerving aspect of the

One of the Hopkinsville goblins reputedly leaned down from the porch roof and snatched at the hair of Billy Ray Taylor.

Suttons' prolonged encounter with the goblins was that these extraordinary beings appeared to be totally immune to bullets. The Suttons scored several successful hits, but on each occasion the goblin simply back-flipped like a circus acrobat and scuttled away on all fours, or, if hit while in a tree, merely floated slowly down to the ground. Eventually,

the Suttons and Taylor became so frightened that they ran out of the house, jumped into two cars and fled at top speed to the police station at Hopkinsville, where they spoke at great length to the local Chief of Police Russell Greenwell, his deputy George Batts and some other officers at the station.

Not surprisingly, the police were thoroughly nonplussed by the Suttons' incredible story, but they were also struck by their genuine terror. Something had clearly frightened these hardy, no-nonsense country people very severely. And so, after persuading the Suttons to return home, Greenwell and the other officers went back with them, but nothing could be found. Yet as soon as the police left the farmhouse and drove back to Hopkinsville, the goblins returned, inspecting the farmhouse and its human contents as before. By sunrise, however, they had gone – and this time they did not come back.

Something that may be an interesting sequel to the Suttons' experience occurred near Gastagh in Vicenza, Italy, on 24 November 1978. Angelo D'Ambros was gathering firewood in the woods when he encountered two small entities that greatly resembled the Hopkinsville goblins and which, like them, floated through the air rather than walking. After he threatened them with a piece of wood, they fled away, but when he chased after them he saw them enter a 2-metre- (6-foot) high domed craft, standing on legs, which promptly flew off into the sky at great speed.

The case of the Hopkinsville goblins has been exhaustively investigated by many different UFO researchers, but no one has currently revealed any evidence, or reason, to suggest that this was a hoax, or even an instance of mass hallucination or misidentification of known animals. Also worth noting is that despite being subjected to extensive public ridicule over the years, not one of the eleven eyewitnesses has ever retracted their story or any portion of it. So if the case *is* genuine, where did the Suttons' amazing visitors come from?

If they are truly extraterrestrial, they are beyond the limits of our world – and the subject of this book. However, as with the visiting Venusians documented earlier (pp.137–139), it is possible that the Hopkinsville entities' undisclosed origin owes more to inner space than to outer space. These large-headed, big-eared, thin-limbed, bug-eyed, diminutive beings bear a very striking resemblance to certain forms of Little People, notably the goblins – hence their ufological nickname. Reading through the UFO literature, moreover, it becomes increasingly apparent that many human encounters with supposed ETs and with Little People share a surprising number of similarities.

Just like fairies, elves and other Little People, a lot of reported ETs are small in size, emit a glowing light or appear within a ball of light, seem to be invulnerable to bullets or suchlike, and can float above the ground. The ability to vanish without trace and to hypnotize (enchant?) their human contacts are further characteristics shared by ETs and Little People.

In many documented cases of humans allegedly abducted by ETs, the person believes that he has been abducted for only a short time, when in reality a considerably longer period has passed by. Once again, this time-lapse scenario is mirrored in traditional folktales, featuring fairy-abducted humans who believe that their visit to Faerie has spanned only a few hours, but ultimately discover that years, even centuries, have flitted by.

The comparison can be taken even further: just as some reports of alien abductions feature bizarre-sounding claims that the ETs have forced their human abductees to mate with them (ostensibly to improve their alien lineage), so too in fairy tales are there many accounts of fairies kidnapping human babies to rear as their own, replacing them with changelings.

Yet where do shared similarities end and shared identities begin? As we saw earlier (p.24), whereas modern-day sightings of traditional Little People are far fewer than in previous centuries, reports of UFOs and ETs are ever-increasing in number. In just over a century, humankind's technological knowledge and capabilities have advanced immeasurably. If Little People are real entities, why should we assume that their capabilities have not advanced too? And bearing in mind that their skills have always far exceeded our own, should we really be too surprised if, while we have progressed only as far as the aeroplane and the manned moon rocket, the Little People of the late twentieth century have developed much more sophisticated flying machines, sleek aerial skycraft that we refer to as UFOs?

These notions may well seem more

*Large-headed, big-eared, thin-limbed, bug-eyed ... traditional images of Little People – seen here in Arthur Rackham's **A House Plagued by Strange Creatures** (1905) – bear a striking resemblance to ETs.*

akin to science-fantasy than factual science, but UFO researchers recognize that the parallels between human encounters with Little People and with supposed ETs are too extensive to be dismissed entirely as coincidence. Consequently, if, as popularly believed by investigators of the Little People, this enigmatic race derives from a parallel

equivalent of our own planet earth, but can travel freely between the two, this could explain visitations by various of today's reputed ETs, such as the Hopkinsville goblins, and perhaps even the notably elfin "Venusians" seen by Samuel Thompson (p.138), dancing just like latter-day Little People near their hovering spaceship.

MOTHMAN

Grey in colour, with a large pair of folded wings, it stood 1.8–2 metres (6–7 feet) tall on two sturdy human-like legs and stared at the approaching car with blazing red eyes that seemed to peer out from the top of its body, because it had no head, or at least no discernible neck delineating a head above its chest. Such was the spine-chilling humanoid apparition that shuffled towards Roger Scarberry, his wife and two friends as they drove by a disused wartime explosives factory close to Point Pleasant, West Virginia, at around 11.30 p.m. on 15 November 1966.

Petrified, they sped away, accelerating to 160 kph (100 mph), but the creature – or a second one – flew after them, emitting eerie high-pitched squeaks and effortlessly pacing their car without even flapping its huge wings. Once they neared Point Pleasant, however, it vanished and when they reached the Mason County courthouse they reported their terrifying encounter to Deputy Millard Halstead. He went back with them to the factory, but nothing was found.

This was not the first recorded sighting of such a creature at Point Pleasant. Driving down Route 2 along the Ohio River in 1961, a car driver and her passenger had been frightened by a very similar creature. It was standing in the middle of the road as the car approached, but suddenly opened its enormous wings, spanning 3 metres (10 feet), and took off vertically into the air.

Nevertheless, it was the Scarberry incident that focused media attention upon this bizarre being, which soon became known as Mothman. During the next 13 months, it was allegedly seen by more than 100 other eyewitnesses in or around Point Pleasant, whose descriptions were mostly consistent with Scarberry's version. By the end of 1967, however, just as abruptly as it had arrived, Mothman apparently departed, for it was seen no more.

Published in 1975, the most comprehensive and thought-provoking documentation of Mothman is John Keel's classic book, *The Mothman Prophecies*, in which he revealed that sightings of this frightening aerial anomaly were not the only disturbing events taking place at that time in the Point Pleasant area. Also on record was a veritable epidemic of UFO reports and cases of macabre animal mutilation, as well as unnerving visits to a number of local homes by sinister and invariably dark-suited, anonymous officials – a mysterious phenomenon in its own right, whose subjects are popularly referred to as Men In Black. Accordingly, Keel and several investigators have proposed that Mothman was a paranormal entity, possibly even an interloper from some other dimension in space and time.

A more conservative line in explanations was taken by biologist Dr Robert Smith from West Virginia University, who proposed that Mothman might have been a vagrant specimen of a very tall, grey-plumaged bird called the sandhill crane *Grus canadensis*. This long-necked species bears scant resemblance, however, to the reputedly neckless Mothman.

Perhaps the most intriguing solution of all was offered in 1988 by the researcher Mark Hall in *Thunderbirds! The Living Legend of Giant Birds*. Hall points out that in the Pacific north-west, the Ozark Mountains in Missouri and the Allegheny Plateau of Pennsylvania (a neighbour of West Virginia), the native American people and also the early Western settlers firmly believed in the existence of a giant species of owl, which they variously termed the great owl, booger owl or big-hoot. No such owl is known to science, but it might well resemble Mothman; unlike various other animals, owls have large eyes that appear red when shining.

Even so, until some physical remains

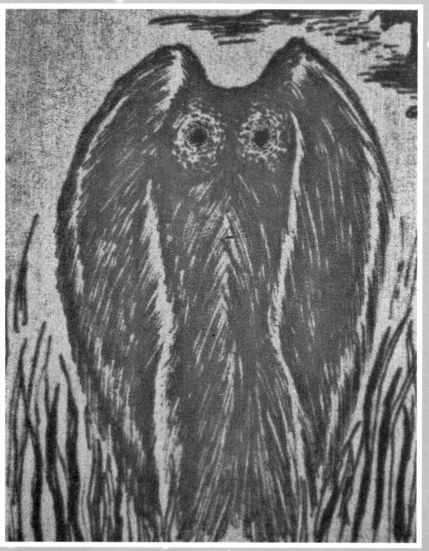

Mothman: humanoid, with blazing red eyes, no discernible neck and enormous wings.

of a big-hoot are obtained, a giant owl is no more acceptable to the zoological community than Mothman itself – whatever it may have been.

✪

THE MAD GASSER OF MATTOON

At around 11 p.m. on 31 August 1944, Mrs Bert Kearney awoke in the bedroom of her home in Mattoon, Illinois, and was surprised to find that it was suffused with a mysterious, sickeningly sweet fragrance. As she later recalled to a local newspaper, this strange scent soon proved to be the sinister herald of a terrifying experience: "At the time I thought that it might be from flowers outside the window. But the odor grew stronger and I began to feel a paralysis of my legs and lower body. I got frightened and screamed."

Neighbours and police searched the area around her house without success, but less than two hours later her husband came home from work and saw a shadowy figure outside their bedroom window. As soon as it saw Mr Kearney, the figure raced away and although Kearney gave chase he was unable to catch up with it. Meanwhile, his wife began to recover from the vapour's evil effects, which proved to be of a swift-acting but short-term nature.

According to Kearney, the mysterious entity was "tall, dressed in dark clothing and wearing a tight-fitting cap". This description would be echoed by many other Mattoon inhabitants during the next 11 days, for although Mrs Kearney (and four unnamed persons earlier that day) were the first, they would not be the last to receive frightening visits from the sinister being who became known as the Mad Gasser of Mattoon.

In each case, the Gasser apparently squirted its incapacitating vapour through an open bedroom window, and all its victims suffered the same temporarily debilitating effects, which also included nausea as well as swelling and burning pains on the face and lips. Yet the determined efforts of the local police to track down this seemingly

"Tall, dressed in dark clothing and wearing a tight-fitting cap", the Mad Gasser of Mattoon was better known to its victims for its strange-smelling, incapacitating vapour.

deranged individual – and a reason for its bizarre behaviour – were all in vain.

On the evening of 5 September, Beulah Cordes and her husband came home to find on their front porch a cloth soaked in a strange-smelling liquid. This induced the characteristic effects of the Gasser's vapour when Mrs Cordes sniffed the cloth out of curiosity. The cloth was sent by the police to Illinois University for analysis, but no results were obtained – strange indeed. Yet the conclusion to this weird case was to prove even stranger.

After 11 days, during which (judging from claims made by Mattoon inhabitants) the Gasser had been active on most evenings but had remained resolutely elusive, Police Chief E.C. Cole issued an official statement dismissing the entire phenomenon as an outbreak of mass hysteria. There had never been any Gasser, gas or visitations: it was all due to

sensationalized reports in local newspapers. Not surprisingly, those who claimed to have been victims of the Gasser were not convinced by this, nor are investigators like Loren Coleman, whose books have generated new interest in this near-forgotten mystery.

After all, if the Mad Gasser really was imaginary, who did Bert Kearney chase? What was the unidentifiable, strange-smelling liquid on the cloth? And how, at least with the earliest cases, could several people – wholly independently of one another, and before the facts of their respective experiences had become publicly known in Mattoon – reveal precisely the same details about their eerie visitations, including the specific scent and effects of the mysterious gas? Today, we are still no nearer to answering any of these questions than the Mattoon constabulary were in 1944 – and that, in itself, is a very disturbing situation.

The Unnatural History of North America

KIDNAPPERS ON THE WING

It was about 8.30 p.m. on 25 July 1977, and 10-year-old Marlon Lowe was running for his life – quite literally. He had been playing with two friends in his family's back garden at Lawndale, Illinois, when suddenly two huge black birds swooped down from the sky and began pursuing one of Marlon's friends, Travis Goodwin. Happily, Travis managed to escape by jumping into the swimming pool, so the deadly winged duo switched their attention to Marlon instead. Marlon ran away from them as fast as he could, but it was not fast enough. As he was running, to his horror he felt the talons of one of the giant birds grip the shoulder straps of his sleeveless shirt, and the next moment the terrified boy – weighing 30 kg (65 lb) – was hauled about 3 metres (10 feet) off the ground.

Screaming and struggling, Marlon shouted at the top of his voice as the bird effortlessly carried him about 12 metres (40 feet) through the air, from the back yard into the front yard. Hearing his voice, his parents Ruth and Jake Lowe came running and so did two family friends working close by. Ruth was first on the scene – the first to witness a horrific sight that froze her

blood. There was her son being abducted by a huge black bird resembling a condor, punching up at its legs with all his might as his feathered kidnapper carried him aloft.

Seconds later, however, one of his punches must have hit home, because the bird suddenly opened its talons and

Marlon Lowe and his mother Ruth after their terrifying ordeal in July 1977.

dropped Marlon on to the ground, before soaring away in the company of its mate. As his mother later told the local newspaper during an interview: "He was hitting at it with his fists. If he hadn't, it never would have dropped him."

The four adults ran to the terrified boy and discovered to their relief that,

except for shock and a frayed shirt where the bird had gripped him, Marlon was none the worse for his incredible experience. In the weeks to come, however, it would take its toll: Marlon frequently suffered nightmares – "He kept fighting those birds all night long," his mother recalled to the press – and the entire family was mercilessly heckled by sceptics and cynics.

But the most dramatic indication of his trauma was also the most visible: within a year, Marlon's coppery-red hair had turned grey.

This is just one of many bizarre accounts on file featuring encounters in North America with giant birds – birds that should be impossible, yet which genuinely seem to exist.

In the case of Marlon Lowe, he and his parents claimed that the bird most closely resembling his abductor was the Andean condor *Vultur gryphus* – a black vulturine species with a wing-span of up to 3.2 metres (10 feet). This species, however, is not native to North America. There is a slightly smaller version, the California condor *Gymnogyps californianus*, which was once widely distributed across the USA, but by 1977 it was virtually extinct in the wild, so this is unlikely to be the culprit either. In any case, the structure of condors' feet is such that they are incapable of grasping and transporting anything as heavy as a 10-year-old boy.

So just what was the mystery bird?

The ancient legends and lore of native peoples throughout North America tell of gigantic vultures or eagles known as thunderbirds. Moreover, in modern times, numerous people in the western USA and Canada have claimed to have seen vulture-like birds with wing-spans of truly colossal proportions – monstrous creatures that would surely be capable of carrying away children, and which readily recall the mythical thunderbirds, yet which cannot be identified with any bird known to be alive today.

For instance, on 10 April 1948 at Overland in Illinois, Clyde Smith, his wife and their friend Les Bacon saw in the sky a huge flying object that they assumed to be a dark-grey aeroplane, until it flapped its wings! Only then did they realize that it was actually a gigantic bird with a wing-span of well over 6 metres (20 feet) – twice that of any living bird recognized by science.

An even closer encounter took place in May 1961, when a New York businessman, piloting his light aircraft along the Hudson Valley River, was buzzed by a bird of stupendous size, soaring close by without flapping its wings. When recalling this hair-raising incident to a local newspaper, he said that the bird behaved "like a fighter plane making a pass".

In his book *Amazing Indeed*, naturalist Robert Lyman mentioned that he had seen one of these birds standing in the middle of a road near Coudersport, Pennsylvania, with its narrow wings outstretched. It stood upright and was about 1 metre (3–4 feet) tall, its plumage was brownish, and its neck and legs were short, but its wings were immense, spanning the entire width of the road. When the bird saw him, it took off; and when Lyman measured the width of the road, he found it to be nearly 7.6 metres (25 feet)!

Many zoologists dismiss such reports as fantasy – even from observers as knowledgeable as fellow naturalists and pilots – but some are less sceptical. This is because only a few millennia ago, birds fitting these creatures' description really did exist in North America. They were huge vulture-like species, with wing-spans ranging from 3.5–5 metres (11–17 feet) and, very aptly, they are known as teratorns, which translates as "monster birds".

Moreover, a mere 5 million years ago, the biggest teratorn of all time was still alive and well in South America – a true monster of a bird known as *Argentavis magnificens* ("magnificent Argentine bird"), whose wing-span did indeed attain an incredible 7–7.6 metres (23–25 feet).

Could such creatures have somehow survived to the present day, inhabiting remote mountain ranges beyond the reach of modern humans and thus remaining undiscovered by science, but observed by native Americans, inspiring their thunderbird legends? If so, there is little doubt that they would readily explain the giant birds currently being reported in this part of the world. And if, through evolution, their feet had become much stronger than those of their fossil ancestors, modern-day teratorns could also explain reports of child-kidnapping by unexplained winged abductors.

Was Marlon Lowe's kidnapper a living fossil – a prehistoric terror awaiting official resurrection by means of scientific recognition of its reality? Until a body of one of these gigantic birds is obtained, or at least until more detailed sightings are made, who can say? It is not very likely, however, that such evidence will be forthcoming in the foreseeable future. After all, if something that seemed to be a rapidly approaching aeroplane suddenly flapped its wings, how many people would stay around long enough to see what it did next?

✵

LEVIATHANS OF LAKE AND RIVER

North America's foremost freshwater mystery beast is undoubtedly Champ, the long-necked, horse-headed monster of Lake Champlain. Sandwiched between New York and Vermont, but extending as far north as the southern tip of Quebec, this immense lake is 175 kilometres (109 miles) long and up to 18 kilometres (11 miles) wide in places.

Inevitably, any attempt to seek even the biggest of monsters in such a sizeable body of water is rather like looking for a moving needle in an extremely large haystack, but this has not deterred investigators from taking up the challenge. Champ's most diligent researcher must surely be Joseph Zarzynski, whose Lake Champlain Phenomena Investigation and definitive book *Champ: Beyond the Legend* have been instrumental in revealing a wealth of important information.

Yet Champ is not a recent phenomenon. Zarzynski has pointed out that reports of an immense aquatic beast inhabiting the lake date back centuries, to when the Iroquois people controlling Lake Champlain's western shore spoke of a huge water-dwelling snake with horns called the chaousarou. By the late 1880s the "Lake Champlain sea serpent", as it was then referred to, had gained its own popular niche in local lore and media accounts, and by the 1970s Champ had become familiar to the international cryptozoological community. Almost 300 eyewitness accounts were on Zarzynski's files by the late 1980s, but at present the most famous piece of evidence remains the Mansi photograph.

On 5 July 1977, Sandra Mansi and her husband Anthony saw what they believe to have been the monster from a distance of 30–45 metres (100–150 feet), somewhere around St Albans, Vermont. Sandra managed to take a colour photograph of it before it submerged. This revealed a dark back, and a long upright neck with a dark head looking away from the camera.

When the photo was analysed by Professor Paul LeBlond, an expert in wave dynamics from the University of British Columbia's Department of Oceanography, he estimated that the lower and upper limits for the portion of the animal *depicted* range from 4.8–17.5 metres (16 feet to 57 feet 4 inches). In other words, this does not include the portion of the animal hidden beneath the water surface, which indicates that whatever it is, Champ is truly of monstrous proportions.

The most popular identity for Champ is a living plesiosaur (as with Nessie, see p.15), which is supported by the morphology of the Mansi photograph's

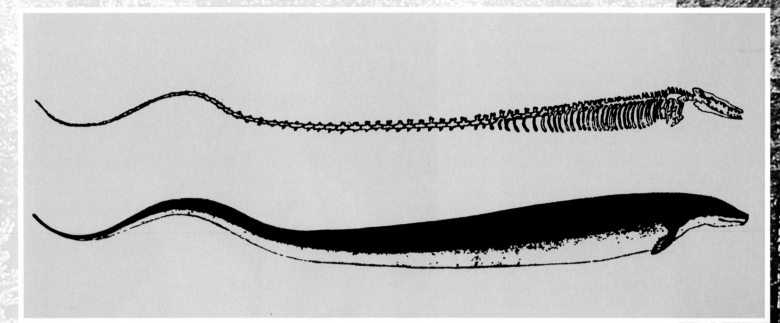

Zeuglodonts – vertically undulating aquatic mammals, like this BASILOSAURUS – are thought to have become extinct some 25 million years ago.

mysterious subject. Not all of North America's lake monsters, however, fit this description.

Very different from Champ is Ogopogo, from Lake Okanagan in British Columbia, Canada. This water monster owes its name, somewhat bizarrely, to an English music-hall song from 1924, entitled "The Ogo-Pogo – The Funny Fox-Trot", which tells of a pixie-headed, banjo-playing monster from Hindustan! As with Champ, however, it had long been known to the native Americans, and the local Okanakane nation called it the naitaka ("lake monster").

Ogopogo eyewitnesses describe an exceedingly elongate, serpentine creature, whose sheep-like head has two ear-like projections, and which undulates vertically, flexing its dark body into a series of perpendicular hoops, as it swims rapidly through the water. Occasionally a forked tail is also seen. Some sightings have been made at relatively close range, but none so close as that of Mrs B. Clark – for while she was swimming near Lake Okanagan's southern shore one morning in mid-July 1974, the monster quite literally bumped into her!

Mrs Clark felt something big and heavy make contact with her legs, and when she looked round she saw a 2.5-metre- (8-foot) long coil or hump, 1.2 metres (4 feet) above the water,

travelling north, away from her, in a slow, leisurely manner. As the water was very clear, she could see a dark-grey body and striped back beneath the surface, with a forked horizontal tail, resembling that of a whale, positioned 1.5–3 metres (5–10 feet) behind the hump. As the hump descended, the tail rose, until its flukes poked up through the surface. She estimated the creature to be 7.6–9 metres (25–30 feet) long, but only 0.9–1.2 metres (3–4 feet) across. Its skin was smooth and hairless. According to Mrs Clark, "this thing looked and acted more like a whale than a fish, but I have never seen a whale that skinny and snaky-looking before … it was definitely not reptilian, and I'm sure it wasn't a fish".

This description corresponds very closely with the predicted appearance in life of the zeuglodonts – those "officially extinct" serpentine whales also proposed by cryptozoologists as a likely identity for the Irish horse-eels (see p.16). Whereas snakes and eels undulate horizontally, zeuglodonts, like other aquatic mammals, would have undulated vertically, matching the many eyewitness reports of Ogopogo. Equally, their tails would have been horizontal, like Ogopogo's, whereas those of fishes and aquatic reptiles are vertical.

Similar in form to Ogopogo is Manipogo, of Lake Manitoba in Canada. This monster came to

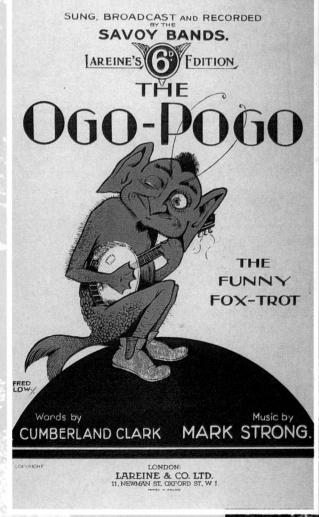

Unique amongst water monsters, the Ogopogo is named after an English music-hall song of the 1920s.

widespread attention on 12 August 1962 when fishermen John Konefell and Richard Vincent photographed what they described as "a large black snake or eel", swimming 45–70 metres (50–75 yards) away from their motorboat. They claimed that about 3.5 metres (12 feet) of the monster's elongate body was visible above the water, and in their photo it resembles a slender black arch, raised *over* the water surface, with a horizontal portion leading from it on each side.

In 1941, Slimy Slim of Lake Payette in Idaho hit the headlines with a flurry of sightings, including one by auditor Thomas L. Rogers, who likened its head to that of a snub-nosed crocodile and estimated its length to be around 11 metres (35 feet) as it undulated through the water.

One final freshwater mystery beast of note from North America is the White River monster seen at Newport, Arkansas. It has inspired many suggested identities, from an alligator garfish, or the world's largest stickleback, to a wandering specimen of the elephant seal. This last-mentioned identity has been proposed by eminent cryptozoologist Professor Roy Mackal. He noted that this giant seal – normally inhabiting the coasts of California and Mexico – might occasionally reach the Gulf of Mexico, enter the mouth of the Mississippi, of which the White River is a major branch, and follow it through to this river.

BIGFOOT

North America's premier mystery beast is unquestionably the bigfoot (sasquatch in Canada) – a giant ape-like creature that walks on its hind legs and has been reported from dense forested regions throughout this continent, but especially from the north-west.

Usually said to stand 1.8–3 metres (6–10 feet) tall and weigh 320–1135 kg (700–2500 lb), the bigfoot, or sasquatch, is habitually bipedal, and has dark skin covered in black or auburn hair. Its face is ape-like with a sloping brow, prominent eyebrow ridges, light-reflecting eyes (usually a nocturnal

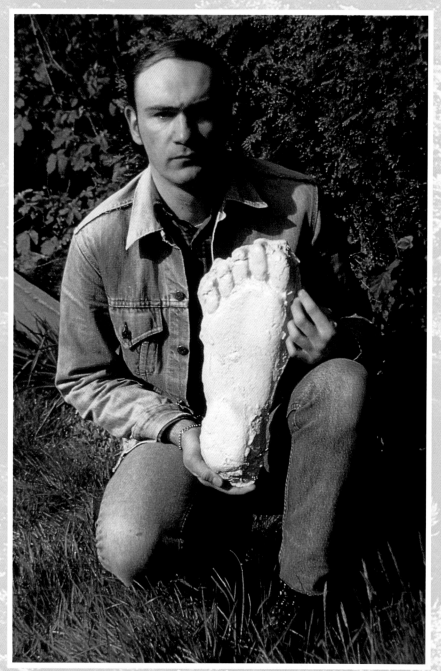

Giant humanoid footprints are a common source of bigfoot evidence. Dr Karl Shuker holds the cast of a print discovered at Grays Harbour, Washington State, in 1982.

adaptation), broad flattened nose and lipless slitted mouth. It has a powerful, muscular chest, very long arms whose paw-like hands have thick fingers and hairless palms, sturdy muscular legs, and no tail. As its name suggests, the bigfoot has very large feet, leaving prints 30–55 cm (12–22 inches) long, with two pads beneath the first toe on each foot.

Over the years, a few intriguing variations upon this basic morphological theme have been reported. In Florida, whose Everglade swamps are reputedly home to a particularly malodorous version of the bigfoot known

evocatively as the skunk ape, strange three-toed footprints have been found, which are very different from the normal five-toed versions. And during the 1960s, many sightings were reported in the Yakima area of Washington state of an extraordinary white bigfoot with reddish eyes; if authentic, could this be an albino bigfoot?

In general, however, the bigfoot bears a strong resemblance to the dzu-teh or giant yeti (pp.115–116). As already discussed, it may well share a common origin and identity with the giant yeti – namely, a surviving

An image of a bigfoot – or of a man in a suit? Like much bigfoot evidence, Roger Patterson's film shot in October 1967 is controversial.

population of the supposedly long-extinct giant primate *Gigantopithecus*, which may have crossed from its known Asian homeland into the New World while the land-bridge connecting Siberia and Alaska still existed.

It must be said that few mystery beasts have a history so bedevilled by hoaxes and controversy as that of the bigfoot. Indeed, virtually every piece of evidence put forward by investigators for the existence of this animal has ultimately been scientifically discredited.

Take, for instance, the well-known film that purportedly portrays a bigfoot seen at Bluff Creek, northern California. This film was shot by Roger Patterson on 20 October 1967 in the company of fellow rancher Bob Gimlin, after allegedly encountering the creature squatting by the river. They had been travelling on horseback, and the horses may have startled the bigfoot, because it suddenly stood up and strode away on its hind legs, glancing back at the two men before disappearing into a forest. Patterson ran after it, shooting with a hand-held 16-millimetre cinecamera. The resulting film, although short and shaky, clearly revealed the creature's conical head, pendulous breasts, dark-brown fur and ape-like form.

Eminent anthropologist Professor Grover Krantz, from Washington State

University, believes that the Patterson film is genuine, stating that a human wearing a bigfoot suit could not achieve the muscle movements and precise striding gait performed by the creature. On the other hand, some special effects film people claim that it is common knowledge in Hollywood that the Bluff Creek bigfoot was a man in a suit. Yet when bigfoot researcher John Green contacted experts at the Disney Studio – always at the forefront of cinematic special effects – for their opinion as to whether the techniques for creating such a film were available in 1967, they told him that they could not have duplicated it at that time.

Also contentious as evidence are the familiar giant humanoid footprints that have often been found following bigfoot sightings in a given area. Some are so detailed that they even exhibit dermatoglyphs (fingerprints). This is the case with those discovered near Tiger Creek in the northern part of Oregon's Blue Mountains by forest patrolman Paul Freeman on 10 June 1982 after spying a 2.5-metre- (8-foot) tall bigfoot close by. Certainly, it would be very difficult to hoax such detailed prints as these. Nevertheless, some very sophisticated instances of chicanery involving bigfoot prints have already been exposed.

Moreover, in an article published by *The Anomalist* in spring 1995, Loren Coleman claims that the highly publicized finding of some 40-cm- (16-inch) long bigfoot prints by workmen at Bluff Creek in 1958 was probably the result of a prank. What makes this so significant, if true, is that reports of such creatures in the USA had previously been few and far between. Not only that, this was the case that earned the creature its name of bigfoot. Hence if this pivotal episode is indeed founded upon a hoax, how dependable are the countless bigfoot sightings and numerous discoveries of giant footprints found in the USA since then?

Hair samples and faecal droppings have also been collected, but these generally turn out to be from other animals, or even of man-made composition. For example, the alleged samples of bigfoot hair obtained during 1987–88 in the Blue Mountains of Washington and Oregon were revealed

by physicist Edward Winn in 1991 to be synthetic modacrylic fibres.

It is not surprising, perhaps, that some bigfoot researchers are beginning to wonder whether there is any convincing evidence at all for the reality of the US bigfoot! In contrast, it remains feasible that Canada's counterpart, the sasquatch, is indeed a valid mystery beast. Here, native American traditions of the creature date back several centuries, as does its name, and there are some very intriguing artefacts associated with these traditions.

These include a sasquatch mask carved from red cedar and dating from 1850–70, which was originally worn by the Niska branch of the Tsimshian nation in British Columbia. Now housed in Harvard University's Peabody Museum, it is the oldest known Canadian sasquatch mask. By offering the closest match to eyewitness descriptions of the creature, it is also the most realistic; other sasquatch masks on record from this region are noticeably stylized.

The bigfoot is dead, long live the sasquatch? Only further researches will tell.

✶

A SURFEIT OF SEA SERPENTS

In early July 1937, the body of a sperm whale brought into Naden Harbour whaling station in Canada's Queen Charlotte Islands was opened up and revealed the carcase of an extraordinary creature inside its voluminous stomach. Although the ingested animal was decomposed, it was still very distinctive. As photographs later revealed, it was 3–3.6 metres (10–12 feet) in total length, had a large camel-like head with downturned muzzle, a long neck, a slender serpentine body with two projections resembling forelimbs, and a fringed tail-like section at the end of its body that may have comprised a pair of hind flippers. Its strange-looking carcase was later discarded, which in the opinion of zoologist Dr Ed Bousfield from the Royal British Columbia

In the nineteenth century, a sea-monster sighting off the Massachusetts coast inspired this vivid artist's impression.

Museum and oceanographer Professor Paul LeBlond from the University of British Columbia was a terrible tragedy. For they believe that this was the corpse of a juvenile Caddy – the popular nickname of a mysterious marine animal known formally as the Cadboro Bay sea serpent, often sighted in the vicinity of Vancouver Island.

As is also true of various North American lake monsters, Caddy has been reported for a long time: the native Chinook nation knew it well, referring to it as the hiachuckaluck. However, it was not until 1933, when it was dubbed "Cadborosaurus" by a local newspaper editor called Archie Wills, that Canada's Western inhabitants became widely

aware of their unusual maritime monster. In recent years, however, reported sightings have increased. One of the most intriguing of these took place on 14 July 1993, when pilots Don Berends and James Wells, flying a Cessna float plane, spied two greyish-blue Caddys together in Saanich Inlet.

When the pilots landed their plane on the surface of the water, the two Caddys swam rapidly away, flexing their bodies into vertical hoops (rather than solid humps) beneath which the pilots could see daylight. Hence they were evidently very slender and serpentine in shape.

It is possible that the pilots disturbed a Caddy mating session, because Dr Bousfield's extensive Caddy researches

indicate that during July (and also late June) this elusive species uses Saanich Inlet as a breeding zone. It is also possible that live young are born at night on beaches.

On 20 April 1995, in the scientific journal *Amphipacifica*, Bousfield and LeBlond published a formal account of Caddy, which they christened *Cadborosaurus willsi*, and provisionally categorized as an undetermined but highly specialized species of reptile. Very few reptiles, however, have ever been able to flex their bodies vertically when swimming. In contrast, the serpent-like zeuglodont whales could have achieved this, and some cryptozoologists (including myself) consider a surviving species of zeuglodont to be a more satisfactory identity for Caddy. Unless another sperm whale disgorges the contents of its stomach, however, we may never obtain the necessary physical evidence with which to learn the truth.

The most famous sea serpent reported recently from the coasts of the United States is another elongate, zeuglodont-type mystery beast, this time from Maryland's Chesapeake Bay, on the Atlantic coast. It first attracted international attention in 1978, when 30 eyewitnesses claimed to have seen a snake-like monster in the Potomac River, near Chesapeake Bay, and was soon afterwards called "Chessie" by reporters. The pace of developments

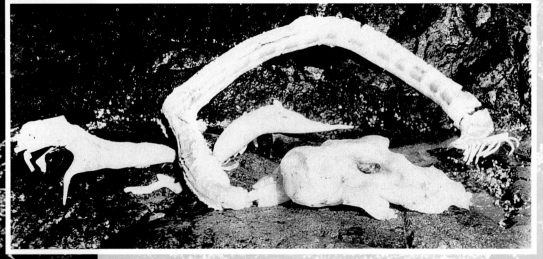

Postcard depicting an unusual marine carcase, possibly of a Caddy, that was found on the beach at Camp Fircom, British Columbia, on 4 October 1936.

quickened in 1982, when Chessie was videoed for three minutes by Robert Frew from his home at Love Point, overlooking the bay, during the early evening of 21 May and at a distance of about 60 metres (200 feet). His wife and two friends saw it too, as it dived and resurfaced near a group of swimmers.

According to Robert Frew, the creature was 9–10.5 metres (30–35 feet) long, but less than 30 cm (1 foot) across, with a series of humps. His film showed three principal surfacings, revealing a head or foot projecting at the front end.

The film was analysed at the Smithsonian Institution in August 1982 but no firm conclusion as to its subject's identity was reached. All seven of the participating scientists, however, gained the strong impression that it was a living object.

ARE THERE GIANTS IN THE EARTH?

Stories abound of gigantic human skeletons or other remains unearthed in various parts of North America. In November 1856, for instance, several local newspapers included detailed accounts of a decayed human skeleton claimed by eyewitnesses to be 3.28 metres (10 feet 9 inches) tall, which had been exposed by some labourers while ploughing Sheriff Wickham's vineyard in East Wheeling, now in West Virginia. It was soon dismissed as a hoax, however, when one of the newspapers announced that three bullets had been found in its skull. Yet these "bullets" were not described; hence they might simply have been lead or copper pellets. And there is still the identity of the giant bones themselves to consider. Sadly, however, the final resting place of this earthly giant is unknown, so we are unlikely to discover the truth.

The skeleton of a 3.6-metre- (12-foot) tall goliath was revealed at Lompock Rancho, California, in 1833 by soldiers digging a pit for a powder magazine. This specimen was further distinguished by its remarkable double row of teeth and by the abundance of huge stone axes, carved shells, and porphyry blocks bearing abstruse symbols associated with it. The skeleton and artefacts were secretly reburied, and their locality "lost", when locals began venerating them.

In 1911, several mummified remains of mysterious red-haired humans ranging from 2–2.5 metres (6½ feet to over 8 feet) tall were disinterred in Lovelock Cave, 112 kilometres (70 miles) north-east of Reno, Nevada, by a guano mining operation. These substantiated the local Piute Indians' legends of such people, which they called the Si-Te-Cahs. Yet scientists proved oddly reluctant to investigate these remains and eventually most of the bones were simply discarded by the miners. What was left was salvaged by various local people, only for most of it to be destroyed in a fire. Happily, however, one of the giant Lovelock skulls, almost 30 cm (1 foot) tall, is preserved with some related bones and artefacts at the Humboldt Museum in Winnemucca, Nevada, and various Lovelock artefacts are also held at the Nevada State Historical Society's museum at Reno.

The most distinctive American giants, however, were found in the 1880s at Tioga Point, near Sayre in Bradford County, Pennsylvania, as Robert Lyman recounted in *Forbidden Land*:

> *Dr G.P. Donehoo, State Historian and a former minister of the Presbyterian Church in Coudersport, together with Prof. A.B. Skinner of the American Investigating Museum, and Prof. W.K. Morehead of Phillips Andover Academy, uncovered an Indian mound. They found the bones of 68 men which were believed to have been buried about the year 1200. The average height of these men was seven feet, while many were much taller. On some of the skulls, two inches above the perfectly formed forehead, were protuberances of bone, evidently horns that had been there since birth. Some of the specimens were sent to the American Investigating Museum.*

One might expect that giant human skeletons with horned skulls could not be overlooked or forgotten. Yet according to Jim Brandon's book *Weird America*, no one at the museum has any knowledge of these specimens – which must surely rate as something of a mystery in itself!

Goliath: stories of giants exist in many cultures.

Giant skull, rare surviving evidence of the Lovelock Cave discovery.

THE FLORIDA GLOBSTER – A GIGANTIC OCTOPUS?

On 30 November 1896, Herbert Coles and Dunham Coretter were cycling along Anastasia Beach near St Augustine in eastern Florida when they spotted the decomposing carcase of a huge sea creature, half-buried in the sands. Resembling a gigantic pear-shaped sack, pale pink in colour, the carcase was 5.5 metres (18 feet) long, 3 metres (10 feet) across, just over 1 metre (3½ feet) thick, and was estimated to weigh 5–7 tonnes. It also bore seven arm-like structures, six of which ranged in length from around 7 metres (23 feet) to over 11 metres (almost 37 feet), despite being incomplete; the seventh was just a stump, no more than 1.2 metres (4 feet) long. The next day, the carcase was examined by local surgeon Dr DeWitt Webb, who later took photos of it. Before the end of 1896, the waves

had carried it back out to sea. Shortly afterwards it was beached again, but by then it no longer had any arms.

Webb and other eyewitnesses were convinced that this was the corpse of a truly colossal octopus, and after reading Webb's accounts Yale University zoologist Professsor Addison Emery Verrill agreed with them. Verrill believed that in life this monstrous creature had weighed 18–20 tonnes, and that the span of its tentacles had reached 45–60 metres (150–200 feet), i.e. almost seven times greater than that of the world's largest officially recognized species of octopus! Consequently, he formally named this Floridian colossus *Octopus giganteus*.

A little later, however, Verrill examined some samples of the carcase's tissues, preserved by Webb, and announced that these resembled whale blubber. As a result, he retracted his identification of the creature as a giant octopus, claiming instead that the carcase was merely the upper portion of a sperm whale's head. Apart from some bottled remains stored in the Smithsonian Institution, for several decades afterwards it was as if the Florida globster (the informal name by which it is now widely known) had

never existed – until 1957, that is.

This was when its controversial history was revived in a published account by Florida Marineland curator Forrest G. Wood, which in turn led to a histological re-examination of its preserved tissues by cytobiologist Dr Joseph Gennaro from Florida University. In 1971, his findings were made public and aroused great interest, for according to Gennaro the globster's remains contained connective tissue similar if not identical to that of octopuses.

This restoration of the Florida globster as a giant octopus was consolidated in 1986 by protein analyses conducted by biochemist Professor Roy P. Mackal at Chicago University. These revealed that its tissues were composed principally of the connective protein collagen, as would be expected from a very large aquatic invertebrate. Moreover, the specific proportions of certain amino acids comprising this collagen were closer to those of octopuses than any other animals studied by Mackal, including their relatives the squids.

All of this suggested that Verrill's initial identification had been correct after all. Then, in April 1995, a team of zoologists from Maryland University led by Professor Sidney K. Pierce revealed the results of their own recent microscopical and biochemical study of the globster's tissues. According to these, the specific chemical composition of the collagen was mammalian, thereby bringing the sperm whale identity back into contention.

However, as Dr Gennaro later pointed out, for many years the globster's tissue samples had been stored in an unknown preservative, which may well have distorted their chemical composition, thus rendering impossible a conclusive identification of the globster.

In any event, these samples are not the only evidence to consider when reflecting upon the possible reality of gigantic octopuses. There are many compelling eyewitness accounts on file concerning the existence of such creatures in several oceanic regions, notably around the Bahamas, Bermuda and Kiribati (formerly the Gilbert Islands).

One of Dr DeWitt Webb's photographs of the dead sea creature subsequently known as the "Florida globster".

THE ICEMAN COMETH ... AND GOETH!

In mid December 1968, cryptozoologists Dr Bernard Heuvelmans and Ivan T. Sanderson visited a farm near Winona, Minnesota, and gazed into a glass-topped refrigerated coffin to observe, sketch and photograph what was destined to become one of the most controversial of all mystery creatures. Entombed within the ice was a male humanoid figure, 1.78 metres (5 feet 10 inches) tall, and lying on its back. Distinguishing it from any typical human figure, however, were its oval (rather than hourglass) torso, its extensive covering of hair (comparable to that of the gorilla and chimpanzee), its conspicuously long and sturdy fingers and toes, very long arms and noticeably large hands and feet. Further inspection by the two cryptozoologists revealed that the strange entity had been shot: the bullet's passage had dislodged its left eye from its socket and had blown away the back of its head.

Nicknamed "the iceman", it had been exhibited in a touring sideshow by the show's proprietor Frank Hansen, who had invited the two scientists to his farm for a private viewing. Hansen claimed, however, that the iceman was not his, but was instead owned by an anonymous, reclusive millionaire. As to its origin, Hansen gave several different answers, ranging from a party of Soviet whalers finding it floating in its block of ice within Kamchatka's Sea of Okhotsk, to Hansen himself shooting it in a Minnesota forest.

At first, the scientific community was intrigued by this enigmatic ice-entombed being, which seemed to resemble Neanderthal man, believed extinct for at least 30,000 years. Indeed, in a formal scientific paper published in 1969, Heuvelmans christened it *Homo pongoides* ("ape-like man"). He believed, and still believes today, that it was a modern-day Neanderthal – probably shot in Vietnam where reports of ape-men often occur, and then smuggled into the United States in one of the "body bags" being used to bring back the bodies of American soldiers killed during the Vietnam war. However, when the FBI allegedly became interested in the iceman, presumably because it was a humanoid entity that had been shot, Hansen withdrew it from display for a time.

When it reappeared, he announced that this was not the original iceman but a model of it. Certainly, the "new" iceman was visibly different from the original one. Such a substitution, however, was hardly likely to enhance its claims for credibility, and scientists began to propose that the original iceman was probably also a model. Indeed, in 1981 it was alleged that expert model-maker Howard Ball had personally constructed it. Heuvelmans, on the other hand, is adamant that the corpse he and Sanderson examined in its icy coffin was genuine and he recalls that they could even detect the odour of rotting flesh filtering up through the ice. The second iceman, the known model, is still being exhibited today, but the mysterious original has never been seen again. Was it, too, just a model, a clever hoax? Or was it the zoological discovery of all time? Sadly, it is unlikely that we shall ever know.

Ivan T. Sanderson made this sketch of "the iceman" in 1968. Long arms and large hands and feet are conspicuous features.

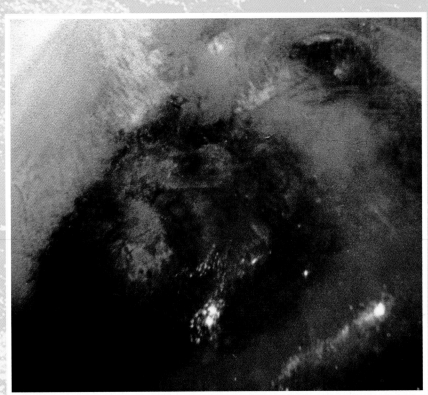

An ape-like humanoid: was "the iceman" a modern-day Neanderthal?

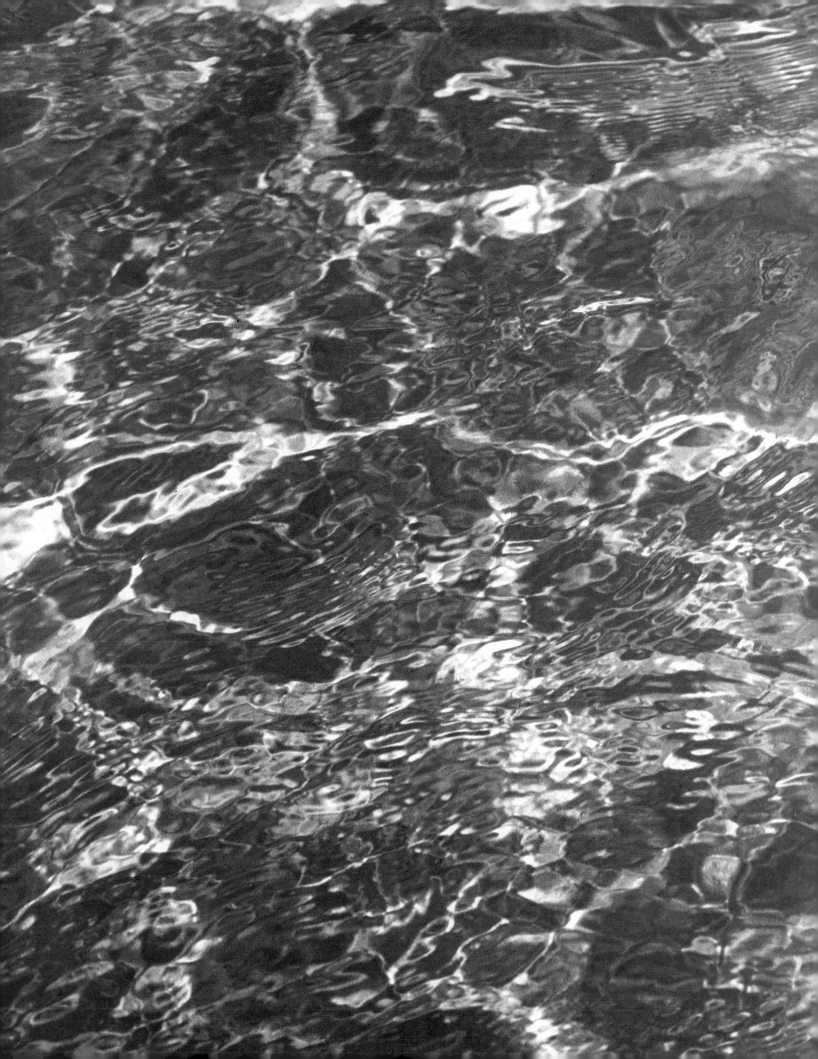

Continents, Coincidences and Curiosities

ATLANTIS

In his books *Timaeus* and *Critias*, the famous philosopher Plato (c.428–c.348 BC) wrote of a vast island continent called Atlantis. Believed to be situated to the west of the Pillars of Hercules (the Straits of Gibraltar) and originally inhabited by a highly advanced civilization, it had been destroyed over nine thousand years earlier by violent earthquakes and floods. This had occurred within the space of a single day and night, and the continent had sunk beneath the depths of the seas. According to Plato, his sources for this account were the works of an Athenian scholar called Solon, who had learnt of it when he visited priests and archives (now lost) in Egypt in c.600 BC.

Since then, numerous theories have been aired regarding the erstwhile locality of Atlantis. Suggestions have included such far-flung, varyingly feasible sites as Greenland, Spitzbergen, Malta, the Azores, Anatolia, Mongolia, Sweden, Heligoland, Nigeria, Mexico, Brazil and South Africa.

Naturally, one might expect that the most reasonable site for Atlantis would be in the mid-Atlantic. Yet there has been no geological upheaval consistent with the sinking of a continental land mass here for at least several million years.

In academic circles, one of the most popular theories is that Plato's account was inspired by the relatively abrupt collapse of Crete's once-mighty Minoan empire and that this had been caused by the cataclysmic volcanic explosion of the Aegean island of Thera, whose modern-day remnant is Santorini. Yet researchers concede that there are many

Plato's account of Atlantis was based on ancient Egyptian sources.

notable discrepancies between Crete's history and Plato's account of Atlantis – not least of which is that Atlantis supposedly vanished nine thousand years before Solon's time, whereas Thera was destroyed a mere nine hundred years before. In any case, there is no certainty that Thera's eruption and the Minoan civilization's collapse

was a direct cause-and-effect situation.

In 1968, however, a dramatically new Atlantean locality was revealed – and not in the Mediterranean, but within the Atlantic Ocean itself. The location was the Bahamas, where a local diver called Bonefish Sam showed Dr J. Manson Valentine – a Miami zoologist who was also a keen amateur archaeologist – an underwater anomaly well known to local tourist guides and fishermen but seemingly unknown to scientists. Nowadays known as the Bimini Road (though more similar to a low wall), it was situated in shallow water at Paradise Point, about a kilometre (half a mile) to the west of North Bimini Island, and in the words of Valentine, it comprised:

... an extensive pavement of rectangular and polygonal flat stones of varying size and thickness, obviously shaped and accurately aligned to form a convincing artifactual pattern ... Some were absolutely rectangular and some approaching perfect squares.

The longest row of these stones (each stone weighing between one and ten tonnes) ran for nearly 500 metres (1600 feet) and ended in a 90 degree bend. Nevertheless, not everyone shared Valentine's belief that the Bimini Road was of human construction. In 1970, archaeologist Professor John Hall from Miami University pointed out that

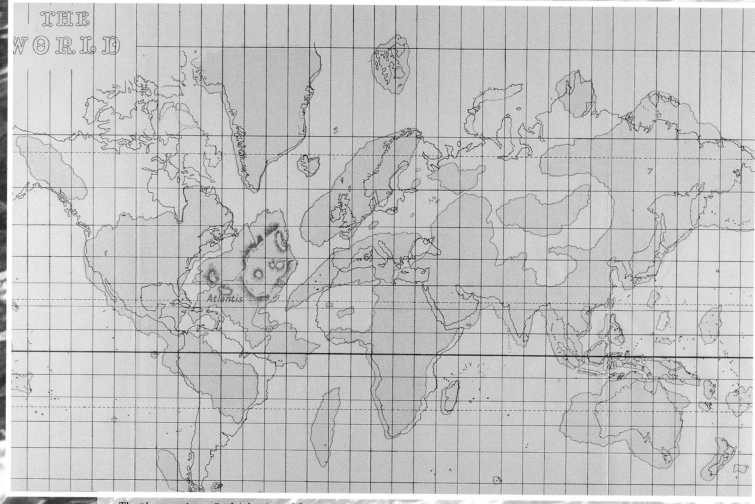

*The "lost continents" of Atlantis and Lemuria particularly interested the Theosophical Society (see page 89), which published this map in W. Scott Elliott's **The Story of Atlantis and the Lost Lemuria** (1896).*

layers of rock with regular block-like fractures like the Bimini examples can be formed by natural means and constitute a well-documented phenomenon known as Pleistocene beach-rock erosion and cracking.

However, the Bimini Road was not the only unexpected discovery made in this area of the Bahamian sea-bed. In 1975, Dr David D. Zink, author of *The Stones of Atlantis*, discovered a stone building block containing an unequivocally man-made tongue-and-groove joint. And several fluted marble columns have been found here by Count Pino Turolla (yet marble is not native to the Bahamas). Sceptics of the Atlantis theory have dismissed these discoveries as ballast from historically recent shipwrecks (noting the presence nearby of a modern-day packing crate).

Even so, there is still no conclusive evidence that ballast formed from items such as these has ever been utilized. As for the Bimini Road, there is a theory that can combine both of the opposing views. What if this structure is indeed of natural origin, but was purposefully used by a vanished race of people? In 1970, Dr R. Cedric Leonard explored some enigmatic temple-like ruins sighted off Andros Island, near Bimini. Investigations of Bimini's underwater mysteries are still continuing: one day their true story may finally be known.

Perhaps the most intriguing correlation between this site and Atlantis derives from the many Atlantis-related predictions made by the famous American psychic Edgar Cayce, for these include the following prophecy:

A portion of the temples [of Atlantis] may yet be discovered under the slime of ages of sea water near Bimini ... Expect it in '68 and '69; not so far away!

Cayce died in 1945, more than 20 years before the discovery of the Bimini Road – in 1968.

JAMES DEAN – RIDDLES OF A REBEL'S DEATH

It was a September evening in 1955, and Alec Guinness, destined to become one of Britain's greatest stars of stage and screen, had arrived in Los Angeles to make his first Hollywood film, *The Swan*. While looking for a table at a restaurant, he and his companion, scriptwriter Thelma Moss, met a 24-year-old American actor in jeans and a sweatshirt who invited them to join him. First of all, however, he asked them to come and see something, which proved to be a shining, silver-coloured racing car, a Porsche 550 Spyder, that he had just bought and was his pride and joy. It was certainly very eyecatching, but for

James Dean (left) with Rock Hudson and Elizabeth Taylor at a 1955 Hollywood press lunch to publicize **Giant**, *the film he completed just days before his death. Inset: Jimmy's car, a Porsche 550 Spyder, which he nicknamed "Little Bastard".*

some inexplicable reason Guinness felt uneasy. As he recalled many years later in his autobiography *Blessings in Disguise*, he couldn't shake off the feeling that there was something sinister about it.

Suddenly, almost as if he were someone else, merely listening to the words, rather than being the person actually uttering them, Guinness found himself earnestly asking this young fair-haired actor never to get into the car. As he spoke, Guinness looked at his watch, and then said: "It is now ten o'clock, Friday the 23rd of September, 1955. If you get in that car you will be found dead in it by this time next week."

A little startled, the youth laughed, and Guinness apologized for his strange outburst. Seven days later, however,

shortly before six o'clock on the evening of 30 September, his unnerving prediction was fulfilled: during the hours that followed, Guinness and the whole world would be stunned to learn of the young actor's untimely death, killed instantly in a collision with a black Ford limousine near the tiny Californian town of Cholame while driving his new silver car to a race at Salinas.

The actor's name? James Dean.

Guinness was not alone in feeling uneasy about Jimmy's car. A few days before Jimmy set off in it, on what would prove to be his final drive, Ursula Andress, a former girlfriend, pleaded with him to change his mind: "I feel something about it. Don't go!" Jimmy asked her to accompany him, but she refused. That was the last time she saw him alive.

These are just two of many eerie coincidences linked with the tragic death of one of the most charismatic actors of all time, who seemed destined to become one of the greatest actors too, until he lost his life while driving what proved to be a singularly ill-fated car. For Jimmy was only the first of many to experience what has been dubbed "the curse" of his Porsche Spyder, which more than lived up to Jimmy's own name for it, "Little Bastard".

After Jimmy's death, car customizer George Barris purchased the crushed wreck of "Little Bastard" to salvage any parts that had not been damaged in the crash. As it was being unloaded in his garage, however, it somehow fell off its platform and hit one of his mechanics, breaking the man's leg. Shortly

Wreckage from the accident in which Jimmy was killed; "Little Bastard" survived in various forms, causing further catastrophes.

afterwards, a sports car driver bought two of its tyres and fitted them to his own vehicle: while he was driving it, both tyres inexplicably burst, the car skidded off the road and its driver was almost killed.

In October 1956, "Little Bastard" was directly involved in three separate accidents that took place in a single race at Pomona, California. The car being driven by one of the competitors, a surgeon called Dr William Eschrich, had recently been fitted with the engine from "Little Bastard". During that race, Eschrich barely escaped serious injury when his car overturned on a bend. Standing nearby at the time was policeman Bob Miller, who was hit in the face by one of Eschrich's wheels when it flew off in the accident. Tragically, physician Dr Troy McHenry was not so lucky as Eschrich and Miller. The back swinging arms holding his car's rear-end were from "Little Bastard", and during this same race he was killed instantly when his car unexpectedly went out of control and smashed into a tree.

Several months later, lorry driver George Barkuis was transporting "Little Bastard" when his truck ran off the road. Nevertheless, he was saved from certain death by being thrown clear – only to be killed when this deadly car fell on top of him. And in a further incident, "Little Bastard" was one of many cars contained inside a garage that mysteriously caught fire. All of the cars were gutted, except for "Little Bastard", which was virtually unscathed.

In 1960, while travelling back to Barris by train from a show in Miami, "Little Bastard" vanished, apparently stolen. Thus the chain of catastrophes associated with this jinxed car was finally at an end – or was it? After all, what happened to the thief who stole "Little Bastard"? Did he live long enough to enjoy his ill-gotten (and ill-starred) prize, I wonder?

In the years since James Dean's death, countless unsubstantiated stories of a supernatural, sensationalistic nature have circulated. These include claims that people have been contacted by Jimmy from beyond the grave, that he was not really killed but was severely disfigured and was smuggled away to a secret clinic, and even that his ghost has been seen driving a spectral "Little Bastard" along that ill-fated stretch of road near Cholame in a recurring repetition of his fatal crash, ending with the sounds of the collision. Make of such tales what you will.

What *is* fully substantiated is that Jimmy was well known for his quirky sense of humour, often wilfully dark, to shock and startle. When photographer Dennis Stock accompanied him in February 1955 on a visit to Fairmount, Indiana, where he had spent much of his youth, Jimmy decided to pose for some photos lying in an open coffin at Hunt's Funeral Parlour. In a picture taken by Sanford Roth, another photographer friend, he placed his head in a noose, and hung limply from it, as if his neck were broken. Presumably it is just an unpleasant coincidence that Jimmy's next (and final) return to Fairmount would also feature him inside a coffin at Hunt's Funeral Parlour, but this time as a corpse – with a broken neck.

Jimmy's razor-sharp, laconic wit, coupled with his passion for contemplation and analysis, have yielded a fund of memorable quotes, but for poignant accuracy few can match the line ad-libbed by him during an interview for a road safety television commercial, filmed less than a fortnight before his death. At the end of the commercial, the interviewer asked him for any advice to offer the viewers. Modifying his scripted reply, Jimmy quipped: "Take it easy driving. The life you might save might be *mine!*" Who could have believed that one of his last screen lines would be so chillingly prophetic?

Giant was Jimmy's last film, and was responsible for a very grotesque aspect of his death. Many people were shocked to learn that when his body was removed from his car's crumpled wreck after the collision, his face resembled that of an elderly man. However, Jimmy's final scenes in *Giant* had been as Jett Rink when old and dissipated, and as part of the make-up artists' procedure to achieve this illusion the hair on his forehead had been shaved off, giving him a receding hairline that aged him considerably. Just seven days after completing his work on *Giant*, Jimmy had set off to the race at Salinas. His hair hadn't had time to grow back, and so an ironic paradox was created in which a young actor whose untimely death ensured that he would remain forever youthful had died in the guise of an old man.

Jimmy once said: "I have a hunch that there are some things in life we just can't avoid. They'll happen to us, probably because we're built that way – we simply attract our own fate, make our own destiny." In life, one of Jimmy's greatest passions was bull-fighting – he even possessed the blood-stained cape of a real matador – but it would find expression in his death too, through a truly bizarre, savage coincidence. For according to John Howlett's book *James Dean: A Biography*, in the fatal crash Jimmy's body had been impaled, "torn open on the steering wheel, like a bullfighter on the horns".

✪

THE MOVING STONES OF DEATH VALLEY

In a locality with a name like Death Valley, it is singularly ironic (or perversely apt, maybe) that what is normally inanimate elsewhere is

The moving stones of Death Valley: a Californian rock legend.

notoriously animate here.

Death Valley is one of California's most familiar national monuments, due in no small way to the scattering of stones on a dried-up lake in this valley known as the Racetrack playa; for these are the famous moving stones, which travel considerable distances across the Racetrack's hardened surface, seemingly of their own volition. Just as the stones themselves vary greatly in size, from pebbles to half-tonne boulders, their furrowed tracks differ very appreciably in form and length, and include zigzags, straight lines, gentle curves and distances ranging from a few metres to many hundreds.

For many years, the valley's roaming rocks bewildered the scientific world. In 1968, however, geologists Dr Robert Sharp and Dr Dwight Carey from the California Institute of Technology embarked upon a seven-year study of

this phenomenon, at the end of which they concluded that it could be satisfactorily explained by the occurrence of a specific set of ground and weather conditions – namely, the presence of strong winds following sufficient rainfall to cause a slippery surface on the Racetrack. As Dr Carey subsequently explained:

The wind is able to pick up the rock and start it moving. It pushes aside the very slippery mud and slides along on the firm surface. It's probably moving a couple of feet per second as it rides off across the playa, and after a hundred, two hundred feet of movement, or sometimes just a very little movement, the stone will eventually come to rest as the wind dies down. I believe it's basically changes in the wind during the time when the rock is moving that cause the stone trails to be so variable.

Until very recently, this mechanism was widely accepted as the explanation for the curious mobility of Death Valley's stones and rocks. In 1995, however, geologist John Reid from Hampshire College in Amherst, Massachusetts, offered a conflicting, alternative solution. He revealed that four years earlier, he had taken a party of students to the valley at a time when the set of conditions proposed by Sharp and Carey as the impetus for rock movement was prevalent there. Yet although Reid and his students were slipping across the Racetrack's surface with alarming ease, the rocks remained stubbornly immobile. Despite all their efforts, none of the members of the party was able to set any of the rocks in motion either.

Accordingly, Reid has suggested that the rocks will indeed move when blown by a strong wind, but only if they are frozen into an ice sheet, the ice's low coefficient of friction countering the resistance to movement created by the rocks' jagged, weathered surfaces. From moving stones to skating rocks? Only when someone is able to devise a means of directly recording their movements is science ever likely to know for sure.

BALL LIGHTNING AND SPOOKLIGHTS

It was summer 1958, and William Becker, now professor and industrial design researcher at Illinois University, was camping with five high-school friends in the upper Minnesota regions north of Grand Marias. One night during a heavy rainstorm, while sharing the back room of a deserted cabin with one friend, Becker was amazed to see a glowing ball of light quite literally squeeze through a small gap above the windowsill and float into their room. Slightly larger than a basketball, with a bright yellow-white perimeter but a darker orange core that contained writhing worm-like shapes, it slowly descended to the floor and glided silently over the rug. When it reached the wall, it shrank and vanished, but almost immediately a loud firecracker-like retort echoed from the other side of the wall.

During a thunderstorm one day in April 1915, a man was standing by a window in his home at Columbia, Missouri, when he heard a sound like a shotgun blast. Moments later, his telephone clicked and out of its mouthpiece emerged a small bubble-like sphere of light that floated towards him and then rolled around the windowsill before disappearing.

Marfa Mystery Lights
Over 100 years of unexplained flickering lights
Location: Mitchell Flats   Photo Date: 9/86
Photo Specifications: SLR w. 50mm lens at f1.8
Exposure: Less than 3 minutes   Film: EL 400
Researcher/Photographer: 1986 James Crocker

TEXAS
Marfa

The Marfa lights dart then hover in an animate display that defies imitation by earthbound or reflected light.

On 25 August 1965, a basketball-sized ball of light, orange-red in colour, unexpectedly shot through the patio's fibreglass screen at the home of Clara Greenlee and her husband at Dunnellon, Florida. Aghast but armed, Clara whacked their fiery intruder with a fly-swatter and the luminous orb dropped to the floor, exploding with the sound of a rifle shot.

While watching television in an upstairs bedroom at her home in Rockville, Maryland, one February afternoon in 1989, Doris M. Humphrey suddenly noticed several small globes of white light, ranging in size from a marble to a ping-pong ball, hovering and dancing along the lengthy cord leading from the television to the wall outlet. They even swooped down into her wastepaper bin, inside which one loop of the cord had fallen, and then came out again and moved towards an artificial fireplace containing electric logs. Although the logs were not switched on, the tiny globes danced in the fireplace opening and then coalesced into a single sphere that bobbed up and down a few times before vanishing behind the logs.

These are just a few of the countless reports on file describing ball lightning – a mystifying phenomenon recorded throughout the world, yet particularly prevalent in North America. Ball lightning is exceedingly varied in form, but "typical" examples are spherical, can be any colour and range in size from marbles to basketballs. They frequently occur during thunderstorms, can materialize within an enclosed building, sometimes make a buzzing or hissing noise and leave behind a smell variously likened to sulphur or ozone. Their existence spans a few seconds to several minutes, and they generally float slowly but with a distinct "sense" of direction, rather than passively drifting. Some vanish silently, others with a loud explosion. They can cause great damage to inanimate objects, but rarely injure humans.

For many years, scientists dismissed ball lightning as an optical illusion – an after-image on the eye's retina resulting from a lightning flash. Such opinions were revised, however, when a dramatic case was witnessed by an extremely qualified eyewitness. On 19 March 1963,

Professor R.C. Jennison from the Electronic Laboratories at Kent University was aboard an Eastern Airlines flight from New York to Washington when an electrical storm enveloped the plane. Jennison reported that he saw a glowing ball of light with a diameter of just over 20 cm (8 inches) emerge from the pilot's cabin and float down the aisle, remaining about 75 cm (2½ feet) above the floor. It was also observed by an air hostess, who watched it disappear towards the toilet at the end of the aisle.

Many identities have been offered for ball lightning, including spheres of plasma, globes sustained by nuclear reaction, burning orbs of gas, forked lightning somehow compressed into a spherical form, and even tiny meteorites of antimatter. Today, Ohio scientists J.F. Corum and K.L. Corum are able to produce small balls of lightning in the laboratory, using a process involving high-voltage radio frequency. Japanese scientists too can create plasma globes, but there is still much to discover regarding this enigmatic phenomenon.

Very different from ball lightning are spooklights, which lack the former's potent, fiery power and more closely resemble will-o'-the-wisps (caused by marsh gas spontaneously igniting). North America has many famous examples, including the Marfa lights, frequently reported just east of this Texan town, in the direction of the Chinati mountains on the Mexican border. These resemble flickering yellow lanterns or headlights, about half as big as a basketball, darting rapidly through the air, sometimes hovering for a while and then vanishing. Although some reports may indeed be based upon unrecognized sightings of vehicle headlights, others have occurred in areas where there are no roads, and in many cases their animate displays effortlessly defy any imitation by earthbound or reflected headlights.

Even more eerie were the dancing balls of pulsating blue light that formerly frequented the graveyard at Silver Cliff, Colorado. In a detailed *New York Times* report for 20 August 1967, eyewitness W.T. Little revealed that several mundane explanations have been offered, including phosphorescence (caused by fungi) emitted by the graveyard's rotting

wooden tombstones and fences, glowing mineral ores in the ground (Silver Cliff is an old mining centre), and even the reflection of house lights from nearby homes. The last-mentioned theory, however, was disproved one night when every house switched off its lights and even the street lamps were extinguished, but the blue balls of light danced on regardless in the graveyard. In recent years, however, they have not been reported.

In contrast, the Brown Mountain lights of North Carolina are still eminently visible, variously described by eyewitnesses as "globular, glowing red, like toy fire-balloons", "a pale white light with a faint halo around it", or "not unlike a star from a bursting skyrocket". As noted by William R. Corliss in his invaluable *Handbook of Unusual Natural Phenomena*, they generally appear singly in succession, rising over the mountain's level ridge, then abruptly vanishing. Sometimes several appear together, and whereas their typical "lifetime" is less than a minute, they have been known to remain stationary above the ridge for up to 20 minutes. Once again, reflected headlights is a popular but unsatisfactory "official" solution.

It has been noted by many investigators, moreover, that the activity of some spooklights is almost intelligent, sometimes disconcertingly so – as in cases featuring balls of light that follow or entice people, then move out of their way when challenged. Could they be glowing swarms of insects? Or should we be looking towards Constable's sky-beast theory (pp.135–137) for an answer?

❂

ABRAHAM LINCOLN, THE PARANORMAL PRESIDENT

The following words were spoken to his wife and some friends by a man describing to them an eerie, disturbing incident that had recently happened to him:

Abraham Lincoln, photographic portrait c.1862.

dream was murdered, on 14 April 1865. Afterwards, exactly as he had foreseen, his body did indeed lie in state in the East Room of the White House, and for a very good reason. The murdered dreamer was none other than Abraham Lincoln – the first President of the USA to be assassinated.

This is just one of many remarkable events with distinctly paranormal overtones that occurred during Lincoln's life – and even after his death too. For several visitors to the White House claim to have encountered his ghost there. Somewhat appropriately, the first such report appears to be from a First Lady – President Calvin Coolidge's wife, Grace, who said that she saw Lincoln looking out of a window in the Oval Office.

Another noteworthy sighting was by Queen Wilhelmina of the Netherlands, during a visit to President Franklin D. Roosevelt. One day, someone knocked on the door of her bedroom at the White House, and when she opened it she was amazed to see Abraham Lincoln standing outside in the hall, wearing his famous top hat and typical clothes dating from his own period of office. Roosevelt later informed her that the bedroom which she was occupying was referred to as the Lincoln Room and had been the scene of several previous sightings of the former president. One of Roosevelt's secretaries had even seen Lincoln sitting on the bed in this room, pulling on his boots. Several photographs purportedly depicting Lincoln's ghost have been publicized over the years too, but all of these have ultimately been exposed as fakes.

Even more macabre than Lincoln's prophetic dream of his own death are stories that a spectral version of the funeral train that took his body to Illinois for burial appears each year and follows this same route. According to a report in the *Albany Times*:

About ten days ago I retired very late to bed and soon began to dream. There seemed to be a death-like stillness about me. Then I heard subdued sobs, as if a number of people were weeping. I thought I left my bed and wandered downstairs. There, the silence was broken by the same pitiful sobbing but the mourners were invisible. I went from room to room. No living person was in sight but the same mournful sounds of distress met me as I passed along. I was puzzled and alarmed.

Determined to find the cause of a state of things so mysterious and so shocking, I kept on until I arrived at the East Room. There I met with a sickening

surprise. Before me was a catafalque on which rested a corpse wrapped in funeral vestments. Around it were stationed soldiers who were acting as guards and there was a throng of people, some gazing mournfully upon the corpse, whose face was covered, others weeping pitifully.

"Who is dead in the White House?" I demanded of one of the soldiers. "The President," was his answer. "He was killed by an assassin."

Despite the disturbing nature of his words, no one paid a great deal of attention to them, until, just a few days later, the man who had dreamed this

It passes noiselessly. If it is moonlight, clouds cover the moon as the phantom train goes by. After the pilot engine passes, the funeral train itself with flags and streamers rushes past. The track seems covered with black carpet and the coffin is seen in the center of the car, whilst all about it in the air and on the train behind are vast numbers of blue

President John F. Kennedy greets crowds in Dallas moments before his assassination on 22 November 1963. A bizarre set of coincidences surrounds the lives – and deaths – of Presidents Kennedy and Lincoln.

coated men, some with coffins on their backs, others leaning upon them.

Just a legend? Perhaps. A fully confirmed fact, on the other hand, is that Lincoln's life was inexplicably connected by an uncanny array of coincidences – some trivial, others tragic – to that of another assassinated US President, John F. Kennedy.

When he was shot, President Kennedy was travelling in a Lincoln car, manufactured by Ford; President Lincoln was in the Ford Theatre when he was shot. Kennedy was advised not to go to Dallas by his secretary, who just

happened to be called Evelyn Lincoln. Both presidents were shot in the back of the head, while travelling with their wives and after predicting their own deaths less than a day before. Kennedy had earlier told his wife that no one would be able to prevent it if someone wanted to kill him; Lincoln had earlier told one of his guards, W.H. Crook, that he was convinced there were people who wanted to kill him and that no one would succeed in stopping them. Morbid pessimism, or dire prophecy?

In any event, both were indeed assassinated: Kennedy by someone shooting from a warehouse who then

ran into a theatre; Lincoln by someone shooting in a theatre who then ran into a storage barn. Both killers were themselves murdered too. A hundred years separated the election of the two future presidents to Congress (1846 and 1946 respectively) and also their election to the presidency (1860 and 1960). Not even their vice-presidents escaped this curious chain of coincidences, for both of them were Johnsons – Lincoln's was Andrew Johnson, Kennedy's was Lyndon Johnson.

Lincoln and Kennedy were clearly linked by fate – but, tragically, not by good fortune.

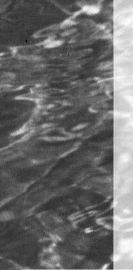

MYSTERIES OF THE *TITANIC*

On 14 April 1912, the 46,000-tonne liner the RMS *Titanic*, at that time the largest ship ever built and claimed to be unsinkable, was sailing from Southampton to New York on its maiden voyage. Just after 11.40 p.m., south-east of Newfoundland in the North Atlantic, the ship struck a lone iceberg: within hours, the *Titanic* and the great majority of its passengers and crew had been condemned to a watery grave on the ocean floor.

Of the 2207 people on board, only 705 survived the sinking of the *Titanic* – one of the greatest maritime disasters known in peacetime. The event was also associated with an unprecedented array of curious coincidences, as exhaustively analysed by George Behe in *Titanic: Psychic Forewarnings of a Tragedy*, which documents and assesses over a hundred examples.

One of the most famous of these concerns a novel entitled *Futility*, written by Morgan Robertson, in which a massive ocean liner called the SS *Titan*, said to be unsinkable and sailing from Southampton on her maiden voyage across the Atlantic, was sunk by an iceberg, killing most of the 2500 people aboard. Reading this, one would naturally assume that Robertson's novel was directly inspired by the true-life sinking of the *Titanic*. In fact, it was written in 1898 – 14 years *before* that tragedy took place! Nor is this unique: another fictional story anticipated the same event by several years too. It was written by a journalist called W. T. Stead, but this instance of penned prediction incorporated an even more chilling twist in its tail: Stead was one of the passengers who died when the real *Titanic* sank!

Yet another example of supposed precognition occurred one Sunday morning in Canada when the Reverend Charles Morgan, minister of the Rosedale Methodist Church in Winnipeg, Manitoba, fell asleep and dreamed vividly yet wholly unexpectedly of turbulent waves far out at sea, crashing beneath a dark sky. Strangest of all was that throughout this baffling dream, he could clearly hear the strains of a near-forgotten hymn, one that was hardly ever sung at that time. Suddenly, he woke up, but the hymn's theme remained in his mind. Then, as he dozed again, the dream returned – accompanied once more by the same hymn.

When he awoke the second time, the minister was sufficiently moved by his mystifying, disquieting experience to begin his service that evening with the hymn that had infiltrated his dream. For a church so far inland, it must have seemed to his congregation to be a highly inappropriate choice, because the hymn was 'For Those in Peril on the Sea'. Little did anyone realize at that time just how tragically apt, indeed prophetic, a choice it actually was – they were singing it on the evening of 14 April 1912.

*"Throughout the day there had been reassurances that the **Titanic** was being towed to port ..." By Tuesday 16 April, the **New York Times** had details which revealed the full grim extent of the tragedy.*

*Of the 2207 people on board, only 705 survived the sinking of the **Titanic**.*

One evening not long before midnight in April 1935, a seaman called William Reeves was keeping a look-out on board a tramp steamer sailing from Tyneside to Canada, when for no apparent reason his mind began to dwell on the terrible fate of the *Titanic*. A feeling of great unease swept over him, and as it did so, a very meaningful date suddenly screamed inside his head – 14 April 1912. Not only was this the date of the *Titanic*'s sinking, it was also his own birthday. But that was not all – the name of his own ship shattered his thoughts as well. It was the *Titanian*. Nothing could be seen ahead, but this flurry of uncanny, ominous coincidences crowding his mind harried him unceasingly like a phalanx of restless ghosts.

He sensed danger, horrific impending disaster, and shouted out in alarm to stop the ship. His cry was heard and heeded – and when he and the other crew members peered through the inky darkness, they discovered to their horror that they had been about to steer directly into a huge iceberg, just one of several towering nearby in invisible deadly silence.

In 1995, a very different *Titanic*-related mystery was aired in *The Riddle of the Titanic*. Robin Gardiner and Dan van der Vat argued that the ship that went down on that fateful evening was not the *Titanic* at all, but was in reality its identical twin sister, a notoriously accident-prone vessel called the *Olympic*. According to their theory, this substitution was a desperate attempt to defraud the company insuring these ships – a financial scam that went horribly wrong, transforming one of the world's greatest hoaxes into one of its most hideous tragedies.

*Shortly before her maiden voyage, the newly built **Titanic** emerges from Baird's shipyard in Belfast.*

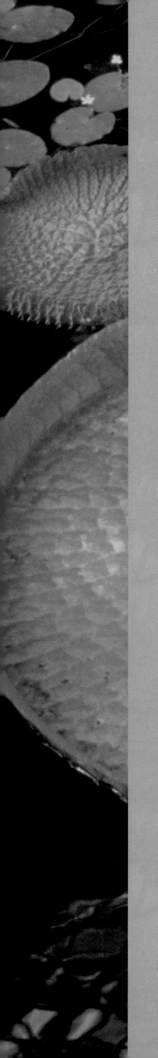

❂ Chapter 6 ❂
Mesoamerica and South America

RIDDLES FROM THE RAINFORESTS

IN 1924, THE EXPLORER LIEUTENANT-COLONEL PERCY FAWCETT WROTE: "BETWEEN THE OUTER WORLD AND THE SECRETS OF ANCIENT SOUTH AMERICA A VEIL HAS DESCENDED." THESE COMMENTS ON THE MYSTERIES HELD BEYOND SCIENTIFIC REACH WITHIN THIS CONTINENT'S VAST JUNGLES AND CLOUD FORESTS ARE EQUALLY APPLICABLE TO THE MANY ENIGMAS AND ANOMALIES OF MESOAMERICA, CONSISTING OF MEXICO AND CENTRAL AMERICA. ACCOMPANY ME NOW AS I ATTEMPT TO LIFT THE EDGES OF THIS VEIL A LITTLE, FOR WHO CAN SAY WHAT WE MAY FIND ON THE OTHER SIDE?

Bermuda Triangle

GULF
OF
MEXICO

Alux (mystery
dwarf-like pygmies)

Zombies

PUERTO
RICO

HAITI

Chupacabras (blood-sucking,
nausea-inducing monster)

CARIBBEAN SEA

BARBADOS

Sisimite (ape-man)

BELIZE

Moving coffins

Crystal skull

d-eating
mpire plant

Xipe
(ape-man)

Dog-devouring
vine

NICARAGUA

Mask of
ape-man

COSTA RICA

PANAMA

Las Bolas Grandes
(giant stone balls)

Vanishing
St Vincent
Islands

El Dorado

Loys's ape

COLOMBIA

Vasitri (ape-man)

VENEZUELA

Golden city
of Manoa

GUYANA

Maipolina
(walrus-like monster);
Camoodi
(horned anaconda)

SURINAM

Monkey-trapping tree

Didi
(ape-man)

Golden island of Manoa

Vanishing
Sarah Ann Island

ECUADOR

Rock-melting plant

PERU

Tarma (ape-man)

Giant anacondas

BRAZIL

Isnachi
(giant monkey)

Lt-Col. Percy Fawcett

Glowing mummies

Mapinguary

Nazca lines

Tiahuanaco

BOLIVIA

SOUTH

PACIFIC

OCEAN

Blue-skinned
humans

PARAGUAY

Yaquaru
(water tiger)

Minhocão
(giant worm-like beast)

Ellengassen

CHILE

Vanishing Davisland
archipelago

ARGENTINA

URUGUAY

Minhocão
(giant worm-like beast)

Andean wolf

SOUTH

ATLANTIC

OCEAN

Key to Phenomena

FLYING

WATER

ELEMENTS

LAND ANIMAL

HUMAN

SITES

PARANORMAL

FALKLAND
ISLANDS

Vanishing Aurora Islands
and Isla Grande

Lost Worlds, Lasting Secrets

Nazca Lines

For the world's largest work of art to be also the world's least visible work of art may seem like a contradiction in terms. Yet the Nazca lines of Peru are both of these things, and more.

In September 1926, a team of archaeologists led by Professor Julio C. Tello was digging at Cantallo, near an expanse of desert in southern Peru called the Nazca Plain, when two of its members climbed a hill close by and made an extraordinary discovery. To their amazement, they saw that the desert at Nazca resembled the sketchbook of a giant, for it was intricately patterned with thousands of straight lines, curves, geometrical shapes and even various animal outlines. Yet all were of such enormous size that their shapes could be discerned only when viewed from above. At ground level, they simply resembled long shallow grooves, and even then could be perceived clearly only when observers stood astride them.

Consequently, the lines had hitherto been largely ignored. Indeed, as Stuart Gordon noted in *The Paranormal*, the Pan American Highway had been built through this desert region without anyone even noticing these designs. During the 1930s, however, the archaeologists' discovery was confirmed and expanded upon by accounts and

photographs obtained from Peruvian Air Force pilots flying over these fascinating patterns. The markings extend across about 1300 square kilometres (500 square miles) and are nowadays referred to as the Nazca lines. Pottery fragments found in association with them date their creation to somewhere between 300 BC and AD 540.

On a vast scale, the complex designs in the Nazca lines are visible only from the air.

The Nazca Plain is covered with dark stones, and its designs were created simply by selectively removing some of these stones, thereby exposing the paler yellowish-white soil beneath. In this way, the distinctive pale lines appear upon an otherwise dark surface. In other words, the actual nature of these lines is quite mundane; what makes them so astonishing is their extraordinary

accuracy, bearing in mind not only that their dimensions are colossal but also that their shapes can be recognised only from the air.

For instance, some of the straight lines are up to 8 kilometres (5 miles) long, yet on average they do not deviate more than 3 metres (10 feet) in every mile. Moreover, even though several of the designs are both enormous and extremely complex – portraying a variety of different animals, including a condor-like bird, a whale, a spider, even a hummingbird – when viewed from the air they are perfectly formed, with no distorted or otherwise inaccurate outlines.

How could such perfection be achieved? And what was the function of these enigmatic earthworks anyway? Such questions have preoccupied a generation of researchers captivated by "Nazca linealogy", foremost of whom is unquestionably Maria Reiche. This German mathematician has spent most of her life studying the Nazca lines, beginning in the 1940s with fellow devotee Professor Paul Kosok from Long Island University, New York, and continuing alone after his death in 1959. Kosok believed that the Nazca lines had astronomical significance, that they comprised a form of celestial calendar, and Reiche's researches supported his conclusion. Some of the lines seem to mark the seasonal appearance of various constellations, whereas certain others pin-point the locations of sunrise and sunset at the two equinoxes and the summer solstice. But was this their only purpose?

Many others have since been suggested. It is known that the Incas gained spiritual solace from walking along specially laid-out lines called ceques, so perhaps the Nazca people who long preceded them produced the Nazca lines in order to derive a similar benefit. Another popular explanation links the lines to irrigation and the identification of water sources. Alternatively, they could have been symbols of ownership or kinship, each line or series belonging to a different family, with the larger and more elaborate examples owned by the more important members of the community. As for the animal pictographs, these may have comprised nature and fertility symbols to be venerated accordingly, or perhaps they represented a form of art. Rather more imaginative ideas have sprung from the novel hypothesis that the lines

functioned as landing strips or refuelling centres for alien spacecraft.

As for the anomaly that their shapes can be appreciated only when viewed from the air, an American airline executive called Jim Woodman has come up with one line of conjecture. In 1975 he flew over the Nazca lines in a special hot-air balloon called *Condor I*, which he had purposefully constructed using materials that would have been available to the Nazca people. His aim was to demonstrate that they could have produced balloons for travelling over the desert, thus obtaining aerial views during their creation of the lines and thereby explaining the lines' amazing accuracy. Yet there is no independent evidence to support such a possibility, and other workers have shown that this accuracy could have been readily achieved using wholly terrestrial methods of marking out the lines with cord and sticks, and working from small-scale originals.

Perhaps the greatest wonder of the Nazca lines is that they have survived at all. This is due to a fluke

combination of favourable meteorology and biology. Even by desert standards, the Nazca region is extremely dry and there is very little wind, so erosion is not a problem, and vegetation is so sparse that the lines are in no danger of becoming overgrown.

✡

EL DORADO

Led respectively by German explorer Nikolaus Federmann, Spanish conquistador Sebastian de Belalcazar, and Spanish explorer Gonzalo Jimenez de Quesada, three separate expeditions from Europe converged in 1539 upon a region of Colombia inhabited by the Chibcha people. Here Quesada was destined to found Bogotá, Colombia's present-day capital. However, the expeditions' principal goal then was to find a very different city – El Dorado, the fabled city of gold, spoken of by many South American peoples but hitherto undiscovered by the West.

Ironically, Quesada and company succeeded in their quest for El Dorado's identity, but without fully realizing it. They learnt that during the Chibchas' coronation ceremony, the new king was anointed with sticky earth followed by a liberal sprinkling of gold, thus coating him from head to foot in a gleaming gilded "skin". This was the real El Dorado – not a golden city, but a golden man. He would sit aboard a raft, placed upon the nearby Lake Guatavita and laden with resplendent golden gifts for the powerful god who supposedly inhabited this sacred lake. Once El Dorado had dropped his people's gifts into Guatavita's deep waters, he would immerse himself in the lake until his glittering covering had washed away – yielding a further tribute to the water deity – and then return to the shore to begin his reign.

Notwithstanding this revelation, some European explorers vainly continued to search for a wondrous golden city, spurred on by stories of Manoa – an idyllic magical island floating upon a great salt lake and brimming with golden artefacts of every kind. This wonderland has even been sought in modern times – its suggested

THE GLOWING MUMMIES OF PERU

In a short account published by *Strange Magazine* in 1992, merchant seaman Curtis A. Rowlett recalled a recent conversation with a fellow sailor (identified only as J.P. in the periodical). The sailor claimed that in spring 1989, while awaiting repairs to his ship in Peru, he had met a local pilot with a very interesting tale to tell. According to the pilot, there was a mysterious cave near the Nazca Plain that contained five small mummies which glowed in the dark. Moreover, anyone who touched them developed strange open sores on their fingers. J.P. planned to visit this cave with the pilot and see the mummies for himself, but his ship's repairs were completed that same day, so he missed the opportunity to do so. Just a sailor's yarn – or yet another Nazca-related anomaly?

Above:
The real El Dorado was a "golden man" ceremony which installed new chiefs of the Chibcha people.
Left:
At the height of the ceremony the chief would dive, covered in gold dust, into the waters of Lake Guatavita.

nineteenth century – and the departure of the Auroras! During the 1820s, a number of vessels visited their documented location, but the islands had vanished without trace. Their most celebrated seeker was the explorer Captain James Weddell, who diligently cruised back and forth in the vicinity plotted very precisely by Bustamente, but he failed to find them. Nevertheless, one or two claimed observations were made by other voyagers during later years, including a sighting in December 1856 by the brig *Helen Baird*, and what appears to be the anomalous Auroras' final bow, when two islands were spied in the correct area by Captain B.H. Hatfield aboard the *Gladys* in June 1892.

Another phantom of the Falklands is the Isla Grande, said to lie just north of the Auroras, along the forty-fifth parallel. It was first reported in 1675 by Antonio de la Roche, who also discovered South Georgia, but like its three southerly compatriots it has resisted all modern-day attempts to relocate it. Some researchers now dismiss it as nothing more than a poorly seen projection jutting out from the South American mainland.

Rather more difficult to explain away is the disappearance of an archipelago, as in the case of Davisland. This was the name given by cartographers to a group

localities have included southern Surinam, south-eastern Venezuela and Brazil's Mato Grosso (proposed by lost explorer Lt-Col. Percy Fawcett) – but there is no more evidence for its reality than for a city of El Dorado.

sketched and even named them – New Island (the most northerly), Low Island (the central one) and Southernmost Island. In his survey, he noted that they were cold, dark and partly snow-covered.

Then came the arrival of the

✦ VANISHING ISLANDS

Islands that mysteriously vanish into thin air are commonplace in mythology and fairy tales, but quite a few true-life examples are also on record, particularly from South American waters. Of these, the most famous – or infamous, perhaps – are the Aurora Islands. This tantalizing trio reputedly lay midway between the Falkland Islands and South Georgia, and were first reported in 1762 by the whaler *Aurora*, though no one went ashore to explore them. Several other ships also recorded seeing them during the later years of the eighteenth century. In 1794, J. de Bustamente, captain of the Spanish corvette *Atrevida*, meticulously charted,

The tribulations of terra firma: St Brendan is said to have mistaken a whale for an island, and landed on it.

of islands of uncertain number sited about 800 kilometres (500 miles) west of Chile and reported in 1687 by Captain John Davis and his crew. Yet despite repeated searches, no one else ever found them.

Nevertheless, during one such search, by the Dutch Admiral Roggeveen, a very significant discovery *was* made: this was Easter Island, and its enigmatic giant statues (pp.197–199), spotted on Easter Sunday 1722. An intriguing link between this island and vanished Davisland has been proposed by archaeologist Professor J. MacMillan Brown, who speculated that Easter Island was the sacred cemetery of the unknown inhabitants of Davisland. However, as this latter chain of islands appears to be permanently lost, it is unlikely that his idea can be pursued further.

Another phantom island reported in Easter Island's general vicinity is Podesta, as well as an unnamed isle spied by the S.S. *Glewalon* in 1912, and yet another, Sarah Ann Island, recorded far to the west of Ecuador. None can be found today. Nor can the St Vincent Islands (not to be confused with the single Caribbean island of St Vincent), which were discovered off Panama's west coast by Antonio Martinus in 1789, and inhabited for a time not long afterwards by Father Santa Clara, a Californian priest. Also worth noting is the evanescent Island of Brasil, if only to point out that despite its name, it shares no geographical link with Brazil. Instead, its rare appearances occur off the west coast of Ireland!

✵

LT-COL. PERCY FAWCETT – AN EXPLORER LOST IN GREEN HELL

On 20 April 1925, at the onset of what proved to be his final, ill-fated expedition in Brazil's Mato Grosso, British explorer and soldier Lieutenant-Colonel Percy Harrison Fawcett relayed

Lieutenant-Colonel Percy Harrison Fawcett, British explorer and soldier.

the following message to London by the Overland Brazilian Telegraph in Rondonia:

I have but one object: to bare the mysteries that the jungle fastnesses of South America have concealed for so many centuries. We are encouraged in our hope of finding the ruins of an ancient, white civilisation and the degenerate offspring of a once cultivated race.

On 29 May, 57-year-old Fawcett

reported his position (Lat. 11° 43' S; Long. 54° 35' W) at Dead Horse Camp in the Xingú Basin to the North American Newspaper Alliance funding his foray, and signed off by saying, "You need have no fear of any failure". Those were the last words ever received from him by the outside world. After marching boldly into the jaws of the Mato Grosso's green hell, his three-man party was entirely engulfed by it.

Even as a youth, Fawcett had been obsessed by the idea that ancient cities far older than the Egyptian civilization

The Mato Grosso, a vast impenetrable land which still holds the secret of Fawcett's lost expedition.

awaited discovery in untraversed parts of the world, particularly South America. He also believed that the legendary continent of Atlantis had really existed. Weaving these strands together, and supplementing them with information gathered from the many indigenous peoples that he had encountered during several explorations of South America's verdant interior, he formulated the notion that if such cities could be found, they would surely be the relics of an advanced white race that had fled from the doomed Atlantis before it sank beneath the ocean waves and had settled in the forests of South America. Here, Fawcett believed, the Atlanteans had survived, but their society had ultimately degenerated. Eventually, only the stony husks of their once-magnificent temples and palaces remained, still illuminated by everlasting globes of light – the last vestige of the Atlanteans' highly sophisticated scientific accomplishments.

In Rio de Janeiro, Fawcett had found an old Portuguese report of the forgotten discovery in 1753 of the ruins of a stone city, enclosed by a wall, deep in the Mato Grosso. And on 20 April 1925, accompanied by his son Jack, aged 21, and a cameraman called Raleigh Rimell, he set out on his ill-fated expedition from Cuyaba to relocate this city and prove its Atlantean connections.

Since the disappearance of Fawcett's party, several teams have attempted to trace their footsteps, and a welter of contradictory stories have emerged. Some eyewitnesses claimed that they had seen the three men living with various indigenous peoples several years after their disappearance. During the 1930s and 1940s, a half-white, blue-eyed Kuikuro Indian boy called Dulipe was even said by some to be Jack's son by an Indian wife. In 1952, however, Dulipe was exposed as a freak partial albino, wholly unrelated to Jack and the innocent victim of a journalistic hoax.

In August 1946, explorer Orlando Vilas Boas tape-recorded a supposed confession by the chief of the Kalapalos Indians that his people had killed all three men – a claim substantiated five years later by the supposed discovery of Fawcett's skeleton in their territory. According to Miriam Tildesley, however, who examined the skeleton, it seemed to be at least a hundred years old, and

THE MYSTERY OF THE MELTING ROCKS

Archaeologists in Latin America have often speculated upon the techniques responsible for the fine precision with which the huge stones used in constructing these lands' ancient cities were carved, given the stones' remarkably tight fit against one another. Although most experts believe that relatively ordinary procedures would have achieved this result, there is a possibility that one quite extraordinary technique also played its part.

Since the early 1980s, French polymer chemist Dr Joseph Davidovits has been researching the startling prospect that some ancient civilizations, including the creators of the Bolivian city of Tiahuanaco (pp.174–5), had developed a process by which crushed rock could be melted, moulded into a given shape (such as a huge cube or an elaborate statue) and then hardened to yield the required object. This would eliminate the laborious task of precision-carving solid blocks of rock into stone cubes for constructing buildings, or into ornamental sculptures.

Davidovits claims that even today witch-doctors in Bolivia are known to powder rock, add natural chemicals to break it down, and then mould the slurry into amulets of solid stone. He has also successfully created his own synthetic rock or geopolymer that can be melted, shaped, then

The fortress of Sacsayhuamán. Did the Incas have the technology to melt rocks?

rehardened. His laboratory contains several shelves groaning under the weight of statues moulded from artificial rock, but most archaeologists remain unconvinced.

Testimony for the "melting" theory was also recorded by Professor Hiram Bingham, during his Peruvian expeditions that culminated in his sensational discovery of the lost Incan city of Machu Picchu in 1911. Bingham recounted stories by the local peoples about a special plant whose juices melted rock, enabling it to be worked into tightly fitted masonry.

In *"Things"*, Ivan T. Sanderson included data on this subject collected by Lt-Col. Percy Fawcett. One item concerned a man who had trekked 8 kilometres (5 miles) through virgin forest along the Pyrene River in the Peruvian province of Chuncho, only to discover at the end of his trek that his metal spurs had been corroded away. He mentioned this to his host, a local rancher, who asked if he had walked through a dense patch of plants with red fleshy leaves, growing about 15 cm (1 foot) high. When the man told him that he had, his host informed him that these were to blame, and were "the stuff the Incas used for shaping stones".

whereas Fawcett had long ago lost two teeth in his upper jaw during a vigorous football match, the upper jaw of the skeleton's skull still possessed both of them.

Somewhere in the Mato Grosso is the secret of Fawcett's disappearance, but this vast land is so impenetrable even today that there is little chance of ever uncovering the truth.

TEOTIHUACÁN AND TIAHUANACO – NEW WORLD CITIES OF AGE-OLD MYSTERY

Situated some 50 kilometres (30 miles) north-east of present-day Mexico City but not to be confused with Tenochtitlán (the Aztecs' capital, upon whose ruins the Spaniards founded Mexico City),

Teotihuacán was, at the pinnacle of its success in c.AD 500, the largest city in the New World, and the sixth largest in the entire world. Standing on a plateau 2300 metres (7500 feet) high, it gained its modern-day name – roughly translating as "city where men become gods" – from the Aztecs, who discovered it 700 years after its demise. A commercial and religious centre laid out in a precisely defined grid system and functioning as the capital of a mighty civilization that spanned almost a millennium, this magnificent metropolis was 20 square kilometres (8 square miles) in area and housed up to 200,000 people. At its heart was a colossal processional route known to the Aztecs

as the Avenue of the Dead. This route linked all three of Teotihuacán's most spectacular features – the 66-metre-(216-foot) high Pyramid of the Sun (Mexico's largest pyramid), the smaller Pyramid of the Moon, and the Citadel containing the Temple of Quetzalcoatl.

Teotihuacán is believed to have originated in c.150 BC (though its site may have been first occupied as far back as c.4000 BC), reaching its zenith of influence over Mesoamerica in the Xolalpan Phase (AD 450–650). It was mysteriously destroyed by fire in c.AD 750.

Almost 4000 metres (13,000 feet) above sea level, Tiahuanaco's ruins are situated approximately 20 kilometres

The Eygptian connection: pyramids in Teotihuacán have led to speculation about ancient links between the Old World and the New. At Tiahuanaco (inset), the face of Con-Tici Viracocha still bears witness to a powerful civilization.

(12 miles) south of Lake Titicaca, just inside Bolivia's border with Peru. During the late nineteenth century, many of the spectacular stone buildings and statues of this once-opulent city were demolished as a source of stone for the construction of Bolivia's present-day capital, La Paz (about 95 kilometres further east), but this was not the first desecration and destruction of Tiahuanaco. Five cities successively flourished and fell here, each built upon the ruins of the previous one. The first was founded in c.1700 BC, the last met its unexplained demise in AD 1200.

Tiahuanaco was the shimmering pearl of a civilization whose influence encompassed the southern highlands of Bolivia and Peru, and extended as far as northern Chile, but was apparently an economic and religious empire rather than one based upon military domination. One of Tiahuanaco's most famous surviving relics is the Gateway of the Sun. Standing 3 metres (10 feet) high, weighing many tonnes, and hewn from a single block of andesite, it bears the elaborately carved form of Con-Tici Viracocha – the ancient weeping god of Tiahuanaco.

Modern archaeological research has revealed much of these two great cities' former history and glory, but the identities of their respective creators remain veiled in shadow. Today, the consensus is that they were probably indigenous to the New World, but not so long ago the much more radical idea that ancient Egyptians may have travelled to the New World and set in motion these lands' great civilizations was widely espoused. Moreover, this concept received an added boost when Thor Heyerdahl constructed an Egyptian papyrus reed boat called *Ra II* and sailed across the Atlantic from Africa to Barbados to prove that such a journey was indeed possible. Supporters of the Egyptian connection also pointed out that ancient Egyptian reed boats are almost identical to those traditionally used on Lake Titicaca; they also emphasized the similarities between Egyptian and New World pyramids.

Even so, do developmental parallels like these between two widely separate cultures genuinely constitute proof that the cultures must have once been in contact with one another? Or are such parallels simple yet valid demonstrations that because there are only a limited number of ways to achieve any given objective, examples of similar development occurring wholly independently among widely separate cultures will inevitably occur?

Unfortunately, the evidence uncovered so far from Teotihuacán and Tiahuanaco offers more ambiguities than answers. As a single example of this, there are indeed many structural similarities between the pyramids of these New World cities and those much older versions in Egypt. Yet whereas the Egyptian pyramids evolved from tombs, New World pyramids evolved (generally, but not always) from temple platforms.

Whether the architects of Teotihuacán and Tiahuanaco were of New World or Old World origin is still undecided. Only the lingering stony relics of these ancient cities know for sure, and like stones everywhere else they are remaining resolutely silent.

KING SOLOMON'S MINES

Traditional localities proposed for this legendary treasure trove have been sited in Africa or the Middle East. During the 1970s, however, Dr Cyrus Gordon from the Department of Mediterranean Studies at Brandeis University, Massachusetts, put forward a much more distant provenance for consideration – South America. He claimed that the Phoenicians knew of Brazil, calling it the island of iron: and iron is indeed a major Brazilian export.

Moreover, in 1966, a retired United States Air Force electrician called René Chabbert discovered in Brazil's National Archives a remarkable letter written in 1753 by some Portuguese explorers of Brazil claiming to have found Solomon's fabled gold mines. That letter inspired Chabbert to begin more than two decades of research, culminating in his conviction that he has detected signs of the mines' grey stone vaults in satellite photographs taken by United States meteorologists over a dense expanse of Brazilian rainforest. Scientists, however, are not convinced, pointing out that water as well as stone will appear grey in such photos, and officials at Brazil's National Archives discount the letter as a hoax by a person or persons unknown.

An oppressive ruler, King Solomon created wealth at a high price for many ordinary people in Judah and Israel.

Monstrous Mysteries

LOYS'S APE AND OTHER NEOTROPICAL MAN-BEASTS

Officially, South America has no apes. This is why the extraordinary creature depicted in an excellent photograph taken by a geologist while exploring this continent is so controversial.

Its story began one day in 1920, while Swiss geologist Dr François de Loys was leading an expedition through the rainforest on the border between Venezuela and Colombia. Suddenly, two strange ape-like creatures stepped out of some bushes just ahead of them, walking on their hind legs, lacking tails and standing approximately 1.5 metres (5 feet) tall. The creatures seemed greatly angered by the sight of the geologists and moved closer, as if to attack them. In order to protect themselves, the geologists had no option but to shoot at these animals, killing one of them, which proved to be a female. The other, presumably a male, turned and fled.

Unable to identify the large ape-like primate, and equally unable to carry its heavy body very far, they propped it into a sitting posture on a wooden crate,

placing a pole beneath its chin to keep it upright, and photographed it. Tragically, most of the photos were later lost when the geologists' boat capsized while they were travelling down a river, but one first-class picture did survive and is

Loys's ape: officially there are no apes in South America.

reproduced here. Some time after the expedition's return to Europe, Loys published an account of the strange ape-men in an *Illustrated London News* article (15 June 1929). This included the photo and it astounded the scientific world.

One French zoologist, Professor

George Montandon, was convinced that it depicted a genuine species of South American ape, the first ever known, which he formally christened *Ameranthropoides loysi* ("Loys's American ape"), but others were more sceptical. As the creature bore an overall resemblance to the familiar spider monkeys, they concluded that this is what it was, despite its much greater size, more robust body and dissimilar dentition (Loys claimed that it had fewer teeth than all known species of spider monkey). They even disputed Loys's statement that it was tailless, and suggested that he may have deliberately cut off or hidden its tail when photographing the animal, to make it look more like an ape.

Today, Loys's ape is virtually forgotten outside cryptozoological circles. Yet the existence of such creatures is apparently well known to the native people in many parts of Central and South America, who call them by a variety of different local names, including the shiru (Colombia), sisimite (Belize), vasitri (Venezuela), didi (Guyana), xipe (Nicaragua) and tarma (Peru). Certainly, there is no good evolutionary reason why the South American primates should not have given rise to an ape-like form equivalent to the Old World anthropoids.

In 1987, mycologist Gary Samuels from the New York Botanical Gardens

Some zoologists dismissed Loys's ape as the spider monkey ATELES PANISCUS.

was kneeling down on a forest floor in Guyana when he looked up to see a hairy 1.5-metre- (5-foot) tall ape-man walking by on its hind legs, apparently unaware of Samuels's presence, crouched on the ground. As it walked it uttered an occasional "hoo" cry. This was presumably a didi.

A rare opportunity to obtain the skeleton of a similar creature may have been lost in 1968. This was when a xipe was allegedly trapped in a cave by a group of Nicaraguan peasants, who then set fire to the bushes around it. It is claimed that they found its scorched skeleton inside the cave afterwards, but no one seems to have preserved it.

What *is* preserved, however, at Chicago's Field Museum of Natural History, is a distinctly ape-like "mask", carved in stone by the Guetar Indians of Costa Rica (AD 1200–1500). And statues of gorilla-like entities have been discovered amid ruined cities half-hidden beneath the foliage in the rainforests of Central and South America.

No less interesting than accounts of elusive ape-men is the possible existence in South America of an undiscovered giant monkey. Reports collected by on-site zoologist Dr Peter Hocking from several different Indian tribes suggest that the forests of Peru conceal a monkey the size of a chimpanzee but with a very short tail and a face like a baboon. According to local people, it is known as the isnachi and is very rare, but is in any case avoided whenever possible because of its ferocity. One of its most characteristic activities is to rip apart the tops of chonta palm trees in order to procure the tender vegetable matter inside. This means that its presence within a given locality can be swiftly confirmed merely by finding trees damaged in this way, because no other creature is strong enough to do this.

Most mysterious of all are the alux, reported from the Yucatán Peninsula in Mexico. The males are described as dwarf-sized humanoids with jet-black beards and clad in a dress-like garment, known as a hupile, worn by the mysterious Mayas. Occasionally, female alux are also seen, with very long dark hair and wearing a similar garment to the males.

Late one evening in 1977, a bearded 1-metre- (3-foot) tall alux was seen in the ancient walled city of Mayapán (the Mayas' former capital) by the city's current caretaker, a young modern-day Mayan called Xuc. The alux had a disproportionately large head and was wearing a hupile and carrying a large machete over its shoulder. As Xuc drew nearer, however, the angry alux bombarded him with a barrage of small clay pellets before disappearing into the shadows of the night.

Interestingly, investigator Bill Mack has noted that many ruined Mayan temples in Yucatán are fronted by one or more tiny stone "houses" with doorways less than a metre (3 feet) high. According to orthodox science, these odd structures are votary shrines, but the modern-day Mayas claim that they were the homes of favoured alux.

WILDLIFE OF THE WEIRD, BUT VERY WONDERFUL, VARIETY

Some of the strangest but potentially most sensational mystery animals on record have been reported from the secluded rainforests, mountains and rivers of South America.

For many years, zoologist Dr David Oren from the Goeldi Museum in Brazil has been following up local reports from the dense Mato Grosso region of Amazonia in his longstanding search for an exceedingly odd creature called the mapinguary. According to the local Indians, it has red fur and when squatting on its hind legs is as tall as a man; it leaves strange footprints that seem to be back-to-front and faecal droppings similar to those of horses; it emits loud shouting cries and is said to be invulnerable to bullets.

Dr Oren feels that this description closely matches that of an officially extinct ground-living sloth called a mylodontid. This is known to science not only from fossils and preserved faecal droppings (which are indeed horse-like), but also from some remarkable mummified individuals several millennia old, yet still covered with reddish-brown fur. From these specimens, zoologists know that mylodontids had bony nodules in their skin that would have served as effective body armour (perhaps explaining the mapinguary's invulnerability).

The Indians also claim that the mapinguary has an extra mouth, in the centre of its belly, and that, when threatened, it releases a hideous stench that suffocates its attackers. This may sound quite bizarre, but Oren suggests that these descriptions might simply refer to some form of gas-secreting gland, used for defence. If one day he finds a mapinguary, it could well prove to be the largest living mammal native to South America; and if it really is a ground sloth, it will resurrect from extinction one of the most peculiar

Claims that this mysterious pelt (held here by cryptozoologist Dennis Vrettos) comes from a hitherto-unknown species of wolf remain controversial.

Lorenz Hagenbeck was visiting a market in Buenos Aires when he saw a very unusual dog pelt for sale. Although somewhat reminiscent of the maned wolf's fur, with a very dense mane-like covering over its neck, it was much longer, thicker and darker over the body, as seen here in this previously unpublished photograph. Its colour graded from black on the upper parts to dark brown on the neck and under parts, and its ears were much smaller and rounder than those of the maned wolf.

Learning that this strange pelt was from a mysterious form of dog reputedly native to the Andes (and noticing that three other pelts just like it were also for sale at this market), Hagenbeck purchased it. When it was subsequently examined by German scientists they concluded that it seemed to be a hitherto-unknown, mountain-dwelling equivalent of the maned wolf. One of these scientists, pioneering cryptozoologist Dr Ingo Krumbiegel, also found a strange canine skull of Andean origin that may have come from such a beast. In 1949, based upon the skull and the skin, he published a formal description of this elusive maned wolf of the mountains, calling it the Andean wolf *Oreocyon* (since changed to *Dasycyon*) *hagenbecki*.

No further skins or skeletal remains were obtained, however, and in later years hair analyses were conducted that pointed towards a domestic sheepdog as a possible identity (or at least as an ancestor) for the Andean wolf. Yet with the recent development of comparative

groups of mammals ever known. A similar beast, locally termed the ellengassen, has also been described from Patagonia.

Equally extraordinary is the minhocão, a huge worm-like beast said to be 23 metres (75 feet) long (but this is no doubt an exaggeration), with black scaly skin and two tentacle-like structures on its head. Reported from Uruguay and Paraná, southern Brazil, this grotesque creature spends much of its time underground. However, its existence is readily betrayed by the dramatic effects of its stupendous subterranean excavations, which will often cause the sudden collapse of hillsides and roads, and are sometimes deep enough to divert the course of rivers.

Zoologists have previously attempted, very unsatisfactorily, to identify the minhocão as an undiscovered species of enormous lungfish, or even a surviving glyptodont – an immense armadillo-like mammal believed to have died out at least 10,000 years ago. As I discussed in my book *In Search of Prehistoric Survivors*, however, a much more compatible identity for it is a gigantic form of caecilian – a limbless worm-like amphibian of subterranean, burrowing life-style. These creatures are already represented in South America by several modest-sized species, some of which do indeed have scaly skin and a pair of tentacles on their head.

Greatly resembling a fiery-furred fox on stilts, the maned wolf *Chrysocyon brachyurus* is native to the Patagonian pampas. Officially, this extremely distinctive animal has no particularly close relatives among other species of wild dog – or has it?

In 1927, German animal dealer

*The minhocão may be a gigantic form of caecilian (*HYPOGEOPHIS ROSTRATA*).*

DNA techniques it is surely time now to re-examine this tantalizing pelt, to determine conclusively whether *Dasycyon hagenbecki* is actually a wolf in sheepdog's clothing after all.

No less mysterious is the maipolina of the Maroni River at Maripasoula, Guyana. A greatly feared beast that supposedly inhabits caves and hollows in the river bank, it is said to be about 3 metres (10 feet) long, with short fur that is fawn in colour on top (plus a paler dorsal stripe) and whitish underneath, large eyes, drooping ears, clawed feet, a cow-like tail, and – most noticeable of all – a pair of huge tusks resembling those of a walrus. Attempts have been made to equate this animal with a giant form of otter, but these are frustrated by its incongruous tusks and also by its cow-like (hence tufted?) tail and drooping ears.

Another walrus-lookalike, but with shaggy yellow fur, has been reported from the rivers of Paraguay, where it is termed the yaquaru or water tiger. Interestingly, similar creatures have been described from tropical rivers in central Africa too, and cryptozoologist Dr Bernard Heuvelmans has boldly postulated that these may be surviving sabre-tooth tigers specialized for an amphibious existence. In South America, normal terrestrial sabre-tooths certainly survived up to around 10,000 years ago. Could some still exist here today, but adapted for an aquatic life-style as suggested by Heuvelmans for the African mystery beasts? South America evidently has ample surprises still in store for any real-life Professor Challengers.

BOTANY OF THE BIZARRE

A botanical monster reminiscent of the supposedly man-eating tree of Madagascar (p.101) has been reported from parts of Central America. In an issue of *Sea and Land* from 1887, J.W. Buel called it the ya-te-veo tree, and described it as having a short thick trunk with immense spine-like shoots at its summit that bear dagger-shaped

*The Venus flytrap (*DIONAEA MUSCIPULA*) has a reassuringly modest appetite.*

thorns along their edges. These shoots hang down to the ground and appear lifeless, until an unwary person walks between them, towards the trunk itself. Then, without warning, the shoots rise up and entwine themselves around him, pressing him on to the trunk's surface where they instantly impale him with their long thorns and crush him until his body is drained of blood, which is rapidly absorbed through the tree's surface. This is just one of several controversial meat-eating plants reported from tropical America but whose reality remains unverified.

On 27 August 1892, for example, the *Illustrated London News* reported a dog-devouring tree in Nicaragua. Apparently, a naturalist called Dunstan had been seeking plant specimens in swamps surrounding Lake Nicaragua when he heard his dog cry out in agony. Running to his assistance, Dunstan found to his horror that the dog was enmeshed in a fine network of rope-like roots and fibres, comprising a bizarre type of vine, almost black in colour and secreting a thick sticky gum. Only with very great difficulty did Dunstan succeed in cutting through the vine's clinging fibres to release his dog, and after he had done so he saw that the animal's skin was covered in sucker marks, where the vine had seemingly pierced its flesh and sucked its blood. The natives knew this macabre species well, and told Dunstan that it could drain the nourishment from a large lump of meat in as little as five minutes.

A comparable form, referred to locally as the snake-tree, has supposedly been recorded from an outlying spur of Mexico's Sierra Madre. According to the claims of a traveller who came across it during the late nineteenth century, a bird that perched on one of its branches was immediately seized by it and crushed, its blood being absorbed

through the plant's surface until its corpse was dry. After watching this grisly spectacle, the traveller rashly touched one of its branches: the branch immediately closed upon his hand, and with such force that he tore his skin when wrenching his hand away!

What may well have been the same, still-unrecognized species was encountered by the famous French explorer Byron de Prorok in early 1933, when he led an expedition into the almost impenetrable jungle region of the Chiapas, in southern Mexico. Just two hours after first entering the forest, their guide, Domingo, pointed to a huge plant and when de Prorok looked at it closely he saw to his astonishment that the plant had captured a bird. This had alighted upon one of the leaves, which had promptly closed, its thorns penetrating the bird's body. Domingo referred to this deadly species as the "plante vampire".

Even more recently, during the early 1970s, Brazilian explorer Mariano da Silva came upon a particularly dramatic flesh-eater of the floral variety while searching for a settlement of Yatapu people on the Brazilian border with Guyana. This species allegedly releases a very distinctive scent that is particularly attractive to monkeys, luring them to it and enticing them to climb its trunk –

*Evading vicious vines is the stuff of derring-do. This illustration accompanied 'The Purple Terror' by Fred M. White in **Strand Magazine**, September 1899.*

whereupon its leaves totally envelop them, rendering these hapless creatures invisible and inaudible to anyone witnessing this vile spectacle. Three days or so later, the leaves open again, and from them drop the bones of their victims, from which every vestige of flesh has been stripped. This resembles the activity of a giant-sized Venus flytrap, but so far science has still to receive a specimen for examination.

✷

GIANT ANACONDAS

For many years, the longest reliably reported anaconda *Eunectes murinus* on record was deemed to be an 11.5-metre- (37½-foot) specimen killed by petroleum geologist Robert Lamon while leading a party exploring for oil in the llanos of the upper Orinoco River in eastern Colombia; it was documented in 1944 by herpetologist Dr Emmett R. Dunn from Haverford College, Pennsylvania. In a *Bulletin of the Chicago Herpetological Society* paper for September 1993, however, zoologists Dr Raymond Gilmore and Dr John Murphy revealed that this snake had actually measured only a little over 7 metres (24 feet), indicating that Dunn's report had been in error.

Yet even if this specimen had truly measured 11.5 metres, it would still have been effortlessly overshadowed by certain others reported over the years, especially from parts of Amazonia. Here, colossal anacondas far greater in size than any officially verified by science are so well known to the local people that they have even been given their own specific name – the sucuriju gigante.

One of these outsized snakes was encountered in 1907 by Lt-Col. Percy Fawcett (see pp.172–173) while he and his expedition were voyaging along the Rio Abunã close to its confluence with the Rio Negro, near the southern border of western Brazil. Without warning, the triangular head of an immense anaconda, followed by several feet of its undulating body, surfaced almost under the bow of his canoe and began to

emerge on to the river bank.

Fawcett immediately shot the creature, killing it outright, then went ashore to examine its carcase. This, he claimed, was of prodigious length: "As far as it was possible to measure, a length of forty-five feet lay out of the water, and seventeen feet in it, making a total length of sixty-two feet." He also noted that the Araguaya and Tocantíns swamps harbour a huge black version, known as the dormidera ("sleeper") after the loud snoring noise that it makes.

Even more enormous was the monstrous specimen that slithered ashore in 1948 and secreted itself amid Fort Tabatinga's fortifications on the River Oiapoc in the Guaporé territory. According to a report in a Rio de Janeiro newspaper, which also featured a photo of the snake, it measured a stupendous 35 metres (115 feet), and a team of soldiers sent to dispatch it fired at least 500 machine-gun bullets into its

body before it was killed. Tragically for science, its gargantuan carcase was rapidly pushed back into the river afterwards.

As an added distinction, some Guyanan giant anacondas are said to be horned too, and these specimens are called camoodi by the locals.

Biomechanically speaking, gigantic anacondas are not impossible, because their great weight would be effectively buoyed as long as they remained in the water. Moreover, many extra-large anaconda skins have been formally documented, but as snake skins can be easily stretched, these are unreliable sources of evidence for the reality of such creatures. In contrast, there are still many reports of living giant anacondas that cannot be dismissed quite so readily (even when we have excluded evident hoaxes and exaggerated estimations of size). After all, an anaconda skin cannot be stretched while the anaconda is still in it!

Fortunately, when Lt-Col. Percy Fawcett encountered a gigantic anaconda under similar circumstances, he was rather better prepared.

Tropical Magic

THE CRYSTAL SKULLS OF DOOM

One day in 1927, teenager Anna Mitchell-Hedges was assisting her adoptive father, a British explorer called F.A. "Mike" Mitchell-Hedges, in his excavations at the ruined Mayan city of Lubantum in British Honduras (now Belize), when she made a momentous discovery. Digging in a temple, she spied something shining beneath its altar. It proved to be a life-sized model of a human skull, meticulously sculpted from a lump of pure quartz rock crystal. The lower jaw was missing, but three months later this was also found by Anna, buried just a metre or more away from the skull's hiding place. Thus reads the official history of what is variously termed the Mitchell-Hedges crystal skull or the Skull of Doom – and what is deemed by many to be the most astounding work of art ever created by human hand.

This fascinating artefact has been in Anna's ownership ever since she discovered it; but it is not unique. A second life-sized skull hewn from rock crystal is also on record: this one has been owned since 1898 by the Museum of Mankind in London (part of the British Museum), which purchased it from Tiffany's, the famous New York jewellers, for £120.

The craftsmanship of these two skulls is truly exemplary. After comparing their respective measurements with those of a real human skull, in July 1936 eminent British anthropologist Dr G.M. Morant documented his findings in the scientific journal *Man*, commenting:

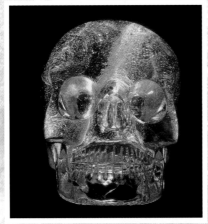

The two crystal skulls of doom are thought to be related. This one is held by the Museum of Mankind in London.

Not one of these measurements would be at all exceptional for an actual skull except the orbital index ... which appears to be slightly removed from the human range for this character. At the same time the other measurements are in remarkably close accordance.

When the two crystal skulls are directly compared with each other, however, certain differences can be perceived. Whereas the lower jaw of the Museum of Mankind's skull is an intrinsic component of this sculpture, the Mitchell-Hedges skull's lower jaw was fashioned as a separate item, which can be moved up and down when fitted to the skull. Leading on from this difference, the Museum skull is more stylized in form, whereas the Mitchell-Hedges skull is much closer to a naturalistic anatomical rendering.

Indeed, this latter specimen corresponds so precisely with the genuine article that when illuminated by radiant sunlight it is as if the bony substance of a real human skull has been magically vitrified, transformed into crystalline fire. Most spectacular of all, however, are its prismatic eyes, which are so skilfully fashioned that they effectively concentrate light in a manner that imparts an uncanny luminescence throughout the entire skull. Yet none of its glistening surfaces betrays even the vaguest hint of how this astonishing artefact was manufactured. In contrast, one of the teeth of the Museum skull bears what may be a slight mark made by a powered cutter.

In his paper, Morant claimed that it was "impossible to avoid the conclusion that the crystal skulls are not of independent origin ... it is safe to conclude that they are representations of the same human skull [quite possibly a female specimen], though one may have been copied from the other". If so, he considered it likeliest that the less precise Museum skull had been copied from the more finely detailed Mitchell-Hedges skull.

Perhaps only marginally less remarkable a wonder than the skulls themselves is our extraordinary dearth of knowledge concerning their origins, the identities of those who fashioned them, and the possible functions of such mesmerisingly macabre effigies. To begin with, much doubt has been publicly aired by several researchers concerning the circumstances surrounding Anna Mitchell-Hedges's alleged discovery of the crystal skull at Lubantum. Pointing out that the day she found it just so happened to be her seventeenth birthday, they have speculated that her father may have deliberately planted the skull for her to find, as a birthday surprise. Yet if this is true, where did he obtain it?

On 15 September 1943, the skull was put up for auction at Sotheby's in London by Sydney Burney, a local art dealer. It did not reach its reserve price, however, and Anna's father bought it for £400. He later claimed that some time *before* the auction he had given it to Burney as security on a loan, and thus by purchasing it at the auction he was merely redeeming what already belonged to him. Sceptics, however, point out that Morant's paper, published seven years before the auction, referred to this skull as "the Burney skull", and did not mention Mitchell-Hedges. Is it possible, therefore, that the story of Anna's finding of the skull at Lubantum is a fabrication on the part of her father (whose fondness for story-telling was widely known), and that the skull had first come into the ownership of the Mitchell-Hedges family only when it was bought from Burney at the auction by Anna's father?

According to gemmologist G.F. Kunz, the second crystal skull had been brought from Mexico to Europe by a Spanish officer some time before France's occupation of Mexico in the mid 1860s, and was sold to an English collector. When he died, it changed owners several times until it was purchased by Tiffany's and thence by the British Museum.

In his autobiography *Danger My Ally*, Anna's father claimed that the "Skull of Doom" was "at least 3,600 years old and according to legend was used by the high priest of the Maya when performing esoteric rites. It is said that when he willed death with the help of the skull, death invariably followed. It has been described as the embodiment of all evil." In their book, *The Mayan Prophecies*, Adrian G. Gilbert and Maurice M. Cotterell proffered the evocative suggestion that this skull may have been used by the high priest as an elaborate burning glass in the Mayan fire ceremony. They proposed that if the priest held its exactly carved form at a certain angle to the sun, it would act like a lens, emitting a bright tongue of fire via the refraction of sunlight through its opened mouth. Perhaps this explains its mobile lower jaw.

As for the Museum skull, anthropologist H.J. Braunholtz asserted in 1936 that its stylized form, with circular eye sockets and ill-defined teeth, was typical of late Aztec art.

More recently, however, several other possible sources for the rock crystal used in the skulls' manufacture have been put forward, including Brazil, Cavalaveras County in California, and Peru. In addition, the skulls may actually have been manufactured rather more recently than originally assumed, and far away from whatever source of rock crystal was used: Japan, Qing Dynasty China, and even Renaissance Europe have been proposed as likely possibilities.

Of the two crystal skulls, the Mitchell-Hedges specimen has inspired the greater public fascination, for according to crystal expert Frank Dorland, who studied it for six years, it is uniquely associated with some very bizarre reports and phenomena. As summarized in Time-Life's lavish volume *Feats and Wisdom of the Ancients*, Dorland claimed that this skull:

... sometimes changed color or filled with a cottony haze; that it produced an "elusive perfume" and strange tinkling sounds; that images of mountains, temples, and other objects appeared within it; and that an aura once surrounded it for several minutes.

Others who saw the skull while it was on loan to Dorland reported similar phenomena. Some observers even attested that while they were gazing at it, their pulse quickened, their arm and leg muscles tightened, and their eyes were physically tugged in their sockets. Dorland believes that these effects are not physical but hallucinatory, somehow triggered by the skull's crystal structure. It is little wonder indeed that it is called the Skull of Doom.

THE GIANT STONE BALLS OF COSTA RICA

Like the scene of an unfinished game of marbles played by a long-vanished race of Titans, the Diquís Delta of Costa Rica is liberally strewn with an array of stone orbs. Known as Las Bolas Grandes ("The Giant Balls"), numbering well over a thousand in total and occurring in association with pre-Columbian artefacts, some of these granitic globes are only a few centimetres in diameter, but many are colossal – up to 2.5 metres (8 feet) across and weighing more than 16 tonnes.

Yet their very existence remained unknown to the outside world until the 1930s, when the dense vegetation covering the delta was levelled in order to establish banana plantations here and its secret spheres were finally exposed. Six decades have passed by since then, but science is still unable to explain how these giant orbs were created – by humankind or by nature?

They have been extensively studied by several archaeologists, notably Dr Samuel Lothrop from the Peabody Museum at Harvard University, and everyone has marvelled at their near-perfect spherical shape, regardless of size. One of the largest balls, with a diameter of 2 metres (6½ feet), deviates in its circumference by only 1.27 cm

Dr Samuel Lothrop made extensive studies of Las Bolas Grandes following their discovery in the 1930s. This is one of his photographs, showing the balls in their original location.

or ½ inch (i.e. approximately two-tenths of 1 per cent). Yet the identity of the long-vanished sculptors responsible for precision stone carving of such an exceptionally high standard as this remains a mystery.

Nowadays, the general consensus of opinion is that the Bolas Grandes embody a canny combination of human and natural design. Great quantities of geometrically accurate stone spheres measuring up to 3.3 metres (11 feet) in diameter yet derived from wholly natural, volcanic processes have been discovered in Mexico. Although they lack the professional external finish displayed by the Costa Rican balls, these Mexican examples eloquently demonstrate that Mother Nature is capable of some impressive feats of mechanical engineering.

Also relevant to this line of speculation is the fact that the granite from which the Costa Rican balls are carved is not indigenous to the Diquís Delta. Hence their raw material clearly originated from elsewhere; yet there is no evidence to suggest that the nearest

The balls vary in size. Some are smaller than footballs, others more than 2 metres (6½ feet) across.

source (and even that is many kilometres away) has ever been quarried. At present, therefore, the origin of their stony substance is yet another mystery associated with these giant orbs.

Taking all this into account, researchers consider it likely not only that Costa Rica's nameless sculptors

were inspired by natural spheres comparable to those of Mexico, but also that some such spheres were imported from foreign parts to the Diquís Delta. There they were directly used by these artisans, improving upon nature's originals to produce the mathematically precise, expertly surfaced versions that we now know as the Bolas Grandes.

Even if all this is true, however, we have still to explain *why* they carved these balls. What was their function – indicatory, symbolic? Perhaps we are looking too deeply for answers: is it too heretical or unscientific to suggest that they were wantonly ornamental?

"That blank face with the dead eyes..." American ethnographer Zora Neale Hurston took this photograph of zombified Felicia Felix-Mentor in Haiti in 1937.

ZOMBIES

Belief in zombies – the living dead – is widespread throughout the voodoo-ridden West Indian country of Haiti, on the island of Hispaniola, to such an extent that even the poorest peasants willingly pay large sums of money for heavy slabs of stone to be placed over their relatives' graves. This is to prevent their corpses from being stolen by evil sorcerers, called bokors, who magically restore them to an eerie half-life as zombies and then take them to remote areas where they are put to work as slaves. Although they can eat, breathe and move, zombies are incapable of thinking for themselves, and have no knowledge of who they once were or of anything else concerning their previous life.

All of this sounds like something from a cheap horror movie, but there are dozens of confirmed cases of zombies and zombification on file, spanning countless years. In 1980, for example, a police officer saw a female zombie ambling mindlessly through a village under his supervision, and recognized her as Natagette Joseph – a woman whom he had pronounced dead in 1966, when she was aged about 46.

Back in October 1936, an almost naked female zombie was found wandering close to a roadway in Haiti's Artibonite Valley. After being transferred to the authorities, she was formally identified by her father and her brother as Felicia Felix-Mentor, who had died from a quick-acting fever in 1907 and had been buried. What makes this case so interesting is that it was the first to feature a Western investigator.

While under surveillance at the hospital at Gonaives, Felicia was visited by the American ethnographer Zora Neale Hurston, who photographed and studied her closely during the visit.

Hurston was later to record: "The sight was dreadful. That blank face with the dead eyes. The eyelids were white all around the eyes as if they had been burned with acid. There was nothing you could say to her or get from her except by looking at her, and the sight of this wreckage was too much to endure for long."

By far the most celebrated of all zombie cases, however, is that of Clairvius Narcisse – the only zombie to become a television star! One day in 1980, Angelina Narcisse was shopping in the market-place of l'Estère, her home village, when suddenly a voice whispered into her ear the boyhood

nickname of her long-dead brother Clairvius. He had died from fever on 2 May 1962 at the Albert Schweitzer Hospital, Deschapelles in the Artibonite Valley, and had been buried the next day at a cemetery north of l'Estère. Bearing in mind that his nickname was known only to immediate members of their family, and had not even been used by any of them since childhood, Angelina was naturally startled to hear it. She was far more startled, however, when she turned round to see who had uttered it – for there, albeit a little shaky on his feet and somewhat bleary-eyed, stood Clairvius!

Not surprisingly, Angelina promptly fainted, but after recovering she confirmed that it was indeed her supposedly dead brother. His identity was also verified by other members of their family, by over 200 l'Estère residents and by his ability to answer correctly many detailed questions about his boyhood that would have baffled everyone but the real Clairvius.

This extraordinary episode attracted such widespread media interest that even the BBC arrived from Britain and made a television film about it. But most important of all, here was a zombie that, unlike others previously investigated, was still sufficiently alert and articulate to be able to reveal how he had actually become a zombie, and what had happened to him afterwards.

It turned out that he had fathered many illegitimate children but had refused to provide financial support for them, and he had also argued violently with his brother over a land dispute. As a result, his brother had hired a bokor to zombify Clairvius. This had been achieved by surreptitiously feeding him a secret poison that had initially produced fever-like symptoms but soon sent him into a death-like trance, in which he was fully conscious yet wholly paralysed, with ghostly skin pallor and a near-imperceptible heartbeat. Even when examined by two different doctors he appeared to be dead, and so he was buried – alive!

Not long afterwards, his body, still paralysed, was dug up by the bokor, who gave him a second type of drug that rendered him sluggishly mobile but prevented any type of clear, decisive thought. Once this had been administered, Clairvius was savagely beaten and was then taken away to the north of Haiti, where he spent the next two years as a slave, working alongside other zombies and constantly abused by their sadistic sorcerer master. He might never have escaped, but one day another zombie somehow awoke sufficiently to attack and kill the bokor. Once the bokor was dead, their periodic intake of the mind-controlling drug ceased, and in the case of Clairvius he gradually began to remember who he was and what had taken place. During the following years, he roamed from one region to another, but after

learning that his brother had died he returned to l'Estère, where he met his sister Angelina.

This astonishing account was of keen interest to American biologist Wade Davis, working at that time in the Harvard Botanical Museum, who was eager to uncover the biochemical identities of the mysterious substances used in zombification – immobilizing, then reviving and brainwashing those victims selected by bokors for this purpose. After visiting Haiti to research the subject and to collect samples of the substances, Davis ascertained that the immobilizing poison contained two very noteworthy constituents. One was tetrodotoxin, a very effective nerve poison inducing rapid, profound paralysis, and commonly obtained from puffer fishes. The other was a fluid containing a potent anaesthetic and hallucinogen, secreted by the skin glands of the highly poisonous cane toad *Bufo marinus*. Davis has recounted his findings in a fascinating book, *The Serpent and the Rainbow*.

As for the resuscitating, mind-controlling drug, this was datura, obtained from the aptly named zombie cucumber *Datura stramonium*. Already known in other contexts to Western pharmacological researchers and also referred to as the thorn apple or jimson weed, its effects include delusions, mental confusion, disorientation, amnesia, and (if taken in sufficient doses) an impenetrable stupor – all typical zombie characteristics. Yet there was clearly more involved here than just this drug, because even when it was no longer administered the zombies rarely regained their normal mental state, remaining perpetually in a twilight world of semi-consciousness until the advent of true death.

In relation to this, Davis noted that if the paralysed, buried victims awaiting zombification are left in their coffins for any considerable period before being exhumed, they will experience oxygen starvation, resulting in irreversible brain damage that enhances datura's mind-numbing activities. The reason why Clairvius Narcisse became relatively lucid once his doses of datura ceased must, therefore, be because he had not been left in his coffin long enough to suffer

any significant degree of oxygen starvation before being dug up by the bokor.

An interesting side-discovery was made by Davis during his zombie revelations. Far from being innocent victims of evil bokors, it seems that those transformed into zombies were often people who had caused trouble themselves and, as a result of this, an angry relative or a jealous neighbour had sought revenge by hiring a bokor to turn them into zombies as a punishment.

From Davis's remarkable findings, it is clear that the traditional nightmarish concept of zombies as rotting corpses magically resurrected to life is nothing more than superstition, made real only by horror movies and pulp novels. Nevertheless, in one sense zombies can still be equated very accurately with the living dead. After all, to be drugged into immobility, pronounced dead and then buried alive in a coffin, exhumed by sorcerers and maintained ever afterwards in a constant state of brainwashed, brutalized servitude – if that isn't a fate worse than death itself, a veritable living death, then what is?

BLUE MEN OF THE MOUNTAINS

Almost 6000 metres (20,000 feet) above sea level, high in the Andean mountains of Chile, lives a community of miners whose members can be instantly distinguished from miners elsewhere in the world, and for a very good reason: their skin is bright blue!

These extraordinary people were brought to scientific attention by physiologist Dr John West from the University of California's School of Medicine at San Diego, who discovered them during a mountaineering trip. At first, the secret of their blue-coloured skin was a complete mystery, but over a period of time Dr West's studies uncovered the answer.

The miners' blue hue stems from oxygen deficiency at the lofty altitude at which they live (some 750 metres, or 2500 feet, higher than the previous

The high Andes of Chile are home to a mining community living some 750 metres (2500 feet) higher than the previous record altitude for long-term human survival.

record for long-term human survival), coupled with their active life-style. These two factors collectively induce the miners to produce greater than normal amounts of the oxygen-transporting blood pigment haemoglobin. This is bright red when oxygenated, carrying oxygen from the lungs to the body organs via the arteries; but it is blue when deoxygenated, travelling from the body organs back to the lungs via the veins.

Deoxygenated haemoglobin imparts a blue colouration to skin when present in the high concentration exhibited by these miners, because its colour is more readily visible through the skin than is the red shade of oxygenated haemoglobin.

Blue-skinned people are not unique to Chile. In Perry County, Kentucky, USA, there is a community characterized by (and nowadays very famous for) their pale-blue skin. Their history began in c.1800, when a boy with blue-tinted skin was born in France but later migrated to the USA, becoming resident on the relatively inaccessible, little-frequented banks of Perry County's Troublesome Creek in the Ozark Mountains. Here he married a local woman and raised a family, whose members exhibited their father's curious trait.

This suggested that whereas the Chilean miners' blue skin is a product of direct physiological adaptation to unusual environmental conditions, in the case of the Troublesome Creek family an inherited mutant gene was responsible. And sure enough, as a result of longstanding inbreeding among the small, isolated community living here, the blue-skin trait persisted, producing a localized population of blue-skinned people.

During the 1960s, this fascinating case attracted the attention of Kentucky University haematologist Dr Madison Cawein. His studies revealed that the biochemical fault caused by the mutant gene, and resulting in the Troublesome Creek denizens' blue skin, was an inability to synthesize the enzyme that breaks down metahaemoglobin – a respiratory blood pigment that is distinctly blue-brown in colour. As it

happens, however, this condition can be simply but successfully treated by the regular administration of methylene blue, a common antiseptic that reverses the mutant gene's effect, thus transforming blue skin into normal pink skin.

CHUPACABRAS

Since the 1970s, the Caribbean island of Puerto Rico has witnessed some decidedly bizarre events featuring a mystifying entity called the chupacabras ("goatsucker").

"Goatsucker" is also an alternative name for a group of inoffensive nocturnal birds more commonly known as nightjars, but judging from the Puerto Rican accounts, the chupacabras is not a bird and is anything but inoffensive! So far, it has been blamed for the savage deaths of many dogs, cats and livestock animals, even creatures as large as cattle and horses, whose grossly mutilated

Grisly gourmet: the chupacabras or "goatsucker" is a grotesque predator with a penchant for blood and mutilation. Has it escaped from a genetic engineering laboratory, as some people believe?

corpses have later been found drained of blood and minus various body organs that have been ripped out. In what must surely be the most grotesque incident from this particular category of chupacabras reports, however, the "victim" was a stuffed teddy bear, which the creature had reputedly destroyed at a house in Caguas before leaving behind a slimy puddle and a piece of rancid white meat on the windowsill!

The chupacabras's attacks upon animals are sinister enough, but its encounters with humans are infinitely stranger, as Scott Corrales has revealed in his invaluable 71-page report, *The Chupacabras Diaries*. At 6 a.m. on 26 March 1995, Jaime Torres was walking through a field containing a flock of sheep owned by farmer Enrique Barreto of Orocovis when he allegedly saw a chupacabras lying along a branch on a nearby tree, looking down at him. According to Torres, it had a round head, dark grey face, elongated black eyes, delicate jaw and small mouth. Even more distinctive, however, was its pigmentation: just like a surrealistic

chameleon it changed colour even as Torres stared at it, fluctuating from purple to brown to yellow. Yet its most bizarre talent was still to be revealed.

Suddenly, as Torres continued to look up at it, the chupacabras's head began to rock from side to side and the creature emitted an eerie hissing sound; as it did so, Torres became very dizzy, almost fainting. Losing no time, the creature dropped down from the tree and rapidly disappeared through the undergrowth, leaving its queasy observer far behind.

This same locality had previously been the site of a very similar encounter. In that case a police officer had been investigating a dead sheep on Barreto's estate when he spied a bipedal creature, 1 metre or so (3–4 feet) tall, with bright orange-yellow eyes peering at him from a shadowy area nearby. When the officer attempted to pursue this apparent chupacabras, however, he was instantly overcome by such an acute yet wholly unheralded attack of nausea and headache that he was forced to

abandon the chase and needed to be assisted by his partner back to their patrol car.

In another incident, the investigator Jorge Martín learnt that a Mrs Quiñones of Naranjito had recently seen a chupacabras the height of a three-year-old child, standing by some hedges. True to form, its gaze caused her to feel so nauseous that she was unable to follow when it fled away.

Based upon a considerable corpus of eyewitness descriptions, the chupacabras seemingly stands about 1–1.5 metres (3–5 feet) tall, with large slanted eyes (sometimes said to glow orange or red), bare holes instead of lobed ears, tiny holes in place of true nostrils and a small lipless mouth. It has thin arms with three clawed fingers on each hand and muscular legs with three clawed toes on each foot (reminiscent of South Carolina's equally mystifying Lizard Man, p. 131). Its furry body is grey mottled with darker blotches, and glowing spines run from the crown of its head down the entire length of its back and continuously change colour.

No creature known to science bears the slightest resemblance to this entity, which has encouraged eyewitnesses and others to propose a number of more imaginative identities; these range from a UFO-originating alien to a grotesque, top-secret product of genetic engineering that has somehow absconded from its laboratory confines. Scientists have attempted to explain away the chupacabras's livestock kills as the work of escapee monkeys that are indeed known to exist here, but monkeys do not suck blood, they do not change colour and they certainly cannot render people physically ill simply by gazing at them. Little wonder that Scott Corrales has named this entity the paranormal predator of Puerto Rico.

As a tantalizing tail-piece, the two issues of *Strange Magazine* for 1995 contained reports by Corrales on the alleged corpse of a small but quite extraordinary entity that had been killed in Puerto Rico during the 1980s by a cattle rancher. Apparently, the rancher's farm had suffered many incidents of grisly animal livestock mutilations, so he had been mounting a vigil with two friends on the night in question when, to their amazement, four of these beings had entered his stables and had begun levitating one of his heifers! The slain creature's three companions escaped.

The reports' accompanying photo, one of 22 obtained by Jorge Martín from a Mr Rafael Baerga, depicts a creature strongly reminiscent of a chupacabras, sharing its round head, large slanting eyes, small lipless mouth, tiny nostrils, apparent lack of ears, and thin arms. However, the corpse's clawed hands each have *four* fingers, not three. Biologists to whom Martín showed the photos were unable to identify the creature, citing many noteworthy morphological idiosyncrasies when ruling out monkeys or a human foetus as realistic possibilities. At present, the unnamed cattle rancher who shot it is refusing to submit its corpse for formal analysis in case it is confiscated, so its identity remains unresolved.

THE BERMUDA TRIANGLE

The Bermuda Triangle has received intensive coverage and attention from the media world. Whether it actually exists in the real world, however, is another matter entirely.

According to a plethora of speculative reports, articles and books that appeared on this subject during the late 1960s and 1970s, the Bermuda Triangle is a mysterious expanse of sea in the western Atlantic where a disproportionately high number of ships and aircraft have supposedly vanished without trace over the years; this includes more than a hundred since 1945. The outermost geographical limits claimed for its baleful effects can be mapped to yield a triangle that links up the tip of Florida, Puerto Rico and Bermuda, thereby earning it its name, which was coined in 1964 by Vincent Gaddis, a veteran American investigator of mysteries.

Countless theories proposing how and why the Triangle exerts such deadly power have been aired. These range from attacks by sea monsters, abductions by extraterrestrials or subaquatic Atlanteans, and freak killer waves of gargantuan proportions, to sudden releases of methane bubbles from frozen lattices of ice on the sea-bed, a black hole beneath the waves, geomagnetic anomalies, and a giant submerged crystal warping the space around its victims (as suggested by Charles Berlitz in his bestseller *The Bermuda Triangle*).

One of the most frequently reiterated cases in the Bermuda Triangle file featured five US Navy Avenger torpedo-bomber planes called Flight 19. The squadron vanished while flying over this area of sea in bad weather on the evening of 5 December 1945, after setting off in good flying conditions that afternoon on a routine training mission from the Fort Lauderdale Naval Air Station. A Martin Mariner search plane sent to look for them also went missing.

Many accounts of this incident claim that in a series of strange messages transmitted by the bombers' leader, Lieutenant Charles C. Taylor, before

*The **Marine Sulphur Queen**, which disappeared in 1963, is one of many vessels which have supposedly been lost without trace inside the Bermuda Triangle.*

their disappearance, he stated: "We seem to be off course ... everything is wrong ... strange ... even the ocean doesn't look as it should ... it looks like we are...." No further words were received. Yet when this was investigated by Lawrence D. Kusche, a research librarian at Arizona State University and author of the much-acclaimed book *The Bermuda Triangle – Solved*, he found that there was no evidence whatsoever to suggest that Taylor had ever spoken those words.

An official Navy report concluded that both of Taylor's compasses had failed and he had mistaken his squadron's position, led astray by the similarity in appearance between the Bahamas and the Florida Keys (the islands that they should have been flying over). In trying to relocate their correct position, he and his squadron would have run out of fuel, crashing into the sea that night. The darkness would have hidden any debris from search parties. At 7.50 p.m., the SS *Gaines Mills* sighted a plane catching fire above the sea near Daytona Beach before hitting the water and exploding. This is believed to have been the lost search plane.

Kusche and other serious researchers have also exposed significant discrepancies between popular reports of many additional Bermuda Triangle cases and the verifiable facts concerning them. Indeed, as David Group emphasizes in *The Evidence for the Bermuda Triangle*, it is very apparent that the supposed "evidence" is principally founded upon factual errors, misinterpretations and overt distortions of the facts behind the cited cases. Almost all of these cases, in fact, can be readily shown to have a perfectly natural rather than an unnatural explanation.

Perhaps the most telling blow to the much-hyped Bermuda Triangle was struck by the shipping insurers, Lloyd's of London, in a letter of 4 April 1975 to the magazine *Fate*: "According to Lloyd's Records, 428 vessels have been reported missing throughout the world since 1955, and it may interest you to know that our intelligence service can find no evidence to support the claim that the 'Bermuda Triangle' has more losses than elsewhere."

THE MOVING COFFINS OF BARBADOS

One of the most famous unsolved Caribbean mysteries features the unnervingly mobile coffins formerly housed in the Chase family's vault at Christ Church, in the south-west of Barbados. The vault was purchased in 1807 by Thomas Chase, a plantation owner, and by 1812 three members of his family had died. The first two had been entombed inside its walls without incident, but when the vault was opened again to admit the coffin of the third, attendants were shocked to discover that the two coffins already present had apparently been disturbed, for their positions had changed. From then on, with the sole exception of Thomas Chase's own burial on 9 August 1812, each time that a member of the Chase family died and the vault was reopened, similar scenes of disarray met the eyes of the ever-increasing throng of morbid onlookers eager to view this macabre sight for themselves.

Yet there were no footprints in the sand covering the vault's floor, and even secret seals deliberately hidden by investigators were found not to have been tampered with when next the vault was opened. Only the positions of the coffins changed, nothing else.

In 1820, the mystery was brought to an unresolved end when Viscount Combermere, Governor of Barbados, ordered all the coffins to be removed and reburied in fresh graves nearby. Many explanations have been offered for their unwonted restlessness, including seismic tremors, poltergeist activity, flooding and even an elaborate Masonic hoax, but none has been verified. All that we do know is that the Chase family's "haunted vault" has remained empty ever afterwards, and its coffins have shown no desire to wander since their reburial.

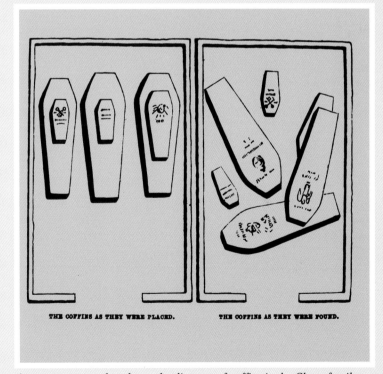

THE COFFINS AS THEY WERE PLACED.　　THE COFFINS AS THEY WERE FOUND.

A contemporary plan shows the disarray of coffins in the Chase family vault after their last disturbance, in 1820.

Migo
(water monster)

NEW
BRITAIN

PAPUA NEW GUINEA

Artrellia
(giant mystery monitor lizard)

Devil-pig

MURRAY
ISLANDS

Booya stones

Burrunjor
(living dinosaur?)

Le Serrec's
sea serpent

Kulta
(modern dinosaur?)

Min-min lights

AUSTRALIA

Yarri
(Queensland tiger)

Ayers Rock (Uluru)

Yowie (man-beast)

Living thy

Mirrii dogs

Giant mystery
monitor lizard

Giant AEPYORNIS egg

Yuurii/bitarr

Lord of the Deep
(giant shark)

Giant AEPYORNIS egg

"Jaws" (yarri?)
carcase

Bunyip

Bunyip

Bunyip

Mass stranding
of electra dolphins

Nyol, net-net, pot-koorok
(ancestral spirit entities)

Living thylacine

Mass stranding
of pilot whales

Bunyip

TASMANIA

Maero (man-beast)

Fireman/
surviving upland moa

The islands of Oceania are scattered across an
area too vast to show here in detail. The following
phenomena do not appear on this map:

EASTER ISLAND

   Giant stone statues

FIJIAN ISLANDS

   Fire-walking

   Vélé (mystery pygmies)

HAWAIIAN ISLANDS

   Menehune (mystery pygmies)

   Nawao (man-beast)

   Musical spheres of light

   Barking beach

KIRIBATI (ARORAE)

   Taani-kanimomoi (whistling ghosts)

POLYNESIA

   Lost Pacific continent of Mu

SAMOA

   Death clicks

SOCIETY ISLANDS (RAIATEA, TAHITI)

   Fire-walking

TUAMOTU ARCHIPELAGO

   Lord of the Deep (giant shark)

VANUATU

   Vui/wui (man-beast)

◈ Chapter 7 ◈

Australasia and Oceania

ISLANDS OF THE STRANGE AND UNCANNY

IN TRADITIONAL MYTHS AND LEGENDS, ISLANDS HAVE ALWAYS BEEN MYSTERIOUS PLACES OF MAGIC AND WONDER, SET APART BY AN ALLURING ARRAY OF INSULAR ENIGMAS AND ANOMALIES. THIS IS EQUALLY TRUE IN THE REAL WORLD OF AUSTRALASIA AND OCEANIA, AMONGST WHOSE MYRIAD ISLES, SET IN THE TROPICAL SEASCAPE OF THE SOUTH PACIFIC, THE STRANGE AND THE INEXPLICABLE AWAIT DISCOVERY.

*Mass stranding
of pilot whales*

EW ZEALAND

Surviving giant moa

*Pseudoplesiosaur
carcase*

Key to Phenomena

 FLYING

 WATER

 ELEMENTS

 LAND ANIMAL

 HUMAN

 SITES

🞸 PARANORMAL

The Ancient Ways

AYERS ROCK – THE MYSTICAL ALLURE OF ULURU

To Westerners and Western science, it is Ayers Rock – the world's largest natural monolith. Situated about 320 kilometres (200 miles) south-east of Alice Springs in the Northern Territory of Australia, this enormous block of arkose sandstone stands 348 metres (1142 feet) high and is up to 3 kilometres (2 miles) long. In addition, it may extend 6 kilometres ($3^1/_4$ miles) down beneath the earth's surface, thus concealing the greater part of its true bulk in a fashion akin to a terrestrial iceberg.

To the aboriginal peoples of Australia, however, it is called Uluru and constitutes the most sacred site on this vast island continent. It is a place of pilgrimage across the arid desert for aboriginals from every region of Australia. Technically, Uluru is owned by two local tribes, the Yankunitjatjara and the Pitjantjatjara, and many of the caves around its perimeter, which measures over 8 kilometres (5 miles), contain sacred paintings depicting the Dreamtime.

The Dreamtime is the aboriginal concept of Creation – when the world and all that it contains came into being. It was a time very different from today, peopled by gods and heroes whose bodies and songs gave rise to the mountains, the lakes and the stars, and by ancient spirit beings and magical beasts (see p.196) that populated the lands with Australia's unique fauna and

Ayers Rock: to Australia's aboriginal peoples the most sacred place on earth.

flora. And every crack, every pebble, every rocky outgrowth on Uluru is invested with a specific Dreamtime story or meaning for its aboriginal guardians.

In recent times, however, this belief has come into conflict with a modern Western threat – tourism. Uluru is famed for its spectrum of highly photogenic colour changes each

morning as the rising sun bestows ever more sunlight upon its craggy surface, transforming its sable evening tones into deep mauve and thence into a shimmering pink hue. This magnificent sight has drawn White Australians and tourists from overseas to visit Ayers Rock in their millions every year, but not all are satisfied merely to see its awesome majesty. All too often, tourists decide to take back home a souvenir of Uluru – sometimes a pebble, sometimes a sizeable lump of rock.

Needless to say, in the eyes of the aboriginal peoples such acts are a desecration and have caused great consternation, but Uluru appears to be solving the problem in its own mystical but highly effective manner. In February 1996, Julian Barry, senior ranger at Ayers Rock, revealed that numerous tourists are returning their pilfered souvenirs (sometimes personally, more often by post), convinced that they are cursed and have brought them bad luck.

One Londoner claimed that shortly after taking a piece of rock from Uluru, he was struck down by gout; an American cited the sudden ill-health of his mother after bringing home a rocky souvenir from Uluru; many others have suffered bankruptcy. Are these mere coincidences, or is the magic of the Dreamtime still as potent today as it was in the beginning?

ANCESTRAL BEINGS AND SPIRIT BEASTS

According to the Dreamtime (Creation) myths of Australia's aboriginal tribes, in the early days of the world there were many strange types of ancestral spirit entities. These magical beasts and beings are dismissed by modern science as fantasy, but the aboriginals firmly believe that they still exist today – if you know where to look for them.

The Wiradjuri aboriginals who live in the central west of New South Wales say that some of this region's lonely stretches of countryside and even its rivers are frequented by hairy dog-like animals known as the mirrii or mirriuula. These magic animals are often quite small when first seen, but the longer you stare at them, the larger they grow! They can often grow to the size of a calf or even a pony in just a few moments, and then, without warning, they will disappear. Some mirrii dogs are dangerous, because when they see someone they will follow him and try to lure him into the depths of their river.

The Wiradjuri also speak of the yuurii, which are hairy little men and women, no more than a metre (3 feet) tall, but with long fingernails and big teeth. The yuurii men have long beards too. The Gumbangirr aboriginals, who also live in New South Wales, call these tiny people the bitarr and say that they particularly enjoy playing with aboriginal children.

The aboriginals of Victoria are familiar with some other types of mysterious pygmy. The nyols are small, stony-grey humanoid beings who allegedly inhabit caverns in the deep rocks beneath the surface of the land, but occasionally they come up above ground to frolic and play amid the shadows of dusk. In contrast, the net-nets have brown skin, long sharp claws instead of fingernails and live among the rocks above ground. Stranger still is the pot-koorok, a small man-frog with great webbed feet, long mobile fingers and a wet pear-shaped body. It dwells in rivers and deep pools. Arnhem Land's rock crevasses may still be home to stick-like spirits known as the mimi, similar in form to Queensland's quinkins – embodiments of lust.

And then there is Old Red-Eye. This is the name given to an often insubstantial entity, or one of only vaguely human form, that can materialize anywhere, at any time, and

This aboriginal rock painting in northern Queensland depicts the stick-like quinkin spirits.

which can mesmerize a person with a fixed glare from its bright red eyes. Time stands still for the victims of Old Red-Eye, held in thrall for however long it chooses to gaze at them, and even if they should succeed in calling out for help, no one is ever able to hear them.

Even more sinister is the yara-ma-yha-who. According to aboriginal folklore, this is a tiny toothless frog-like man that lives in fig trees and has suckers on its hands. If any children should see it, they must run away at once, because the yara-ma-yha-who is a merciless vampire, who will immediately jump down on top of them from out of the tree, clasp them with its suckers and drain them of their blood!

Mirrii dogs, net-nets, pot-kooroks, yara-ma-yha-whos and the other magical dream beasts are rarely reported nowadays, for their time was long ago – but time is never still, and one day theirs may come again.

✷

EASTER ISLAND, LAND OF THE LONG-EARS

Lying roughly 4350 kilometres (2700 miles) east of Tahiti, 4200 (2600) west of Valparaiso in Chile and 3200 (2000) south-west of the Galapagos Islands in the south Pacific, Easter Island is the world's loneliest inhabited locality, as Thor Heyerdahl observed in *Aku-Aku*, recording his 1955–56 expedition here.

The island first became known to the Western world when it was discovered by the Dutch sea voyager Admiral Jacob Roggeveen on 5 April 1722; this was Easter Sunday, hence the island's Western name. Ever since then, Easter

Island has attracted great scientific interest, owing to its enigmatic giant statues (moai), numbering around a thousand. Who made them, and why?

Researchers now believe that Easter Island was first settled in c.AD 400, and for several centuries afterwards the islanders created skilfully carved, sun-oriented terraces and small statues. These resembled various pre-Columbian Andean examples (i.e. dating from the period before Columbus's discovery of the New World). By AD 1100, however, they were converting the terraces into ceremonial platforms (ahu), and were creating the first stone giants, carved directly from the crater walls of Rano Raraku, a dormant volcano.

These statues were slid down the hillside into a standing position, where they were completed and polished before being taken to the ahu and placed on top of them, facing inland. Their function remains controversial, but according to modern-day islanders they were monuments to dead rulers and were once infused with benevolent supernatural power (mana). Intriguingly, various geomagnetic anomalies have been recorded from Easter Island, so could it be possible that these monoliths acted as foci for healing earth energy, as proposed for standing stones in Britain and elsewhere in the world?

At first, the statues varied in form from one another, but later examples all depicted the same man (whose identity is unknown). Each was carved only as far down as the top of his legs, and portrayed him with a heavy brow, lantern jaws, jutting chin, aquiline nose, very long ear-lobes and a red topknot (pukao) on his head. The topknots were carved from a small volcanic cone called Puna Pau. Most statues weighed 25–40 tonnes and stood 3.5–7.5 metres (12–25 feet) tall, but over the years they were carved ever larger by the islanders: one incomplete example still lying inside the crater at Rano Raraku weighs about 270 tonnes and is around 21 metres (70 feet) long.

This is only one of about 400 unfinished statues found in the crater. The reason why these were never completed was a violent civil war on the island, between the Hanau Eepe or Long-Ears, who were apparently the ruling class, and the Hanau Momoko or

Early Easter Island statues vary in form, but later examples – such as this, near the Rano Raraku crater – portray the same unknown man.

Wooden tablets and a lost language: could these solve the riddle of how civilization sprang up in one of the world's most remote places?

Short-Ears, who were their underlings. In 1680, the war culminated in a battle on the Poike peninsula, in which the Short-Ears triumphed, killing all but one of the Long-Ears, and 42 years later the island's long period of isolation from European contact came to an end with its discovery by Roggeveen. In 1774, Captain Cook arrived, and found that some time in the previous 50 years the stone giants had been knocked off their platforms during fresh outbreaks of war and were lying haphazardly on the ground – but far worse was to follow in 1862.

This was when a Peruvian slave ship abducted most of Easter Island's men, transporting them back to Peru to work in the mines. The majority died, and of the few that survived and were returned to their island home following the intervention of Tahiti's bishop, all were infected with smallpox. Inevitably, this virulent disease decimated Easter Island's already much-depleted population: by 1877 it totalled a mere 111 people. One of the many consequences of this terrible saga of suffering was the death of every islander who could read their unique picture writing (called rongo-rongo and carved on wooden slabs). Even today, it

remains undeciphered. In 1888, Chile claimed Easter Island and since then the population of native islanders has gradually increased, so that they now number more than 2000. Around 30 of the giant statues have been erected again too, by visiting scientific teams.

But where did the very first inhabitants of Easter Island come from? According to traditional schools of thought, they originated solely from the Polynesian islands to the west, whose inhabitants in turn came from Asia. Thor Heyerdahl, however, was not convinced that this was the entire story, and during his researches on Easter Island in the mid-1950s he obtained some intriguing evidence to support his conviction that migration to this far-flung outpost may also have occurred from the east, by pre-Inca people from Peru.

The evidence on Easter Island that Heyerdahl has cited in favour of his hypothesis includes: the presence here of a freshwater plant called the totora reed native to Lake Titicaca in the Andes, and also the Andean sweet potato; early Easter Island drawings of reed boats and statues that recall versions found in the ancient city of Tiahuanaco near Bolivia's border with Peru; the former presence of sun worship here and in early Peruvian cultures; the existence here and in Andean cultures of fair-skinned red-haired people; plus the occurrence of the stone giants' long ear-lobe characteristic in Andean legends about the Tiahuanacan deity Con-Tici Viracocha. Demonstrating that such a migration would have been possible in those far-off days, Heyerdahl had previously built an early-Peruvian-style balsawood raft (named the Kon-Tiki) and sailed across the Pacific from Peru to the Tuamotu Archipelago in his famous voyage of 1947.

Geographer Robert Langdon has also offered support for this notion by disclosing in 1988 that tapioca, derived from South America's manioc plant, had been found to be part of the Easter Island people's diet as long ago as 1770, by an expedition led by Captain Felipe Gonzalez. Unfortunately, this notable fact subsequently became obscured owing to a mistranslation of manioc's local name in 1908 by historian Bolton

Corney within his definitive account of the expedition – an error that remained uncorrected until Langdon's revelation 80 years later.

Even so, the notion of ancient South American settlement here is still not fully accepted in scientific circles, so the mystery surrounding the origins of Easter Island's civilization remains unresolved. Ironically, the answer to this riddle may already exist, locked away in the various surviving samples of Easter Island's cryptic rongo-rongo language, but until (if ever) the key to its linguistic secret is uncovered, we shall never know for sure.

FIRE-WALKING

Originally a rite of spring, and performed in many parts of the world, including India, Greece, South Africa and California, fire-walking is most popularly associated with Polynesia, especially the Society Islands and the Fijian Islands. In 1901, engineering scientist Professor S.P. Langley from the Smithsonian Institution witnessed a classic demonstration of fire-walking in Tahiti, performed by a native priest from the

neighbouring Society island of Raiatea. The demonstration featured a trench measuring 6.4 metres (21 feet) long, 2.75 metres (9 feet) across and about 0.6 metre (2 feet) deep, filled with radiant basalt rocks piled on top of blazing logs. The priest and several of his acolytes strode steadily but very briskly over this trench four times, with no resulting injury. Yet when Langley levered one of the rocks out of it and into a bucket of water, the water churned and frothed so violently that a considerable quantity boiled over the sides.

In 1950, Dr Harry B. Wright of Philadelphia observed a similar fire-

Many fire-walkers expose the soles of their feet to temperatures as high as 800°C.

walking ceremony, performed annually by the people of Mbengga, one of the smaller Fijian islands. Before the fire-walk began, Wright examined the feet of the participants, to determine whether they had been treated with any protective substance, but he found no evidence to suggest this. Paradoxically, he did discover that although these people experienced no injury or pain whatsoever when walking across their trench of fiery rocks, their feet displayed normal sensitivity to the approach of a lighted cigarette and also to a pinprick.

Many other fire-walking demonstrations have been closely monitored by scientists, who confirm that the walkers' feet have not been treated in any way, that the temperature of the rocks has been shown to be as high as 800°C, and that even untrained Westerners can successfully perform fire-walking – as long as they firmly believe that they will not be harmed by the fire. How can this astonishing accomplishment be explained?

The answer seems to be a subtle blend of several different interacting factors. The soles of the feet of native fire-walkers are very thick and calloused, which would reduce injury. Moreover, during an investigation in

1935, the English psychical researcher Harry Price noted that physical contact between the *entirety* of each of the walker's feet and the fiery rocks lasts no more than half a second at a time (hence actual contact by any *specific* part of that foot is even less). Thus there is insufficient time for the feet to be burnt, especially if the total length of the walk is itself brief. Tellingly, after watching some local people undertake a three-second fire-walk at the 26th annual meeting of the Ceylon Association for the Advancement of Science, Dr Carlo Fonseka challenged them to perform a 30-second fire-walk: they all declined to do so.

As Professor Jearl Walker, a physicist at Cleveland State University in Ohio, has pointed out, a phenomenon very relevant to fire-walking is the Leidenfrost effect. This is the process whereby a liquid exposed to intense heat will instantly form a protective, insulating boundary layer composed of steam. It allows us all to indulge in a very simple form of fire-walking – when we snuff out a candle with a wet finger. And sure enough, many observers at fire-walking ceremonies have noted that the walkers often moisten their feet before performing the walk.

Psychology is also most important. Westerners performing fire-walking after convincing themselves that the glowing rocks will not harm them not only escape injury but also experience feelings of euphoria. This suggests an enhanced secretion by the brain of endorphins – natural pain-killers that impart an elevated sense of happiness and well-being. As shown with stigmata (pp.73–75) too, the power of the mind is indeed a potent force.

✶

BOOYA STONES

In Steven Spielberg's classic adventure film *Indiana Jones and the Temple of Doom*, starring Harrison Ford, the eponymous hero embarks upon a quest to regain some stolen sacred stones that are able to radiate an eerie glowing light. All this, of course, is fiction – whereas the booya stones from the Murray Islands are an extraordinary fact.

The Murray Islands are situated in the Torres Strait, separating the Cape York peninsula in Queensland from Papua New Guinea. The booya stones (of which at least three were known)

Stones that radiate an eerie glowing light: more than just enjoyable film fantasy?

were formerly retained by the Murray Islands' priesthood, who had apparently passed them down from generation to generation since time immemorial.

These remarkable objects have been researched in detail by Australian travel writer Ion Idriess, who revealed that they emitted a blue light of such intensity that when it was concentrated into a beam by a special holding device and pointed at a human, an X-ray effect was observed and it was invariably followed by that person's death. Idriess speculated that they may have been lumps of pure radium, but their identity has never been conclusively ascertained, for with the onset of European control in Australasia, the Murray Islands' priests hid their revered stones in secret caves. Perhaps a real-life Indiana Jones is needed, to rediscover not only their hideaway but also the key to their formidably potent power.

✦

WHISTLING GHOSTS AND DEATH CLICKS

During the first half of this century, Sir Arthur Grimble was an administrator in the Gilbert and Ellice Islands (now the independent Pacific republics of Kiribati and Tuvalu respectively), and it was here that he encountered the whistling ghosts of Arorae, a tiny coral isle in the Southern Gilbert group.

Towards the end of a long sea voyage to Arorae, Grimble was told by fellow passengers that his friend Tabanea, the sorcerer of Tarawa, had died two evenings before from a sudden stroke. Yet Tabanea had been in good health when Grimble had last seen him a week earlier, and there had been no ship in the area recently to bring news from Tarawa anyway. Consequently, Grimble dismissed the story as unfounded gossip; but when he arrived at Arorae, he received precisely the same account from a wholly independent source. Once again, however, Arorae had not been visited recently by anyone, so where had such a rumour originated?

In the Gilbert Islands, ancient understandings put the paranormal into context.

Making enquiries, Grimble learnt that on Arorae it had come from an extremely old wise-woman called Nei Watia, who had in turn received it from a mysterious but entirely infallible source – the taani-kanimomoi, or whistlers. These are supposedly the ghosts of recently dead relations, who inhabit the air and fly up and down the islands, seeing and hearing everything that happens and passing news of their findings to people who can understand their whistling speech.

Wishing to learn more about these remarkable entities, Grimble visited Nei Watia, and once he was inside her thatched shack she called out to the whistlers. Immediately, the entire shack was filled with a shrill multitudinous whistling, like a host of invisible crickets or strident disembodied

birdsong. It occurred at the same time as Nei Watia was speaking, thereby ruling out ventriloquism.

Perplexed but still not convinced, Grimble eventually departed Arorae, aboard a boat homeward-bound for Tarawa. As soon as he docked at Tarawa, however, he was met by a throng of people who informed him that his friend Tabanea had unexpectedly died – from a stroke and at the exact time reported (via Nei Wadia) by the whistling ghosts of Arorae.

A comparably bizarre phenomenon has also been documented from Samoa. Instead of whistling ghosts that spread news, however, it features the sudden onset of loud and persistent clicking sounds throughout the house of someone who is about to die.

Dragons and Devil-Pigs

TANTALIZING TIGERS

Since the 1800s, reports have regularly emerged from the rainforested areas of northern Queensland (and occasionally from elsewhere in Australia too) that tell of confrontations by aboriginal people and Western settlers with a large and notoriously savage tiger-like beast whose existence has still not been formally verified by science. Reputedly the size and shape of a leopard, but strikingly marked with blackish-grey and white hoop-like bands around its body, it has a distinctly feline head, very prominent, peculiarly tusk-like teeth at the front of its mouth, and is able to climb trees. The aboriginals have always known of this creature, and call it the yarri; to Westerners here, it has become known as the Queensland tiger.

Of the many yarri sightings currently documented, one of the most detailed examples, which graphically conveys not only the morphology but also the menacing demeanour of this mystifying animal, is a pre-1930s encounter by P.B. Scougall and G. de Tournoeur. They had been riding from Munna Creek towards Tiaro when they spied:

... a large animal of the cat tribe, standing about 20 yards [18 metres] away,

astride of a very dead calf, glaring defiance at us, and emitting what I can only describe as a growling whine. As far as the gathering darkness and torrential rain allowed us to judge he was nearly the size of a mastiff, of a dirty fawn colour, with a whitish belly, and broad blackish tiger stripes. The head was round, with rather prominent lynx-like ears, but unlike that feline there were a tail reaching to the

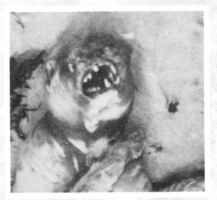

"Jaws": could this extraordinary fanged animal corpse be that of a yarri?

ground and large pads. We threw a couple of stones at him, which only made him crouch low, with ears laid flat, and emit a raspy snarl, vividly reminiscent of the African leopard's nocturnal 'wood-sawing' cry. Beating an angry tattoo on the grass with his tail, he looked so ugly and ready for a spring that we felt a bit 'windy'; but on our making a rush and cracking our stockwhips he bounded

away to the bend of the creek, where he turned back and growled at us.

This description does not match that of any living species of animal discovered by science so far, but since almost all of Australia's native mammals are marsupials, this formidable beast is most probably one too. In fact, a mere 10,000 years ago, a much greater variety of Australian marsupials existed than does today, and these included a leopard-sized feline version known as the marsupial or pouched lion *Thylacoleo carnifex*, whose fossil remains have been found in Queensland and several other mainland regions.

Very significantly, reconstructions of *Thylacoleo*'s appearance when alive, based upon studies of its fossils, portray a creature bearing a remarkable resemblance to eyewitness descriptions of the yarri; it shares the yarri's size, shape and even its strange tusk-like teeth. Since *Thylacoleo* is believed to have been a tree-climbing species (also like the yarri), it may have been striped too, for effective camouflage. Accordingly, some zoologists, including myself, strongly believe that the yarri may prove to be a living species of pouched lion.

Ironically, many yarris have allegedly been killed by farmers and hunters during the past two centuries, but because it was formerly a familiar

The thylacine or Tasmanian wolf THYLACINUS CYNOCEPHALUS, *which officially became extinct in 1936.*

creature to them (it is apparently much rarer nowadays), no one ever thought to preserve a carcase for scientific examination. There is, however, a unique photo that may portray just such a specimen.

In or around 1975, some beachcombers found an extraordinary, highly decomposed animal corpse in a beach and sand-dune area near the Margaret River in south-west Australia. They did not attempt to salvage it, but they did take one photo of it, vividly capturing its prominent tusk-like teeth; these have earned their demised owner the nickname "Jaws". Never before published, this sole photo of Jaws, kindly made available to me by Australian cryptozoologist Kevin Farley, is reproduced here. Could Jaws have been a yarri?

A major problem with such an identity is that whereas Jaws's tusk-like teeth are true fangs (i.e. canine teeth), those of *Thylacoleo* were enlarged incisors. Consequently, if the yarri is a living *Thylacoleo*, its dentition would not match Jaws's. Having said that, however, we cannot be certain (in the absence of a body) that the yarri is indeed a living *Thylacoleo*.

According to Farley, no one at the Australian Museum or the Queensland

Museum has been able to identify Jaws from the photo; like the yarri itself, therefore, it remains an enigma.

Very different from the Queensland tiger, but no less controversial, is the Tasmanian tiger – better known as the thylacine or Tasmanian wolf *Thylacinus cynocephalus*. Living up to its nickname as the world's most common extinct animal, the thylacine is regularly reported by eyewitnesses, and not only in Tasmania itself (where this striped, dog-like marsupial officially became extinct in 1936) but also on the Australian mainland (where it supposedly died out around 2500 years ago).

According to national park ranger Charlie Beasley, for example, on 25 January 1995 he had a sighting of a thylacine for about two minutes in some light forest inland from St Helen's in north-east Tasmania. Sandy-brown in colour, it was described by Beasley as "about half the size of a fully matured German shepherd dog, it had stripes over its body from about half-way down". This is an accurate verbal portrait of a thylacine.

Since 1993, a very similar beast has been reported from Queensland's Sunshine Coast too. One evening in March 1995, dentist Dr Lance Mesh was driving along the southern slopes of the

Buderim rainforest with his 10-year-old daughter Samantha when he saw "a strange-looking dog with stripes ... it was striped and like a combination of a goldy, brindly cat and dog. It was medium-sized and had a prominent bump above the eyes".

After reading about Mesh's sighting in Brisbane's *Sunday Mail* of 18 June, Ron West of Pomona came forward to announce that he and his wife had seen a creature fitting the thylacine's description too. They saw it one evening near their home, while it was sniffing a dead animal lying upon the road. According to their account, the creature was tan in colour, with very distinctive, darker stripes around its tail region, and stood about 60 cm (2 feet) tall. After a few moments, it "almost sauntered, loped off the road and into the scrub".

Taking into account the noteworthy fact that, whereas they have their own specific names for various other Australian mystery beasts, the aboriginals do not seem to have one for these thylacine-like animals, some investigators believe that even if such creatures really are thylacines they are not survivors of the native Australian version. Instead, it has been suggested that they could be descended from escapee Tasmanian thylacines, which were once kept in captivity on the mainland as zoo exhibits or even as exotic pets.

✷

New Guinea Novelties

Many major zoological surprises may well await disclosure amid New Guinea's vast yet sparsely explored jungles. During an expedition led in 1906 by Captain Charles Monckton to Mount Albert Edward in Papua, two of its members, Police Constable Oina and Private Ogi, were sent on ahead to investigate a newly discovered path. Unfortunately, Oina and Ogi somehow became separated from one another, and while attempting to find Oina, Ogi encountered two animals so strange that he referred to them afterwards as devil-pigs.

Ogi claimed that they were 1.4 metres (4½ feet) long and about a metre (3 feet) high, very dark in colour, with cloven feet, a horse-like tail and a very long nose. This description does not match any animal known in New Guinea today. Yet similar creatures have been sighted here by other explorers too. The closest correspondence among living species is with the tapirs – those long-snouted Malayan and South American relatives of horses and

An early stone sculpture of what may be a palorchestid features on this Papua New Guinea postage stamp.

rhinoceroses – but they do not have cloven feet. Furthermore, as most of New Guinea's mammals are marsupials, Ogi's devil-pigs most probably were too; tapirs, on the other hand, are not.

Interestingly, as recently as 6000 years ago, some tapir-like marsupials did exist. Belonging to a now-extinct family of large herbivorous species called diprotodonts, they were known as palorchestids, and in general shape and size these creatures would have very closely matched Ogi's description of the devil-pigs. At present, however, palorchestid fossils have been uncovered only in Australia, not in New Guinea. Nevertheless, there are some curious stone sculptures made by early people and found in Papua's Ambun Valley that depict a peculiar long-nosed mammal tentatively identified by Australian mammalogist James Menzies as a palorchestid. Possibly, therefore, these marsupial tapirs did indeed exist here at one time – and in view of Ogi's encounter, perhaps they still survive here today.

In January 1994, a Japanese television team journeyed to the island of New Britain, just north of Papua, in search of a strange water monster known locally as the migo, which is said to inhabit Lake Dakataua. Shaped like a horseshoe, the lake is about 425 metres (1400 feet) in diameter, approximately 9 metres (30 feet) deep, and, surprisingly, does not appear to contain any fishes. This, however, was fortuitous for the team – which included renowned American cryptozoologist Professor Roy P. Mackal as scientific advisor – because it means that the migo has to spend more time at the surface than other lake monsters tend to do, in order to feed upon the abundant flocks of waterfowl settling here.

As a consequence, the team succeeded in filming a migo, which was estimated by Mackal to be over 10 metres (33 feet) long, extremely serpentine in shape, and moving at a speed of 4 knots, by vertical undulations of its body. This mode of swimming implies that it is a mammal, because true snakes and fishes generally can only undulate horizontally. There is, however, only one type of mammal that fits the migo's description and that is a highly specialized form of elongate whale called a zeuglodont, which officially died out around 25 million years ago. Living zeuglodonts have also been proposed by

cryptozoologists as the identity of various other snake-like water monsters, including the Irish horse-eels (p.16), Ogopogo from Lake Okanagan in Canada (p.147), and Caddy the Cadboro Bay sea serpent (p.149).

From the late nineteenth century onwards, many eyewitness reports have emerged from New Guinea's eastern, Papuan portion – and also from northern New South Wales and Queensland in Australia – that describe sightings of huge dragon-like creatures. With long sturdy bodies and very lengthy, tapering tails, they apparently resemble the varanids or monitor lizards, but are said to be up to 8 metres (27 feet) long. In comparison, the Komodo dragon *Varanus komodoensis*, the world's largest known species of living monitor, rarely exceeds 3 metres (10 feet).

Accordingly, such reports were disbelieved by zoologists for many years, but in 1980 a specimen of the Papuan "dragon", known locally as the artrellia, was captured alive during "Operation Drake", a scientific expedition led by explorer Lieutenant-Colonel John Blashford-Snell. Although it was only a very young individual, measuring a mere 1.87 metres (6 feet 1½ inches), it solved the mystery of the

Captured alive in 1980, the Papuan "dragon" was in fact a known species of monitor lizard, Salvadori's monitor VARANUS SALVADORII.

artrellia's identity, for it was shown to belong to a species previously documented by science – Salvadori's monitor *Varanus salvadorii*.

As it happens, this species was already known to attain a greater maximum length than the Komodo dragon: the longest fully authenticated specimen of Salvadori's monitor currently on record was a male that measured 4.75 metres (15 feet 7 inches), verified by researcher Michael Pope. However, it is much less sturdy, which is why the Komodo dragon is referred to as the *largest* monitor species. Now that the artrellia has been shown to be real, however, the eyewitness reports of giant dragons in Papua indicate that in future years some considerably larger (as well as longer) specimens of Salvadori's monitor may well be discovered there.

In contrast, since this species is not known to exist at all in mainland Australia, the dragons reported there have been cautiously compared by some zoologists to an officially extinct giant Australian monitor – *Megalania prisca*. So could this species still be alive today?

Until recently, apparent similarities between Australia's mystery dragons and *Megalania* encouraged such speculation, but new fossil evidence suggests that *Megalania* probably bore a prominent crest on its head. This is a feature that has never been mentioned by anyone claiming to have seen a living giant monitor in Australia. *Megalania*, therefore, may not be the correct identity for these reptiles after all. Back to the cryptozoological drawing board!

BUNYIP

The bunyip is Australia's most famous mystery beast, but according to aboriginal lore there are at least two visibly distinct types of this elusive freshwater creature, and this categorization is closely mirrored in accounts of sightings by Western eyewitnesses too.

The most commonly reported type has a dog-like head and may be reminiscent of a seal, but is usually said to have a long shaggy coat. In April 1872, the *Wagga Wagga Advertiser*

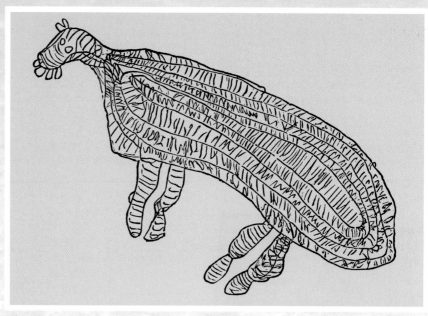

This aboriginal drawing of a bunyip was made in 1848. It shows an animal with a covering of either scales or feathers.

published a first-hand description of one such beast, lately encountered in Midgeon Lagoon, 26 kilometres (16 miles) north of Narrandera in New South Wales. According to one of the three men who stood watching it while it remained in view at the water surface for half an hour, it was:

... half as long again as an ordinary retriever dog; the hair all over its body was jet-black and shining, its coat was very long, the hair spreading out on the surface of the water for about five inches [13 cm], and floating loosely as the creature rose and fell by its own motion. I could not detect any tail, and the hair about its head was too long and glossy to admit of my seeing its eyes; the ears were well marked.

One morning in November 1821, E.S. Hall spotted a jet-black bunyip with a bulldog-like head in the marsh running into Lake Bathurst South, New South Wales, from a distance of only 90 metres (100 yards). A bulldog-headed bunyip with black shaggy fur like the Midgeon Lagoon specimen, and estimated to be 1.2–1.4 metres (4–4¹/₂ feet) long, was observed during the autumn of 1852 in Lake Tiberias, Tasmania. Another Tasmanian specimen, this time frequenting Great Lake, was almost bumped into by Charles Headlam and a friend as they were rowing across the lake; it was about the size of a fully

grown sheepdog, with two small wing-like flippers that it made good use of as it swam through the water, staying at the surface until it was out of sight.

The second category of bunyip appears to be much rarer, and is readily distinguished from the first by its long neck, sometimes said to be maned. Perhaps the most detailed description of a long-necked bunyip appeared in a letter published by the *Sydney Morning Herald* on 16 June 1847. Written by George Hobler, a local settler, it documented the sighting made some weeks earlier by a young herdsman. The man had been working on a cattle station at the edge of a large reedbed about 20 kilometres (12 miles) from the junction of the Lachlan and Murrumbidgee Rivers in New South Wales. While searching for some cows in a flooded area of this reedbed, he unexpectedly encountered a strange animal grazing there. According to Hobler's report:

... it was about as big as a six months' old calf, of a dark brown colour, a long neck, and long pointed head; it had large ears which it pricked up when it perceived him; had a thick mane of hair from the head down the neck, and two large tusks. He turned to run away, and this creature equally alarmed ran off too, and from the glance he took at it he describes it as having an awkward shambling gallop; the forequarters of the

animal were very large in proportion to the hindquarters, and it had a large tail, but whether he compared it to that of a horse or a bullock I do not recollect. He took two men to the place next morning to look for its track, which they describe as broad and square, somewhat like what the spread hand of a man would make in soft muddy ground.

Sceptics of bunyip reports have sought to explain them away as misidentifications of seals, but any seal with the head of a bulldog and long shaggy fur, or one with a long hairy neck, a large tail and a herbivorous grazing life-style, would itself be a very remarkable creature, and unquestionably new to science.

Intriguingly, although Australia's marsupials are very varied in form, they do not include any aquatic species. Could the bunyips be two undiscovered examples? If so, they may be derived from a once-diverse family of plant-eating marsupials termed diprotodonts. Officially extinct, in both body form and life-style they collectively paralleled several different hoofed animals, including cattle, pigs, rhinos and even tapirs. Perhaps there were some amphibious species too, mirroring hippos and certain bovine swamp-dwellers, which have persisted into modern times, owing to the security afforded by their watery domain?

THE YOWIE AND OTHER ISLAND MAN-BEASTS

Australia's answer to the Mongolian almas, Himalayan yetis, North American bigfoot, Chinese yeren, Venezuelan vasitri and other reported man-beasts from around the globe is the yowie – a tall tailless gorilla-like entity covered in long hair, walking on its hind legs, and allegedly spied on numerous occasions by aboriginal and Western eyewitnesses alike.

In *Out of the Shadows*, Australian cryptozoologists Tony Healy and Paul Cropper included many such accounts,

The Bambala yowie: an artist's impression of a creature that Charles Harper claimed to have seen in south-east New South Wales in 1912.

including the following example, which is of particular worth as its eyewitness is a Queensland National Parks and Wildlife ranger. He asked for his identity not to be disclosed, but the incident itself took place during March 1978, near to the Antarctic Beech tree grove in the Springbrook region of south-east Queensland.

The ranger had heard what he assumed to be an escaped pig, rooting among the trees, but when he investigated, he spotted a hairy black

gorilla-like beast about 3.5 metres (12 feet) away. Very muscular and sturdy in build, it stood about 2.25 metres (7½ feet) tall, with a flat, black shiny face, two big yellow eyes, a hole for a mouth, a short thick neck, human-like fingers and a covering of short black hair over the dark shiny skin on its hands, feet and body. Suddenly, it emitted a foul stench that made the ranger vomit, and as he did so the yowie turned sideways and disappeared. After informing his boss, the ranger was told not to publicize his sighting in case it attracted hunters to the area, anxious to bag a beast that officially does not exist.

In contrast, the ranger no longer has any doubt about the yowie's reality:

The point I want to make is that there is no fiction about my experience. I saw this beast in daylight, about 2 o'clock in the afternoon. Before I might have agreed they were comic-book stuff – but no more. They exist alright. The reason they aren't seen more often is that most people who go for bushwalks make a noise. I didn't make a noise because I was trying to stalk what I thought was a pig.

Some cryptozoologists have suggested that the yowie may be a marsupial of some kind. Proposed identities range from an elusive marsupial equivalent of an ape-man or ape (this latter identity has also been offered for a quasi-anthropoid mystery beast from New South Wales called the yahoo), to a giant species of wombat – though this scarcely corresponds with the creature encountered by the ranger!

Alternatively, the yowie may be a modern-day descendant of *Homo erectus*, which was both ancestral to and contemporary (for a time) with modern man *Homo sapiens*. But even if this is so, how did *Homo erectus* reach the island continent of Australia? According to anthropologist Dr Charles Reed from Illinois University, the two species of human may actually have lived together, and when modern man made the first raft-borne journeys to Australia around 40,000 years ago, *Homo erectus* went along too. It is possible that, later, *Homo erectus* reverted to a wild state there, thus becoming what we now call the yowie.

Island man-beasts may not be restricted to Australia. As recently as 1846, the Maoris of Fjordland in New Zealand's South Island were still claiming that this region harboured a small hairy man-beast called the maero or macro, with long claw-like nails and adept at tree-climbing. Similar entities have also been reported from Malaita, one of the Solomon Islands. The Laudari Mountains on Guadalcanal, another member of the Solomons group, reputedly harbour a tall man-beast

called the mumulou, with long nails and long straight hair.

According to ancient beliefs still prevalent in the Hawaiian archipelago, long before modern humans reached these islands they were inhabited by a race of pygmy-like people called the menehune. A few of these people are alleged to survive here even today, unlike a large hairy man-beast termed the nawao, which has apparently died out. Unconfirmed accounts of cone-headed pygmies called vélé carrying tiny hand-clubs have emerged from Fiji; and some of Vanuatu's islands (formerly the New Hebrides) supposedly house man-beasts known as vui or wui, which are said to resemble satyrs and have the hooves and tail of a goat (but see p.48).

✪

Dwarf Moas and Giant Eggs

Endemic to New Zealand but believed to be long extinct, those famous flightless birds known as the moas hit the headlines in a very surprising manner during the early part of 1993. This was when hotelier Paddy Freaney and two fellow hikers claimed that on 20 January they had encountered a *living* 2-metre- (6-foot) tall moa, in the

In this engraving, a DINORNIS moa is shown with the much smaller kiwi.

Craigieburn mountain range of South Island. According to their description, it had brown and grey feathers, a long neck, partially unfeathered legs and huge feet, thus resembling certain ostrich-like species of moa (*Dinornis* spp.) that supposedly died out at least 300 years ago.

Freaney succeeded in obtaining a photo of the bird as it ran away, but the image of the creature itself was very blurred; even after computer enhancement it was so indistinct that many scientists refused to believe that it depicted a bird at all, suggesting instead that it might simply have been a red deer, or even a couple of hikers standing next to one another! Undeterred by their scepticism, however, Freaney is currently seeking sponsorship for launching a full-scale expedition to seek out the creature that he and his two colleagues saw, and prove that it was indeed a living moa.

The problem faced by anyone willing to believe in the existence of a population of 2-metre-tall moas (the likelihood of only a single specimen existing is very remote) is explaining how such large birds could have survived undetected by science since their "official" extinction three centuries or more ago. Far more plausible is the modern-day persistence of one of the smaller, less conspicuous moas, such as the turkey-sized upland moa *Megalapteryx didinus*, which probably resembled a giant kiwi and is believed to have survived until at least as recently as the mid-1800s. Indeed, in 1848, Australian bird painter John Gould noted:

I have reason to believe that a third and much larger species of Apteryx *[kiwi] is still living in the Southern or Middle Island; at least the sealers who annually visit those shores affirm that such a bird exists; it is known to them by the name of the Fireman, and is said to be about three feet in height.*

The still-unidentified fireman earned its name from its call, which resembled the sound made by the large wooden rattles used as fire alarms by nineteenth-century firemen in New Zealand. This mysterious bird was also said to have spurred feet, a

*Not surprisingly, the great elephant bird AEPYORNIS MAXIMUS laid monstrous eggs.
More extraordinary is the survival of two of them in Australian sand dunes
– a distance of 4000 miles and at least 400 years from their Madagascan origin.*

characteristic not shared by any known species of kiwi, but on record from *Megalapteryx*.

In 1978, a Japanese scientific team led by Professor Shoichi Hollie arrived in Fjordland, South Island, to investigate whether *Megalapteryx* did still survive. They were armed with a very ingenious lure, a tape-recording of this miniature moa's voice, created by computer, using reconstructions of its throat anatomy based upon fossilized remains. Despite being broadcast many times through sound amplifiers, however, its call did not receive a reply.

Perhaps the most unusual case involving giant birds features two enormous eggs found near to one another but more than 60 years apart, and astonishingly far from their site of origin. The story began in 1930, when rancher's son Vic Roberts and a friend found a colossal egg, with a diameter only marginally under 30 cm (1 foot), amid some sand dunes about 450 metres (500 yards) from the sea at Nannup, in the Scott River region of Western Australia's southernmost tip. In 1962, it was examined by Australian naturalist Harry Butler, who identified it as the egg of a monstrously large, extinct flightless bird called the great elephant bird *Aepyornis maximus* – an identity confirmed by the Western Australian Museum, who later received it on permanent loan from Roberts.

What makes this identity so extraordinary is that the elephant birds lived only on the island of Madagascar, at least 6500 kilometres (4000 miles) away from Western Australia! They died out about 400 years ago but their eggs or fragments from them are often found buried beneath the island's sands. To explain how one of these eggs could come to be found on an Australian coastline, scientists have suggested that it must have been transported from Madagascar upon the prevailing ocean currents; it is known that the Indian and Southern Oceans happen to converge at the very coastal point where the egg was found.

Supporting this explanation was the discovery of a second elephant bird egg further along the same Australian coastline in March 1993. It was dug out of some sand at Cervantes by three children – Jamie Andrich (aged nine), Kelly Pew (eight) and Michelle Pew (six) – after they had initially mistaken it for a very large smooth rock. With a circumference of 81.78 cm (32.2 inches), the Cervantes specimen is even bigger than the Scott River egg.

Following a ruling made by the Western Australian Government Crown Law Department that under the Lands Act of 1968 it belonged to the crown, the Cervantes egg became the property of the Western Australian Museum, where it is now on display. However, an ex gratia goodwill payment of AUS $25,000 has been made to the families of the three children, in recognition of their surprising discovery's scientific significance.

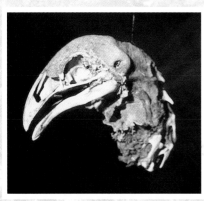

Preserved head and neck of the upland moa (MEGALAPTERIX DIDINUS).

✻

IN SEARCH OF SEA MONSTERS

It was 12 December 1964 when photographer Robert le Serrec claimed to have spotted and photographed an astonishing sea monster lying in shallow sea water near Hook Island, in Australia's Great Barrier Reef. According to his description, it resembled a gigantic tadpole, measuring at least 20 metres (over 65 feet) in length, with a very wide head and tapering body, and it appeared to have a gaping wound in its left flank. As le Serrec attempted to film it, however, it raised its head – and when a 20-metre-long sea monster raises its head, it is best not to stay around to see what it is going to do next! – so he fled away at once in his boat. He returned a little later, but the beast had gone, presumably back into deeper water, and was not seen again.

Some scientists consider that the entire episode may have been a hoax, but cryptozoologist Ivan T. Sanderson wondered whether the creature (if it really did exist) could have been a gigantic species of swamp-eel. Also called synbranchids, swamp-eels are very strange fishes with no close relatives, but they do resemble miniature versions of the Hook Island beast.

Just as weird, and certainly no less wonderful, was the polychromatic plesiosaur (or something very like one) observed through a telescope for half an hour one afternoon in mid-October 1939 by Leading Seaman Cecil W. Walters and a colleague while aboard HMAS *Kurumba*, sailing north-west of King Sound. Travelling at about 20 knots, the creature possessed a small head with at least one ear-like structure and a flickering tongue, a 3-metre- (10-foot) long neck, and two humps following behind; its visible length was roughly 30 metres (90 feet).

Even more striking than the great size of this particular sea serpent, however, was its colouration, for according to Walters its brownish-yellow background colour was covered with a network of blotches like a giraffe. Yet whereas a giraffe's blotches are of a sober brown shade, those of Walters's beast were a harlequinesque patchwork of pale blue, green and yellow!

On 25 April 1977, it looked as if a modern-day plesiosaur had finally been procured, when a Japanese fishing vessel, the *Zuiyo Maru*, hauled up a huge rotting carcase of plesiosaurian shape about 50 kilometres (30 miles) east of Christchurch, New Zealand. This identity was eventually disproved, however, when tissue analyses by Tokyo University biochemist Dr Shigeru Kimora revealed that the carcase contained the protein elastodin, which is found only in sharks. Moreover, it is well known that decomposing shark carcases often assume a deceptively plesiosaurian shape: the result is popularly termed a pseudoplesiosaur.

Nevertheless, the sharks may themselves be harbouring an undiscovered sea monster in their midst. The Polynesian fishermen who work along the coasts of New South Wales speak of a highly mysterious but truly immense and ghostly white form of shark that they refer to very respectfully as the Lord of the Deep. According to their description, this formidable creature resembles the ferocious great white shark *Carcharodon carcharias*, but whereas this latter species is not known to exceed 8 metres (26 feet) in length, the Lord of the Deep is said to measure 30 metres (100 feet) or so. Giant sharks of this same frightening form have also been reported from the waters around the South Pacific's Tuamotu Archipelago: eyewitnesses include Zane

Robert le Serrec might have taken more pictures of this extraordinary sea monster, but the monster apparently had other ideas.

This exotic catch looked very like a plesiosaur but was found to be a rotting shark. This misidentification is common enough to earn the shark carcase a special name: pseudoplesiosaur.

Grey, writer of Westerns, who caught sight of one near the island of Rangiroa in the late 1920s.

The concept of a giant carnivorous shark dwarfing even the great white would seem highly implausible, were it not for the uncomfortable fact that at least as recently as 11,000 years ago such a species really did exist. Known as *Carcharodon megalodon*, the megalodon ("big tooth") shark, it is believed to have been up to 17 metres (55 feet) long, and fossil megalodon teeth sometimes exceeding 10 cm (4 inches) long have been obtained. Could the megalodon have survived into the present day? Supporters of this disturbing possibility suggest that it may spend much of its time in the ocean depths, preying upon giant squids, only rarely coming to the surface, thus explaining how it has remained undiscovered by science – but for how much longer?

KULTA AND BURRUNJOR – DINOSAURS OF THE DREAMTIME?

This is how Rex Gilroy, one of Australia's foremost investigators of mysteries Down Under, has referred in his book *Mysterious Australia* to two of this island continent's least-publicized but most fascinating mystery beasts – the kulta and the burrunjor.

According to ancient Central Australian aboriginal lore, the kulta inhabited the great swamps that existed long ago in the far north, browsing inoffensively upon the region's lush vegetation. It possessed a small head, an exceedingly long neck and tail, an enormously bulky body and four sturdy legs. This description is irresistibly similar to that of the sauropod dinosaurs, such as *Diplodocus* and *Apatosaurus*. Yet the aboriginals have no palaeontological knowledge, so how are they able to describe so accurately a type of reptile that officially died out millions of years ago – unless at least one lineage did not die out, but persisted undisturbed in this remote locality right into historic times? Yet whatever it was, it is no longer: centuries ago the swamps dried up, and the kulta died out.

Even more extraordinary, however, is the burrunjor, a terrifying tyrannosaur-like creature named after Burrunjor, a remote expanse of Arnhem Land in northern Australia where, according to longstanding aboriginal testimony, this huge reptilian monster is said to live. Here it is even depicted in local aboriginal cave art, portrayed as a gigantic bipedal creature, and enormous unidentified tracks have been reported from this region. English cryptozoologist Alan Pringle has noted that monitor lizards will sometimes rear up and run for a time on their hind legs, so could this be the true explanation of the burrunjor? Or should we be seeking a living anachronism thriving in the primeval wilderness of Arnhem Land?

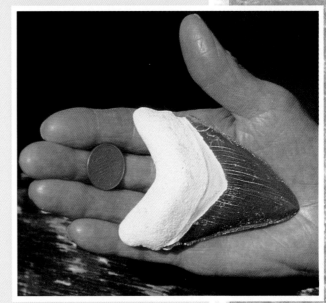

The original owner of this fossil tooth was a giant meat-eating shark CARCHARODON MEGALODON, thought to have been extinct for 11,000 years. Eyewitness reports suggest otherwise.

Secrets of the Islands

MIN-MIN LIGHTS AND THE MUSIC OF THE SPHERES

In the days of Australia's early European settlers, the Min-Min Hotel was a staging post between Boulia and Winton in western Queensland, whose best-known feature for the people living nearby were the ghostly balls of light that regularly flitted through the air, often white but sometimes changing colour. Still seen today and referred to as min-min lights, these are reminiscent of American spooklights and English will-o'-the-wisps, and display a marked if disconcerting tendency to follow and even taunt their perplexed observers.

An example is recorded in *You Kids Count Your Shadows*, a collection of Wiradjuri aboriginal lore and beliefs from New South Wales compiled by Frank Povah. It contains an account of a sheep drover who was checking his flock on horseback one evening when a blue min-min light appeared over his shoulder, and persistently followed him during his work. In exasperation, he chased after it, still on horseback, but was unable to catch up with it. He gave up and began riding home, whereupon the min-min cheekily appeared over his shoulder again!

The aboriginals fear the min-mins,

believing that they can lure people to their doom, drain their lives away, or even steal their minds, but reports of their activity suggest an inquisitive rather than a hostile attitude to humans – not that this is any easier to explain rationally!

Min-min investigator Dr Jack Pettigrew has shown that distant vehicle

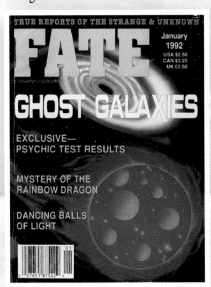

Mystery lights, featured here on the cover of **Fate** *magazine, continue to fascinate.*

headlights can appear much closer than they really are on cold, still nights, owing to a mirage-like inversion effect that bends their glow from over the horizon so that they seem to be floating near an observer elsewhere. Yet this cannot explain reports such as the one given

above, in which the min-min *actively follows* the observer. As with American spooklights (p.160), some researchers have boldly proposed that min-mins comprise a form of sentient energy. An alternative view, put forward by Paul Devereux, a longstanding investigator of these and other 'earthlights', is that they are the result of geomagnetic energies manifesting from geological faults, and may even interact with the electrical fields of the human brain, taking on whatever form is consciously or unconsciously bestowed upon them by the mind of the observer.

Perhaps the most extraordinary mystery lights of all are those reported from Waimea, on the island of Hawaii. Resembling spheres of heavy fog, they not only pulsate and manifest themselves roughly in phase with the new moon, but also emit an ethereal musical sound.

THE PORTUGUESE KANGAROO

According to the textbooks, the first Europeans to land in Australia and explore its unknown interior were the Dutch, during the early 1600s. For although the Portuguese dominated the East Indies during the previous century,

there is supposedly no evidence that they actually landed in Australia and witnessed any of its unique fauna before the Dutch explorers arrived. In fact, there is an intriguing question mark over this long standing assumption.

In the 1590s, the great Portuguese cartographer Cornelis de Jode published his famous atlas of the world, *Speculum Orbis Terrae*, whose ornately engraved title page depicts four animals. Three of these are a horse (top left), a camel (top right) and a lion (bottom left); but what is the creature in the bottom right of the page? Intriguingly, with a long tail, muscular hind legs, short forelegs and – most remarkable of all – a distinctive pouch containing two small offspring, it bears more than a passing resemblance to a kangaroo!

Yet this was before anyone from Europe had explored Australia. True, the likeness to a kangaroo is far from exact, but it is nevertheless sufficiently similar to suggest that the engraving was based upon a verbal description from someone who had genuinely seen one.

Presumably, then, some Portuguese travellers did visit Australia before the Dutch, perhaps setting sail from the island of Timor, a Portuguese colony in those days. After all, a beast as novel in form as the kangaroo, with no physical counterparts elsewhere in the world, is much too strange to have been invented by even the most imaginative human mind!

MU – AN ATLANTIS OF THE SOUTH PACIFIC?

Ideally, with a total surface area of around 176 million square kilometres (68 million square miles), the vast Pacific Ocean offers far more scope for the erstwhile existence of a subsequently submerged continent than does the much smaller Atlantic Ocean – a favoured site for lost Atlantis. Moreover, claims have indeed been made for the one-time occurrence of a Pacific Atlantis, known as Mu. However, the foundations for these claims seem shaky to say the least.

The most detailed documentation of this vanished land flowed from the pen (not to mention the imagination) of a former Bengal Lancer called Colonel James Churchward. He wrote four Mu books, mostly during the late 1800s though they did not begin to appear in print until 1926, with the publication of *The Lost Continent of Mu*. The opening lines of that volume succinctly set the scene for what was to follow:

The Garden of Eden was not in Asia but on a now sunken continent in the Pacific Ocean. The Biblical story of creation – the epic of the seven days and the seven nights – came first not from the peoples of the Nile or of the Euphrates Valley but from this now submerged continent, Mu – the Motherland of Man.

Churchward claimed that the priest of a Hindu temple in India (or Tibet – its site fluctuates from one locality to another in Churchward's books!) had shown him four sacred tablets of stone, on which were carved arcane writings in a hitherto unknown script – Naacal, the language of Mu. Deciphering these writings by gazing intently at them until their meanings helpfully revealed themselves in his mind, Churchward learnt that Mu had once been a mighty continent on which humankind had first arisen, around 50 million years ago (as compared with the current estimate of 4 million years suggested by palaeontological evidence). Mu's sizeable land mass had extended 9600 kilometres (6000 miles) from the Marianas and the Hawaiian archipelago southwards to Fiji, Tonga, Tahiti and Easter Island, yielding a Polynesian parallelogram.

Inhabited by a highly advanced civilization of 64 million inhabitants (comprising ten different races of which the dominant one was of Aryan appearance), Mu was an idyllic empire whose noble people eventually spread throughout the world, initiating all other human civilizations. About 12,000 years ago, however, a combined onslaught by cataclysmic earthquakes, volcanic eruptions and tidal waves destroyed this great continent, causing it to sink beneath the Pacific. The same fate befell one of its Atlantic colonies, known as Atlantis, a thousand years later. Today, all that is left of Mu is the sprinkling of Polynesian islands in the South Pacific.

Sceptics of this scenario, however,

A cataclysmic demise: the end of Mu as James Churchward pictured it.

were swift to expose the many geological and historical inaccuracies and anachronisms with which Churchward's books were liberally strewn. Further discouraging any would-be believers is the strange fact that no researcher other than Churchward has ever seen the Naacal tablets; moreover, he never fully reproduced their inscriptions and he never identified the temple in which they were supposedly retained.

Equally uninspiring are the claims of another Mu supporter – Augustus Le Plongeon, a nineteenth-century French physician who was the first person to excavate the Mayan ruins in Mexico's Yucatán peninsula. He attempted to translate the *Troano Codex*, one of only three Mayan books that had not been destroyed by a Christian zealot called Diego de Landa, the Spanish Bishop of Yucatán. The result was a fascinating but thoroughly fictitious history of Mu, drawing heavily upon a previous but notoriously inaccurate translation of this same codex by a French scholar called Abbé Charles-Etienne Brasseur.

Today, most scientists dismiss Mu as a joke – and who can blame them? In 1959, a report claimed that an archaeologist had found documents in Mexico that had been left there long ago by a priest from Mu. However, the report's credibility was severely dented when the archaeologist's name, Reesdon Hurdlop, was shown to be an anagram of Rudolph Rednose!

✪

New Guinea's Phoenix and the Lost Birds of Paradise

The gloriously beautiful phoenix bird of Middle Eastern mythology has come to symbolize resurrection, and for good reason. Situated at the very top of a palm tree in ancient Egypt and constructed from aromatic leaves, a wonderful nest is set alight by a stray spark of fire, flying from the hooves of the sun god's steeds of the sky as they

Bensbach's bird of paradise Janthothorax bensbachi: *scientifically written off and consigned to oblivion?*

draw his radiant chariot through the heavens. Scarlet flames instantly envelop the nest in a fiery shroud of scorching destruction, yet at the very heart of this blazing inferno the phoenix stretches out its magnificent wings as it dances amid the flickering flames surrounding it on all sides, until eventually nest and bird alike are nothing more than a crumbling pile of smouldering embers. In 500 years' time, however, a new phoenix is reborn from the ashes of its predecessor, whereupon it collects the nest's cinders and seals them in myrrh, which it then encapsulates within an egg-shaped package of aromatic leaves, before flying to the temple of the sun at Heliopolis. Here it solemnly places its fashioned egg on the altar as a sacred offering, and afterwards flies away to Paradise, returning to earth in another 500 years to commence the cycle of self-destruction and resurrection again.

This wonderful legend (of which many variations exist) has captured the imagination of scientists and poets alike, who have earnestly sought to uncover whether the phoenix had any basis in reality. During centuries of discussion and dispute, all manner of identities have been considered, ranging from the purple heron, golden pheasant and golden eagle, to the peacock, various exotic parrots, and even rooks holding their wings over smouldering stalks of straw as a strange form of stimulant. During the 1950s, however, a team of

Australian scientists visiting New Guinea stumbled upon what would seem to be the true answer.

Famed for the flamboyant riot of exquisite plumes possessed by the males of most species during the mating season, New Guinea's extravagantly plumaged crow-related birds of paradise did not become known to Western science until the sixteenth century. The team learnt, however, that the people of this island had been trading their feathered skins as far back as 1000 BC, when they were regularly visited by Middle Eastern seafarers from the phoenix's homeland, Phoenicia. The people wrapped the delicate skins in myrrh, fashioned into a protective parcel in the shape of an egg, which was then placed inside a second parcel, of burnt banana leaves. This method of preserving the skins from harm closely mirrors the legend's account of how the resurrected phoenix prepared its offering for the temple of the sun.

Moreover, one bird of paradise whose plumes were very commonly traded was a species called Count Raggi's bird of paradise *Paradisea raggiana*. The male of this species possesses great cascades of blazing scarlet feathers, which it throws up all around itself when it dances during its courtship display – thereby vividly resembling a bird dancing amid a fiery inferno. There seems little doubt that reports of its extraordinary pre-mating dance recounted back home in Phoenicia, with its egg-shaped capsules of preserved plumes offering physical proof of this wonderful bird's reality, ultimately gave rise to the legend of the phoenix.

The celebrated Russian firebird may also have been based upon birds of paradise. In 1961, Soviet scientist Dr V. Kiparsky discussed this thought-provoking concept when contemplating the possibility that their skins had first reached Eastern Europe far earlier in history than previously assumed.

From phoenix to firebird – and both conjured into being by a family of dazzlingly arrayed cousins of crows from the far end of the world. It is fitting that the solution to the origin of the most fabulous of all fabled birds should be as magical as they are themselves.

I have always been amazed (but delighted, of course) that even the worst depredations of the plume trade failed to jettison into extinction any of the birds of paradise. Perhaps, however, I have been a little premature in my assumption. In his book *The Lost Birds of Paradise*, ornithological researcher/painter Errol Fuller recounts the histories of 24 highly controversial forms of birds of paradise that were initially believed to comprise genuine species in their own right, but which were later demoted to the trivial rank of hybrids. Yet almost all of these demotions were executed by a single person – German ornithologist Dr Erwin Stresemann, in a detailed but sometimes opaque scientific paper published in 1930 by *Novitates Zoologicae*.

Reading it, there is little doubt that Stresemann was correct in most instances, but as Fuller convincingly points out, there are at least six discounted species that seem far too distinctive to be adequately explained as crossbreeds. During their short-lived tenure as accepted species, they were respectively known as Elliot's sicklebill *Epimachus ellioti*, Sharpe's lobe-billed riflebird *Loborhamphus ptilorhis*, Rothschild's lobe-billed bird of paradise *L. nobilis,* Duivenbode's riflebird *Paryphephorus duivenbodei*, Bensbach's bird of paradise *Janthothorax bensbachi*, and Ruys's bird of paradise *Neoparadisea ruysi*. In each case, it is hard to imagine how the particular parental species proposed for it by Stresemann could create such a bird, since it seems to possess many features lacked by both "parents".

What makes this finding especially disturbing, however, is that only a handful of specimens at most (and sometimes just one) are on record for each of these controversial birds of paradise. Consequently, echoing the apt title of Fuller's book, if they should somehow be shown one day to be valid species after all, the discovery may be of little more than academic interest, because it is quite possible that they are irretrievably lost. Tragically, during their many decades in taxonomic anonymity, these forgotten phoenixes of the New Guinea forests may well have become extinct.

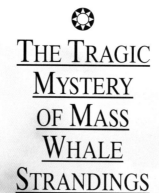

THE TRAGIC MYSTERY OF MASS WHALE STRANDINGS

In 1959, 200 electra dolphins *Peponocephala electra* inexplicably but fatally beached themselves at Crowdy Head, near Taree in New South Wales, Australia. In mid-1980, about 60 pilot whales *Globicephala melaena* became stranded on Treachery Beach, near Seal Rocks, also on the coast of New South Wales. Almost 200 pilot whales died after beaching themselves near Bicheno on Tasmania's east coast in September 1992 – the third mass stranding of pilot whales on Tasmanian beaches in 12 months, collectively involving over 430 individuals.

This is just a small sample of the grim statistics testifying to the tragic reality of mass strandings – often labelled "mass suicides" in media reports – on coastal beaches by certain species of whale and dolphin. Such strandings have been reported from coasts in many parts of the world, but seem particularly frequent around Australia and New Zealand.

Nor are they a relatively recent phenomenon. Reports of beached whales were being documented as long ago as the fourth century BC, by the philosopher-scientist Aristotle, who confessed that he could not explain why they should occur. And even in modern times, zoologists have only recently begun to unravel the mystery behind this behavioural enigma.

Yet there has been no shortage of ideas. As noted in *New Scientist* (12 February 1987) by Dr Margaret Klinowska, a marine mammal specialist at the University of Cambridge, England:

Suggestions include: suicide; entering shallow water to rub the skin, or to rest; reversion to some primitive instinct to seek safety on land; confusion of sonar echoes in shallow water; parasites of the inner ear preventing the whales from receiving sonar echoes; brain infections,

Pilot whales tragically stranded on a beach. Dr Margaret Klinowska has identified locations which are "black spots" for whale beachings.

leading to disorientation; attempts to use ancient migration paths now closed by geological changes; population pressure; pollution; radar, TV and radio transmissions; earthquakes; storms; phases of the Moon; and probably others that I have not yet heard of.

Klinowska's own researches led her to a conclusion that is nowadays widely supported in the scientific community – namely, that the stranding of whales results from errors in their own map-reading. She discovered that there are certain "accident black spots", such as the Australian examples cited above, where strandings are particularly common. Moreover, these "black spots" are areas where lines of geomagnetic variation (known as magnetic valleys) are blocked by islands or cross the coastline instead of running parallel to it.

This is of great significance, because it is believed that many species of whale use geomagnetic variations as navigational aids when cruising through the seas, often overriding other sensory stimuli. Accordingly, one might expect that coastal species of whale, which spend much of their lives close to shore, would rarely become stranded because they will be familiar with localized geomagnetic anomalies of the "accident black spot" variety. In contrast, oceanic species, such as pilot whales, would surely have little or no knowledge of them, and hence will be readily lured into these geomagnetic traps if they swim into coastal waters. And sure enough, both of these expectations correspond precisely with logged records of whale strandings – few featuring coastal species, many featuring oceanic species.

There can surely be few sights more despairing than a herd of beached whales floundering helplessly as their great weight, no longer buoyed by water, threatens to crush their chests and lungs. Happily, however, not all cases end in tragedy. In 1992, 49 killer whales beached themselves on the coast of New South Wales, but 35 were saved by human intervention. In November 1993, about 100 pilot whales were rescued and released back into the sea after becoming stranded on Farewell Spit, a beach at the northern tip of New Zealand's South Island. Most marvellous of all, however, was an incident in September 1983, when 80 pilot whales stranded on Tokero Beach in New Zealand were refloated by a team of human rescuers, and were then guided back out to sea by a school of local dolphins!

THE BARKING BEACH OF KAUAI

In the district of Mana, on the south coast of Kauai in the Hawaiian archipelago, there is a range of tall sand dunes that runs for nearly 2 kilometres (just over a mile) almost parallel to the sea. At its easternmost limit, the range ends in a dune more symmetrical than most of the others, resembling a broadened, truncated cone on its land side. In a paper published by the American journal *Science* in 1890, H. Carrington Bolton reported:

The sands on the top and on the landward slope of this dune (being about 100 yards [91 metres] from the sea) possess remarkable acoustic properties, likened to the bark of a dog. The dune has a maximum height of 108 feet [33 metres], but the slope of sonorous sand is only 60 feet [18 metres] above the level field on which it is encroaching. At its steepest part, the angle being quite uniformly 31°, the sand has a notable mobility when perfectly dry; and on disturbing its equilibrium it rolls in wavelets down the incline, emitting at the same time a deep bass note of a tremulous character.

These remarkable sands also attracted the interest of Dr James Blake, from the California Academy of Sciences, who conducted a microscopical investigation of their structure:

... the grains are chiefly composed of small portions of coral, and apparently calcareous sponges. They are all more or less perforated with small holes, mostly terminating in blind cavities, which are frequently enlarged in the interior, communicating with the surface by a small opening. The structure of the grains [in Blake's opinion] fully explains the reason why sounds are emitted when they are set in motion. The mutual friction causes vibrations in their substance, and consequently in the sides of the cavities; and, these vibrations being communicated to the air in the cavities, the result is sound ... The sand must be dry, however, in order to produce sound; for, when the cavities are filled with water, the grains are incapable of originating vibrations.

The most significant contribution of Kauai's barking beach to the scientific appreciation of mineralogical curiosities like these is its succinct revelation that the acoustic quality of sonorous sands is wholly independent of their chemical composition. For whereas more than a hundred other famous examples of sonorous sands are siliceous in content, those of Kauai are composed of calcium carbonate.

A FINAL WORD

I began this book by recalling the belief of one eminent scientist, Albert Einstein, on the subject of the mysterious. Let me end it now by recollecting the thoughts of a second one, British geneticist J.B.S. Haldane, on this same subject, as expressed in his *Possible Worlds*:

Now, my suspicion is that the universe is not only queerer than we suppose, but queerer than we can *suppose ... I suspect that there are more things in heaven and earth than are dreamed of, in any philosophy. That is the reason why I have no philosophy myself, and must be my excuse for dreaming.*

Bibliography

Adamski, George, *Inside the Space Ships*, Abelard-Schuman, New York, 1955.

Adamski, George and Leslie, Desmond, *Flying Saucers Have Landed*, T. Werner Laurie, London, 1953.

Allan, John, *Mysteries*, Lion Publishing, Tring, 1981.

Alway, Carol *et al.*, *Strange Stories, Amazing Facts*, 2nd edition, Reader's Digest, London, 1984.

Ash, Russell *et al.*, *Folklore, Myths and Legends of Britain*, Reader's Digest, London, 1973.

Bader, Chris, *Strange Northwest*, Hancock House, Blaine, 1995.

Baring-Gould, Sabine, *Curious Myths of the Middle Ages*, Longmans, Green, London, 1892.

Beer, Lionel, *The Moving Statue of Ballinspittle and Other Related Phenomena*, Spacelink, London, 1986.

Behe, George, *Titanic: Psychic Forewarnings of a Tragedy*, Patrick Stephens, London, 1988.

Benwell, Gwen and Waugh, Arthur, *Sea-Enchantress: The Tale of the Mermaid and Her Kin*, Hutchinson, London, 1961.

Berlitz, Charles, *The Lost Ship of Noah*, Putnam, New York, 1987.

Blundell, Nigel and Hall, Allan, *Marvels and Mysteries of the Unexplained*, Tiger Books International, London, 1993.

Bord, Janet and Colin, *The Evidence for Bigfoot and Other Man-Beasts*, Aquarian, Wellingborough, 1984.

Bord, Janet and Colin, *Alien Animals*, revised edition, Panther, London, 1985.

Bord, Janet and Colin, *Ancient Mysteries of Britain*, Grafton, London, 1986.

Bord, Janet and Colin, *Modern Mysteries of Britain: 100 Years of Strange Events*, Grafton, London, 1987.

Bord, Janet and Colin, *Modern Mysteries of the World: Strange Events of the 20th Century*, Grafton Books, London, 1989.

Bord, Janet and Colin, *Atlas of Magical Britain*, Sidgwick & Jackson, London, 1990.

Bord, Janet and Colin, *Life Beyond Planet Earth?*, Grafton, London, 1991.

Brandon, Jim, *Weird America*, E.P. Dutton, New York, 1978.

Briggs, Katharine, *A Dictionary of Fairies*, Allen Lane, London, 1976.

Brookesmith, Peter (ed.), *The Unexplained: Mysteries of Mind, Space and Time*, 13 vols, Orbis, London, 1980–83.

Brookesmith, Peter (consultant), *Bizarre Phenomena*, Reader's Digest, Pleasantville, 1992.

Caldwell, Harry R., *Blue Tiger*, Duckworth, London, 1925.

Cardinall, Allan W., *In Ashanti and Beyond*, Seeley, Service, London, 1927.

Carmichael, Alexander, *Carmina Gadelica*, 2 vols, Norman MacLeod, Edinburgh, 1900.

Churchward, James, *The Lost Continent of Mu*, reprinted by Paperback Library, New York, 1969.

Clark, Jerome, *Unexplained!*, Visible Ink, Detroit, 1993.

Clark, Jerome and Coleman, Loren, *Creatures of the Outer Edge*, Warner, New York, 1978.

Coghlan, Ronan, *The Encyclopaedia of Arthurian Legends*, Element, Longmead, 1991.

Cohen, Daniel, *Encyclopedia of Ghosts*, Michael O'Mara, London, 1984.

Coleman, Loren, *Mysterious America*, Faber & Faber, London, 1983.

Coleman, Loren, *Curious Encounters*, Faber & Faber, London, 1985.

Coleman, Michael H., *The Ghosts of the Trianon*, Aquarian, Wellingborough, 1988.

Coleman, Ray, *McCartney – Yesterday and Today*, Boxtree, London, 1995.

Collins, Andrew, *The Circlemakers*, ABC Books, Leigh-on-Sea, 1992.

Constable, Trevor J., *Sky Creatures*, Pocket Books, New York, 1978.

Cooper, Joe, *The Case of the Cottingley Fairies*, Robert Hale, London, 1990.

Corliss, William R., *The Unexplained: A Sourcebook of Strange Phenomena*, Bantam, New York, 1976.

Corliss, William R., *Handbook of Unusual Natural Phenomena*, Sourcebook Project, Glen Arm, 1977.

Corliss, William R., *Incredible Life: A Handbook of Biological Mysteries*, Sourcebook Project, Glen Arm, 1981.

Corliss, William R. *et al.*, (consultants), *Feats and Wisdom of the Ancients*, Time-Life Books, Alexandria, 1990.

Corrales, Scott, *The Chupacabras Diaries: An Unofficial Chronicle of Puerto Rico's Paranormal Predator*, Samizdat Press, Derrick City, 1995.

Costello, Peter, *In Search of Lake Monsters*, Garnstone Press, London, 1974.

Cruz, Joan C., *The Incorruptibles*, Tan Books, Rockford, 1977.

Currer-Briggs, Noel, *The Shroud and the Grail*, Weidenfeld & Nicolson, London, 1987.

David-Neel, Alexandra, *With Mystics and Magicians in Tibet*, Bodley Head, London, 1931.

Davis, Wade, *The Serpent and the Rainbow*, Collins, London, 1986.

Delgado, Pat and Andrews, Colin, *Circular Evidence*, Bloomsbury, London, 1989.

Devereux, Paul, *Earth Lights*, Turnstone Press, London, 1982.

Devereux, Paul, *Earth Lights Revelation*, Blandford Press, London, 1989.

Dinsdale, Tim, *The Leviathans*, 2nd edition, Futura, London, 1976.

Douglas, Adam, *The Beast Within: A History of the Werewolf*, Chapmans, London, 1992.

Edwards, Frank, *Stranger Than Science*, Ace, New York, 1959.

Edwards, Frank, *Strange World*, Lyle Stuart, New York, 1964.

Evans, Hilary and Grant, Reg (consultants), *UFO, The Continuing Enigma*, Reader's Digest, London, 1992.

Evans, Hilary, Shuker, Karl P.N., *et al.*, (consultants), *Almanac of the Uncanny*, Reader's Digest, Surry Hills, 1995.

Fairley, John and Welfare, Simon, *Arthur C. Clarke's World of Strange Powers*, Collins, London, 1984.

Fairley John and Welfare, Simon, *Arthur C. Clarke's Chronicles of the Strange and Mysterious*, Collins, London, 1987.

Fate, St John, Minnesota, No. 1, 1947–present.

Fawcett, Percy H., *Exploration Fawcett*, Hutchinson, London, 1953.

Floyd, E. Randall, *Ghost Lights and Other Encounters With the Unknown*, August House, Little Rock, 1993.

Forman, Joan, *Royal Hauntings*, Fontana, London, 1987.

Fort, Charles, *The Complete Books of Charles Fort*, reprinted by Dover, New York, 1974.

Fortean Times, formerly *The News*, London, No. 1, 1973–present.

Freeman, David N., Robinson, Thomas L., *et al.*, (consultants), *Mysteries of the Bible*, Reader's Digest, Pleasantville, 1988.

Fuller, Errol, *The Lost Birds of Paradise*, Swan Hill Press, Shrewsbury, 1995.

Furneaux, Rupert, *The Tungus Event*, Panther, London, 1977.

Gaddis, Vincent H., *Mysterious Fires and Lights*, David McKay, New York, 1967.

Gardiner, Robin and Vat, Dan van der, *The Riddle of the Titanic*, Orion, London, 1995.

Gilbert, Adrian G. and Cotterell, Maurice M., *The Mayan Prophecies*, Element, Longmead, 1995.

Gilroy, Rex, *Mysterious Australia*, Nexus, Mapleton, 1995.

Gordon, Stuart, *The Paranormal: An Illustrated Encyclopedia*, Headline, London, 1992.

Gould, Rupert T., *A Book of Marvels*, Methuen, London, 1937.

Grant, John, *Unexplained Mysteries of the World*, Quintet Books, London, 1991.

Gray, Affleck, *The Big Grey Man of Ben MacDhui*, 2nd edition, Lochar, Bankhead, 1989.

Grimble, Arthur, *A Pattern of Islands*, John Murray, London, 1952.

Group, David, *The Evidence for the Bermuda Triangle*, Aquarian, Wellingborough, 1984.

Haining, Peter, *The Monster Trap and Other True Mysteries*, Armada, London, 1976.

Haining, Peter, *Ancient Mysteries*, Sidgwick & Jackson, London, 1977.

Haining, Peter, *The Legend and Bizarre Crimes of Spring Heeled Jack*, Frederick Muller, London, 1977.

Haining, Peter, *The Man Who Was Frankenstein*, Frederick Muller, London, 1979.

Haining, Peter, *A Dictionary of Ghosts*, Robert Hale, London, 1982.

Hall, Mark A., *Thunderbirds! The Living Legend of Giant Birds*, M.A.H.P., Bloomington, 1988

Hamel, Frank, *Human Animals*, William Rider, London, 1915.

Hancock, Graham, *The Sign and the Seal*, William Heinemann, London, 1992.

Hancock, Graham, *Fingerprints of the Gods*, William Heinemann, London, 1995.

Healy, Tony and Cropper, Paul, *Out of the Shadows: Mystery Animals of Australia*, Pan Macmillan Australia, Chippendale, 1994.

Heuvelmans, Bernard, *On the Track of Unknown Animals*, Rupert Hart-Davis, London, 1958.

Heuvelmans, Bernard, *In the Wake of the Sea-Serpents*, Rupert Hart-Davis, London, 1968.

Heyerdahl, Thor, *Aku-Aku*, Allen & Unwin, London, 1958.

Hippisley Coxe, Antony D., *Haunted Britain*, Hutchinson, London, 1973.

Hitching, Francis, *The World Atlas of Mysteries*, Collins, London, 1978.

Hogue, John, *Nostradamus: The New Revelations*, Element, Longmead, 1994.

Howlett, John, *James Dean: A Biography*, Plexus, London, 1975.

Hughes, David, *The Star of Bethlehem Mystery*, Dent, London, 1979.

Izzard, Ralph, *The Hunt for the Buru*, Hodder & Stoughton, London, 1951.

Keel, John, *The Mothman Prophecies*, E.P. Dutton, New York, 1975.

Keith, Jim (ed.), *Secret and Suppressed*, Feral Horse, Portland, 1993.

Kingsley, Mary H., *West African Studies*, Macmillan, London, 1899.

Koch-Isenburg, Ludwig, *Through the Jungle Very Softly*, Viking Press, New York, 1963.

Kranz, Grover S., *Big Footprints*, Johnson Books, Boulder, 1992.

Kusche, Lawrence D., *The Bermuda Triangle Mystery – Solved*, New English Library, London, 1975.

Laurentin, Rene, *The Apparitions of the Blessed Virgin Mary Today*, 2nd edition, Veritas, Dublin, 1991.

LeBlond, Paul H. and Bousfield, Edward L., *Cadborosaurus: Survivor from the Deep*, Horsdal & Schubart, Victoria, 1995.

Leonard, R. Cedric, *Quest for Atlantis*, Manor, New York, 1979.

Luce, J.V., *The End of Atlantis*, Thames & Hudson, London, 1969.

Lyman, Robert R., *Amazing Indeed: Strange Events in the Black Forest*, Vol. 2, Potter Enterprise, Coudersport, 1973.

McClure, Kevin, *The Evidence for Visions of the Virgin Mary*, Aquarian, Wellingborough, 1983.

McClure, Kevin, *Visions of Bowmen and Angels*, privately published, St Austell, 1992.

Mackal, Roy P., *The Monsters of Loch Ness*, Macdonald and Janes, London, 1976.

Mackal, Roy P., *Searching for Hidden Animals*, Doubleday, Garden City, 1980.

Mackal, Roy P., *A Living Dinosaur? In Search of Mokele-Mbembe*, Brill, Leiden, 1987.

Maclean, Charles, *The Wolf Children*, Allen Lane, London, 1977.

Maclellan, Alec, *The Lost World of Agharti*, Souvenir Press, London, 1981.

MacManus, Dermot, *The Middle Kingdom: The Faerie World of Ireland*, Max Parrish, London, 1959.

McNally, Raymond T. and Florescu, Radu, *In Search of Dracula: A True History of Dracula and Vampire Legends*, New York Graphic Society, New York, 1972.

Marshall, Richard *et al.*, *Mysteries of the Unexplained*, amended edition, Reader's Digest, Pleasantville, 1988.

Meaden, Terence, *The Goddess of the Stones*, Souvenir, London, 1991.

Meaden, Terence (ed.), *Circles from the Sky*, Souvenir, London, 1991.

Ménatory, Gérald, *La Bête du Gévaudan*, Imprimerie Chaptal et Fils, Mende, 1976.

Michell, John and Rickard, Robert J.M., *Phenomena: A Book of Wonders*, Thames & Hudson, London, 1977.

Michell, John and Rickard, Robert J.M., *Living Wonders: Mysteries and Curiosities of the Animal World*, Thames & Hudson, London, 1982.

Mitchell-Hedges, Frederick A., *Danger My Ally*, Elek, London, 1954.

Morgan, Elaine, *The Aquatic Ape*, Souvenir Press, London, 1982.

Morrison, Tony, *Pathways to the Gods: The Mystery of the Andes Lines*, Michael Russell, London, 1978.

O'Donnell, Elliott, *Haunted Britain*, Rider and Company, London, 1949.

Pardoe, Rosemary and Darroll, *The Female Pope: The Mystery of Pope Joan*, Crucible, Wellingborough, 1988.

Phillips, Graham, *The Search for the Grail*, Century, London, 1995.

Picknett, Lynn, *The Encyclopaedia of the Paranormal: The Complete Guide to the Unexplained*, Macmillan, London, 1990.

Picknett, Lynn and Prince, Clive, *Turin Shroud: In Whose Image?*, Bloomsbury, London, 1994.

Povah, Frank, *You Kids Count Your Shadows*, privately published, Wollar, 1990.

Ravenscroft, Trevor, *The Spear of Destiny*, Corgi, London, 1974.

Rickard, Robert J. M. and Kelly, Richard, *Photographs of the Unknown*, New English Library, London, 1980.

Riese, Randall, *The Unabridged James Dean: His Life and Legacy from A to Z*, Contemporary Books, Chicago, 1991.

Robin-Evans, Karyl, *Sungods in Exile*, Neville Spearman, London, 1979.

Rogo, D. Scott, *Miracles: A Parascientific Inquiry into Wondrous Phenomena*, Dial Press, New York, 1982.

Rogo, D. Scott and Clark, Jerome, *Earth's Secret Inhabitants*, Tempo, New York, 1979.

Russell, Eric F., *Great World Mysteries*, Dobson, London, 1957.

Sanderson, Ivan T., *Abominable Snowmen: Legend Come to Life*, Chilton, Philadelphia, 1961.

Sanderson, Ivan T., *"Things"*, Pyramid, New York, 1967.

Sassoon, George and Dale, Rodney, *The Manna Machine*, Sidgwick & Jackson, London, 1978.

Scrutton, Robert, *The Other Atlantis*, Neville Spearman, London, 1977.

Scrutton, Robert, *Secrets of Lost Atland*, Neville Spearman, London, 1978.

Shackley, Myra, *Wildmen: Yeti, Sasquatch and the Neanderthal Enigma*, Thames & Hudson, London, 1983.

Shuker, Karl P.N., *Mystery Cats of the World: From Blue Tigers to Exmoor Beasts*, Robert Hale, London, 1989.

Shuker, Karl P.N., *Extraordinary Animals Worldwide*, Robert Hale, London, 1991.

Shuker, Karl P.N., *The Lost Ark: New and Rediscovered Animals of the 20th Century*, HarperCollins, London, 1993.

Shuker, Karl P.N., *Dragons: A Natural History*, Aurum Press, London, 1995.

Shuker, Karl P.N., *In Search of Prehistoric Survivors: Do Giant 'Extinct' Creatures Still Exist?*, Blandford Press, London, 1995.

Shuker, Karl P.N., *From Flying Toads to Snakes With Wings: In Search of Mysterious Beasts*, Llewellyn Worldwide, St John, 1996.

Shuker, Karl P.N. (consultant), *Man and Beast*, Reader's Digest, Pleasantville, 1993.

Shuker, Karl P.N. (consultant), *Secrets of the Natural World*, Reader's Digest, Pleasantville, 1993.

Singer, Stanley, *The Nature of Ball Lightning*, Plenum Press, New York, 1971.

Skinner, Bob, *Toad in the Hole: Source Material on the Entombed Toad Phenomenon*, Fortean Times, London, 1986.

Smyth, Charles P., *Our Inheritance in the Great Pyramid*, 4 editions, W. Isbister, London, 1864–80.

Smyth, Frank, *Ghosts and Poltergeists*, Aldus, London, 1976.

Soyka, Fred and Edmonds, Alan, *The Ion Effect*, E.P. Dutton, New York, 1977.

Sox, H. David, *File on the Shroud*, Coronet, London, 1978.

Spencer, John, *The UFO Encyclopedia*, Headline, London, 1991.

Stemman, Roy, *Atlantis and the Lost Lands*, Aldus, London, 1976.

Stommel, Henry, *Lost Islands*, University of British Columbia Press, Vancouver, 1984.

Stoneley, Jack, *Tunguska: Cauldron of Hell*, Star, London, 1977.

Strange Magazine, Rockville, Maryland, No. 1, 1987–present.

Tame, David, *The Secret Power of Music*, Turnstone Press, Wellingborough, 1984.

Temple, Robert K.G., *The Sirius Mystery*, Sidgwick & Jackson, London, 1976.

Toibin, Colin (ed.), *Seeing Is Believing: Moving Statues in Ireland*, Pilgrim Press, Mountrath, 1985.

Truzzi, Marcello (consultant), *Into the Unknown*, amended edition, Reader's Digest, Pleasantville, 1988.

Truzzi, Marcello (consultant), *Transformations*, Time-Life, Amsterdam, 1989.

Truzzi, Marcello *et al.* (consultants), *Mystic Places*, Time-Life, Amsterdam, 1987.

Underwood, Peter, *Dictionary of the Occult and Supernatural*, Fontana, London, 1979.

Watson, Lyall, *Supernature*, Hodder & Stoughton, London, 1973.

Watson, Lyall, *Heaven's Breath: A Natural History of the Wind*, Hodder & Stoughton, London, 1984.

Watson, Lyall, *The Nature of Things: The Secret Life of Inanimate Objects*, Hodder & Stoughton, London, 1990.

Weiss, Suzanne E. (ed.), *Great Mysteries of the Past*, Reader's Digest, Pleasantville, 1991.

Welfare, Simon and Fairley, John, *Arthur C. Clarke's Mysterious World*, Collins, London, 1980.

Welfare, Simon and Fairley, John, *Arthur C. Clarke's A–Z of Mysteries: From Atlantis to Zombies*, HarperCollins, London, 1993.

West, John A., *Serpent in the Sky: The High Wisdom of Ancient Egypt*, Wildwood, London, 1979.

Westwood, Jennifer (ed.), *The Atlas of Mysterious Places*, Guild, London, 1987.

Wignell, Edel (ed.), *A Boggle of Bunyips*, Hodder & Stoughton, Sydney, 1981.

Wilkins, Harold T., *Mysteries of Ancient South America*, Rider, London, 1946.

Wilson, Colin and Grant, John, *The Directory of Possibilities*, Webb & Bower, London, 1981.

Wilson, Colin and Damon, *Unsolved Mysteries, Past and Present*, Headline, London, 1993.

Wilson, Ian, *The Turin Shroud*, Victor Gollancz, London, 1978.

Wilson, Ian, *The Bleeding Mind*, Weidenfeld & Nicolson, London, 1988.

Wood, Manfri F., *In the Life of a Romany Gypsy*, Routledge & Kegan Paul, London, 1973.

Woodward, Ian, *The Werewolf Delusion*, Paddington, London, 1979.

Zarzynski, Joseph W., *Champ: Beyond the Legend*, revised edition, M-Z Information, Wilton, 1988.

Zink, David D., *The Stones of Atlantis*, Englewood Cliffs, New Jersey, 1978.

Zink, David D., *The Ancient Stones Speak*, Jonathan-James, London, 1979.

Index

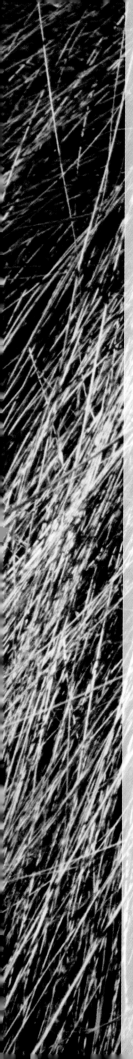

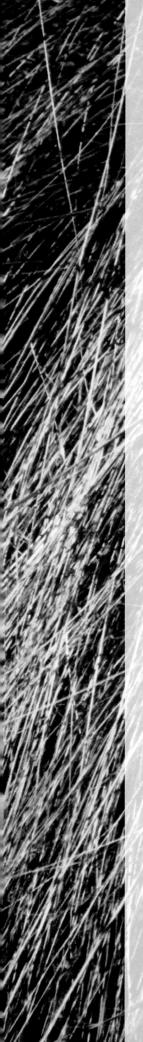

Acknowledgements

I wish to thank most sincerely the following people and organizations for their much-appreciated encouragement and assistance during my preparation of this book:

Academy of Applied Science (Concord, New Hampshire), Arcturus Books, Trevor Beer and Endymion Beer/*Athene*, John "Ace" Bonar, Sylvia Bongiovanni, British Library, British Museum (Natural History), Owen Burnham, Cassell Publishers, *Cat World*, Mark Chorvinsky/*Strange Magazine*, Loren Coleman, Paul Cropper, Mike Dash, Jonathan and Alison Downes/*Animals and Men*, *Enigmas*, Excalibur Books, Kevin Farley, *Fate Magazine*, Angel Morant Fores, *Fortean Times*, Errol Fuller, Blade Galentine, Bill Gibbons, J. Richard Greenwell, Bob Hay, Tony Healy, David Heppell, Isabela Herranz, Dr Bernard Heuvelmans, Professor Shoichi Hollie, Tyson Hughes, International Society of Cryptozoology, Gerard van Leusden, Dr John A. Long, Professor Roy P. Mackal, Debbie Martyr, Dr Ralph Molnar, Joan Moore, Steve Moore, Richard Muirhead, Carina Norris, Sally Parsons, Michael Playfair, Alan Pringle,

Michel Raynal, Bob Rickard, Dr Robert H. Rines, Ron Scarlett, Paul Screeton/*Folklore Frontiers*, Steven and Frances Shipp/Midnight Books, Mary D. Shuker, Paul Sieveking, Malcolm Smith, Lars Thomas, the late Gertrude Timmins, We Remember Dean International (WRDI), *Wild About Animals*, Jan Williams, Susan Wood and the late Gerald L. Wood, World Explorers Club and the Zoological Society of London.

I would like to offer an especial vote of thanks to my editors Tessa Rose and Sarah Larter, and also to picture researchers Sharon Hutton and Maja Mihajlovic, at Carlton Books; to Barry Sutcliffe, Andy Jones and Clare Eastland at Topics; to Janet and Colin Bord, and the Fortean Picture Library; and to my agent Mandy Little of Watson, Little Ltd, for breathing life into this creation of mine. I am truly grateful.
Anyone interested in mysteries and unexplained phenomena should seriously consider subscribing to the following publications:

Animals and Men (Editor: Jonathan Downes), 15 Holne Court, Exwick, Exeter, Devon EX4 2NA, England
Athene (Editor: Endymion Beer), Tawside, 30 Park Avenue, Barnstaple, Devon EX31 2ES, England
Cryptozoology (Editor: J. Richard Greenwell), The International Society of Cryptozoology, PO Box 43070, Tucson, Arizona 85733, USA
Enigmas (Editor: Isabela Herranz), Editorial America Iberica SA, Miguel Yuste, 26, 28037 Madrid, Spain
Fate (Editor: Terry O'Neill), PO Box 64383, St Paul, Minnesota 55164-0383, USA
Fortean Times (Editors: Bob Rickard, Paul Sieveking), John Brown Publications, The Boathouse, Crabtree Lane, Fulham, London SW6 6LU, England
Strange Magazine (Editor: Mark Chorvinsky), PO Box 2246, Rockville, Maryland 20847, USA

Picture Credits

The publishers would like to thank the following for their kind permission to reproduce pictures used in this publication:

AKG London 14(b), 48(tr), 60(t), 82; **Academy of Applied Science, R H Rhines, USA (1975-95)** 15(t); **British Film Institute Slide Collection** 200(b); **Bruce Coleman (Orion)** 39(t), 89, 103(l),178; **Beinecke Rare Book and Manuscript Library, Yale University** 51(c), 52(tl); **Booth Museum, Brighton** 13(b); **Bridgeman Art Library** 74, 86,102; **British Museum (Museum of Mankind)** 3(tr), 83; **Carlton Books (Ian Jones)** 52(br); **Caters News Agency** 13(t), 71(t); **Charmet** 58(b), 59(tr); **Corbis** 145, 157(t), 162, 163, 164, 188, 190(tr), 190(b); **Philippa Coxall/Wild About Animals** 118; **Enigmas Magazine, Spain** 3(tl), 199; **Robert Estall Photo Library** 29(t); **Frank Lane Picture Agency** 46(t), 49(b), 83(b), 119(t), 125, 159, 172(t), 179(br), 180(t), 195, 216(br); **Fortean Picture Library** 3(br), 4, 5(bl), 6, 7(bl), **(A Barker)** 11(c), 12(t&b),15(b), 16(t), 24(t),

25(t), 27(tr), 37(t&b), 43(c), 61(tr), 63(c), 66(b), 70(t), 83(t), 91, 94, 96, 100, 112, 131, 132, 133(l&r), 134, 137, 140, 142, 143, 147(t&b), 148, **(René Dahinden)**149, 150(t&b), 152, 153(t&b), 160, 171(br), 173(box), 177, 180(br), 181, 185(t), 193(box), 198(t), 204(tl), 205(l), 205(br), 206(tl), 207(r), 208(b), 210(l), **(Taiyo Fisheries, Tokyo)** 211(tl), 211(br), 213(b), 214(tl); **Errol Fuller** 215(t); **Illustrated London News** 185(b); **Hulton** 110, 117(b), 123; **Humbolt Museum, Nevada** 151(b); **Images Colour Library** 3(bl), 5(tl), 7(tr), 17(tr), 18(b), 19(t), 21(c), 23(tr), 29(b), 30(t), 38(tl), 47(br), 84, 108, 111, 107, 196, 197, 198(b), 199(b); **Manchester City Art Gallery** 22(t); **Mansell Collection** 53(t), 69(br), 72, 73(t), 81, 88, 99, 124, 151(t); **Mary Evans Picture Library** 5(tr), 33(c), 35(t), 38(tr), 44(bl), 47(t), 54(t,bl & br), 55(t), 57(t), 61(bl), 65(tl), 65(br), 67(t), 69(tl), 79, 113, 136, 138, 156, 165(t&b), 139, 141, 155, 172(t), 186, 214(br); **Maureen Gavin Picture Library** 35(b), 68(t), 175(box), 201(tr); **David Miller (under direction of Dr R P Mackal)** 92(tl); **Mirror Syndication International**

87, 127; **Novosti** 125(t); **Popperfoto**, 22(b), 75(t), 80, 109, 115, 116, 126; **Pictorial Press** 49(t); **Réunion des Musées Nationaux, Paris** 103(r); **Rex Features** 26(t), 48(tl), 56(bl), 64(t), 157(inset), 158; **Ronald Grant Archive** 101; **Scotland in Focus** 36(b); **Solo Syndication** 28(t); **Science Photo Library (David Parker)** 28(b), **(David Scharf)** 25(br), **(National Library of Medicine)** 45(br), 135; **Tim Sell** 92(bl), 93(t & b), 95(t, cr & br), 97(t), 117(t), 121; **Dr K P N Shuker (Institute of Cryptozoology, USA)** 119(b), 179(tl), 203(b), **(Wellington Museum)** 209(bl); **Paul Sieveking** 97(b); **South American Pictures/Tony Morrison** 169, 171(cl & tl), 174(inset bl); **Tony Stone Images** 31(t); **Strange Magazine, USA** 170(box); **Werner Forman Archive** 174(br); **Western Australian Museum, Perth** 209(tl).

Thanks to Tim Sell for illustrations